W9-AZZ-064

Business Intelligence in Microsoft SharePoint 2013

Norman P. Warren
Mariano Teixeira Neto
Stacia Misner
Ivan Sanders
Scott A. Helmers

Published with the authorization of Microsoft Corporation by:
O'Reilly Media, Inc.
1005 Gravenstein Highway North
Sebastopol, California 95472

ISBN: 978-0-7356-7543-8

1 2 3 4 5 6 7 8 9 LSI 8 7 6 5 4 3

Printed and bound in the United States of America.

Microsoft Press books are available through booksellers and distributors worldwide. If you need support related to this book, email Microsoft Press Book Support at *mspinput@microsoft.com*. Please tell us what you think of this book at *http://www.microsoft.com/learning/booksurvey*.

Microsoft and the trademarks listed at *http://www.microsoft.com/about/legal/en/us/IntellectualProperty/ Trademarks/EN-US.aspx* are trademarks of the Microsoft group of companies. All other marks are property of their respective owners.

The example companies, organizations, products, domain names, email addresses, logos, people, places, and events depicted herein are fictitious. No association with any real company, organization, product, domain name, email address, logo, person, place, or event is intended or should be inferred.

Acquisitions and Development Editor: Kenyon Brown

Production Editor: Rachel Steely

Editorial Production: Octal Publishing, Inc.

Technical Reviewer: Carl Rabeler

Copyeditor: Bob Russell, Octal Publishing, Inc.

Indexer: BIM, Inc.

Cover Design: Twist Creative

Cover Composition: Karen Montgomery

Illustrator: Rebecca Demarest

Contents at a Glance

Contents

What do you think of this book? We want to hear from you!

Microsoft is interested in hearing your feedback so we can continually improve our
books and learning resources for you. To participate in a brief online survey, please visit:

microsoft.com/learning/booksurvey

Chapter 7   Using PowerPivot for SharePoint 2013   189

What do you think of this book? We want to hear from you!

Microsoft is interested in hearing your feedback so we can continually improve our
books and learning resources for you. To participate in a brief online survey, please visit:

microsoft.com/learning/booksurvey

Introduction

Welcome to *Business Intelligence for Microsoft SharePoint 2013*. Whether you are a SQL Server business intelligence (BI) developer, a SharePoint Administrator, or a data scientist, this book shows you how Microsoft is delivering on its commitment to provide useful and actionable insights by way of BI to its customers. It provides a quick dive into new Microsoft SharePoint 2013 BI features and offerings and complementing new SQL Server 2012 BI features and tools.

This book provides a getting started guide for many of the SharePoint application services dedicated to BI. Additionally, it introduces features for managing SQL Server 2013 Reporting Services Power View reports and Excel 2013 PowerPivot in SharePoint.

The SharePoint Server 2013 application services that provide functionality to the BI stack include the following:

- **Excel Services**   A SharePoint Server 2013 service application that you can use to manage, view, interact, and consume Microsoft Excel client workbooks on SharePoint Server.

- **Visio Services**   A service with which users can share and view Visio diagrams on a SharePoint website. This service also makes it possible for you refresh and update data-connected Microsoft Visio 2013 diagrams from a variety of data sources.

- **PerformancePoint Services**   A performance management service that you can use to monitor and analyze your business. This service provides flexible, easy-to-use tools for building dashboards, scorecards, reports, and key performance indicators (KPIs).

Integrating Microsoft Office 2013, SharePoint Server 2013, and SQL Server 2012 provides the following tools and feature sets, primarily for self-service BI:

- **PowerPivot in Excel 2013 and SharePoint 2013**   A SharePoint 2013 application service (included in SQL Server 2012) and an extension to Excel that adds support for large-scale data. It includes an in-memory data store as an option for Analysis Services. Multiple data sources can be merged to include corporate databases, worksheets, reports, and data feeds. You can publish Excel documents to SharePoint Server 2013.

- **Power View in Excel 2013 and SharePoint 2013**   With Power View, the Excel user can easily and quickly turn raw data into beautiful visualizations that reveal patterns and relationships that exist in that data.

SharePoint administrators, business users, and BI developers, as well as other users and consumers of BI, will want to understand each of these client tools and services and how they work together to bring BI to more people through SharePoint.

Who this book is for

In a sense, this book is written to the data scientist. What is a data scientist? A valid description would be someone who has 25 percent business knowledge, 25 percent analytics expertise, 25 percent technological capabilities, and 25 percent visualization experience. The following table describes the breakdown of skills.

Part of a data scientist	Skills taught in this book
25 percent business knowledge	We explain the reasons for business intelligence (Chapter 1) and when and where you would use each tool (Chapter 2). We also explain where "big data" fits (Appendix B).
25 percent analytics experience	We show you the new analytic and reporting features in Excel 2013 (PowerPivot and Power View), PerformancePoint, and Visio. We provide steps on how to use them with a data warehouse database.
25 percent technological capabilities	We explain how to connect to the data, model it, and automate a data refresh (Chapter 3). We also give you the resources to install the complete stack (Office 2013 + SQL Server 2012 + SharePoint 2013) for making all the tools come together (Appendix A).
25 percent visualization	All the tools have visualization features. In particular, Power View in Excel 2013 (Chapter 5) shows how to very quickly create visualizations from the data that is pulled into PowerPivot in Excel 2013.

Although anyone interested in using advanced tools to gather and present BI can benefit from this book, it should also prove especially valuable to the SharePoint administrators, business users, and BI developers.

SharePoint administrator/developer

Just as a SQL BI developer peeks into SharePoint 2013 products, we want SharePoint administrators to peek into the tasks involved in developing BI solutions and getting to trusted data. A SharePoint administrator must be aware that you typically can't just "turn on" BI in SharePoint or in SQL Server; rather, you must set up some processes or use existing, trusted data. A SharePoint administrator should also be aware of the newest BI features and tools as well as existing technologies, and have some idea of how to set them up. In this book, we give SharePoint administrators an overview of the latest available BI tools and how they work with SharePoint 2013. This book strives to give SharePoint administrators an understanding of the work and expertise required for an extensive range of possible BI implementations.

Your advantage is that Microsoft is delivering on its promise to simplify the integration of self-service BI tools. Your other advantage is that as a SharePoint expert, you already know how to construct the self-service concept.

Business user and data scientist

In this book, the term "business user" describes people who are eager to understand the technologies that can help them, their teams, and their company or organization to measure, explore data, analyze, forecast, and report on the most important aspects of their business by using the company's business data.

A business user might also be a technical decision-maker, deciding which products work best for the individual, team, or organization. By understanding how technology and business needs meet through reporting, measuring, analyzing, and more, we hope that business users will see a return on investment through increased accountability and better alignment with organizational goals.

Using SharePoint 2013 and other stand-alone tools, business users can benefit from learning about the end-to-end process for surfacing and presenting insights to decision-makers. Business users know that trusted insights can change behavior and decisions, which can ultimately help to lead a company in the right direction.

Business users who can benefit from the integrated BI tools offered by Microsoft Office, SharePoint, and SQL Server include the following:

- Data scientists

- Business analysts

- Business decision-makers

- Knowledge workers

- Line workers

- ...and more

Note that the data scientist is a new role that is being deployed in companies. As you will find, this book does not specifically target one group because we are aware that in many situations IT professionals and business users wear more than one hat.

Each of the preceding roles has its own unique accountabilities. For each role, we provide simple examples showing how to create BI end results such as the following:

- Reports

- A dashboard in PerformancePoint Services

- KPIs that can be presented by using various tools

- PivotTables in Excel

End users might also want to know how to do some tricks in SharePoint, such as how to add a rating system in a SharePoint list, view a blog post, implementing collaborative decision-making in SharePoint 2013, or rating BI assets.

BI developer

Put simply, the BI developer's task is to establish trusted data sources (tabular data and Online Analytical Processing [OLAP] cubes) in SQL Server for the various services (Excel, Visio, PerformancePoint) and for PowerPivot and SQL Server Reporting Services. Broadly, BI developers can also help with report design, training, and back-end maintenance such as deploying models and automating a data refresh. All of these things are covered in this book. BI developers also help to create connections to the trusted data sources and help ensure that the data is the right data.

Organizational BI begins by establishing a single source for trusted data. If users cannot trust the data that's in front of them to make decisions, they won't trust the tools that deliver the data. They will abandon those tools to seek some other way to get the right data, which likely means abandoning their considerable investment in those tools, in both time and money, to invest in new ones.

Data can come from a variety of sources, and in many cases, companies have spent lots of money and time to establish a repeatable Extract, Transform, and Load (ETL) process. This requires a BI developer who knows something about data warehouses (SQL Server), integrating data from various sources by using SQL Server Integration Services, and developing Transact-SQL (T-SQL) procedures. If a company decides that creating OLAP cubes is worth the effort, it will also hire (or train) SQL Server Analysis Services experts to do the job. Microsoft has provided the tools to tie all this data together, and this book can help you use them to get the best value from your data management tools.

Using the information in this book, BI developers can help decide which tools to use to surface the data. They can also communicate closely with the SharePoint Administrator for cases in which trusted data must be shared.

In this book, the authors provide a longer discussion about the new SQL Server 2012 Business Intelligence Semantic Model (BISM) model, and a shorter discussion of SQL Server Analysis Services OLAP cubes, because OLAP cubes are the ideal data sources for organizational BI using Performance-Point Services, for data sources used by the other services (such as Excel Services, Visio Services, and others). The BISM model applies more to "personal BI" using PowerPivot in Excel and SharePoint and Power View in Excel and SharePoint.

How this book is organized

This book gives you a comprehensive look at the various features that you will use. It is structured in a logical approach to all aspects of using BI tools that integrate with SharePoint 2013.

Chapter 1, "Business intelligence in SharePoint 2013," introduces BI for SharePoint 2013. BI is a difficult concept to pin down precisely, because it covers a wide range of products and technologies and thus means slightly different things to different people. This chapter discusses exactly what the authors mean by the term "business intelligence," the Microsoft approach to BI, and how SharePoint fits into the picture.

Chapter 2, "Planning for business intelligence adoption," provides instruction on which tool to use. People often ask which tools they should use when trying to select among a variety of Microsoft offerings. They're often confused and need information as to why they might want SQL Server Reporting Services in SharePoint over PerformancePoint Services, or why they might use the Excel 2013 PowerPivot Add-in instead of Excel or Excel Services. After all, each product connects to a database and surfaces data from an OLAP cube.

The difficulties of making such decisions are compounded because different teams and companies are at different stages in their ability to surface data to business users for optimal decision making. Overall, this chapter prepares you for adoption of the right tools for the right job by answering questions about which tools to use, clarifying the purposes and capabilities of the various products, and helping you choose which ones are most appropriate for your situation.

Chapter 3, "The lifecycle of a business intelligence implementation," discusses the process and approach to formalizing a self-service scenario, as described in Chapters 4 and 5, to importing a PowerPivot model into Visual Studio and deploying to SQL Server 2012 Analysis Services.

Chapter 4, "Using PowerPivot in Excel 2013," introduces PowerPivot in Excel 2013. The PowerPivot and Data Model experience is designed to feel as seamless as possible to an Excel user. Because PowerPivot and the Data Model use the xVelocity engine, it extends Excel so that you can work with millions of rows. Moreover, operations—even with huge volumes of data—are fast! Aggregations that might have taken a day to calculate in SQL Server Analysis Services take only seconds in PowerPivot. In this chapter, you'll see how to mash-up data from different sources, share that data securely via SharePoint, create Data Analysis Expressions (DAX) queries, and more.

Chapter 5, "Using Power View in Excel 2013," introduces another enhancement to Excel: Power View. Using Power View, the Excel user can easily and quickly turn raw data into beautiful visualizations that reveal patterns and relationships existing in that data. These visualizations can use data imported into an Excel workbook's Data Model or the more advanced PowerPivot model. This chapter shows you how to add Power View sheets to a workbook, work with each type of visualization supported in Power View, and use interactive features such as drilling, animated scatter charts, highlighting, and filtering.

Chapter 6, "Using Excel Services in SharePoint 2013," provides instruction for sharing your Excel file in SharePoint 2013. Most BI begins in Excel, which can be considered the most pervasive BI tool that exists. But, sharing Excel files has always been a huge challenge. Excel Services not only provides the ability to share Excel-based content safely and securely, it also adds powerful management capabilities. Such features as the PivotTable and PivotChart in Excel improve the look and feel of how data is presented. Among several hands-on examples, you'll see how to create a PivotTable and slicers to provide slice-and-dice capability on the screen for analysis, and how to add your PivotTable to a simple dashboard webpage so that you can share it.

Chapter 7, "Using PowerPivot in SharePoint 2013," introduces you to PowerPivot for SharePoint and its functionalities that take Excel Services to the next step. This chapter demonstrates how to publish a PowerPivot workbook to SharePoint and how to schedule data refreshes, how to use workbooks as data sources for other applications, and it explains how IT professionals can manage PowerPivot for SharePoint by using the PowerPivot Management Dashboard.

Chapter 8, "Using PerformancePoint Services," shows the exciting solutions that PerformancePoint Services offers in its ability to show a dashboard that reflects KPIs, such as the available disk space of managed servers. This chapter explains how to create a dashboard with scorecards, KPIs, reports, and connections to data sources.

Chapter 9, "Using Visio and Visio Services," demonstrates the business intelligence value that Visio offers. You've probably used Visio to create flowcharts, or perhaps network diagrams, or maybe an org chart or a floor plan. But, should Visio be an integral part of your BI solutions? The goal of this chapter is to provide a "yes" answer to that question by demonstrating the BI value that Visio offers, both by itself and when integrated with the products described in other chapters in this book. You will see examples that employ colorful, data-rich diagrams that you can view with a web browser and that update automatically when the underlying data changes.

Chapter 10, "Bringing it all together," helps you capitalize on the concepts and products discussed in all the preceding chapters by walking through the steps to create a dashboard that shows data from various sources, such as Excel Web Access Web Parts.

Appendix A, "Installing and configuring scripts to run a demo environment," provides system requirements for your demo environment; detailed setup and configuration instructions, including downloadable scripts; and helpful screen captures so that you can get up and running quickly to work through the book's exercises. We also provide instructions for configuring SQL Server 2012, Share-Point Server 2013, and Office Professional 2013, along with links to relevant sites.

> **Note** Trial versions of SQL Server 2012, SharePoint Server 2013, and Office Professional 2013 are available for evaluation from Microsoft. For information, please visit *http://technet.microsoft.com/en-us/evalcenter/*.

Appendix B, "Microsoft and 'Big Data'", introduces you to "Big Data" and the role SharePoint 2013 plays and will play in getting value from Big Data investments. We provide instruction for how Microsoft HDInsight integrates with Hadoop to query and visualize data. You will learn how the tools described in this book are relevant to getting value from disparate data sources and (un)structured data.

What's not covered in this book

Even though this book covers a wide range of products, it doesn't cover everything. We chose to concentrate instead on those technologies that we believe make up the core Microsoft BI tools. Three of the following BI tools are a part of SharePoint Server 2013, and one of them Reporting Services, is part of the SQL Server 2012 platform, offering strong reporting and report management features in SharePoint.

This brief section explains which technologies we chose not to discuss, but if these technologies also suit your needs, you might consider how you can implement them.

Access Services

Microsoft Access is a relational database management system. Software developers and data architects can use Access to develop application software, and "power users" can use it to build individual and workgroup-level applications.

Access Services is a service application with which you can host Access databases within SharePoint Server 2013. Through Access Services, users can edit, update, and create linked Access 2013 databases, which are then both viewed and manipulated by using either a web browser or the Access client. In other words, Access Services extends "access" to Access so that even users who don't have the Access client installed on their desktop can perform operations with the Access application through Access Services.

An Access web app is a new type of database that you build in Access and then use and share with others as a SharePoint app in a web browser. After you create the Access App, you can import data from Access desktop databases, Excel files, Open Database Connectivity (ODBC) data sources, text files, and SharePoint lists. Because all data is now stored in SQL Server, you can use a tool of your preference to create reports. You are able to connect to the SQL database by using ODBC and can take advantage of existing skillsets you might have—for example, Excel, and Power View.

There is a self-service element to Access that lets users incorporate rapid application development (RAD) principles to more quickly create data-driven websites without coding in Microsoft ASP.NET. This is attractive to smaller companies that have fewer IT resources—sometimes only one or two IT workers. Access and Access Services also become attractive to larger companies when projects are prioritized into already-full IT development schedules, or when users want to provide a very quick proof-of-concept data-driven website.

SQL Server 2012 Reporting Services in SharePoint

SQL Server 2012 Reporting Services (SSRS) with SharePoint integration has several new features, including support for Power View, SharePoint mode for support of SharePoint 2013, a new version of Reporting Services Add-in for SharePoint 2010 and 2013, and the ability to interact with reports in Apple Safari on iOS devices. Although we include a chapter about Power View in Excel 2013, we don't discuss thoroughly Power View in SharePoint nor do we discuss SSRS Report Builder.

SSRS Report Builder is a report-authoring tool with which you can create ad hoc reports quickly. The tool helps report creation, collaboration, and consistency by enabling business users to create and share report components that can be accessed via a shared component library.

We didn't quite omit this topic entirely; Chapter 3 includes a somewhat longer summary of what SQL Server Reporting Services is.

Business Connectivity Services

Microsoft Business Connectivity Services (BCS) provides read/write access to external data from Line-of-Business (LoB) systems (such as Microsoft Dynamics, Oracle, or Siebel), web services, databases, and other external systems from within Microsoft SharePoint 2013. SharePoint 2013 has product features that can use external data directly, both online and offline. BCS enables tools such as Microsoft Visual Studio 2013 and Microsoft SharePoint Designer 2013 to help make connections to the external data. Improvements to SharePoint 2013 include Open Data Protocol (OData) support and support for self-contained apps for SharePoint—developers can package Business Data Connectivity (BDC) models in an app for SharePoint.

> **Note** OData is an industry-standard web protocol that is used to access data from external systems.

Duet Enterprise

You might have asked, "How is Duet Enterprise different from BCS if it connects to Enterprise Resource Planning data?" Duet Enterprise is an application built on the SharePoint 2013 platform, and it uses BCS in conjunction with SAP data. Duet Enterprise was developed jointly by two companies: SAP and Microsoft. SAP is a German software company known primarily for its SAP Enterprise Resource Planning and SAP Business Objects products. Duet Enterprise enables all employees to consume and extend SAP applications and data through SharePoint 2013 and Office 2013. Duet Enterprise combines the collaboration and productivity supported by SharePoint and Office with the business data and processing functionality of SAP applications.

For SAP users, Duet reduces the learning curve and provides wider access to enterprise information and policies, resulting in greater user adoption. As a result, organizations can increase corporate policy compliance, improve decision-making, and save time and money. We mention the product here because there are a lot of SAP customers and a lot of SAP data; making that data available to many users was previously difficult or impossible.

Duet's plan is to continue developing interoperability between SAP and SharePoint in areas such as system management, single sign-on, and more. By blending the worlds of process and collaboration, end-to-end solutions will form as tools and feature extensions become available.

 More Info To learn more, go to *http://www54.sap.com/solutions/tech/collaboration-content-management/software/duet-enterprise/index.html.*

Web analytics

Web Analytics in SharePoint Server 2010 has been discontinued and is not available in SharePoint 2013. Analytics processing for SharePoint 2013 is now a component of the Search service.

The reason for the change is this: a new analytics system was required for SharePoint 2013 that included improvements in scalability and performance, and that had an infrastructure that encompasses SharePoint Online. The Analytics Processing Component in SharePoint 2013 runs analytics jobs to analyze content in the search index and user actions that are performed on SharePoint sites.

SharePoint 2013 still logs every click in SharePoint sites and still provides a count of hits for every document. User data is made anonymous early in the logging process and the Analytics Processing Component is scalable to the service.

This analytics data is used in SharePoint 2013 to provide new item-to-item recommendation features; to show view counts that are embedded in SharePoint 2013 and Search Server user interface; to provide a report of the top items in a site and list; and to influence the relevancy algorithm of search.

Even though Social features and Search in SharePoint 2013 are not BI tools, you should consider how to use them to help make BI reports, data dictionaries, and other BI assets more discoverable. More sharing and conversations around BI assets will help you to take advantage of collective and interactive discoveries from insights.

Conventions used in this book

This book presents information by using conventions designed to make the information readable and easy to follow.

- Each exercise consists of a series of tasks, presented as numbered steps, listing each action you must take to complete the exercise.

- Boxed elements with labels such as "Note" provide additional information or alternative methods for completing a step successfully.

Companion content

Chapters in this book include exercises by which you can interactively try out new material learned in the main text. Sample projects are in their post-exercise formats and can be downloaded from the following page:

http://aka.ms/BI_SP2013/files

Follow the instructions to download the file. The following chapters include content that you can use:

Chapter	Description of content
Chapter 3	Solution files for AdventureWorks model in SQL Server Data Tools
Chapter 4	Completed Excel 2013 file with a PowerPivot model
Chapter 5	Completed Excel 2013 file with a Power View report
Appendix A	Scripts and sample databases (see note)

Note Trial versions of SQL Server 2012, SharePoint Server 2013, and Office Professional 2013 are available for evaluation from Microsoft at *http://technet.microsoft.com/en-us/evalcenter/*.

System Requirements

Appendix A provides Windows PowerShell scripts and instructions to install and configure trial versions of SQL Server 2012 SP1, SharePoint 2013, Office 2013, and sample code. The software and configuration described are necessary to complete the practice exercises in this book. Additionally, you will need the following hardware to complete the practice exercises in this book:

- A 64-bit computer, 4 cores for small deployments (fewer than 1,000 users)

- 16 GB of RAM for medium deployments (between 1,000 to 10,000 users)

- 80 GB of available hard disk space

- Internet connection to download software or chapter examples

Depending on your Windows configuration, you might require Local Administrator rights to install or configure.

Acknowledgments

Norm Warren would like to first thank his wife, KarAnn, and his five children for their patience while writing the book. He would also like to thank the people who have helped contribute in one way or another to this book. They include the coauthors of this book, Ancestry.com manager Eric Rios, Technical Reviewer Carl Rabeler, and other reviewers at Microsoft.

Mariano would like to thank Kay Unkroth, program manager, Lee Graber and Ben Levinn, developers (all from the Analysis Services team at Microsoft), for shedding light on the darkness. And, most importantly, he would like to thank his family—Bárbara, Sofia, and Miguel—for their support and love.

Stacia would like to thank Sean Boon for his insights about Power View in addition to everyone involved in this book—the authors, the editorial team, and the production team.

Scott would like to thank Marilyn, Sara, and Julie for coping with his absence while working on his chapter, especially because writing it fell in the middle of a six-month-long project to write *Microsoft Visio 2013 Step by Step*. Thanks also to Kenyon Brown for the invitation to join Norm, John, Mariano, and Stacia on this project, and to Krishna Mamidipaka for his insightful comments on the chapter in progress.

The Authors
May, 2013

Support and feedback

The following sections provide information on errata, book support, feedback, and contact information.

Errata

We've made every effort to ensure the accuracy of this book and its companion content. Any errors that have been reported since this book was published are listed on our Microsoft Press site at *oreilly.com*:

http://aka.ms/BI_SP2013/errata

If you find an error that is not already listed, you can report it to us through the same page.

If you need additional support, email Microsoft Press Book Support at

mspinput@microsoft.com.

Please note that product support for Microsoft software is not offered through the addresses above.

We want to hear from you

At Microsoft Press, your satisfaction is our top priority, and your feedback our most valuable asset. Please tell us what you think of this book at:

http://www.microsoft.com/learning/booksurvey

The survey is short, and we read every one of your comments and ideas. Thanks in advance for your input!

Stay in touch

Let's keep the conversation going! We're on Twitter at: *http://twitter.com/MicrosoftPress.*

CHAPTER 1

Business intelligence in SharePoint

This chapter introduces the definition of business intelligence (BI) and explains why it is important to you, your team, and your organization. It also discusses the platforms and tools used to deliver pervasive BI for a wide variety of users. At the end of the chapter, we provide a peek at what you can do with BI in SharePoint.

This book is a collaborative effort to show how Microsoft and Microsoft SharePoint BI offerings can help businesses and technical personnel solve common business problems.

BI in SharePoint is less about a specific technology or product tailored to the needs of a small percentage of users, and more about a "buffet" of offerings that can aid customers who are trying to solve a specific problem. One common customer complaint is that much of the published documentation and content is too product-specific, which makes it difficult to get the big picture. Providing that big picture while also providing quick how-to instructions for getting started is one rationale for this book.

Even more important, customers need to know which Microsoft offerings they should choose from the buffet to address which problem. Perhaps one day, the handful of tools that offer a method for creating key performance indicators (KPIs) will merge into a single product, but for now, customers are confused and need guidance as to when they should use Microsoft SQL Server Reporting Services in SharePoint 2013 rather than PerformancePoint Services, or why they would use PowerPivot for Excel 2013 instead of Microsoft Excel or Excel Services. Chapter 2, "Planning for business intelligence adoption," offers this guidance, looking at the tools from several angles, including a BI maturity model.

Leading up to BI

So, exactly what does "business intelligence" mean? We could provide a simple, tool-centric definition, but we have decided to give you the context that can help you make the most sense of what BI is, why it's important, and what forces are propelling its integration into nearly all aspects of companies.

It's fitting to introduce BI with an observation made by Steven R. Covey in his book *The Seven Habits of Highly Effective People* (2004, Free Press). He observed that an airplane that travels from Boston to Los Angeles is off-course for 90 percent of the journey, but the airplane successfully reaches its destination because the pilot makes continuous course corrections based on instruments that monitor the flight and provide feedback.

Much like an airplane, if a company is not steered, it will likely be off course most of the time. Figure 1-1 shows an example of the analogy. Most companies have a goal or destination, sometimes called a vision, and to reach that destination, they rely on business insights. These insights are provided by instruments or measurement tools that help monitor and analyze past, current, and projected future performance. They give managers the information that they need to make changes, or "course corrections." Insights come in the form of reports, scorecards, KPIs, dashboards, and other information vehicles, supported by a concept called "trusted data."

FIGURE 1-1 A visual analogy of BI as the cockpit of an aircraft.

Tools such as these as well as others can help a company see the relationships between their business and its highest priorities and strategies. Decision-makers want the visual experience that dashboards offer so that they can determine at a glance whether they're driving their company toward its destination.

Fortunately, airplanes are predictably more successful at reaching their destinations than companies are in successfully reaching their goals. Is this success due to the science and precision of the measurement tools used in the aviation industry?

Over the years, weather conditions, patterns, and other variables that affect flight and direction—originally considered immeasurable—have become increasingly more measurable and accurate. New instruments were developed and produced to give pilots precise location coordinates.

Now, the same is occurring for businesses. In his book *How to Measure Anything: Finding the Value of "Intangibles" in Business* (2010, Wiley), Douglas W. Hubbard lists a few real-life examples of variables that companies previously chose not to measure because they were presumed to be immeasurable, including the following:

- The flexibility to create new products

- Management effectiveness

- Productivity of research

- Risk of bankruptcy

- Quality

Accounting professionals and academics, including Robert S. Kaplan, Baker Foundation Professor at Harvard Business School, have developed methodologies for measuring many elements in business that were previously thought of as immeasurable in the performance of companies. Kaplan and David Norton proposed the concept of a Balanced Scorecard (BSC) as a means of measuring the performance of a business strategy. The BSC encapsulates the following four main areas that capture performance metrics:

- **Financial** Measures of profitability and market value to satisfy owners and shareholders

- **Internal business processes** Measures of efficiency and effectiveness for producing a product or service

- **Customer satisfaction** Measures of perceived quality, low cost, and other related factors to show how well a company satisfies its customers

- **Innovation and learning** Measures of a company's ability to develop and utilize human resources to meet strategic goals in the present and future

These areas can be referred to as Finance, Operations, Sales, and Human Resources. Or, to condense even further, you can refer to them simply as *FOSH metrics*.

Additional perspectives can include community and social impact, government relations, and others. These measures of success are sometimes called critical success factors. The BSC and other methodologies, such as Six Sigma,[1] help companies to follow the pattern shown in Figure 1-2.

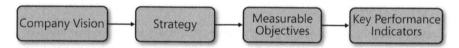

FIGURE 1-2 From company vision to key performance indicators.

A *company vision statement* or *mission statement* is important for getting a company to focus on what makes it successful. There is an old saying, "You must stand up for something, or you will fall for everything." The vision statement helps a company filter which voices it will listen to, because the vision defines its purpose and reason for existence. Typically, upper management communicates the vision or mission statement to the company.

---

[1] Originators of Six Sigma: *http://web.archive.org/web/20051106025733/http://www.motorola.com/content/0,,3079,00. html*.

A strategy is a set of policies, procedures, and approaches to business that is intended to produce long-term success. The strategy reflects the mission of the company.

The mission is also used to develop measurable objectives. When established, objectives help determine KPIs, which are quantifiable measurements that reflect critical success factors.

KPIs make it possible to monitor the metrics that are aligned with principal objectives. Then, managers or employees can analyze issues that surface from data that indicate conditions in need of more attention (these were once called "exception reports"). Action can then be taken to "correct the course" so that the company reaches its destination. As you will see in this book, in addition to KPIs, visualizations that include interactive charts and graphs, maps, bubble charts and more prove to become very powerful because they change behavior and lead to more data drive-decisions.

For illustration purposes, the following example shows how an organization—Adventure Works Bike Company—designs a KPI, turning data into actionable information:

- **Mission:** To design, build, and market bikes to meet the needs of the mountain bike community

- **Strategy:** To improve customers' satisfaction

- **Objective:** To increase repeat customer store sales by 20 percent

- **KPI:** The number of quarterly repeat customer sales

To achieve the objectives, the decision-makers in the Adventure Works Bike Company ask the following questions about the business:

- What has happened? (monitoring)

- What is happening? (monitoring)

- Why is it happening? (analyze)

- What will happen? (forecast based on analyzing)

- What do we want to have happen? (new hunches spurring new actions based on what you know)

Part of the problem when trying to arrive at the answers to these questions is that much of the data needed is in a raw format stored in Line-of-Business (LoB) systems and other disparate, disconnected business areas. Chapter 3, "The lifecycle of a business intelligence implementation," explains how companies accomplish providing access to this data in a usable form.

Beware of losing sight of what matters most

Companies that develop a vision or mission statement (define who they are and what success is), make goals, and monitor those goals can then re-evaluate and flourish. This approach is used by corporations, teams, departments, and not least, individuals (us). Unfortunately, what happens often is that organizations lose focus of the vision and are deterred or distracted.

The result of focusing on the wrong things

This is illustrated in the experience of a tragic airplane accident[2] that occurred more than 36 years ago. In the middle of the night, a Lockheed 1011 jumbo jet fatally crashed into the Florida Everglades. All vital parts and systems of the airplane were working perfectly, and the plane was only 20 miles away from its landing site.

During the approach, a green light failed to illuminate, and the pilots discontinued the approach. The aircraft was set to a circular holding pattern over the pitch-black Everglades while the crew focused on investigating the failed light. The pilots became so preoccupied with the light that they failed to notice the plane was gradually descending toward the dark swamp. By the time someone noticed what was happening, it was too late to avoid the disaster.

The malfunctioning light bulb didn't cause the accident; it happened because the crew placed its focus on something that seemed to matter at the moment, causing them to lose sight of what truly mattered most.

The tendency to focus on the insignificant at the expense of the profound can happen not only to pilots but to companies, departments, teams, and individuals. Sometimes the things that distract are not necessarily bad; in fact, they often seem right.

As you will see, BI helps bring to life the mantra, "what is measured gets managed." We believe it is worth the time and efforts to ensure that you are measuring the right things. When you know what to measure, you can stay on course and not be distracted by the insignificant.

What is BI?

Simply put, BI comprises the tools that help companies to execute performance management. Performance management can be defined as a series of organizational processes and applications designed to optimize the execution of business strategy.

In this book, we extend this definition of BI to include tools that help individuals, teams, and organizations simplify information discovery and analysis, making it possible for decision-makers at all levels of an organization to more easily access, understand, analyze, collaborate, and act upon information—anytime and anywhere.

In this way, to improve organizational effectiveness, Microsoft BI tools make it possible for you to create and manage information through an integrated system that includes core business productivity features, such as collaboration tools, search capabilities, and content management.

This book provides high-level information about the available tools so that you can determine which tools can best help you reach your destination as an individual, team, or organization.

---

[2] The Crash of Flight 401 (source: *http://aviation-safety.net/database/record.php?id=19721229-0&lang=en*).

The need for BI today

This following story[3] illustrates the importance of winnowing the data that's truly relevant from massive amounts of raw data and explains how to incorporate that important data into a BI solution:

> *Two men formed a partnership. They built a small shed beside a busy road. They rented a truck and drove it to a farmer's field where they purchased a truckload of melons for a dollar per melon. They drove the loaded truck to their shed by the road, where they sold their melons for a dollar per melon. They drove back to the farmer's field and bought another truckload of melons for a dollar per melon. Transporting them to the roadside, they again sold them for a dollar per melon.*
>
> *As they drove back toward the farmer's field to get another load, one partner said to the other, "We're not making much money on this business, are we?"*
>
> *"No, we're not," his partner replied. "Do you think we need a bigger truck?"*

You'll probably agree that we don't need a bigger truckload of information. Like the partners in the story, our bigger need is a clearer focus on how to value and use the information we already have. Today's workplace tends to inundate people with information instead of using the right amount of data to focus on the right problems.

The amount of data that businesses accumulate will continue to grow, and Microsoft and other companies will continue to develop better methods for moving, storing, retrieving, and displaying that data in meaningful ways. Companies must continue to increase their capacity to discover useful data, which will likely come from various systems and will require planning and collaboration to utilize effectively. Best practices must be developed for converting that relevant information into different forms or visualizations that can help provide insights and change behavior. See Appendix B, "Microsoft and "Big Data"," to learn how Microsoft is positioning itself to extract, structure, and get value from Big Data.

In the words of Bill Baker, former general manager of BI applications for the Microsoft Office Business Platform, "There is no substitute for getting the design right, getting the data right, training your users, and in general providing them the least amount of data and the most amount of guidance."

T.S. Eliot, in his poem, "Choruses from The Rock," described the situation as an "endless cycle" in which "wisdom" is "lost in knowledge" and "knowledge" is "lost in information."

Focusing on good BI addresses the problem of losing wisdom in knowledge and losing knowledge in information. And, as you might have experienced in the work place, bad patterns can seem like an endless cycle. BI simplifies information discovery and retrieval, making it possible for decision-makers at all levels of an organization to more easily access, understand, analyze, share, and act on information by helping them reach insights. Insights provide the impetus to improve the behavior of individuals, teams, and organizations. "Insights" is the word Microsoft uses to encapsulate what SharePoint 2013 provides to customers in the way of BI.

---

[3] Do you think we need a bigger truck? (Source: *https://www.lds.org/general-conference/2001/04/focus-and-priorities?lang=eng*).

What is self-service BI?

Self-service business intelligence (SSBI) is an approach to data analytics by which business users can access and work with corporate information without large investments and involvement from the IT department. The self-service approach makes it possible for end users to create personalized reports and analytical queries while freeing up IT staffers to focus on other tasks, potentially benefiting both groups.

IT must still set up self-service BI so that users can take advantage of the underlying data systems that help make trusted data available (discussed in Chapter 3), deploy the tools, and provide enough assistance and training to execute a successful implementation.

It should be noted that self-service BI does not replace corporate BI; rather, it supplements it by providing business users with the features and tools that simplify creating interactive analytics.

Microsoft's vision for BI and self-service BI

It continues to be Microsoft's vision to provide BI tools that give *all* employees access to the data required for making informed decisions. Employees must also have the flexibility to work in familiar ways, using tools such as Excel and Microsoft Visio. The fact that Microsoft continues to deliver tools that are self-service and meant for all is most evident with the release of Excel 2013, for which the SQL Server 2012 code base for the latest ad hoc reporting tool, Power View, has been included as an option for users. Also, PowerPivot is no longer a separate download but part of Excel 2013. If you think about how many people use Excel, you can easily see that it is the most commonly used BI tool.

The analytical paradox states, "Those who make the most decisions have the least information. Those who make the fewest decisions in the middle of the organization have the most information."[4] Employees on the front line have the ability to take action on insights derived from analytical capabilities but rarely have the information required to reach those insights on their own. They must ask the IT department—and then get in line when requests for information from systems are backlogged. Figure 1-3 summarizes Microsoft's vision and the direction it has taken to deliver BI to people to help them solve the analytical paradox (source: *http://www.slideshare.net/nicsmith/ business-intelligence-deck-final*).

Modern computing power is making BI more and more available to all employees in an organization so that they can make faster, more informed decisions. Microsoft has worked hard to deliver on the vision and strategy by building the tools that are highlighted in this chapter and in this book.

---

[4] Joey Fitts (*http://vimeo.com/11756037*), author of the book *Drive Business Performance: Enabling a Culture of Intelligent Execution.*

Microsoft Vision & Strategy
Democratizing Business Intelligence

Improving organizations by providing business insights to all employees leading to better, faster, more relevant decisions

- Delivered through a familiar environment
- Integrated into a business productivity infrastructure
- Built on a trusted & extensible platform

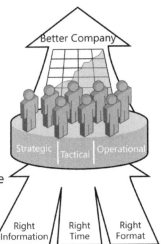

FIGURE 1-3 The Microsoft Vision and Strategy.

Figure 1-3 illustrates the flow of right information being delivered at the right time and in the right format and to the right people. Finding the right amount of information to deliver is critical so as not to overwhelm business users and, at the same time, help them stay focused. The flow of information in the illustration touches three decision levels: Strategic, Tactical, and Operational. Each of these is described as follows:

- **Strategic** At the executive level, decisions are made that center around what a company is going to do at large, comprising choices such as product lines, manufacturing methods, marketing techniques, and channels.

- **Tactical** Decisions made at this level support the strategic decisions made at the executive level. At this level, analysts examine whether forecasts meet the financial targets set forth in the one-to-five-year plan. If they do not, the elements of the forecasts must be changed. For example, a financial forecast is created in part for the purpose of measuring and monitoring against a firm's own general targets as compared to investor expectations. Investor expectations are based on a number of variables, which include industry average, the economy, and so on.

At this level, pro forma statements are used to accomplish the following objectives:

  - Estimate the effect of proposed operating changes, which makes it possible for managers to conduct "what-if" analysis.

  - Anticipate the firm's future financing needs.

  - Forecast free cash flows under different operating plans, forecast capital requirements, and then choose the plan that maximizes shareholder value.

- **Operational** Operational decisions comprise those made daily by all employees to support tactical decisions. Their impact is immediate, short term, short range, and usually low cost. The consequences of a bad operational decision are usually minimal, although a series of bad or sloppy operational decisions can cause harm. But when taken together, operational decisions can have an impact on the success of the company realizing its vision.

Is all of this just another attempt toward a "BI for everyone" utopia? We don't believe it is. We think it is important for you to be aware of the work that might be necessary to prepare data so that insights can be made available to more people—people in positions to do something about problems or make adjustments toward a better company. We believe it's worth your time to review the BI maturity model discussed in Chapter 2, which gives you an idea of where your department or company is in terms of making trusted data available and of having a culture geared toward executing on intelligence. The BI maturity model leads to a well-supported, concerted effort to get data from systems in a state that can be trusted to help support agile decisions.

Many companies use Excel for gathering BI and yet still have an infinite number of "versions of the truth." Also, companies often have some people who are louder than others or have more clout, so those are the folks who end up getting what they need from the IT department to create reports. Others know how to create more visual reports and, as a result, are more successful in getting their data in front of the decision-makers, even when their data is not validated.

We wouldn't have written this book if we didn't genuinely believe that you can make a difference in this space to help make the promises of BI become reality.

What SharePoint does for BI

SharePoint Server 2013 can be used with SQL Server reporting and BI tools to make BI data available in meaningful ways. SQL Server provides the primary data infrastructure and BI platform for giving report authors and business users trusted, scalable, and secure data.

Many good reasons support the partnering of SQL Server and SharePoint product groups to integrate products such as PowerPivot and SQL Server Reporting Services, with which you can share and organize BI assets in SharePoint lists and document libraries.

The following is a list of benefits that SharePoint Server products provide:

- If users have adopted SharePoint, they are accustomed to self-service site creation and design and thus will more likely move toward self-service reporting and analytics, particularly with Power View and PowerPivot in Excel.

- Source data refresh is configured and scheduled in SharePoint. From the Central Administration website, you have interactive reports that help you to manage and analyze all scheduled jobs that refresh source data. For more information see Chapter 7, "Using PowerPivot for SharePoint 2013."

- Users can capitalize on the scalability, collaboration, backup and recovery, and disaster recovery capabilities inherent in SharePoint 2013 to manage BI assets created in PowerPivot, Excel, Visio, Report Designer, Power View, Report Builder, and PerformancePoint Dashboard designer.

- Use of trusted locations limits access to PerformancePoint Services content types, Excel Services, and Visio Services files.

- When security and data source connections are established, publishing to a SharePoint website is a quick way to share BI assets that ultimately help employees make better decisions, faster.

- In SharePoint Server, with Analysis Services SharePoint Mode and PowerPivot, Excel Services, Visio Services, and PerformancePoint Services functioning as service applications, Visio Web Drawing files, Excel workbooks, and PerformancePoint dashboards and dashboard items are stored and secured within SharePoint lists and libraries, providing a single security and repository framework.

The BI stack: SQL Server + SharePoint + Office

The architectural diagram presented in Figure 1-4 (described in detail on the Microsoft TechNet site in "Architecture for Business Intelligence in SharePoint Server 2013") provides another, more technical visual aid for how each of the pieces work together.

The following is a very brief summary of what's new for BI in SharePoint 2013.

- Ad hoc report authoring in the browser by using Power View

- In Excel 2013, the SQL Server 2012 code base for the latest ad hoc reporting tool, Power View, is included. Also, PowerPivot is no longer a separate download but is an integral part of Excel 2013.

Report authoring is discussed in the next section. Report viewing can occur in just about any browser, in Microsoft Office, on Windows 8 phones and other table devices (such as Surface and iPad), and in SharePoint Search.

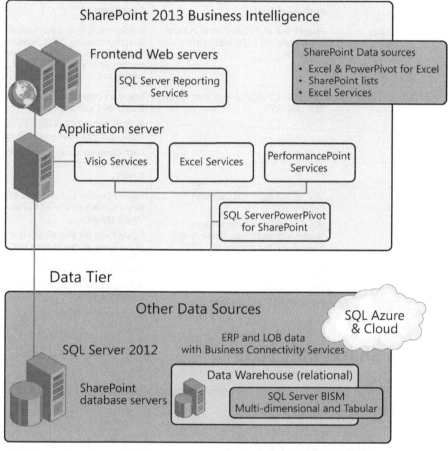

Presentation Tier

Report viewing
Browser, Microsoft Office, mobile, and Search

Report authoring
Browser (PowerPilot), Microsoft Office, PerformancePoint Dashboard Designer, and more

Application Tier

SharePoint 2013 Business Intelligence

Frontend Web servers

SQL Server Reporting Services

SharePoint Data sources
- Excel & PowerPivot for Excel
- SharePoint lists
- Excel Services

Application server

Visio Services

Excel Services

PerformancePoint Services

SQL ServerPowerPivot for SharePoint

Data Tier

Other Data Sources

SQL Azure & Cloud

SQL Server 2012

ERP and LOB data with Business Connectivity Services

SharePoint database servers

Data Warehouse (relational)

SQL Server BISM Multi-dimensional and Tabular

FIGURE 1-4 SharePoint 2013 Services for BI.

Authoring in Microsoft BI tools

When it comes to SharePoint and BI, the essential objective is to have the ability to create insights in the authoring tools that are spread among Office, SharePoint, and SQL Server (see Table 1-1) and then to share the results in charts, reports, dashboards, and KPIs. These insights can be shared with the organization, the team or community, or with the individual via a browser.

TABLE 1-1 Microsoft BI authoring tools and platforms

Product or platform	Authoring tool	Comments
Microsoft Office 2013 desktop applications	PowerPivot and Power View in Excel 2013, Visio 2013 (Professional or Premium)	Before publishing a worksheet to SharePoint using Excel Services or Visio Services, you must have already authored and—if applicable—connected to a data source.
SharePoint Server 2013	Dashboard Designer and Web Parts that offer KPIs	You start Dashboard Designer from a SharePoint website. BI Web Parts are available to use individually to create simplified KPIs. Each client tool also provides Web Parts to extend your ability to render reports.
SQL Server 2012	SQL Server Reporting Services Report. SQL Server Data Tools (Visual Studio with same functionality as PowerPivot but deploy to SSAS) Excel: consumes Analysis Services/Tabular data via an ODC or BISM connection file PowerPivot for SharePoint	Report Builder and Report Designer was originally designed to help you create reports. PowerPivot for SharePoint is a SharePoint shared service that integrates PowerPivot into your SharePoint environment. Access a deployed SSDT project via a connection file.

Examples of BI in SharePoint 2013

The following sections look at ways that you can take advantage of SharePoint 2013 features for developing and strengthening your BI capabilities.

PerformancePoint and the BI stack

Figure 1-5 demonstrates how a solution using PerformancePoint Services in SharePoint 2013, integrated with SQL Server 2012, provides KPIs that drive decisions in an IT department. The IT Operations scorecard shows how simple it is to see where database space, as a percentage, is not meeting its target. After the following illustration is a brief explanation that maps what is going on under the hood.

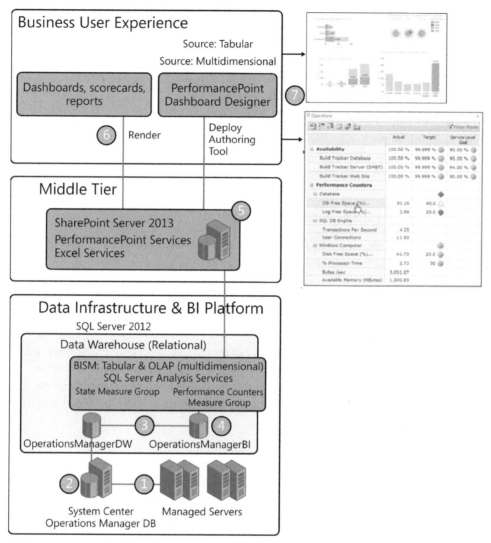

FIGURE 1-5 From SCOM to PerformancePoint.

1. System Center Operations Manager (SCOM) collects monitor state and performance counter data from managed servers.

2. The Operations Manager database collects data from the managed servers. Data is pre-aggregated and stored in tables designed to support production reporting requirements.

3. A small subset of data in the Operations Manager data warehouse (OperationsManagerDW) is transformed and loaded into the BI framework database (Operations Manager BI). This database contains the star schemas for the Analysis Services Online Analytical Processing (OLAP) cubes. Alternatively, users can load data into a tabular model from the data warehouse to make data available in either a pivot table in Excel 2013 or in Power View in Excel 2013.

4. Analysis Services OLAP cubes are built and processed from data stored in the Operations Manager BI database.

5. Data from the OLAP cubes is used to populate PerformancePoint Server scorecards, dashboards, and analytic reports. These components are originally created by using the PerformancePoint Services 2013 Dashboard Designer.

6. Scorecards, dashboards, and analytic reports are made available to the user community through SharePoint Server. After the scorecards, dashboards, and analytic reports are initially created and deployed, they should not need to be deployed again. These components are refreshed as new data becomes available in the OLAP cubes.

7. Alternatively, data that is stored in the tabular database is made available to authoring tools such as Excel 2013 and Power View in Excel 2013.

The IT Operations scorecard on the right side of Figure 1-5 reveals (flagged by the red diamonds) that free-space targets for the database are not being met.

Power Pivot and BISM Model: A Fulfillment Report for Tracking Products

This example demonstrates the ease and simplicity of creating an interactive Power View report. But, don't misunderstand; getting to trusted data is not as simple as this example might illustrate. The data that supports it has been massaged, reviewed, and more over the course of several months. This is a high-level view of the process and steps for getting to a successful product fulfillment dashboard.

The story and report requirements

A team at the call center for Lucerne Publishing manages the fulfillment of orders; specifically, high-end user-created books. These books are created online with existing family pictures in the form of images and often content from individual social networking sites. The team needed an interactive report with which it could manage the fulfillment of orders by monitoring the various states of an order as they relate to the fulfillment of that order. This helps it manage third-party vendors who assist in fulfilling a book order.

Choosing a tool, introducing self-service BI, and planning for adoption

After having an understanding of the team culture, existing infrastructure, and having chosen a tool-set for BI, as described in Chapter 2, the IT team chose to set up self-service analytics by using Power View and underlying data from their data systems, imported into PowerPivot in Excel 2013.

Understanding the culture   The call center at Lucerne Publishing is an important part of the company that maintains a healthy autonomous culture. One user close to all of the teams had already learned PowerPivot and Power View and was available to assist users with learning and adoption of new reporting options. The team was well aware that if they approached other teams in the company, they would likely be put in a waiting period for lack of resources and priority.

BI maturity   Users were already accustomed to using Reporting Services reports for filtering, searching, and analyzing data to manage the order fulfillment. They wanted a report with interactive visuals for analysis and actionable insights.

Discovering a visual concept for a report

The manager of the company data servers had a good understanding of the team's needs and what a visual, interactive fulfillment bar chart should look like. They further investigated by searching on Bing/images for more examples. Figure 1-6 presents just one example that was found. Quickly, the goal was set to create a similar report with Lucerne Publishing data.

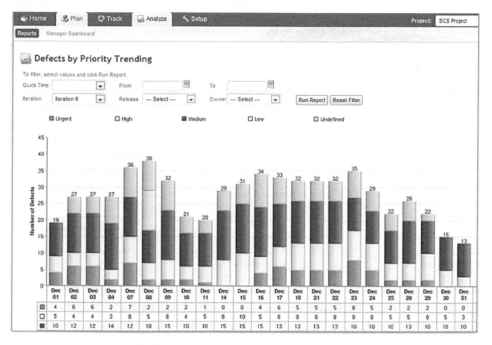

FIGURE 1-6 An example of fulfillment chart located by Bing Search.

Tip A great method for brainstorming on chart types and uses is to search on Bing/images with keywords specific to your need.

The steps to implementation

What follows are high-level descriptions of the steps to take to implement the described fulfillment report.

Determine data sources and importing data

In this example, there is data ready for reporting. Because the data server developer understands the need for a report and existing SQL Server Reporting Services (SSRS), reports are already supported by the data he manages; thus, this is not as difficult process. Of course, every use case is different and data preparation might be more work-intensive.

Import data into PowerPivot, explore data, and design

PowerPivot in Excel 2013 is the choice for creating proof-of-concepts and for making ad hoc reports. Users are able to schedule a data-refresh in SharePoint. Sometimes, the next logical step is to formalize the PowerPivot report by importing it into the tabular modeling tool in SQL Server Data Tools (SSDT). At that point, you can automate a data-refresh (or processing) on a more flexible schedule.

You will find that exploring data in the PowerPivot window is fast and simple. You can filter on columns and quickly determine what additions should be made to the model by way of calculated columns and measures such as calculations.

In this case, the SQL table already updates the all-important date/time stamp for each status of the fulfillment process. Occasionally, however, you will perform a Data Analysis Expressions (DAX) formula to enrich the data. Figure 1-7 shows is an example of a simple calculated column to provide in a Pivot Table or Power View the duration of time from when the PO was created to Rendered (or printed), in a user-friendly format.

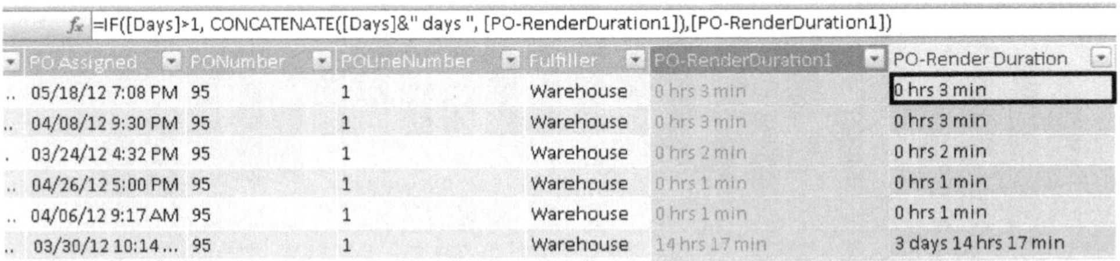

	f_x =IF([Days]>1, CONCATENATE([Days]&" days ", [PO-RenderDuration1]),[PO-RenderDuration1])					
▼ PO Assigned ▼	FONumber ▼	POLineNumber ▼	Fulfiller ▼	PO-RenderDuration1 ▼	PO-Render Duration ▼
.. 05/18/12 7:08 PM	95	1	Warehouse	0 hrs 3 min	0 hrs 3 min
.. 04/08/12 9:30 PM	95	1	Warehouse	0 hrs 3 min	0 hrs 3 min
. 03/24/12 4:32 PM	95	1	Warehouse	0 hrs 2 min	0 hrs 2 min
.. 04/26/12 5:00 PM	95	1	Warehouse	0 hrs 1 min	0 hrs 1 min
.. 04/06/12 9:17 AM	95	1	Warehouse	0 hrs 1 min	0 hrs 1 min
.. 03/30/12 10:14 ...	95	1	Warehouse	14 hrs 17 min	3 days 14 hrs 17 min

FIGURE 1-7 PowerPivot Window and DAX for showing time between PO and Rendering.

Here are the equations used to calculate Seconds, Minutes, Hours and Days.

Days:

```
=IF(ISBLANK([Rendered]), 0, FLOOR(1. * ([Rendered]-[PO Assigned]), 1))
```

Hours:

```
=IF(ISBLANK([Rendered]), 0, FLOOR(MOD(24. * ([Rendered]-[PO Assigned]), 24), 1))
```

Minutes:

```
=IF(ISBLANK([Rendered]), 0, FLOOR(MOD(24. * 60 * ([Rendered]-[PO Assigned]), 60), 1))
```

Seconds:

```
=IF(ISBLANK([Rendered]),0, 24. * 60 * 60 * ([Rendered]-[PO Assigned]))
```

Concatenating:

```
=CONCATENATE(MyCanvas[PO-RenderHours]&" hrs ", [Minutes]&" min")
```

Figure 1-8 depicts a finished view of the PivotTable in Excel 2013, where you will test your measures and calculated columns.

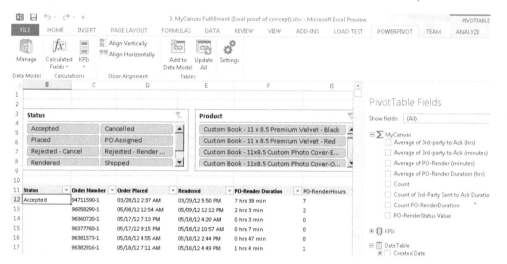

FIGURE 1-8 A pivot table showing data for Lucerne Publishing.

Create the Power View report

The next step is to create a Power View report from the data collected in PowerPivot in Excel 2013. Refer to Chapter 5, "Using Power View in Excel 2013," to learn how to create reports in Power View. There are also excellent articles for creating user-friendly reports and dashboards.

Publish to SharePoint

As a best practice, publish the Excel 2013 workbook with a PivotTable and Power View example so that users can explore the data in the PivotTable and discover the mechanisms in Power View for analyzing via the cross-filtering slicers and visuals (Figure 1-9).

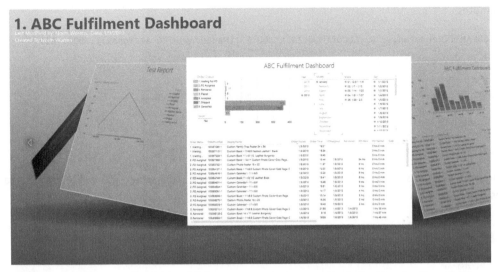

FIGURE 1-9 The Lucerne Publishing fulfillment report in presented in Power View for SharePoint.

Modify according to user needs

You modify the report by working on the model. For example, you might simplify or clarify labels or add value by simplifying the data table for time intelligence and showing the time difference between each state of an order.

Automate and formalize in SQL Server Data Tools

The data for this particular report needs to be refreshed every 15 minutes, and for this reason we need to import the PowerPivot into SQL Server 2012 Data Tools, deploy to Analysis Services, and set up a job that refreshes the data more frequently. We also want to optimize the data-refresh by creating partitions and only refreshing the *MyCanvas_Current* partition, and processing (refreshing) the partition, *MyCanvas_Historical*, only once.

This process is all described in Appendix B.

Sharing with other teams (building user adoption)

Your efforts to promote an extremely useful report should not end until you have shared the report with other team managers. You now have an example and some code from which you can draw and reproduce with other teams. This specific example was reproduced for DNA fulfillment and vendor management analytics and reporting.

Capture what customers say and how the interactive report helps them take preemptive action on delayed states in the fulfillment process. Make these comments available to other groups that can also benefit.

A summary of the fulfillment example

Figure 1-10 illustrates just one of many examples that can become realities as you either combine or adopt one of several available tools in SharePoint 2013, SQL Server 2012, and Office 2013.

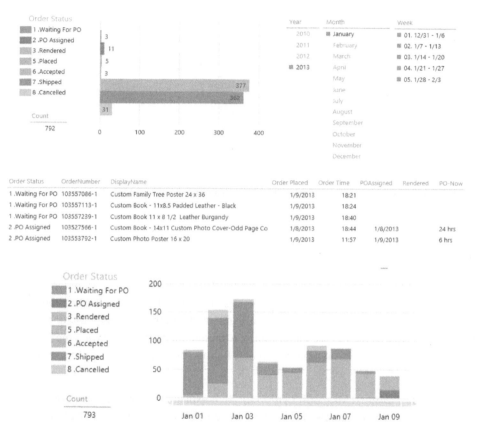

FIGURE 1-10 Power View example of a fulfillment report.

Creating a report by using an Odata feed from a SharePoint list

It's simply amazing to be able to refresh and consume data from a SharePoint 2013 or 2010 list by way of an Odata feed in SharePoint 2013. An extremely useful approach is to provide interactive visualizations to the SharePoint lists to which users have been adding, sometimes for a very long time.

Figure 1-11 shows a list that was updated for three years. From discussions with the users, they asked that the reasons for reshipment be divided into three sections to show responsibility for replacements and reshipments of products.

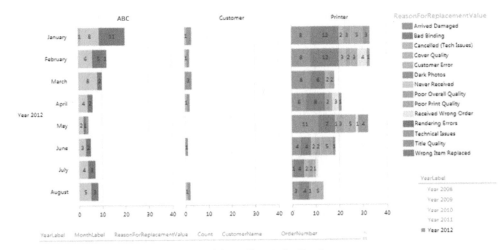

FIGURE 1-11 Power View example derived from SharePoint list data.

Summary

In this chapter, we discussed the purpose and need for BI in a language that is directed at the business user. It showed that companies are much like aircraft in that they have a destination or goal and must constantly react to feedback provided by instruments that measure and monitor the status of various inputs. Those instruments are the BI tools we implement so that we have a method for visualizing metrics that tell us what has happened, what is happening, why it is happening, and what will happen to our business.

The chapter also explained Microsoft's vision for BI. It explained what SharePoint does for BI and provided a couple of examples to show the benefits of using SharePoint 2013 in any BI implementation.

CHAPTER 2

Planning for business intelligence adoption

As described in Chapter 1, "Business intelligence in SharePoint," business intelligence (BI) is a general term used to describe the development of insights from one or more tools that make it possible for data consumers in a company—information workers and decision-makers—to understand what has happened in the past and to compare past events to what is happening now. With these insights, they can set appropriate goals for the company, monitor ongoing progress toward those goals, and take corrective action whenever necessary. This chapter focuses on the reporting and analysis tools that data consumers use to make these insights possible. In turn, these tools rely on a supporting infrastructure of trusted data, described in Chapter 3, "The lifecycle of a business intelligence implementation."

If you're a business user, your primary interaction with a BI solution is with the presentation layer. However, the Microsoft stack includes a variety of tools with overlapping capabilities that can seem confusing at first glance. This chapter can help you to understand how these tools support different scenarios, how your choice of which tool to use for a particular task can change over time, and how to select the right tool for the task at hand.

If, on the other hand, you're a BI developer or SharePoint administrator, this chapter can help you to develop and support a successful BI implementation. You need to understand the different ways that users can interact with data, now and in the future, and the implications of tool selection for the overall architecture. Additionally, you need to consider how tool selection impacts the workload of IT support staff. For example, if you have limited resources, rather than implement products that require IT support to maintain the technical infrastructure and develop complex reports and analytical tools, you might choose to use only those tools that enable self-service BI for business users.

This chapter starts by examining the analysis needs of business user communities and how the Microsoft reporting and analysis tools serve these communities. It then reviews the typical progression of competency with BI within a company and how that progression affects the mix of tools for business users. Finally, it provides a guide to selecting the right tool for the community and analytical requirements applicable to you and describes an action plan for supporting user adoption of BI.

Business user communities

When it comes to BI, business users are likely to have different information needs, depending on their technical skills, the types of decisions they make, and how they need to save and share their insights. In several different ways, business users with common characteristics can be grouped into separate user communities. By understanding the needs of these business user communities from a variety of perspectives, you can select the tools that best support those needs.

Understanding your audience: Casual users vs. power users

One common way to differentiate business users is to separate them into two communities—casual users and power users. Casual users might be department managers, executives, or even external stakeholders such as customers or suppliers. Casual users tend to be infrequent users of BI, perhaps once per week or less, whereas power users are often daily consumers of BI.

Because casual users spend less time with BI, their skill level with BI tools is much lower than that of power users, so the interfaces to such tools must be simple so that they can find the information they need on their own. For these users, a web-based reporting application works well. The tools that help a casual user interact with data and develop insights tend to be very simple and focused on specific sets of data.

But, making tools simple for casual users often makes them too simple for power users, who typically require access to a wide variety of data and need more on-demand analytical capabilities. Power users spend enough time working regularly with BI tools that they develop advanced technical skills. These users, typically business analysts and analytical modelers, need tools that give them the ability to explore the data and create visualizations.

Another way to distinguish casual users and power users is by assessing their familiarity with the data. It's quite possible that a person can be quite knowledgeable about the data in his own department and thus qualify as a power user, requiring a more analytical BI tool for daily work. It's also possible that this same person has access to data in another department but is less familiar with that data. For that situation, this user needs a basic reporting tool that simplifies information access.

In their book *Business Intelligence: Making Better Decisions Faster* (2002, Microsoft Press), Elizabeth Vitt, Michael Luckevich, and Stacia Misner further separate the casual users into two groups: information users and information consumers. Figure 2-1 presents the relationship of all three groups graphically, in which the pyramid shows the relative size of each group.

FIGURE 2-1 The business user communities.

The largest community consists of information users, who rely on standard reports that BI developers publish to a central location. These reports might be accessible either online or in print, depending on the distribution mechanism that the report administrators implement. For this information-user community, SQL Server Reporting Services is a good solution, either running as an independent application or integrated with Microsoft SharePoint Server 2013. It provides a scalable online environment for viewing reports that administrators can secure, and it can deliver reports in a variety of formats on a scheduled basis via email or to a network file share. If information users require only online access to centralized reports, other good options supported by SharePoint Server 2013 include Microsoft Power View in SharePoint, Microsoft Power View in Excel, or PowerPivot for SharePoint 2013 workbooks.

> **Note** Power View in Excel and Power View in SharePoint are similar products, but behave differently online. Both require an instance of SQL Server Reporting Services installed in SharePoint integrated mode. However, to create a Power View in Excel report that is accessible in Excel Services, you start by using Excel 2013 to access an internal data model or a PowerPivot for Excel data model embedded in the same workbook, add a Power View sheet to the workbook, design one or more visualizations, and then publish the workbook to a SharePoint document library, as described in Chapter 5, "Using Power View in Excel 2013." Users can interact with the Power View sheet in a web browser by using features such as filtering and highlighting, but they cannot edit the visualizations, save the Power View sheet separately, or export it to Microsoft PowerPoint. Power View in SharePoint, on the other hand, is the tool you use to create a new Power View report that you store as an RDLX file in a SharePoint document library. If you open a saved Power View report, you can use the interactive features with its visualizations, and you can also edit the report by adding or removing fields or rearranging items. You can also export the report to PowerPoint to create an interactive slide presentation with a live data connection.

Information consumers are the second community of casual users. They tend to explore the data more than the information users, but they lack the expertise necessary to query a database directly. They can get the information they need by working with interactive reports that include parameters for filtering and sorting or those that include options to change the visibility of selected report elements. Interactive reports can also include the ability to present more detailed information, either by displaying the details in the same report or by opening a separate report. Again, Reporting Services is a good choice for meeting the needs of this community. With a proper understanding of the needs of information consumers, a report author can incorporate a variety of interactive features to satisfy those needs. Interactivity in Reporting Services emphasizes navigation within a report and between reports, which is useful but restricts the ability of information consumers to explore the data. If interactive exploration is preferable, Power View in Excel or Power View in SharePoint are good choices because these tools make it possible for business users to easily filter data and change visualizations on demand. Another option is to deploy PowerPivot workbooks to SharePoint, with which users can filter, slice, and sort model-based pivot tables and pivot charts in the browser.

At the top of the pyramid, power analysts are the smallest community. Power analysts might use existing reports as a starting point for analysis, but they also need the ability to define and execute their own queries. In some cases, they might even build reports for the other communities. For example, a power user can use Report Builder to create a report based on their own queries and then publish the entire report (or even individual elements of the report, called *report parts*) for the other user communities to access. Information consumers can build up a customized report from these report parts without knowing anything about how to construct a query or how to design the report part.

As flexible as Reporting Services is when you install it as a native mode report server, its report definition language (RDL) files have limited support for the type of ad hoc analysis that power analysts frequently perform. A more commonly used tool for analysis is Microsoft Excel 2013. A power analyst can group and filter data in a pivot table and create additional calculations to supplement analysis of the data and publish the workbook to SharePoint for others to view by using Excel Services. If analysis requires integrating data from multiple data sources, the power analyst can create a data model in Excel and add Power View sheets for displaying the data model as charts, maps, and other types of interactive visualizations. Furthermore, if the model requires more advanced calculations and modeling operations, the power analyst can use PowerPivot in Excel to enhance the model and use a pivot table to display the data or use the model as a source for Power View in Excel. To share the results of analysis as a report, the power analyst can then publish a workbook with Power View or PowerPivot sheets to SharePoint Server 2013.

Organizational hierarchy

The position of a business user within the organizational hierarchy and the decision-making associated with that role often are a factor in the type of information and the BI tool that the user requires. The higher the business user is in the hierarchy, the more likely that the user is an information consumer, as described in the preceding section. Furthermore, the higher in the hierarchy a user is, the more likely it is that the information that the user relies on is already cleansed and highly processed, is already compatible with data from different sources, and has been restructured for reporting and analysis.

Because this information has long-term value and is vital to strategic planning, a solid BI infrastructure exists to automate the necessary cleansing and processing. Usually, this information is provided to upper management in a summarized, structured format with limited analytical capabilities. Reporting Services can be useful as a delivery mechanism for this type of information online, in print, or via email. Other online viewing options include dashboards and scorecards in SharePoint Server 2013 or PerformancePoint Services.

As business users move closer to the operations of the business, their information needs diverge, depending on the type of work a user performs. People at this level of the organizational hierarchy can be information users, information consumers, or power analysts.

The information requirements of these users differ from those of upper management because these users often combine official corporate data from a BI system with other data either created manually or obtained from external sources. This combination of data might occur only occasionally or might be an ongoing exercise. Either way, this type of quick data mash-up typically has only short-term value, so it's not a candidate for a formal BI implementation. On the other hand, it's a perfect scenario for a data model in Excel or PowerPivot in Excel, which very easily accommodate this type of ad hoc data integration.

> **Note** Both the Excel data model and the PowerPivot in Excel tabular model are desktop versions of the tabular model that was first introduced in the PowerPivot for Excel 2010 Add-in. In turn, the tabular model is one type of the Business Intelligence Semantic Model (BISM). You can publish the desktop tabular models to a SharePoint Server 2013 farm that includes Excel Services and PowerPivot for SharePoint 2013. Microsoft SQL Server 2012 introduced a server version of the tabular model that you can use to host tabular models created in SQL Server Data Tools independent of a SharePoint Server 2013 farm. Conceptually, the desktop and server versions of the tabular model are similar. The differences lie in the features supported in the models and the server infrastructure requirements for centralized storage and access. The other type of BISM is the multidimensional and data-mining model which requires installation of a SQL Server Analysis Services instance. You can learn more about this in Chapter 3.

BI communities

Microsoft has another way of grouping users that focuses instead on how users work with BI and how much collaboration they require. These BI communities and the BI tools designed for each community are shown in Figure 2-2. As the diagram makes clear, some overlap of tools exists between communities.

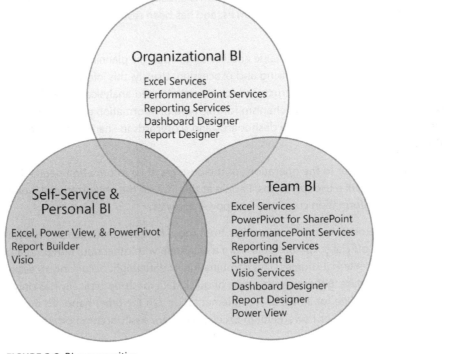

FIGURE 2-2 BI communities.

Organizational BI

Some popular ways to deliver BI to all employees in a company are to provide access to metrics that show progress toward organizational goals or to compare a current state to historical trends. Ideally, users of organizational BI can break down this information to see how their individual departments contribute to current conditions. Because the intended audience of information is the entire company, you can anticipate that the audience consists largely of information users and information consumers. Therefore, an organizational BI solution needs to support only online viewing, with limited interaction.

Typically, this information comes from approved data sources that have been staged, transformed, and restructured into a data warehouse. Ideally, this data has also been incorporated into an Analysis Services cube or tabular model to provide both faster reporting to all business users and more flexible analysis for the power analysts.

Whether the data is stored in a relational database, a cube, or a tabular data model, the three primary tools for consuming this data at the organizational level are Excel Services, PerformancePoint Services, and Reporting Services, which you learn more about in Chapter 3. Excel Services, PerformancePoint Services, and Power View require a SharePoint Server 2013 Enterprise installation, with scalability achieved by setting up a SharePoint farm to distribute the workload. Reporting Services must be integrated into a SharePoint farm to use Power View or can run independently if you do not want to use Power View or SharePoint. All these services require IT support to install and configure the environment.

In organizational BI solutions, business users tend to be consumers of published content rather than contributors. Content contributors are usually BI developers, IT professionals, and in some cases, power analysts. The prevailing concept in organizational BI is to centralize content by using defined standards for layout, naming conventions, and color schemes. This BI can be consumed as is or can be used as base components by power users who aggregate these with other content suitable for a targeted audience.

Each of the tools discussed in this section solves specific problems for organizational BI, starting with the most commonly implemented tool. The following descriptions of each tool aren't intended to be comprehensive; they focus on the features that address specific challenges that organizations face when implementing BI.

Reporting Services   Many organizations start with standard reports by implementing Reporting Services. If it's set up to run in SharePoint integrated mode, Reporting Services relies on the same security model and centralized storage that SharePoint uses, which makes it easier to administer. Report administrators can control how reports execute to balance performance against timeliness of data by setting up a report to run on demand to view current data or to use caching to execute it in advance and minimize the wait time for viewing. Users access reports by using a supported browser—Microsoft Internet Explorer or Mozilla Firefox on a computer running a Windows operating system, or Apple Safari on a computer running a Mac operating system.

Having reports available in a SharePoint document library also makes it easier for business users to find information for online viewing. Users have only one place to go for all corporate information, whether that information is in the form of Reporting Services reports, Excel workbooks, or other content. The interface is simple for users to access because reports are stored like any other content on the SharePoint server, making it a good option for information delivery to a wide audience of casual users. (Even if you run Reporting Services in native mode—without SharePoint Server 2013—the interface remains easy to use.) As an alternative, reports can be sent directly to users via email as often as necessary.

Reporting Services is also popular for its ability to produce pixel-perfect reports. The report author, typically an IT professional, has a high degree of control over the appearance and behavior of report elements to produce just the right layout, whether users view the report online or export it to another format. Also, with some advance thought about the types of questions that a user might ask when viewing a report, the report author can build in parameters for filtering and can add interactive features that lead the user to additional answers.

Crossing over into the team and personal BI communities, Reporting Services also supports a variety of export formats so that any user can save the report in a print-ready format such as a Portable Document Format (PDF) file or to incorporate information into a Microsoft Word document. Moreover, the user can reuse the information in a report simply by using a Web Part to include it in a dashboard. Users with more advanced skills can export report data for further analysis into Excel, or they can set up a report as a data feed for ongoing analysis in a tabular model or PowerPivot in Excel. In addition, BI developers can incorporate reports into PerformancePoint Services dashboards. And reusability doesn't stop there. In companies with mature BI implementations, application developers can embed Reporting Services content in custom analytical applications through application programming interfaces (APIs).

> **Note** Power View in SharePoint is also a feature of Reporting Services that could be part of an organizational BI solution, but it lacks many of the features that are associated with operational reporting that Reporting Services supports with RDL files. We discuss its features as part of a Team BI solution later in this chapter.

Excel Services   Although Reporting Services can produce some reports with complex calculations, it is limited in what it can do. It isn't meant to be a replacement for Excel. On the other hand, Excel isn't meant to be a corporate reporting solution. Although it provides a lot of formatting options and can handle complex calculations, Excel does not support the same control over formatting that's available in Reporting Services, and it has limits on the amount of data that can be stored in a workbook. (If you're creating workbooks with a tabular data model, the limits are much higher.) However, sharing Excel workbooks through Excel Services can be a reasonable reporting alternative for organizations that aren't using Reporting Services.

Excel Services runs as a SharePoint Server 2013 service application. The advantage of using Excel Services is that organizations can take advantage of the SharePoint infrastructure to deliver information contained in workbooks to a wide audience, which is a much better approach than sending them to users through the email system. Users don't need to have Excel or any other type of application or plug-in installed on their computer; they just need to use a supported browser—Internet Explorer, Firefox, or Google Chrome on a computer running a Windows operating system, or Safari on a computer running a Mac operating system. And, because the workbooks are stored in SharePoint, the users need only learn how to use one interface to access any corporate content.

Excel Services also provides a more secure and scalable approach than email distribution. Administrators and content owners can control whether users can only view a document online or whether they can download it. It's also possible to restrict viewing to certain sheets or selected items in the workbook when it's important to hide intellectual property or the detailed data behind a particular cell value. Furthermore, the Excel Services calculation engine handles all the complex calculations for multiple concurrent users, thus sparing hardware resources on the user's computer.

When an Excel workbook sources data from an Analysis Services cube or tabular model, Excel Services supports drilling, filtering, and sorting data in a pivot table. In SharePoint Server 2013, Excel Services now supports replacing data on the pivot table's rows, columns, or filter axes. Overall, the interactivity is better than Reporting Services RDL files can support.

The workbook author can configure the report to accept parameters from the user for another type of interactivity. When the user views the workbook in Excel services, the user can type in the parameter values, which can in turn be input values for a calculation. This feature makes it possible for the user to dynamically change workbook content by using a simple interface.

Another benefit of Excel Services is the reusability of information contained in workbooks for the team and personal BI communities. Users can reference cell values in an Excel workbook published to SharePoint to create status indicators, which are a very simple type of key performance indicator (KPI), having only three possible levels. Also, more advanced users can use workbooks in whole or in part in dashboards by using Excel Web Access Web Parts. Parameters in the workbook can be connected to Filter Web Parts. This means that users can change content for multiple Web Parts on the same dashboard page with a single filter. In addition, an Excel workbook can provide source data for a Chart Web Part.

BI developers can take advantage of Excel workbooks in several ways. Data in a workbook can be a data source for various content types in PerformancePoint Services, whereas a workbook itself can display in a PerformancePoint Services dashboard. For custom web-based analytical applications, application developers can use the Excel Services REST API or the ECMAScript object model to display and interact with workbooks, as described in Chapter 4, "Using PowerPivot in Excel 2013."

PerformancePoint Services   Companies with a clearly defined performance management strategy use PerformancePoint Services to communicate progress toward established goals. The basic dashboard capabilities in SharePoint Server 2013 might be the first step that some companies take as they develop corporate performance analytics, but PerformancePoint Services is preferred for its advanced dashboard functionality. It also includes components such as scorecards, analytical reports, strategy maps, and filters that BI developers and power analysts can use with either PerformancePoint or SharePoint dashboards.

The best data source for PerformancePoint Services components is an Analysis Services cube or tabular model, which delivers the best performance for viewing and interacting with content. With respect to the analytical grid, analytical charts, and decomposition tree, Analysis Services is the only type of data source that these reports can use. The analytical reports are the best way to support drilling and pivoting in a web browser environment. BI developers can structure dashboards to simplify the use of analytical reports for casual users who might feel overwhelmed by the functionality that these reports provide, but the decomposition tree cannot be built in advance. Power analysts who fully understand the data source and the tool's capabilities will appreciate the support for ad hoc analysis in these report types.

Apart from the analytical components in PerformancePoint Services, dashboards and scorecards are simple enough for the casual user to explore. A benefit of using PerformancePoint content types to build dashboards and scorecards is the ability for the BI developer to integrate multiple data sources together so that business users can see related content in one location. For example, rather than opening an Excel workbook to see the established organizational goals and then opening a Reporting Services report to see the current status from an operations data source, the user can instead see the goals and the status side by side in one report, no matter where the source data is actually stored.

Although plenty of advantages are gained by using PerformancePoint Services, some disadvantages must be pointed out. First, the formatting options are limited as compared to Reporting Services or Excel. Second, developers can use PerformancePoint Services dashboards to combine a lot of content built for other purposes and can reuse many PerformancePoint content types in SharePoint dashboards, but that's it. The only other way to reuse content built for PerformancePoint Services is to build custom applications by using the PerformancePoint Services API.

Team BI

An easy way to get started with BI is to focus on a single community within an organization, which might be preferable because it's faster to deliver initially than an organization-wide initiative. The target community might be an entire department or perhaps a small team within a department. Or, it could be a project team in which multiple departments are represented, or it could even be a group of people external to the organization, such as customers.

The key differentiators between team BI and organization BI are the scope of the information provided to the target audience and a greater participation in the content development process by the team community. Consequently, the ideal BI infrastructure provides an opportunity for the team to use the information collaboratively as they work toward a common goal.

Like organizational BI, data for a team BI solution often comes from approved, cleansed, and processed sources and is quite possibly stored in an Analysis Services cube or tabular model. However, the scope of the data tends to be more limited. For example, a data mart built from a single data source might be the primary data of interest for team BI.

Team BI solutions can use the same tools that are prevalent in organizational BI. In addition, team BI might also include SharePoint BI, Microsoft Visio Services, and PowerPivot for SharePoint as additional options for creating and sharing content. Casual users can easily view content produced with any of these tools within SharePoint as part of a dashboard or as individual documents stored in a document library. Power analysts and BI developers typically share responsibility for creating and managing content for team BI.

Let's start by reviewing the three new tools added to the mix. Then, we can revisit the other tools to learn how their usage changes when implemented for team BI communities.

SharePoint BI   SharePoint Server 2013 includes several features that make it ideal for team BI, especially for teams without much existing infrastructure already in place. In fact, after IT has given a team access to a SharePoint site, power analysts on the team can manage content for consumption by the team BI community with relatively little effort. The ease of implementation translates to simple capabilities, but for teams that are new to BI, these simple capabilities might be all that casual users need.

Another benefit of SharePoint BI is the ability to combine content in a single location from team members who use different tools. That way, no one is forced into learning a new tool for content creation or investing in the hardware, software, and processes necessary to support even a small data mart before the migration to a new tool or process is absolutely necessary.

To get started quickly, a SharePoint site collection owner can create a specialized site type called Business Intelligence Center. It includes a set of libraries and supports content types specific to BI such as Excel workbooks and dashboards. It can also store reports if Reporting Services is configured to run in SharePoint integrated mode. In addition, the Business Intelligence Center includes a special document library for data connections that power analysts and BI developers can use to create new workbooks, reports, Visio diagrams, and PerformancePoint content. We use the term SharePoint BI to refer generically to the features supported in Business Intelligence Center because they can be implemented independent of this site type.

We've already mentioned SharePoint dashboards as a way to present workbooks, reports, and PerformancePoint components. Dashboards can include all kinds of other content, such as Visio Services diagrams and Filter Web Parts. They're supposed to be simple enough such that anyone can build a dashboard page, but in reality, power analysts and BI developers are the creators of dashboards.

Filter Web Parts on the dashboard make it easy to customize content on a dashboard page for each user. The same filter value can update multiple Web Parts on the same page. Working with dashboard pages is not difficult when merely adding a group of Web Parts. However, it can be a bit more challenging to configure correctly when attempting to link these Web Parts together for use with a filter, especially if the Web Parts come from different data sources. For this reason, constructing anything but the simplest of dashboards is usually a task assigned to a BI developer.

Visio Services Visio Services provides another way to visualize data. It supports live connections to data sources for use in web-based Visio diagrams that display information ranging from a color-coded status about projects to the current state of processes to the availability of servers, and so on. Conceptually, the purpose of a Visio diagram is similar to that of a dashboard because it helps business users see trends and outliers at a glance.

Visio diagrams are accessible in a document library or can be added to a SharePoint dashboard by using a Visio Web Access Web Part, so they are just as easy for users to consume as any other content available in SharePoint. Like Excel Services with workbooks, Visio Services does not require users to have Visio installed on their computers before they can view a diagram published to SharePoint.

The development of Visio diagrams is in the realm of a specialist who understands how to build them and how to connect the data to the diagram properly by using the Visio 2013 desktop application. Supported data sources for Visio Services include SQL Server, SharePoint lists, Excel Services, Microsoft Access, and any source accessible with an OLE DB or ODBC provider. No other tool provides functionality like Visio Services, so the diagrams are not reusable for team BI outside of SharePoint unless the team develops a custom application.

PowerPivot for SharePoint   PowerPivot for SharePoint is a feature of Excel Services that executes queries and renders PowerPivot in Excel workbooks on demand in a browser. It requires you to install Analysis Services in SharePoint Integrated Mode and register the Analysis Services server in the Excel Services service application. You can also install the PowerPivot for SharePoint Add-in to include the following features: scheduled data refresh, PowerPivot Gallery, Management Dashboard, and the BISM file content type. PowerPivot for SharePoint provides a link between self-service BI and team BI.

Business users—usually power analysts—can publish their PowerPivot in Excel workbooks to SharePoint either in a standard document library or in a specialized document library that displays thumbnail images of workbooks by which users can find the workbook they want without first opening it. Just as with Excel workbooks, administrators and workbook owners can control access and restrict users to online viewing only, thereby protecting the data contained in the workbook.

Beyond making it possible to share information with other team members and supporting concurrent access in a scalable environment, PowerPivot for SharePoint has several other benefits for business users. PowerPivot workbooks do not maintain live connections to the data sources, so a periodic refresh is necessary to keep the information as current as possible. PowerPivot for SharePoint can manage the data refresh process on a schedule and send out notifications if a problem occurs. In addition, PowerPivot for SharePoint can become a data source for another PowerPivot workbook, a Reporting Services report, and any other tool that can use Analysis Services as a data source.

PowerPivot for SharePoint has features for IT professionals, as well. Often, any information that is managed by users rather than IT can go undetected. A user might create a report to answer a one-time question, and then under certain circumstances, the report suddenly can become a mission-critical application that IT knows nothing about. PowerPivot in Excel gives users the freedom to compile information as they see fit, while publishing the results to SharePoint gives IT the ability to use management features in PowerPivot for SharePoint to maintain some oversight over the users' activities. IT can see what data sources are being used, which workbooks are popular, and how many server resources are necessary to render a report for the team community. When appropriate, IT can recommend that a proper BI solution take the place of a PowerPivot workbook.

Excel Services   Excel Services can be just as important to a team BI community as it is to an organizational community, if not more so. To support this community and encourage power users to develop content, IT can supply a set of data source connection files in a data connections library. Power users can then create workbooks, with or without PowerPivot models and Power View sheets, and publish them to a SharePoint document library. Business users are able to view and interact with Excel workbooks, PowerPivot's pivot tables and charts, and Power View sheets in Excel Services.

Reporting Services   As with Excel Services, a good strategy for IT (or power analysts) to adopt in support of team BI is to create and publish reusable content that users can access for team content development. In the case of Reporting Services, three types of content support this strategy: shared data sources, shared datasets, and report parts.

Shared datasets contain the query strings necessary to retrieve data from a data source and hide the technical details from the user who can take the dataset and build up a report completely from scratch by using the Report Builder authoring tool. This tool is much simpler to use than the report designer that BI developers use, providing enough flexibility and freedom for power analysts to construct a report according to their needs but also providing wizards to guide less-technical users through the process of building simple report layouts.

The use of report parts is another option available to further simplify the report development process for users who might otherwise fall into the category of information user. Report parts, as mentioned earlier in this chapter, are individual elements in a report, such as a map, a chart, or a table, that can be published independent of the original report in which they were created. Report Builder includes a Report Part Gallery through which users can browse to locate items that they would like to include in a report and arrange any way they like. Everything necessary for the report part to work is added to the report along with the report part, so the user doesn't need to know how to set up data sources, datasets, or parameters in order to build a report successfully by using report parts. If users have enough technical skill to create a Word document, they probably are capable of building a report entirely from report parts.

Power View in SharePoint   Power View is a component of Reporting Services that is accessible as a self-service, browser-based tool in SharePoint. Users can open a BISM data connection available in SharePoint or connect to a PowerPivot for SharePoint workbook to create a new report that has all the same features available for Power View in Excel. They can save reports in a SharePoint document library for personal use or sharing with others. A power user can publish Power View reports for others to use as a starting point for analysis. Users can export a Power View report to PowerPoint to provide interactive analysis features as long as a live connection to the tabular model is available during a presentation.

PerformancePoint Services   A team BI community can use PerformancePoint Services for department-focused dashboards and scorecards. As with report parts, an IT professional or a designated power user can construct individual components, such as data sources, KPIs, filters, scorecards, and reports that users can employ in a SharePoint dashboard, which would be easier to construct for the more advanced information user or power analyst than a PerformancePoint dashboard.

Self-service and personal BI

The whole point of building BI infrastructures that contain a data warehouse, data mart, Analysis Services cube, or tabular data model is to facilitate users being able to get information when they need it, on a self-service basis. But in many companies, users still rely on standard reports that have limited interactivity. The reports might have parameters with which users can filter the reports, or they might make it possible for the users to continue to extract more detail. Regardless, these reports are typically built to answer one question and not necessarily the next question that the user might have. Thus, when these new questions arise, users wind up going back to IT to get those reports. Successfully implementing self-service can significantly reduce the backlog of report requests that IT handles.

As an alternative, users start looking outside the approved sources because they need to get information to make decisions. They might get information from wherever they can find it internally; they might get it from external business partners; and maybe they'll find some data on industry trends that they can download from an Internet site. In short, they wind up manually compiling a lot of data. The bottom line is that the data they need for making decisions on a day-to-day basis is not being integrated into the corporate system, and that's the problem that self-service BI is intended to solve.

Due to the overlap with organizational and team BI communities, we've already touched on the tools commonly used by this community: Excel, Power View in Excel, PowerPivot in Excel, Report Builder, Power View in SharePoint, and Visio. Casual users are more likely to use Excel and Report Builder, whereas power users might use any of these tools, as applicable to the task at hand. A user can use any of these tools to create a document for personal reference or can share the document with a team BI community by publishing it to a SharePoint document library.

How would a user decide which tool to use? Let's review the characteristics of the documents produced by each tool.

Excel   Excel is a tool commonly preferred by users of all skill levels for ad hoc reporting and analysis. Users can retrieve data from data sources and combine it with manual data. A user can import data and then manipulate the data by creating charts, sorting, filtering, and applying a wide range of calculations from simple to complex. Casual users might use Excel for simple summing and averaging of data, whereas power users might create complex forecasting models or tabular models combining multiple data sources. Power users can also create PivotTables from raw data or from Analysis Services data sources for analysis using aggregate functions to summarize data grouped on rows and columns and using filters and slicers to focus on a subset of data. Although the creation of a PivotTable is generally a task for the power user, a casual user can easily explore a PivotTable that has already been created.

Excel is ubiquitous in many organizations, so most users already have a passing familiarity with this tool. Even if they don't create the workbooks themselves, they can access workbooks from SharePoint and, as long as they have the right permissions, download workbooks for personal use. Then, they can apply calculations, filter the data, and make other changes to the data without affecting the original workbook.

Power View in Excel   Power users and casual users alike can easily create a data model based on one more data sources, even if the data contains more than a million rows. Users don't need to understand relationships between tables created by drawing together data from disparate sources, and Excel can recommend relationships based on its analysis of the contents of data from each source. After creating the data model, users can add a Power View sheet to visualize and explore the data model, as described in Chapter 5. Exploration starts by adding fields from the model to a table, and then converting the table to some other type of visualization, such as a matrix, column chart, pie chart, or map, to name a few. Not only can the user quickly and easily change the visualization, but relationships in the data can be discovered through highlighting data shared across multiple visualizations. Better understanding of trends over time can be discovered through animated scatter and bubble charts. Users can also further explore the data by applying filters to all visualizations or a single visualization on the sheet.

Power View in SharePoint   Business users who can access an existing tabular model through a BISM data connection or a PowerPivot for SharePoint workbook can create their own Power View reports to explore data and save the reports with the .rdlx file extension to a SharePoint document library. Alternatively, they can access a published Power View report and apply filters and highlighting or change visualizations as needed to personalize the report and save it as a new version for personal consumption. The process of creating and interacting with visualizations is very similar to using Power View in Excel. However, when using Power View in SharePoint, users can build a report with multiple views and can export the results to PowerPoint.

PowerPivot in Excel   Power users can extend the Excel data model by adding calculations, hierarchies, and KPIs. Calculations can be added by using the Data Analysis Expression language known as DAX, as described in Chapter 5. This language is Excel-like, which makes it easier for users to create calculations if they're already comfortable with Excel functions. PowerPivot in Excel does make self-service BI easier, but primarily for power users. Casual users benefit most from PowerPivot in Excel when power users publish workbooks to SharePoint.

Report Builder   Report Builder is a desirable tool for users who want to produce a specific type of report layout and also want to store reports in a centralized location, whether for personal use or for sharing with others. Even if a user creates a report for personal consumption and saves it on the report server, the user can subscribe to the report to receive a report with fresh data on a regular schedule.

Visio   Visio is the only tool that provides data-driven diagrams. A business user might link a network diagram to a device configuration database to show real-time status, or might connect a floor plan diagram to an occupancy/vacancy list. In addition, power users and BI developers can use Visio to create diagrams to publish to SharePoint for sharing with a team BI community.

The progression of BI

The Microsoft vision for BI can be summarized simply as the delivery of the right information at the right time in the right format to users at all levels of a company. It's a noble goal, and the Microsoft tools can indeed help companies attain this goal, but not from day one. Instead, the democratization of BI across the organization occurs incrementally. The length of time required depends on many factors, such as the corporate culture overall, management's attitude toward BI, and a support system for users, among others.

An understanding of the typical progression that many companies experience as they expand their use of BI can help in many ways. It can affirm that your company is moving in the right direction, and it can also show you the possibilities that remain for further progression. It can also help you determine which tools are best suited for your current stage and help you to prepare for the next.

The Business Intelligence Maturity Model

Wayne Eckerson developed the Business Intelligence Maturity Model for The Data Warehousing Institute (TDWI) as a means for organizations to benchmark their deployments against other companies. At a high level, the model identifies six stages that mark the progression of BI from a cost center to a strategic asset. As shown in Figure 2-3, by plotting the typical user adoption rate along the six stages of the model, Eckerson's research revealed a bell curve in most organizations in stages 2 and 3. It's important to understand that companies don't necessarily follow a linear progression from stages 0 to 5. Stages often overlap, and the length of time that a company remains in a particular stage can vary.

> **Note** You can download a poster illustrating the Business Intelligence Maturity Model from *http://download.101com.com/tdwi/Poster/TDWI_BI_Maturity_Model_Poster_2005.pdf*. You can also use TDWI's online assessment tool to benchmark your company's BI maturity by completing the survey at *http://tdwi.org/pages/maturity-model/maturity-model-home.aspx*.

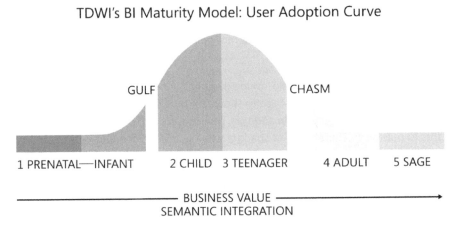

FIGURE 2-3 The TDWI BI Maturity Model.

Notable aspects of the model are the Gulf and the Chasm, which highlight the reality that BI implementations are not likely to proceed smoothly from one stage to another. As Eckerson discussed these findings with BI implementers, he discovered that the inclusion of these two obstacles in the model validated their experience that setbacks in BI implementations and flagging enthusiasm for pursuing pervasive BI are a normal part of the process. Perseverance pays off for teams that can stay focused on the steps necessary to expand the capabilities of their BI infrastructure.

Even within the same company, it's very likely that each department will mature at different rates. That's okay. The good news is that wherever people are, they have tools to support them, they can transition to higher levels of maturity over time, and the tools can adapt accordingly. Each successive step in the maturation process translates into greater business value.

In this section, we provide an overview of the characteristics of each stage of the BI Maturity Model and describe the tools that are useful in each stage.

Stage 0: Prenatal

In the prenatal stage, a company has yet to create a data warehouse to support information requirements. Instead, all reports are sourced from operational systems, with no consolidation of information across systems without special processes in place. That is, there are no formal Extract, Transform, and Load (ETL) processes. Financial applications often have the richest set of reports available in the company and are the primary source for management reports. At this point, the available reports are static, and focus on historical events to help users understand what has happened. Any changes desired by users require customization by IT, although it's not uncommon for such requests to take weeks or months to fulfill.

To transition from the rigid reporting system typical of this stage to a formal BI solution, many companies start by reproducing their existing reports in Reporting Services. Problems associated with responding to requests for customization don't go away by taking this approach. However, with some forethought, with parameterization of reports, users can make changes to the report content, which in some cases might forestall the need for one-off report development.

Stage 1: Infant

When users can't get what they need from the operational reports, they often develop their own solutions, which leads to a proliferation of reports based on Excel spreadsheets or Access databases that users have cobbled together. Such user-developed data collections are also described as *spreadmarts*, *shadow systems*, or *skunkworks* projects.

Executives often enlist analysts to compile briefing books based on these informal data collections. The focus begins to shift from trying to understand what has happened in the past to attempting to understand how past results might influence what happens in the future.

What starts as a compilation of official data for a specific need can grow into a mission-critical solution that people come to rely on, yet it's unmanaged, unsecured, undocumented, fragile, and cannot be audited. It can take a lot of manual labor to gather and manipulate the data, leaving little time to analyze the data collected before a decision from the user is required. The concern of each user in this stage is to produce information that supports personal decision-making. Little regard is given to reconciling results with other users producing comparable information, and no official system-of-record exists to resolve results that disagree.

In this stage, Excel and Access are popular tools. For organizations that have yet to implement a formal BI environment, an Excel data model or PowerPivot in Excel can simplify the effort of gathering and integrating data. But, it doesn't solve the more serious problem resulting from a lack of IT oversight.

The Gulf

The Gulf is the first obstacle that must be overcome before moving into real BI. Prior to this obstacle, executives likely view any efforts to promote BI as just another variation of operational reporting. To progress, they need to understand how BI is necessary to improved business processes and decision-making at all levels of the organization. According to an Aberdeen Group study, one of the benefits of a collaborative BI environment is a 30-percent improvement in business processes as compared to other companies with such an environment. Executive support is critical to experiencing similar improvements.

Users need to understand how the next step in the BI progression can shift their workload from mundane data gathering tasks to analysis tasks that are much more valuable in the long run to employers. If users remain unconvinced, a company can get stuck in The Gulf. Even after crossing The Gulf, companies find that spreadmarts are difficult to completely eradicate and often persist through into the teenager stage.

To successfully cross The Gulf, BI developers should take an iterative and incremental approach, focusing on small projects that are easier to implement rather than trying to build a solution to be all things to all people. Ideally, the first effort should focus on a single source system that contains well-understood data sources. Frequent prototype reviews with users can help the team stay focused on the requirements of this first official BI project. BI developers must remain diligent to counteract scope-creep as user requests continue to outpace the ability of IT to deliver new information.

Fortunately, the Microsoft platform can help here. It's very easy to prototype and develop solutions from those prototypes in an iterative fashion, working closely with the user community to get it right. One option is to build prototypes with Analysis Services to build a model and then use Excel to validate it with users. Another option is to let users model their data the way in which they want to see it by using an Excel data model or PowerPivot in Excel. When users model the data, IT can take the design and reproduce it in Analysis Services, either by importing a PowerPivot model into an Analysis Services tabular model project or by manually recreating the design of an Excel data model or PowerPivot model as an Analysis Services multidimensional model.

Stage 2: Child

At last, the company begins to demonstrate progress with BI, with the first project typically focused on a single subject area. Most companies in this stage have no previous experience with managing BI projects, so the early projects focus on building a data mart without attempting to align metrics with corporate objectives.

The novelty of BI in this stage can generate excitement among users, who are motivated to abandon their labor-intensive past for the new-and-improved way of finding answers to their questions. Power users who understand the business well can learn the new tools quickly so that they can further investigate trends over time to determine why things happened the way they did.

If an organization has yet to start with Reporting Services, this stage is a common place to introduce it to users. The first set of reports is usually based on department-level standard reports that were developed in earlier stages with parameterization and drilldown capabilities built in so that casual users can successfully explore the data. Behind the scenes, the BI team builds a data mart and possibly an Analysis Services cube or tabular model as data sources for these reports.

To support the ad hoc analysis requirements of power users, the BI team gives users access to cubes or tabular models by using Excel. In addition, these users continue to employ Power View in Excel, PowerPivot in Excel, Power View in SharePoint, or PowerPivot in SharePoint to get answers to questions that can't be answered by the data mart.

Stage 3: Teenager

Having successfully implemented BI at a department level during the Child stage, many companies next take steps in an attempt to prevent each department from setting up its own data mart. In the Teenager stage, the company establishes a formal data warehouse not only to consolidate resources but also to bring consistency to BI processes and company metrics. By adding experienced BI practitioners to the team or by engaging consultants, the company begins to formalize BI across departments and to adopt best practices.

During this stage, the BI solution grows to accommodate more casual users, but this growth also results in an increased demand for standard parameterized reports that can be filtered and dashboards that can be tailored to specific audiences. Also during this stage, the use of BI expands to include KPIs to help management monitor progress toward goals.

Reporting Services continues to be a dominant technology in this stage, with greater emphasis on developing reports that can be used in multiple ways by the addition of parameters, including filters that tailor information to the user. Team BI communities also begin to emerge, with power users publishing shared datasets and report parts with which casual users can build their own versions of reports. To promote collaboration, the BI solution expands to include the use of SharePoint for dashboards and possibly PerformancePoint Services for scorecards.

The Chasm

Unfortunately, The Chasm is a more challenging obstacle to cross than The Gulf. If the problem of spreadmarts and independent data marts across the comp have not been addressed by this point, the next step in the maturation process will be exceedingly difficult to obtain. Any change in the company's business strategy can also pose problems for the BI team, but ironically, that's when the organization needs BI most of all.

To successfully move to the next stage, developing a flexible architecture for the company's BI solutions is mandatory. As difficult as it might be, the company must commit a key group of users to the development of a common glossary for terms and calculations used in reports, workbooks, and other BI-related documents. Support from the top down is necessary. One characteristic of The

Chasm is the inevitable struggle between team BI and organizational BI communities. In the end, corporate IT standards must prevail so that the departmental BI systems can properly align at the corporate level.During this stage, self-service BI is perceived to be the goal by many users, but over-reliance on this approach to information management can lead to chaos, with unmanaged reports proliferating throughout the company. Reports developed by one person might be useful to another, but if that other user can't find what he needs, time is wasted to develop a duplicate report.

To counteract this type of problem, the BI team needs to focus on building datasets, data feeds, data models, interactive reports, report parts, and dashboards that address the range of broad questions that users ask regularly. In particular, this is the very type of problem that the self-service BI features in Reporting Services, Excel Services, and PowerPivot for SharePoint are intended to solve. These tools can be introduced during the Teenager stage; however, they can't solve the unification problem, which is typically not a technical challenge but an organizational behavior challenge.

Stage 4: Adult

When a company can successfully define standards, a common set of terms, and consistent rules, it's ready to develop an enterprise data warehouse and move to the Adult stage, which yields several significant advancements in BI capabilities. The enterprise data warehouse is instrumental in the transition of the use of BI from the support of departmental objectives to the support of organizational objectives. Performance management expands beyond the use of dashboards for monitoring processes to include scorecards with which individuals can see how their respective decisions impact corporate performance.

The addition of real-time data feeds as well as forecasting, modeling, and data mining tools makes it possible for users not only to analyze the past to better understand what happened but also to apply that knowledge to the current situation and to anticipate the future. This maturation of BI capabilities facilitates proactive management of the company based on predictive analytics as an alternative to the reactive management approach in earlier stages in which only historical analysis was possible.

Furthermore, the flexibility previously missing in the BI solution architecture finally arrives. Abstraction layers insulate users from changes to the underlying system as alignment of sources continues to occur. Users can now repurpose data and reports to suit their needs rather than wait for BI developers to respond to a new report request.

The Microsoft platform continues to support the BI requirements of a company in the Adult stage. The BI team can roll out PerformancePoint Services, if it hasn't already been implemented in an earlier stage, in support of the new performance management activities. In addition, Analysis Services supports the development of forecasting models, the results of which can be accessed in any of the self-service BI tools.

In terms of tool usage, most of the time casual users still want prepackaged content to monitor events or conditions relevant to their daily tasks. This can be accomplished through dashboards presenting a combination of scorecards, reports, and Excel workbooks. Each of these tools can present a view of the current state, support filtering by which the user can focus on particular items of interest, and provide the ability to extract information in greater detail. The enterprise search capability in SharePoint provides these users with another way to find relevant content. If users still need to create something themselves, they can use Report Builder to create data mash-ups from reusable components in Reporting Services, SharePoint lists, and PowerPivot workbooks published to SharePoint.

Stage 5: Sage

In the final stage, companies establish a BI center of excellence to promote and sustain best practices for the current platform, to support user adoption, and to drive innovation. Rather than maintain the centralized management of BI that emerged in the Adult stage, the company allows departments to assume control once again over BI processes with the mandate that these departmental-level projects adhere to the standards and best practices defined at the corporate level.

BI becomes a strategic asset in this stage, as well, and transitions to a service-oriented architecture. Developers can then use web services to embed BI into Line-of-Business (LOB) applications. The provision of BI to external stakeholders can also become a revenue stream for the company. When this happens, the company continues to make large investments in BI to ensure high levels of service to the external stakeholders.

The entire Microsoft BI stack is in use by the time a company reaches this stage. In addition, the Microsoft platform is fully extensible. Developers can use APIs for any tool in the stack so that customization can occur at every point of the information management process, and they can embed that customization into applications. Even without customization and with no additional configuration necessary, Reporting Services can provide data feeds as a service so that a company can make data available from tabular models, cubes, mining models, or relational data warehouses.

Road map to analytical competition

Another way to view the progression of business intelligence is described by a road map developed by Thomas H. Davenport and Jeanne G. Harris in their book *Competing on Analytics: The New Science of Winning* (2007, Harvard Business School Press). The purpose of this road map is to provide a realistic view of the stages a company often experiences in its quest to derive value from analytics and to outline a strategy for successfully transitioning to higher stages. Figure 2-4 illustrates that the analytics road map proposed by Davenport and Harris consists of five stages that follow a progression similar to the one in the Maturity Model described in the previous section, but one that's more compressed and leads to a more specific outcome. Whereas the Maturity Model views the end state for BI as a pervasive technology and potential revenue stream, the road map considers that the primary goal for BI is to produce a distinct competitive advantage.

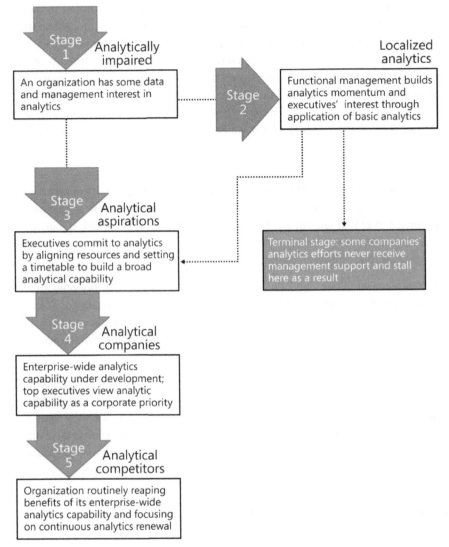

Stage 1 Analytically impaired

An organization has some data and management interest in analytics

Stage 2 Localized analytics

Functional management builds analytics momentum and executives' interest through application of basic analytics

Stage 3 Analytical aspirations

Executives commit to analytics by aligning resources and setting a timetable to build a broad analytical capability

Terminal stage: some companies' analytics efforts never receive management support and stall here as a result

Stage 4 Analytical companies

Enterprise-wide analytics capability under development; top executives view analytic capability as a corporate priority

Stage 5 Analytical competitors

Organization routinely reaping benefits of its enterprise-wide analytics capability and focusing on continuous analytics renewal

FIGURE 2-4 The road map to analytical competition.

Stage 1: Analytically impaired

In the first stage, operational data is not ready for analysis. Reporting directly from operational data is fraught with problems and suffers from data quality issues. To progress to the next stage, management needs to be convinced that better decision-making will result from data that is not only better but also more accessible and actionable. Meanwhile, some technically savvy business users begin compiling data for personal analysis. Excel is often the tool of choice at this stage.

Stage 2: Localized analytics

The work begun by the independent analysts begins to show promise in this stage as they develop new insights that have value for the company. One of two things happens at this point: either executive management agrees that it's time to start formally investing in BI and the company moves to the next stage, or management remains unconvinced and needs more evidence of successful outcomes from analysis before making the commitment.

As a result, the focus of this stage is to gradually build out a BI infrastructure at a local level with minimal investment, such as a department-level, single-subject data mart. Despite the lack of support from executive management, the BI team can use this stage to develop experience before tackling the more comprehensive projects in the next stage. In addition, the department making the investment in BI benefits from the business process improvements resulting from the better analytical capabilities. According to the analytics road map, a company could be in this stage from one to three years.

The BI components in the Microsoft stack are a good starting point for a department-level data mart that could also include a complementary tabular model or cube to support analysis in Power View in SharePoint. Reporting Services can deliver standard reports to department users and provide data feeds for power users to use in Power View in Excel or PowerPivot in Excel for deeper analysis.

Stage 3: Analytical aspirations

When a company is ready to commit to analytics at the corporate level, the focus shifts from the tactical BI solutions found at the department level to a company-wide performance management solution. The challenge at this stage is the integration of various tools and processes implemented across departments and to reach agreement regarding the metrics against which to measure progress. In general, the road map indicates the length of time for this stage can be a few months or up to two years.

In this stage, the Microsoft stack scales from a departmental deployment to an enterprise deployment. The Reporting Services platform remains in place for broad distribution of standard reports. SharePoint and PerformancePoint Services now become tools for monitoring and reporting performance management results. Power users can also now share Power View reports, Power View in Excel, and PowerPivot in Excel workbooks by publishing them to SharePoint and thereby promote collaborative analysis.

Stage 4: Analytical companies

To move into this stage, the company must establish analytics as a priority and the corporate culture must support an ongoing process of experimentation. Management encourages analysts to develop and test hypotheses and to discover new areas worth exploring. The purpose of analytics in this stage is to discover how to use information assets to differentiate the company from its competitors in the marketplace. During this stage, the tools for analysis become more advanced, and developers are tasked with embedding analytics into business processes.

Here, the BI team can exploit the full range of capabilities in the Microsoft BI stack, including the data mining features in Analysis Services. In addition, developers can integrate BI into the LOB applications.

Stage 5: Analytical competitors

At this stage, analytics aren't just helping management run the company better, as evidenced by strong financial performance, but the insights derived from analytics also create a competitive advantage in the marketplace. The use of BI is now widespread across the company and executive management is fully committed to continued investment in BI technologies.

Additional tools are not a major factor in this stage. Instead, the implementation of the Microsoft tools in earlier stages can help foster an environment in which business users at all levels of the organization can find the right information at the right time.

Tool selection

Throughout this chapter, we've identified various characteristics of the user tools, including their appropriateness for different types of users and the suggested level of BI maturity at which each tool can be adopted. We've also pointed out some of the advantages and disadvantages of each tool to help you understand the implications of selecting a tool before you get started on a project. Now, we'll summarize this information and provide some additional pointers so that you have a quick reference for all the tools in one convenient location.

Table 2-1 provides a summary of the tools, with a breakdown of the primary user of each tool by business user community and by BI community. Additionally, the table identifies whether business users (who can be either casual users or power analysts), the power analyst, or the BI developer is responsible for creating content with the tool. Last, the table identifies where the content for the tool can be reused.

TABLE 2-1 A summary of tools

Tool	BI community	Content author	Reusability
Excel	Self-service and personal BI	Business user	Excel Services SharePoint BI PerformancePoint Services
Power View in Excel	Self-service and personal BI	Business user	Excel Services SharePoint BI
PowerPivot in Excel	Self-service and personal BI	Business user	PowerPivot for SharePoint
Excel Services	Team BI Organizational BI	Business user	SharePoint BI PerformancePoint Services Custom applications

Tool	BI community	Content author	Reusability
PowerPivot for SharePoint	Team BI	Business user	Excel Report Builder SharePoint BI PerformancePoint Services Custom applications Any tool that connects to Analysis Services
Report Builder (Reporting Services)	Self-service and personal BI Team BI	Business user	PowerPivot in Excel SharePoint BI PerformancePoint Services Custom applications
Report Designer (Reporting Services)	Team BI Organizational BI	BI developer	PowerPivot in Excel SharePoint BI PerformancePoint Services Custom applications
Power View in SharePoint	Self-service and personal BI Team BI	Power user Business user	PowerPoint
SharePoint BI	Team BI	BI developer Power user	Content not reusable in other tools
PerformancePoint Services	Team BI Organizational BI	BI developer Power user	SharePoint BI Custom applications
Visio	Self-service and personal BI	BI developer Business user	Visio Services
Visio Services	Team BI	BI developer Power user	SharePoint BI Custom applications

Note In the Content author column in the preceding table, the BI developer is omitted in some rows but can often be the primary content author with the respective tool. We've elected to identify the BI developer in this table only when the BI developer is most likely to have the primary role for creating the content.

Excel

Excel is a very popular tool, and many, if not most, analysts are already using it. Excel is familiar even to casual users and, for this reason, it is used for everything from simple To Do lists to complex financial analysis.

You can use this tool to do the following:

- Retrieve data from a source without having query language skills

- Analyze data (that is, group, filter, deep analysis) containing fewer than one million records

- Create pivot tables and charts with limited formatting options

- Apply complex calculations to data

- Create an internal data model as a source for a Power View in Excel visualization by using small or large amounts of data (in excess of one million records) and data from disparate sources

- Publish workbooks to Excel Services to share insights

- Store data for use in SharePoint:

  - Visio web diagram

  - PerformancePoint Services KPI or filter

  - Component in a SharePoint or PerformancePoint Services dashboard

Power View in Excel provides casual and power users with a tool to explore data by using interactive visualizations. You can use it to do the following:

- Explore data in an Excel internal data model or PowerPivot in Excel tabular model

- Visualize data as a table, matrix, chart, map, tile, or card

- Create an animated scatter chart

- Filter and highlight data

PowerPivot in Excel provides power users with a tool that uses familiar Excel features while supporting more advanced analysis. You can use it to do the following:

- Analyze small or large amounts of data (millions of records)

- Integrate multiple data sources when no data mart exists or when analysis needs to incorporate data not found in the data warehouse

- Create pivot tables and charts with limited formatting options

- Apply complex calculations to data

- Reproduce the analytical capabilities that Analysis Services supports without waiting for IT to build a cube

- Prepare a data model for import into an Analysis Services tabular model

- Publish workbooks to PowerPivot for SharePoint to share insights

- Store data for use in Reporting Services as a data source for standard RDL reports and Power View in SharePoint reports

- Store data for use in SharePoint:

  - KPI

  - Visio web diagram

  - PerformancePoint Services KPI or filter

  - Component in a SharePoint or PerformancePoint Services dashboard

Excel Services

Excel Services is a SharePoint service application with which users can share Excel workbooks in a secure, centralized location. The interface is simple for casual users to find and access information.

You can use this tool to do the following:

- Provide users with a way to share large workbooks outside of email, even to users who don't have Excel installed

- Display data in a dashboard-like layout using a familiar interface

- Provide casual users with collaborative workbook editing and limited analysis capabilities in a browser environment

- Protect intellectual property in Excel workbooks

- Embed complex calculation capabilities in custom applications

- Display Power View in Excel visualizations

PowerPivot for SharePoint uses Excel Services and an Analysis Services instance in SharePoint mode to display PowerPivot in Excel workbooks. The PowerPivot for SharePoint Add-in provides management oversight of activity related to these workbooks. Because PowerPivot for SharePoint relies on Excel Services, the familiar, simplified interface helps casual users interact easily with the workbooks and to use the workbooks as a data source by using self-service BI tools such as Report Builder or Excel.

You can use this tool to do the following:

- Make it possible for users to work collaboratively on analytical data compiled in a PowerPivot in Excel workbook

- Automate the process of refreshing the data sources in a workbook

- Provide users with a data source for self-service BI tools

- Discover data sources used in workbooks and monitor workbook usage

Reporting Services

Reporting Services is the best option for delivering standard report content to a wide audience, either online or via email. When integrated with SharePoint, it relies on the same storage and security mechanisms but retains all the features available in native mode.

Casual users can easily access reports and, in some cases, might build their own reports. Power users can participate in the content development process.

Casual users can use Report Builder to do the following:

- Build reports from published report parts by using drag-and-drop

- Build reports from shared datasets (with no need to know the query details) and design a simple table, matrix, or chart by using a wizard

- Apply basic formatting to a report

Power users can use Report Builder to perform the same tasks as casual users and to do the following:

- Connect to data sources and create queries to retrieve data for a report

- Create and publish shared datasets and report parts for use by casual users

- Build reports by using any of the same features supported in the Report Designer available in Business Intelligence Development Studio:

  - Pixel-perfect layout of table, matrix, list, or chart objects

  - Design for online viewing or print format

  - Geospatial mapping

  - Interactive features—sort, filter, deep analysis, drill through, document maps, tooltips

- Provide a data source of PowerPivot in Excel

- Create an entire dashboard layout, displaying data from multiple sources on a single page when the following characteristics are desired:

  - Fine control over the appearance

  - Interactive features already available in Reporting Services

  - Distribution of dashboard in print or other formats

  - Support for subscriptions

- Create content with a specific layout or interactive features for use in a SharePoint or PerformancePoint Services dashboard or in a custom application

BI developers can use Report Designer to perform the same tasks as power users. However, although Report Designer facilitates the BI developer in publishing report parts, it does not provide access to published report parts to use when designing a new report. Report Designer also makes it possible for the Report Developer to work with multiple reports in the same session, whereas with Report Builder, users can work with only one report at a time.

Report consumers can access standard RDL reports in SharePoint to do the following:

- View and interact with a report online

- Export a report to a variety of formats, including data feeds

- Subscribe to a report for scheduled delivery by email or to a network file share

- Configure data alerts to receive email notifications of changes in data values

Power users can create reports by using Power View in SharePoint to share with casual users and to do the following:

- Explore data in PowerPivot for SharePoint or Analysis Services tabular models and cubes

- Visualize data as a table, matrix, chart, map, tile, or card

- Create an animated scatter chart

- Filter and highlight data

- Export a report to PowerPoint

SharePoint BI

SharePoint BI accommodates a variety of sources with which power users or BI developers can consolidate information in a single location even when a formal BI implementation is not yet in place and can change out content when the company eventually develops a data warehouse or Analysis Services cube.

Use this tool to build a simple dashboard to display, and optionally filter, information from multiple sources on a single page (such as workbooks, reports, Visio web diagrams, PerformancePoint Services content, and other content types). Chapter 8, "Using PerformancePoint Services," provides more information about working with SharePoint's BI features.

PerformancePoint Services

PerformancePoint Services is yet another SharePoint service application that supports the development of content types used in performance management solutions that users access in SharePoint. BI developers typically produce the complete solutions by using the Dashboard Designer tool, although power users might also use this tool to contribute content.

Use this tool to do the following:

- Create data sources for use when developing KPIs, scorecards, reports, and filters

- Develop both simple and advanced KPIs

- Create scorecards to display KPIs in asymmetrical or hierarchical structures for use in either a SharePoint or a PerformancePoint dashboard

- Build an analytic grid report or analytic chart report to support browser-based interactive pivoting, drilling, and filtering of data in an Analysis Services cube

- Provide access to the decomposition tree visualization by creating a scorecard, analytic grid report, or analytic chart report

- Build a strategy map as a supplement to a scorecard to illustrate relationships between objectives, goals, and KPIs

- Design filters to use in a SharePoint or PerformancePoint Services dashboard

- Develop a dashboard containing one or more pages by using PerformancePoint content types (scorecard, strategy map, analytic reports, and filters)

Visio Services

Visio Services is the final SharePoint service application that we cover in this book. With it, users can securely share Visio diagrams for viewing in a browser. Because designing data-driven Visio diagrams requires a solid understanding of Visio and the data sources, BI developers will often have the primary responsibility for content development. However, many Visio power users are capable of building information-rich diagrams that visualize data in creative ways. Not all of them will be familiar with Visio Services, so they may require assistance from BI developers with the publishing step.

Use Visio 2013 to do the following:

- Produce web diagrams, optionally linked to a data source, to illustrate a business process, organization chart, floor plan, or almost any other business scenario

- Build a PivotDiagram to visualize for hierarchical data

- Visualize data in any business diagram.

Use Visio Services to do the following:

- Provide a means for users to share Visio diagrams with users who don't have Visio installed

- Embed diagrams in custom applications

- Enable real-time collaboration among users viewing a diagram in Visio Services and those editing it with Visio 2013.

An action plan for adoption: Build it and they might come

In their book *Drive Business Performance: Enabling a Culture of Intelligent Execution* (Wiley, 2008), Bruno Aziza and Joey Fitts describe the "Analytical Paradox":

> *While analysts have the analytic capabilities to derive insights, they lack the ability to directly act upon these insights. Conversely, while employees have the ability to take action, they often lack the ability to derive insights by themselves. The result is that business analysts' request queues are overloaded on a daily basis, and employees end up making decisions which lack insight, timeliness, or both. This situation makes it impossible for organizations to quickly recognize and act upon changing market conditions—to be agile.*

Our purpose in this chapter is to show you how you can use BI to empower employees and reduce the backlog in the request queues of business analysts. However, you can't implement new tools in a BI solution and expect users to come running to embrace that new solution. Your adoption plan needs to capture both the minds and hearts of the user community to ensure that the solution will be successful. One strategy is to start with an evaluation version of the BI tools that you want users to adopt. You can then spend time educating decision-makers about the value of these tools so that they can influence budget allocations for the tools. Remember that by introducing a new reporting tool, you are introducing change and change is often perceived as bad—even if it's good change. This section draws on our personal experiences, each of us having worked in environments where there is push and pull from all perspectives in an organization.

Self-service BI versus traditional BI

Self-service BI is a practice or discipline that is very different than traditional methods for sharing information. Always keep in mind that the purpose of self-service BI is not to replace traditional methods of BI. In many cases, it supplements existing processes to measure business activities and provides another opportunity to deliver on the promise of pervasive BI, thus driving even more metric-driven decision-making in the company.

Often, self-service BI leads to formal BI and proves as an extremely useful method for empowering employees to more analytical insights. Someone once said to Jack Welch, former CEO of General Electric, "You paid me for twenty years for my hands and you could have had my brain for free." The value that employees can have at the front line can be missed simply by not giving them the tools to uncover insights possible with access to the right BI tools.

Lessons learned: Adoption for self-service BI in SharePoint

The principles for encouraging self-service in SharePoint Server are applicable to BI. Therefore, you will find it beneficial to review best practices for adoption of SharePoint. Understand that successful adoption requires not only a plan to manage people, processes, and tools, but also a written plan to train, communicate, and gather feedback. This is an iterative process that includes communicating change, training people on new skills, tools and processes, and gathering feedback for future improvements. A written adoption plan provides the following key benefits:

- It makes you think about how to accomplish self-service goals.

- It gives you something to share with others so that they can share your vision.

- It involves other people so that they can be part of the process of change.

Talk to the users! The adoption plan should be based on an understanding of what success looks like to the group you are working with, what users will do with the results, and how they can take action from what you build. Start from user needs and work backward to provide tools that support those needs. Even when users cannot specify in advance what they really want, it is critical to involve them early and often, as BI tools are considered. Prototypes or proof-of-concepts that use data with which the users are familiar helps them gain confidence in your ability to deliver a solution and the tools they will be using. Remember that users can't always define what they want, but they know it when they see it.

Ask users how they gathered information before they had access to current reports and how they currently arrive at decisions. If you give users the ability to set parameters for analytics modeling, determine the default values to set and confirm that they know when and how to change the parameters to other values. Users can help identify early wins that you or the designer might not have thought of and might provide useful introductions to other potential users and their communities. A user who feels a sense of ownership in report design can become an advocate for the technology and help introduce the technology to a wider audience.

An analytics interface can be visually appealing. However, if the information it conveys doesn't stimulate action, it's not likely to be very effective for improving business operations. A good interface provides sufficient context to let business users know when action might be required and what action to take.

Often BI developers ask, "What do you want to measure?" And many times business users respond, "I don't know." A good place to start is to find out what business users currently measure to know when a problem has occurred or is about to occur. Then, demonstrate how the collection of information can be automated to reduce the time required to put together a report. Show them that by using Power View in SharePoint, they can easily export information for use in PowerPoint presentations.

> **Note** Susan Hanley is an excellent resource for best practices related to user adoption and metrics showing the value of a SharePoint deployment. You can download articles and white papers on these topics from her website at *http://www.susanhanley.com/ white-papers.htm*.

Summary

The chapter described how the various BI tools can work separately or together in different scenarios, for different user communities, and at different stages of maturity with BI capabilities. Don't be overly concerned if you or business users in your company want to start using a certain tool before the maturity model or road map says you're ready for that stage. The whole point of BI is to empower users to access information in any way possible. Just ensure that users aren't trying to use a tool that requires greater technical skills than they possess. If they're willing to learn, support them in their efforts, but don't turn them loose without support, because they might simply give up on all BI out of frustration. For the same reason, don't implement a tool if the necessary infrastructure isn't yet in place or if it doesn't provide the specific functionality that you need. At this point, you should have a better understanding of how the tools available in the Microsoft BI stack work together to support your goals for delivering information to users at all levels of your company, and you should feel better prepared to select a tool. The next chapter explains what you'll need to do to establish the back-end infrastructure to better support many of these tools.

CHAPTER 3

The lifecycle of a business intelligence implementation

There is nothing quite like viewing a diagram to bring about a clear understanding of a process. To that end, Figure 3-1 visually describes the process of business intelligence (BI) implementation, from defining what questions users have of data, to implementing a model that helps users explore data via interactive charts, graphs, and reports. All of these elements in Figure 3-1 are a preview into the lifecycle for bringing insights in useful forms to light. What also follows in this chapter is an approach to outline specific actions, roles, and best practices for incorporating what starts as self-service BI to a more formal approach of BI, or corporate BI.

Figure 3-1 illustrates a portion of each of the following possible scenarios:

■ **Self-service BI**   "Power users" create models and reports and share them by uploading or saving to SharePoint 2013. Users can create data models in either Microsoft Excel or PowerPivot in Excel 2013.

■ **IT-enabled self-service BI**   IT and BI developers build the models or at least provide access to data and SQL queries to power users, who then either extend or build models and build reports.

■ **Corporate BI**   IT promotes models that are created by power users to corporate-sanctioned and managed models by using SQL Server Data Tools and Microsoft SharePoint 2013 to model or extend an existing data model.

In this chapter, we show how to import the PowerPivot data model that is created in Chapter 4, "Using PowerPivot in Excel 2013," and modify it to include a Power View report in Chapter 5, "Using Power View in Excel 2013." The focus is on the new SQL Server Analysis Services tabular model. This is different from our first book *Business Intelligence in SharePoint 2010* (2011, Microsoft Press) in which we show how to create a data warehouse from a transactional database and then create a multidimensional cube.

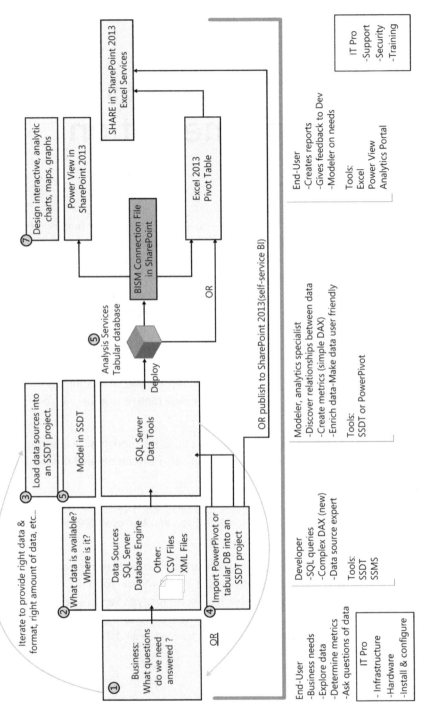

FIGURE 3-1 A high-level, end-to-end BI scenario.

Note Microsoft announced in the last SQL PASS that Power View will be able to build on top of existing multidimensional cube data. This is evidence of Microsoft's commitment to support multidimensional data.

Working together: SQL Server 2012 + SharePoint 2013 + Office 2013

Microsoft SQL Server has traditionally been a one-stop shop for customers seeking to implement BI solutions. As a corporate BI solution, companies use SQL Server to move data from disparate sources in an extract, transform, and load (ETL) process; develop solutions to make multidimensional and tabular data available; and use products such as SQL Server Reporting Services and Excel to build reports from relational, tabular, and multidimensional databases. Figure 3-2 shows a variation of a downloadable poster on TechNet (*http://www.microsoft.com/downloads/details.aspx?familyid=FC97D587-FFA4-4B43-B77D-958F3F8A87B9&displaylang=en*). The illustration shows the larger picture of how SQL Server 2012, SharePoint 2013, and Microsoft Office 2013 work together to deliver data that helps business users.

Note Microsoft BI authoring tools are available in all three layers shown in the Figure 3-2. Some tools come from SQL Server, such as Report Builder; some, like PerformancePoint, are in SharePoint; and others are in Office, including Excel and Visio. To learn more about these tools, see Chapter 2, "Planning for business intelligence adoption."

You use SharePoint Server in conjunction with SQL Server Reporting Services, Visio, PerformancePoint, and Excel to show BI data in meaningful and productive ways. SQL Server provides the primary data infrastructure and BI platform that gives report authors and business users trusted, scalable, and secure data.

Note You can now use PowerPivot in Excel 2013 when you need to "mash-up" data; that is, when your data comes from disparate sources, such as SQL, Teradata or Oracle, spreadsheets, the cloud, and SharePoint lists.

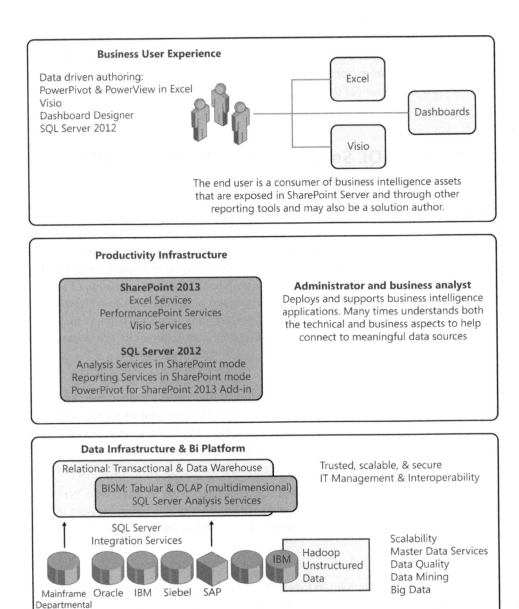

FIGURE 3-2 Platforms for data, sharing, and business user experience.

Figure 3-3 shows another scenario in which Excel's PivotTable Field List—which can be derived from an Excel table, Excel data model, or SQL Server Analysis Services (SSAS; tabular or multidimensional)—is made available in a PerformancePoint dashboard. The tools make data available in a drag-and-drop format for building reports. The data is organized intuitively. The key is that the Excel options require very little IT, thus proving the self-service BI concept.

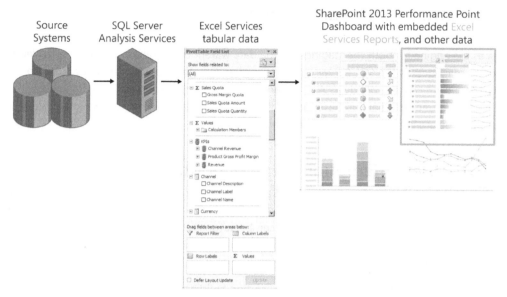

FIGURE 3-3 An end-to-end scenario, with multidimensional data to PerformancePoint Dashboard.

SQL Server 2012 features

This section describes each core element, which are depicted in Figure 3-4, that make up the SQL Server BI features.

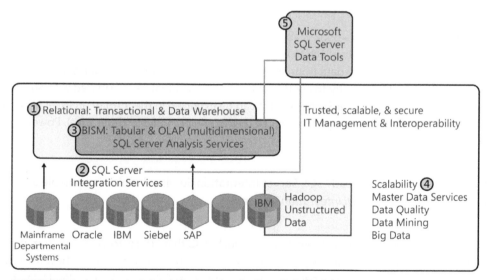

FIGURE 3-4 A closer look at data infrastructure for SharePoint insights.

1   The SQL Server database engine

The SQL Server database engine is the core service for storing, processing, and securing data. It serves as the engine for both the staging and the data warehouse databases. BI data is derived from databases managed by the SQL Server database engine and other database engines. It is also derived from NoSQL solutions, the Windows Azure Marketplace, and other sources. The engine hosts the data warehouse and transactional databases and is the underlying data in Analysis Services (multidimensional and tabular). We explain these later in this chapter.

2   SQL Server Integration Services or other tools

Microsoft SQL Server Integration Services (SSIS) is one tool that gives you data integration and data transformation solutions to help you get to trusted data faster. You can create repeatable data integration by using the ETL process. This process can be automated, moving data from sources such as XML data files, flat files, or relational data sources to one or more destinations. Data from disparate sources must often be cleansed.

Features that make SSIS compelling for ETL solution building include:

- A user interface that helps users move data and perform ETL.

- Wizards for importing and exporting data as well as those that help create a package containing the business logic to handle data extraction, manipulation, and transformation. Workflow elements help process data.

- Runtime debugging so that BI developers can step into code and watch the processes in a package. Reusable event handlers also help developers to create rich, repeatable ETL processes.

On another note, because this book is about SharePoint, it makes sense to mention that SharePoint is also a source system from which to extract and load data. It is becoming increasingly more important to know how to move data from and to SharePoint as companies adopt it to store business data. Some data will be tied directly to another software product that has partnered with SharePoint for sharing. Often, the data from a SharePoint list can be exported in the form of an Excel file or an Open Data Protocol (OData) feed and then pulled into a tabular model in either Excel, PowerPivot, or the SQL Server Data Tools.

> **More Info** To learn more, read "SQL Server Integration Services," which is available at *http://aka.ms/BI_SP2013/SQLIntegrationServices*.

Big Data is sometimes defined as there being so much data that efforts to get value from it needs to be spread across multiple workloads. Big Data as an unstructured data source will become increasingly important. We have created a separate section in Appendix B, "Microsoft and "Big Data," to inform you as to what is here and coming for Big Data, SQL Server integration, and how it will affect SharePoint.

3   The Business Intelligence Semantic Model

With the introduction of the Business Intelligence Semantic Model (BISM), there are now two separate features that serve as Analysis Services databases in Microsoft SQL Server 2012: multidimensional (ROLAP, MOLAP) databases, and tabular (initially introduced in the PowerPivot Add-in, versions 1 and 2). Each database and respective modeling features have the single goal of organizing disparate data into an analytic model that effectively and efficiently supports the reporting and analysis needs of the business.

Tabular modeling is supported by the xVelocity engine (formerly called Vertipaq). You can create a semantic model by using Excel, PowerPivot in Excel 2013, or SQL Server Data Tools (formerly Business Intelligence Development Studio [BIDS]). The result is a multidimensional model, an Excel or Power-Pivot tabular model in a workbook.

The following are some resources that further explain the BISM model:

- *Microsoft SQL Server 2012 Analysis Services: The BISM Tabular Model* by Marc Russo, Alberto Ferrari, Chris Webb (2012, Microsoft Press)

- "What is BI Semantic model (BISM) in SQL Server 2012?," which is available at *http://www. codeproject.com/Articles/506032/WhatplusisplusBIplusSemanticplusmodelplus-BISM-plu*

- "SQL Server 'Denali'-BI Semantic Model (BISM)," which is available at *http://blogs.msdn.com/b/ nikosan/archive/2011/01/24/sql-server-denali-bi-semantic-model-bism.aspx*

Tabular modeling vs. multidimensional modeling

Multidimensional modeling, introduced with SQL Server 7.0 OLAP Services and continuing through SQL Server 2012 Analysis Services, makes it possible for BI professionals to create sophisticated multidimensional cubes by using traditional Online Analytical Processing (OLAP). Multidimensional modeling creates cubes composed of measures and dimensions based on data contained in a relational database. The OLAP engine uses the multidimensional model to pre-aggregate large volumes of data to support fast query response times. The OLAP engine can store these aggregations on disk with multidimensional OLAP (MOLAP) storage or store them in the relational database with relational OLAP (ROLAP) storage.

Tabular modeling, introduced with PowerPivot for Microsoft Excel 2010, provides self-service data modeling capabilities to business and data analysts. The tabular modeling experience is more accessible to these users, many of whom have spent years working with data in desktop productivity tools such as Excel and Microsoft Access.

Tabular modeling organizes data into related tables. If you want to use tabular modeling in SQL Server Data Tools (SSDT) and provide server capacity for processing data, you must install Analysis Services to operate in tabular mode.

> **Note** You can model data without Analysis Services in Excel 2010 by using PowerPivot, Excel 2010, or PowerPivot in Excel 2013. When modeling in Excel, you can share the results in SharePoint 2013.

In tabular mode, you can use the xVelocity in-memory engine to load tabular data into memory for fast query response, or you can use DirectQuery to pass queries to the source database to take advantage of its query processing capabilities. To learn more about DirectQuery, read *Microsoft SQL Server 2012 Analysis Services: The BISM Tabular Model*. Table 3-1 compares the two models.

TABLE 3-1 Comparison of tabular modeling vs. multidimensional modeling

Tabular	Multidimensional
Familiarity Tabular data is familiar to those who work regularly with stored tables in relational databases, Excel, or Access. Calculations are written using Data Analysis Expressions (DAX), which is similar to the Excel formula language.	**Rich Data Model** In its sixth release, the multidimensional model provides extensive functionality to model dimensions and measures for simple and complex datasets found in enterprise data warehouses. Advanced features include many-to-many relationships, parent-child hierarchies, and localization.
Flexibility There is no rigid organization of data into measures and dimensions, which quickens development cycles and requires less data preparation and design.	**Sophisticated Analytics** The advanced calculation and query language, Multidimensional Expressions (MDX), makes it possible for you to create business logic and calculations and to accomplish financial allocations, time-series calculations, or semi-additive metrics.
Uses a column-oriented database which offers query performance improvements. Calculated columns can be added to a table in a tabular model and then, after processing, behave like regular columns.	Stores data in a row-based format and modeled as a series of cubes and dimensions rather than tables.
Tradeoffs Not suited for most solutions that require more complex datasets or business logic. The simpler datasets help to make self-service modeling and analytics possible.	**Tradeoffs** Its complexity leads to longer development cycles and a decreased ability to adapt to changing business conditions.
Queries are much faster at the leaf level.	Queries are faster with aggregated data.

Both modeling tools are structured in a way that mirrors how the users already view their business, so it's intuitive and familiar in the Excel 2013 client experience.

4   Additional BI tools

The SQL Server team is working to maintain and enhance existing tools and features while investigating others that will respond to industry needs and improve end-user experience. This section discusses these.

SQL Server Reporting Services

Microsoft SQL Server Reporting Services (SSRS) and SharePoint 2013 are integrated to include a full range of tools with which you can create, deploy, and manage reports for your organization. SSRS also has features that you can use to extend and customize your reporting functionality.

SSRS includes Power View (independent of Excel 2013) and Report Builder 3.0, both of which you can launch directly from SharePoint Products 2013. You can publish report server content types to a SharePoint library and then view and manage those documents from a SharePoint site.

Because this book is about BI in SharePoint, we should mention why you should use SharePoint for managing SSRS reports. Stacia Misner explains it best in *Microsoft SQL Server 2012 Reporting Services* (2013, Microsoft Press) when she says, "You'll have only one security model to manage and, even better, business users will have only one environment in which to create, find, and share information, whether that information is in the form of reports, lists, documents, or other content types. Furthermore, you can manage reports by using the same content management, workflow, and versioning features that you use for other SharePoint content."

More Info To learn more about SSRS, see "SQL Server Reporting Services," at *http://aka. ms/BI_SP2013/SQLReportingServices*.

Data mining

SQL Server Analysis Services (SSAS) data mining tools provide a set of industry-standard data mining algorithms and other tools that help you discover trends and patterns in your data. Data mining works in SSAS to complement Excel. It helps you to discover surprises in data and often provides a glimpse of "what will happen." This is sometimes referred to as *predictive analysis*. Also, SSAS helps you to validate what you think happened, to support a belief that is based on historic data.

The following Excel add-ins can help you perform predictive analysis:

- Table Analysis Tools for Excel provide easy-to-use features that take advantage of Analysis Services Data Mining to perform powerful analytics on spreadsheet data. For more information, see "SQL Server Predictive Analysis," at *http://www.microsoft.com/sqlserver/en/us/ solutions-technologies/business-intelligence/predictive-analytics.aspx*.

- New to the SQL Server 2012 Excel Add-in is 64-bit capability, a feature for which many have waited that significantly enhances performance.

- With the Data Mining Client for Excel Add-in, you can work through the full data-mining model development lifecycle within Microsoft Office Excel 2010 and Excel 2013, using either worksheet data or external data available through Analysis Services. The data mining add-in requires a connection to either SQL Server Enterprise or BI edition.

5   SQL Server Data Tools

SQL Server Data Tools (SSDT), previously called Microsoft Business Intelligence Development Studio (BIDS), provide several intuitive wizards for building integration, reporting, and analytic solutions within a unified environment. SSDT supports the complete development lifecycle for developing, testing, and deploying solutions. The SSDT development environment uses a Microsoft Visual Studio shell and includes project templates that make it easy to design solutions for ETL processes, cubes, and reports.

The lifecycle of a BI implementation

One way to explain BI concepts is within the context of a BI implementation lifecycle. By looking at the life-cycle, we also provide an approach to integrating corporate and self-service BI and align that approach with the appropriate roles and tools. In some ways, the approach is just as important as the tools. You have probably experienced that it's not *what* you are delivering to business users but *how* you deliver it.

The diagrams in this section gives you a 50,000-foot view of the lifecycle of a BI implementation, from determining what questions must be answered to making data available in the form of interactive visualizations, charts, and graphs. Of course, these diagrams cannot represent all of the possible scenarios or lifecycles that can exist within an organization.

In our previous book, we provided an end-to-end example of the ETL process that involved moving data from a small database to a data warehouse by using SQL Server Integration Services and then building a multidimensional cube. Figure 3-5 shows the parts that were covered in the first book—these are worth your time to review if your team will use multidimensional data for reporting. Investments might have been made and the technology remains very relevant and the ideal data source for organizational reporting.

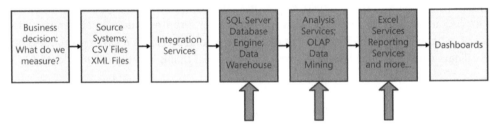

FIGURE 3-5 The process, from measuring to dashboards.

In the example in this chapter, we chose to show the lifecycle of a BI project, presenting trusted tabular data for insights rather than multidimensional data. There are several different use cases. You will also note that the lifecycle for accomplishing an end-to-end scenario is shortened in comparison to using multidimensional data because there is less complexity.

The example in this section is intended only as an illustration of the end-to-end process; it is not necessarily reflective of the reality that companies face. However, for the purpose of learning about the major components of an implementation, which includes subcomponents for each phase, this example is very useful. After the end-to-end example, you can work through a quick hands-on lab to practice creating a project in SSDT and then automating the data processing by using XMLA and SQL Server jobs.

> **Note** "Data processing" and "data refreshing" are used synonymously, although when a PowerPivot report is scheduled, the term is "data refreshed."

Figure 3-6 provides a guide for what we are going to show during this end-to-end example.

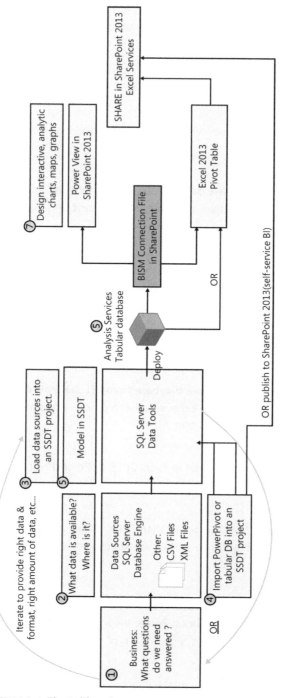

FIGURE 3-6 The BI lifecycle process.

Here is a summary of the process that occurs during the lifecycle of a BI implementation.

- Your "customers" have an idea of what questions they need to answer. This process evolves as analytic-minded business users have opportunities to explore the data.

Tip As users discover new insights that they want to see, ask that they prioritize which are most critical, useful, or insightful.

- As users discover new insights, you will discover what data is needed and begin strategizing on how to prepare that data for modeling.

Tip Try not to lament too much on how database design could have made life easier. Every organization is at a different maturity level. You will discover workarounds and maybe encourage some refactoring.

- How you model the data determines how the client will view data. You enhance the client's view of the data by delivering metrics in the form that they want to see. This is where most of your effort will be expended.

Tip Quickly get a working knowledge of DAX.

- Deploying to Analysis Services puts your model in a database from which clients can consume via a BISM connection file, an ODC connection in Excel, or other methods explained in just a short while in "Step 7: Create a BISM file in SharePoint 2013."

Note This is only one alternative. You can also model in Excel 2013 or PowerPivot in Excel 2013 and publish directly to SharePoint.

- Clients can upload their Pivot tables and workbooks to SharePoint. If they are using Excel 2013, they can share the visualizations they create in their workbooks and Power View reports very easily.

Tip Train users in Power View. It's the most un-Microsoft tool I've ever used. However, there is a return on investment after two to three clicks. Power View is a very ad hoc, very easy, very visual report builder. Consider who will be a champion of this visualization tool.

Step 1: Decide what to analyze, measure, or forecast

Business decision: What questions do we need answered? What is being measured that can provide answers to critical questions we have of the data?

We thought it a little funny that there is a person sitting down for Step 1 in Figure 3-6, as if she is waiting for her report. In many cases the business users are accustomed to getting static reports and perhaps do not recognize their value as a stakeholder or their role in the iterative process of determining what to measure. Additionally, often things are being measured, but the business users don't know how or where to get the data—and if they get it, it is a cumbersome manual process. Additionally, they might or might not realize that the result of their efforts will produce interactive reports rather than static reports, in which case their role is to become more analytically minded by asking questions of the data—to then further the design process for data-driven reports that directly affect decision making.

There are many possible scenarios that drive reports. For example, your company might decide that it wants to answer questions by using data it has collected from transactional systems, or the company wants to improve its forecasting process by collecting the right information by having more reporting flexibility or by giving more people access to information. For example, a common request is to combine transactional data with marketing campaign data. Another is to pull in data from the cloud that is related to demographics or weather. The required steps for these BI initiatives can go wrong in several places. You need to get to what your customer wants, and you want to be effective so that you build the solution that the organization needs.

Discovering and exposing data and determining what to do with the data might be the most important and often the most difficult steps. It's important because you do not want to spend resources collecting data that is not useful. Savvy developers and solution designers must work with users to determine their data requirements in an efficient, iterative manner.

Be patient if they do not know what or how they want to measure. Or, they do not know if there is trusted data available. Deliver prototypes and give them an opportunity to explore data and visualizations. It can take time, but you will gain their trust and they will begin to trust the data.

In our corporate BI scenario, the easier a designer or modeler makes it for users to quickly understand the results of a BI solution, the closer a designer can come to delivering a useful solution. For this reason, one of the multidimensional tools, the SSDT browser, gives developers the ability to see the results of data collection and queries, and it is nearly identical to the viewer in Excel. Additionally, you can view your tabular data results in the Excel client in SSDT.

Finally, because you can import your tabular project from PowerPivot in Excel 2013 into an SSDT project, consider using PowerPivot or Excel to prototype and to give users an opportunity to explore the data before formalizing the data processing or refreshing.

Each of these tools provides great support for prototyping and scope checking.

Step 2: Get to trusted data

After having an idea of what the business user wants answered, you must determine where the data will come from and plan how to collect it. Figure 3-4 represents data from Line-of-Business (LOB) systems, Enterprise Resource Planning (ERP) systems, Customer Relationship Management (CRM) systems, and flat files, such as CSV and XML files. Other sources, such as Excel files and data from Online Transaction Processing (OLTP) systems, are also common and are valuable as raw data sources that can be cleaned and prepared for BI solutions.

An OLTP system can be defined as a relational store that is designed and optimized for computer-based transactions. Transaction processing is information processing one transaction at a time. For example, when an item is purchased at a store, the store logs that purchase as a single transaction in a computer system that uses an OLTP database. An OLTP system records business transactions as they happen and supports day-to-day operations in an organization. Transactional data is the raw data that the business can use as the basis-for-fact data and, later, to calculate measures (in cubes) as discussed in the next section.

As you can see, it's common to draw from multiple data sources to deliver a useful BI solution. It's also common to gather data from multiple OLTP systems. Because of the variety of sources, the data very likely contains a variety of different formats for dates, product and category names, and other data. Inconsistent data types used for the same data, different time periods, and other problems require you to consolidate and cleanse the data.

Before cleansing data, your primary goal is to determine where the data is that you want to extract, clean, and conform. Because the ETL process can be the most resource-heavy, it's also vital that you understand exactly what the users require before you begin. Best practices for understanding user requirements often include a prototyping and iterative back-and-forth discussion among analysts, report users, and developers. It is particularly important to validate that you're collecting the right amount of information at the right time, in the right format, and with the most helpful visualizations.

Far too often, a company starting a BI initiative wants to integrate the enterprise's data right now, so it is reluctant to take the time to design an extensible and universal solution—but not doing so increases the likelihood of unusable solutions that lead to future rework. It is well worth your time to review the methodologies and literature around BI project management solutions in other books and articles.

You deliver the cleansed source data into a dimensional data store that implements querying and analysis capabilities for the purpose of making decisions. There are excellent books and articles on best practices for ETL data. Ralph Kimball is a pioneer for data warehousing and has published much of the original content for ETL and other data warehousing best practices. You can find his books and articles at *http://www.ralphkimball.com*. Anther source is The Data Warehouse Institute (TDWI) at *http://tdwi.org*, which is an educational institution for BI and data warehousing. In addition, the "Information Management" site at *http://www. information-management.com/* provides news, commentary, and offers content serving the information technology and business community.

What is trusted data?

The major focus of this book is on how to use SharePoint Server 2013, integrated with the SQL Server 2012 and Office 2013, to present data to business users. This would be pointless without data you can trust to present to your business user applications. Trusted data comes from business processes occurring in departments such as marketing, finance, e-commerce, and more. It is then transformed for use in decision-making processes. The transformation lets trusted data be delivered in formats and time frames that are appropriate to specific users, reports, spreadsheets, visualizations, and other data-rendering tools.

Data that's incomplete, out-of-date, or poorly documented can destroy users' trust and your credibility. Users who don't have confidence in the data might refuse to use the reports and analyses created from the data. Instead, they might build their own data stores. Moreover, when data is inaccurate or is misinterpreted, individuals, teams, departments, and the company can make misguided decisions.

The solution for trusted data depends on the size of the organization, size of the data, the kind of reports you are delivering, and other variables. But most often, getting trusted data is an involved process that includes a combination of following best practices for data collection, data profiling, and data integration, as well as the application of guidelines from related disciplines, such as data quality, master data management, metadata management, and adding business logic into a data model. The BI maturity model mentioned in Chapter 2, "Planning for business intelligence adoption," shows that making trusted data available across an organization doesn't occur as a single event; it's a process that occurs in stages, and different parts of the organization can be mapped to different maturity levels.

Another way to look at trusted data is as data "approved for viewing" and made discoverable in SharePoint by publishing access points such as connection files. The viewers are business users who range from front-line employees to executive management and external stakeholders.

The broad definition of BI described at the beginning of this book includes both the data warehouse and the tools used to view the data in the warehouse. This chapter explains what a data warehouse is, what the two parts of the BISM model (OLAP and tabular data) are and how they relate to data warehousing, and finally, how Microsoft implements these technologies to deliver the right information and the right amount of information, in the right format, at the right time. In our first book, we walked you through creating a data warehouse and a multidimensional database and cube. We don't abandon the multidimensional content; rather, we put it in Appendix B to make room for the latest tabular technology.

A lot of thought and work goes into warehousing data in such a way that it can be retrieved easily. This chapter provides a broad overview of the steps toward creating trusted data; you can find other resources that provide deeper coverage. Data warehousing and OLAP have developed over decades, and many people have written books about these subjects.

Some companies are engineering new methods for harnessing massive amounts of data (see Appendix B), whereas others rely on more traditional methods that are described well in books such as *The Data Warehouse Toolkit: The Complete Guide to Dimensional Modeling* and the *Data*

Warehouse ETL Toolkit: Practical Techniques for Extracting, Cleaning, Conforming, and Delivering Data (Wiley, 2004) from Ralph Kimball and The Kimball Group. A source for white papers about BI, managing BI projects, and more is TDWI.

It's important to note that data modeling in Excel and PowerPivot were developed by the SQL Server product team in large part to confront the reality that Excel is being used by business users to answer business questions that are to slow coming from traditional corporate BI. Data warehouse and standard SSRS reports move too slowly and do not answer questions fast enough. The traditional corporate BI approach proves too expensive and too rigid for power users trying to answer questions quickly. Work must continue regardless of whether the corporate data warehouse has all of the information. Getting to trusted data faster is the key to success.

The data warehouse

An ideal data source for loading data into a tabular model is a data warehouse and its data marts. In many cases a data warehouse already exists. This will depend on several factors such as the size of your company or the maturity level for business intelligence (discussed in Chapter 2). This optional intermediary step of creating a data warehouse is not shown in the end-to-end diagram in Figure 3-6. Notwithstanding, comprehending the process of preparing data in the form of a data warehouse is worth knowing; otherwise, skip to the next step.

Preparing data in the form of a data warehouse can occur in two phases. First you must design and create a data warehouse in SQL Server. (A number of books have been written on best practices for creating a data warehouse.)

A staging database is created. A staging database is an intermediate storage location used for organizing, cleansing, and transforming data to prepare it for a data warehouse. A staging database helps minimize the impact on the source systems during the ETL process. Basically, you want to get in and out of the data warehouse quickly. If you put everything into a staging database and then if a transformation step fails, you can restart with the data in stages instead of having to go back and touch (impact) the source systems again. The staging database sits between the various sources and the data warehouse.

After creating a data mart or data warehouse, you can use stored procedures or SSIS to create a repeatable ETL process for getting various sources of data into your data warehouse databases. SSIS is a rich tool that performs useful operations such as making the data conform to specifications so that you can use it in applications, to create cubes, or to connect directly to it from reports.

Let's look at some of the components of a data warehouse.

What is a data warehouse?

A data warehouse is a database that functions as a repository for storing an organization's data for reporting and analysis. The core data in the data warehouse typically consists of numeric values that you can aggregate in a number of ways. The data is usually stored in a structure called a *star schema* rather than in a more normalized structure found in typical transactional databases. Querying data can be very resource-intensive, so the data warehouse structure provides much better querying times. Ad hoc queries return summed values, similar to queries that you would perform in a transactional database to create a report.

The data warehouse vs. the data mart

A data warehouse usually contains data from multiple sources and covers multiple subject areas. In contrast, a data mart is subject-specific and contains a subset of data applicable to a specific department or segment of an organization. A data warehouse can contain one or more data marts.

Facts and dimensions

When you work with data warehouses, you quickly learn that the entire discussion centers on facts and dimensions. Data warehousing is about storing the data that people can use to solve business problems—and you determine what data to store by asking questions such as "What number needs to be viewed, and in what manner does the number need to be analyzed?"

The "what" part is typically a number such as the number of products produced, the defect rate, the manufacturing cost, and so forth. These numbers are called *fact data*. The values stored in a data warehouse (or data mart) consist primarily of fact data.

After identifying the "what," you must determine how users should see the fact data. How the user will analyze the fact data becomes the *dimension*. The most common dimension is time, which gives context to the facts that are stored. For example, users might want to see trends in manufacturing costs over time, or they might want to see sales volume over time.

A data warehouse has a different structure than a transactional database. The primary reason for the structure change is to improve the speed of querying the data. Figure 3-7 shows a scaled-down version of a star schema. It also illustrates how fact data and dimensions are made available—from which you would choose report elements to create a report. A report is a subset of the data in the relational database, but as is demonstrated in Figure 3-7, multiple scenarios are available, and the report you want to create is dictated by the data within the facts and dimensions. The schema in the figure shows only one fact and only a handful of dimensions, but in real-world situations, a schema can hold more facts and many, many more dimensions.

The information shown in the report at the bottom of Figure 3-7 could be a prototype for a customer to communicate requirements to a business user. The report communicates one variation of two facts, Quantity and Dollar Sales. The Date column shows how the two facts are aggregated, in addition to the context provided by the dimensions.

Example of a star schema in a data warehouse

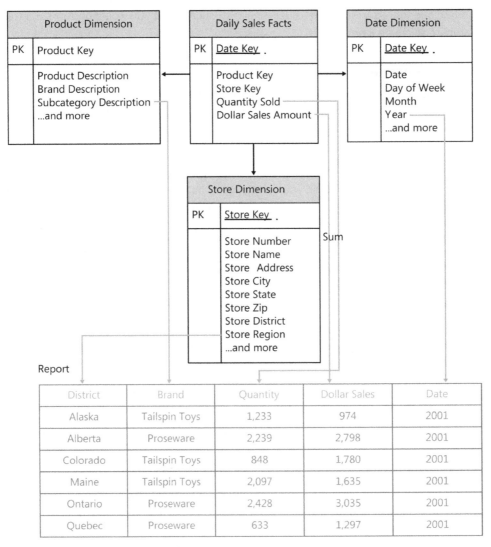

FIGURE 3-7 An example of a start schema.

Moving data by using SSIS

SSIS is a tool that you can use to move data from various sources to the data warehouse. Other BI developers might prefer to clean and load data to the data warehouse by using Transact-SQL (T-SQL) and stored procedures, but SSIS provides a useful alternative to T-SQL and stored procedures because it can support repeatable ETL processes.

This phase can be the most expensive part of your BI solution because it's typically the most time-consuming part of the project. You can expect a lot of surprises in the data, such as missing or invalid values, and cleaning it is typically an iterative process during which misunderstandings are ironed out and data quality issues are resolved. The cost of ETL for any BI solution is also affected by other variables—too many to list them all here—such as the following:

- How well the project is sponsored, starting from the very top (CIO, CEO, and so on).

- The size of the project and business unit. The solution could reach the organization, department, team, and a group of individuals, each of which vary in size.

- The culture and dynamics of the organization, department, and team: how well they are able to communicate requirements, and how well the prototypes are presented. Typically, ETL is an iterative process—and even after that, misunderstandings often lead to changes. A good change-management system helps control the scope of the project and, ultimately, the time and money spent.

The preceding is not an all-inclusive list of variables or considerations. You can find several good books that discuss project methodologies, such as agile BI data warehousing, as well as books explaining how to use SSIS for more than just creating a repeatable ETL solution.

In our previous book, we show you how to create a data warehouse with a simple database. It is worth reviewing to see how transactional data is transformed into a star schema, described in the prequel to this book, *Business Intelligence in SharePoint 2010* (2011, Microsoft Press).

Step 3 or 4: Load data into a SSDT (Visual Studio) project

In this step, you have the option of importing an existing project built in either PowerPivot in Excel 2013 or an existing Analysis Services tabular database, or create a new project and load data and model to fit your user's needs. In other words, by importing from an existing model, you can create or further "mash-up" data from work performed by other analysts, developers, and business users.

Figure 3-8 gives a visual representation of the options available. You can also see the options in Visual Studio (or SSDT) in Figure 3-11.

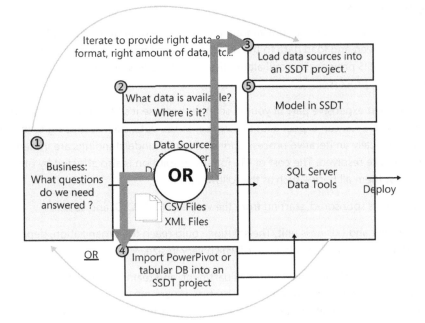

FIGURE 3-8 Step 3 or 4 of the lifecycle.

You must have SQL Server 2012 Data Tools to create a new project and import data into the tabular modeling tool. You can obtain it in one of three ways.

- Install Visual Studio 2012 where SSDT is included

- Install Visual Studio 2010 SP1

- When installing with SQL Server 2012 media, you have the option of including SSDT

After selecting Analysis Services as the default setting for your start page, you will see the options shown in Figure 3-9.

FIGURE 3-9 The Visual Studio start page.

When you click New Project, you are presented with the following three options for creating a tabular project:

- **Analysis Services Tabular Project**   From the outset, you begin to import data and model.

- **Import From PowerPivot**   You can import an existing model from PowerPivot in Excel 2013.

- **Import From Server (Tabular)**   You can import an existing model that has already been deployed to Analysis Services.

Figure 3-10 shows the Table Import Wizard, which is little different from importing data in Power-Pivot in Excel. In fact, the code base is the same, and if you have modeled in PowerPivot, you will have no problem modeling data in SSDT.

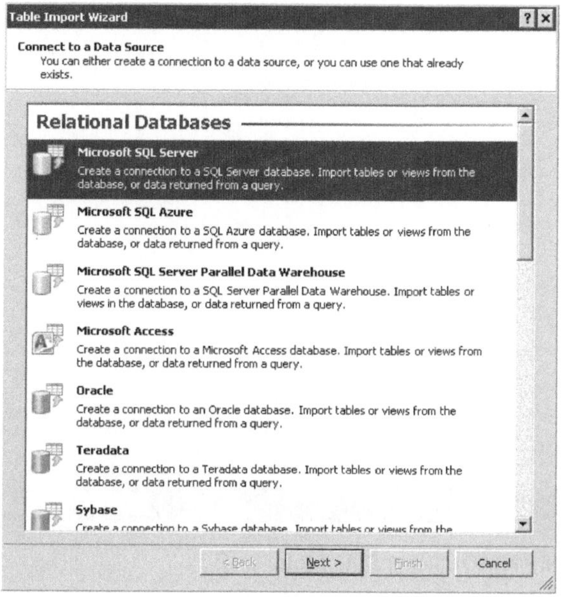

Table Import Wizard

Connect to a Data Source
You can either create a connection to a data source, or you can use one that already exists.

Relational Databases

Microsoft SQL Server
Create a connection to a SQL Server database. Import tables or views from the database, or data returned from a query.

Microsoft SQL Azure
Create a connection to a SQL Azure database. Import tables or views from the database, or data returned from a query.

Microsoft SQL Server Parallel Data Warehouse
Create a connection to a SQL Server Parallel Data Warehouse. Import tables or views in the database, or data returned from a query.

Microsoft Access
Create a connection to a Microsoft Access database. Import tables or views from the database, or data returned from a query.

Oracle
Create a connection to an Oracle database. Import tables or views from the database, or data returned from a query.

Teradata
Create a connection to a Teradata database. Import tables or views from the database, or data returned from a query.

Sybase
Create a connection to a Sybase database. Import tables or views from the

< Back   Next >   Finish   Cancel

FIGURE 3-10 The SQL Server Data Tools with the Table Import Wizard.

If we were to continue with this scenario, we would simply import from the *AdventureWorks* data warehouse, right-click the project file, and then deploy to Analysis Services so that we could create a connection file either in SharePoint (BISM), from Excel (ODC), or RSDS file for SSRS. In this chapter, we show how to import an existing PowerPivot model into an SSDT project.

Import an existing PowerPivot model

In this example, we import an existing model, as described in Chapter 4.

To create a new tabular model project from a PowerPivot for Excel file, perform the following:

1. In SQL Server Data Tools, on the File menu, click New, and then click Project.

2. In the New Project dialog box (see Figure 3-11), in the Installed Templates section, click Business Intelligence and then, in the center of the window, click Import From PowerPivot.

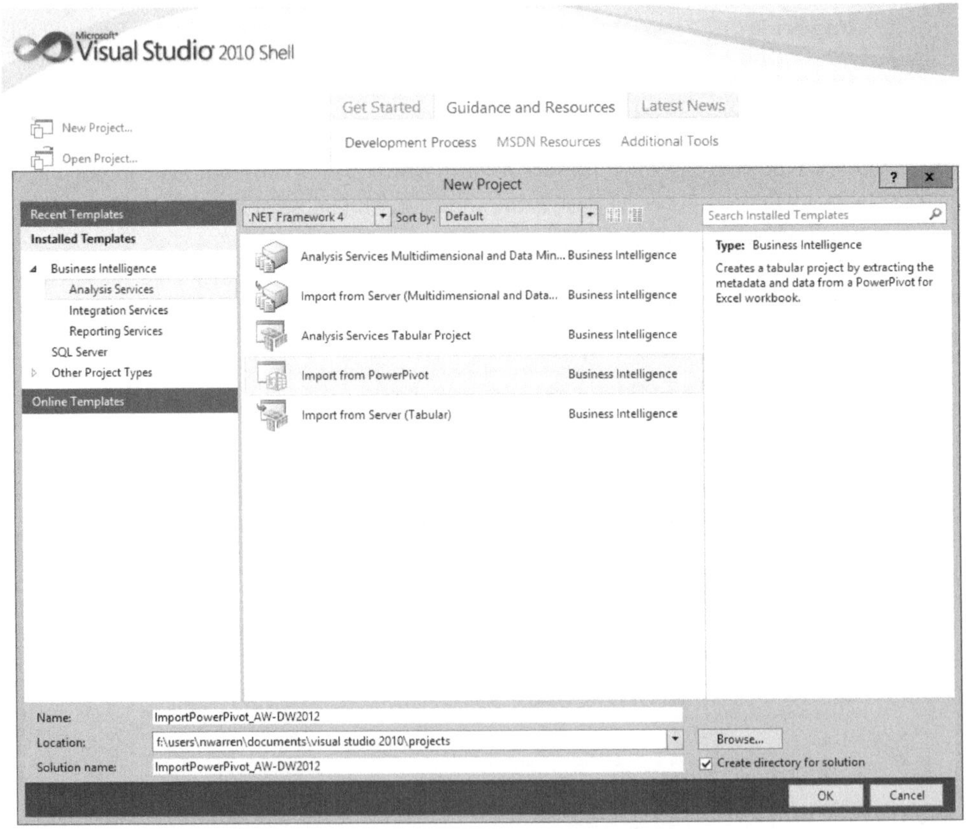

FIGURE 3-11 The Visual Studio 2010 Shell with SQL Server Data Tools.

3. At the bottom of the window, in the Name text box, type a name for the project. Specify a location and solution name in the respective text boxes and then click OK.

When you click OK, you will see the dialog presented in Figure 3-12, which asks where your workspace database will be stored. You will typically want to store this locally even if you deploy to another instance of an Analysis Services tabular database. You do not want your workspace database to take resources from the production server. Also, consider the effects of having multiple workspace databases on a single development server. If multiple developers are using the same workspace database server, you might have multiple copies of the database in memory and on disk.

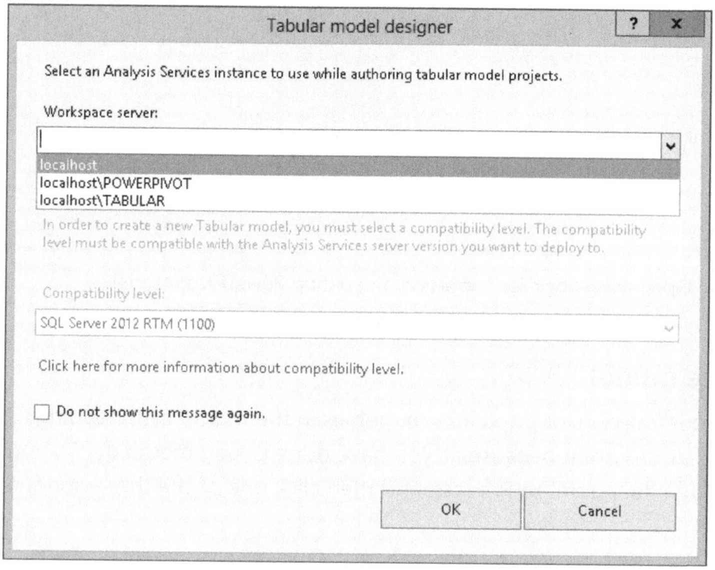

FIGURE 3-12 The Tabular Model Designer dialog box.

Upon selecting the localhost\TABULAR, you are then prompted to select the Excel file that contains the PowerPivot model to import, as shown in Figure 3-13.

> **Tip** It is a good idea to learn more about the workspace database. You can do this at *http:// msdn.microsoft.com/en-us/library/hh230969.aspx*. Also review the white paper, Hardware Sizing a Tabular Solution (SQL Server Analysis Services) at *http://msdn.microsoft.com/en-us/ library/jj874401.aspx*.

4. In the Open dialog box (see Figure 3-13), select the PowerPivot for Excel file that contains the model metadata and data that you want to import, and then click Open.

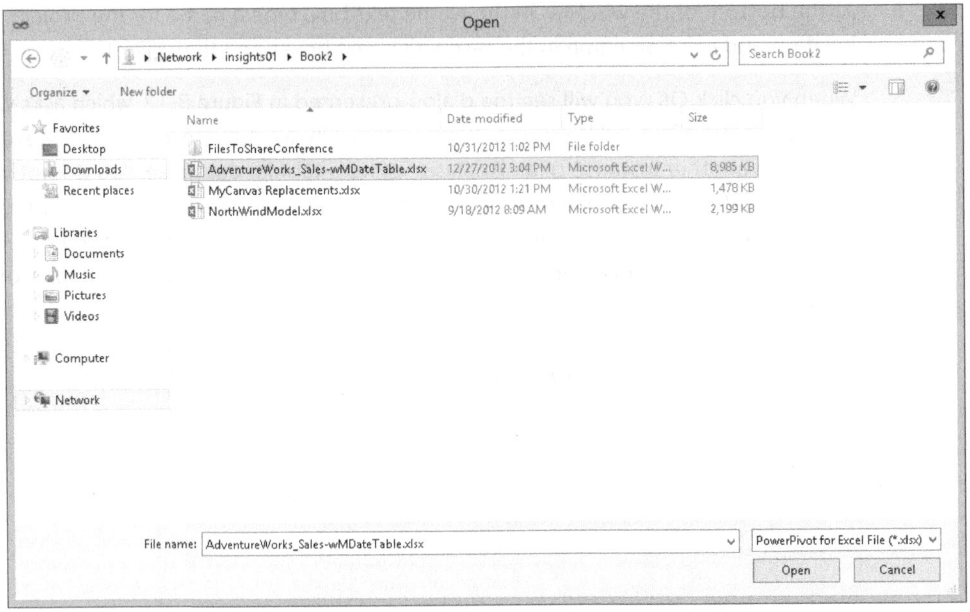

FIGURE 3-13 The Open dialog box for importing an existing PowerPivot model.

Load data into the model

Upon clicking Open, your PowerPivot populates the tables in the model with headings. The data might not be imported at this point because all you have done is load metadata. To import the data, you must select the Model tab, point to Process, and then click one of the three options, as shown in Figure 3-14.

- **Process Partitions**   Use this option if you have created partitions discussed in the next step of modeling or extending and enhancing the existing data model.

> **Note** Excel 2013 does not have partitions.

- **Process Table**   Choose this if you only want to import data from a source into one table.

- **Process All**   Choose this if you want to import all data and data sources into all tables, assuming that you have more than one table.

Model Table Column Tools Window Help

Import From Data Source...
Analyze in Excel
Process ▶   Process Partitions...
Existing Connections...   Process Table
Perspectives ▶   Process All
Roles...
Model View ▶
Show Hidden
Find Metadata ...
Calculate Now
Calculation Options ▶

		DueDac...	ShipDat...	ResellerKey	Employe...	PromotionKey	CurrencyKey	Sale
	20050801	20050813	20050808	403	282	1	100	
	20050801	20050813	20050808	403	282	1	100	
	20050801	20050813	20050808	403	282	1	100	
	20050801	20050813	20050808	403	282	1	100	
	20050801	20050813	20050808	403	282	1	100	
	20050801	20050813	20050808	403	282	1	100	
285	2005	20050801	20050813	20050808	403	282	1	100	
272	2005	20051101	20051113	20051108	403	282	1	100	

FIGURE 3-14 Processing All in SQL Server Data Tools.

Step 5: Model the data

The purpose of data modeling is to organize disparate data into an analytic model that effectively and efficiently supports the reporting and analysis needs of the business.[1] Figure 3-15 shows that modeling is the step just prior to deploying to the Analysis Services tabular database and making the data available to business users.

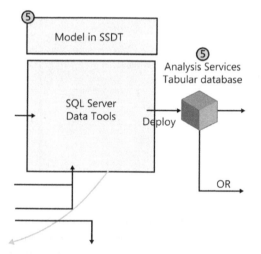

FIGURE 3-15 Step 5 of process diagram.

---

[1] Excerpted from *Microsoft SQL Server 2012 Analysis Services: The BISM Tabular Model.*

As part of the modeling experience, you want to discover useful relationships between tables; create metrics or measures by using DAX; enrich the data such as including a date table for simplifying aggregating by dates or using time intelligence functions; helping the user experience with simpler names; and more. This is the part where the modeler and perhaps developer (if they are not one in the same) will continue the iterative process of understanding user needs, coaching the user to discover insights, and making the right data available by doing things like adding properties specific to the client tools: Excel and Power View. Perhaps the most important time is spent helping the user understand the data by discovering and mapping data sources to business knowledge.

Figure 3-16 shows the relationships in Diagram view. The experience is almost the same as that in PowerPivot in Excel 2013.

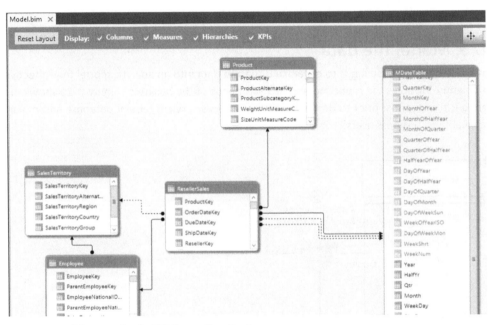

FIGURE 3-16 Diagram view in SQL Server Data Tools.

The tabular modeling experience is simpler than multidimensional modeling and there are tradeoffs as explained, in the section "Tabular models vs. multidimensional models." You were able to see the data modeling experience in the context of preparing a data warehouse with dimension and fact tables. These were brought together to provide options to the business user from which to report.

In our example, the data modeling has already occurred by the user in PowerPivot in Excel 2013, and we import it to extend or enhance the model, or both. For example, a data table was added to the model to simplify and make time-intelligence features available. We can also take advantage of the following benefits of working in SSDT and deploying the model to Analysis Services in tabular mode:

- The preparation of a schedule to automate the processing (data refresh) of the model for as often as is needed.

- The creation of partitions, which is explained later in the next step of deploying the model.

- The creation of roles and the application of dynamic security at the row-level of our tables. (See Securing the Tabular BI Semantic Model at *http://msdn.microsoft.com/en-us/library/jj127437.aspx*.)

- The publishing of a connection file that queries the Analysis Services on a robust server rather than on client-side resources.

> **Tip** We expect more Office Apps, specific to Excel 2013 that will help you to further enhance the user experience with features such as time intelligence. You can find an example of this, a Time Dimension App, at *http://stefanjohansson.org/apps/timedimension/*.

In a broader sense, we performed data modeling when we provided more efficient data processing (or refreshing) by partitioning the table into historical and current sections.

Excel: Test the modeled data

You can immediately see the results of what you have modeled in your tabular project that results from the data that is put into a temporary workspace database by opening the Excel file (see Figure 3-17). Excel queries your immediate workspace database without deploying the model.

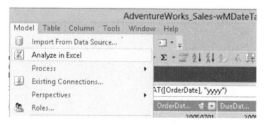

FIGURE 3-17 Using the Analyze In Excel option from SSDT.

Note This chapter does not cover what is considered the self-service modeling process in PowerPivot. But, we encourage you to enable self-service wherever possible by training users to believe that in addition to creating their own reports, they can also perform modeling functions using Excel, PowerPivot, and SSDT. Some users refer to modeling as "mashing-up data".

We also suggest that you review the following two excellent sources for data modeling in which there are sections that provides details such as how to use DAX for enriching data:

- For data models, read *Microsoft PowerPivot for Excel 2010: Give Your Data Meaning* by Marco Russo and Alberto Ferrari (2010, Microsoft Press). A. Kindle Edition.

- For data modeling in tabular, read *Microsoft SQL Server 2012 Analysis Services: The BISM Tabular Model*.

Step 6: Deploy the model to SSAS

After you have developed your model in SSDT or imported an existing model, you are ready to deploy the tabular model to Analysis Services. This is the most exciting part of the process because you will be able to provide the data from which users can create reports. By deploying with the right settings, you make available the data that you and users can consume in Power View in SharePoint 2013 and Excel 2013. Figure 3-18 shows the result in SQL Server Management Studio when you connect to your tabular instance.

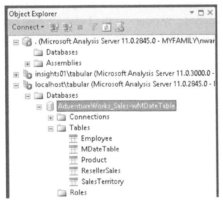

FIGURE 3-18 The SQL Server Management Studio with the *AdventureWorks* tabular database.

What follows are considerations for the server that hosts Analysis Services.

Roles (back-end permissions)

In SQL Server, you must apply roles for those that need access to the data contained in the tabular database. A role is a grouping of users who all perform the same tasks and therefore share the same permissions. When you grant permission to a role to do something, you are granting that permission to all users who are members of that role. "Users" are either Microsoft Windows domain user accounts or local user accounts from the computer on which Analysis Services is installed. Roles can be created and edited in both SSDT and SQL Server Management Studio. If you do not add the user "on the back end" but you do in SharePoint, the user will receive a data source error.

> **Note** Some teams add [domain]\Domain Users to roles and manage security in one place: SharePoint. The risk in doing this is that users can access the data via Excel by connecting to the tabular dataset by using the Data tab.

Figure 3-19 shows that you can add row filters to a role, add members by selecting the Members tab and adding domain users, and that you must set permissions to at least Read. Conveniently, you can also copy a role and build on that. The technical article "Securing the Tabular BI Semantic Model" (*http://msdn.microsoft.com/en-us/library/jj127437.aspx*) gives an example of how to filter rows by using dynamic security.

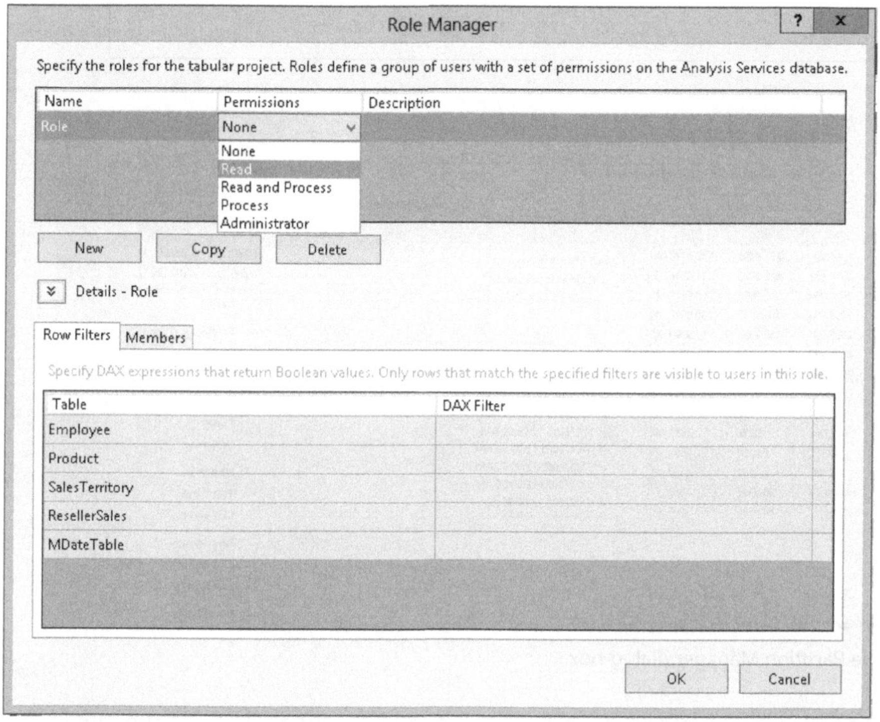

FIGURE 3-19 The Role Manager dialog box.

Partitions

You can reduce the processing time—when data is being loaded into your model—significantly by partitioning the table. This is because when loading data into your model or tabular database, the delta or most recent changes are *not* updated; instead, a new copy of the data replaces the existing. Because you can process partitions separately, you can process one that has historical data and another that processes the most current information. Unlike multidimensional, partitions are (for the most part) processed serially, not in parallel.

Figure 3-20 shows an example of setting up partitions. In this example, there are two partitions, ResellerSales-Historical and ResellerSales-Current. ResellerSales-Historical will filter by date to import all data up to a certain month. This partition only needs to process once. You can use the Reseller-Sales-Current partition to load data into the model on a more frequent schedule.

To open the Partition Manager, on the main menu, click the Table tab and then, on the menu that appears, click Partitions.

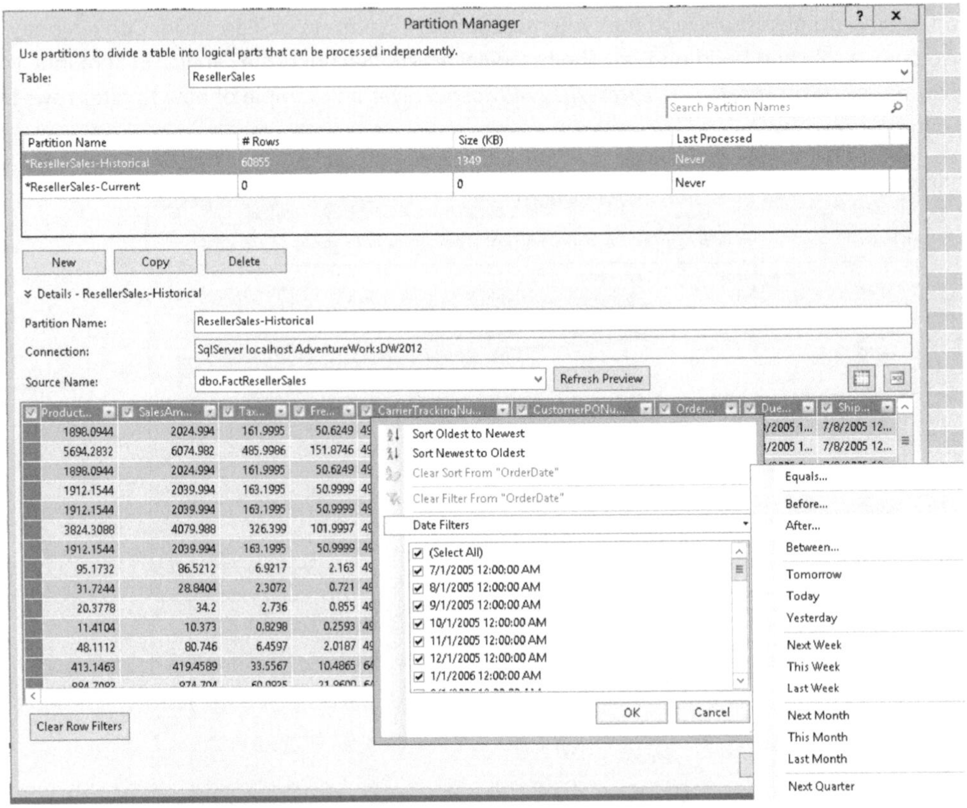

FIGURE 3-20 The Partition Manager dialog box.

If you used a SQL query to import the data, you can modify your query to do the same.

This chapter does not go into depth; rather, it gives you enough to get started. Additional guidance and reasons for developing a partitioning strategy are given in the aforementioned book, *Microsoft SQL Server 2012 Analysis Services: The BISM Tabular Model*.

Automating data processing (refresh tabular data)

After users have explored their data and surfaced useful insights, they might find that they want data loaded to the tabular database more frequently than what the "guided" self-service experiences in PowerPivot and SharePoint 2013 offer. This might be the primary reason for moving some PowerPivot projects to SSDT and deploying to a tabular database rather than a PowerPivot database in Analysis Services. Here are some details to remember about refreshing data:

- Users cannot set a data refresh schedule more frequent than every 24 hours in SharePoint for PowerPivot in Excel 2013 files that you upload.

- Users can now refresh back-end data on demand from both Excel 2013 and PowerPivot.

Prepare to automate data processing

1. In SQL Server Management Studio, connect to SQL Server engine.

2. Create a credential. (For more information on how to do this, go to *http://msdn.microsoft.com/en-us/library/ms190703.aspx*.)

   A credential is a record that contains the authentication information that is required to connect to a resource outside SQL Server. Most credentials include a Windows user and password.

3. Create a Proxy. (For more information on how to do this, go to *http://msdn.microsoft.com/en-us/library/ms175834.aspx*.)

4. A SQL Server Agent proxy account defines a security context in which a job step can run. Each proxy corresponds to a security credential. To set permissions for a particular job step, create a proxy that has the required permissions for a SQL Server Agent subsystem and then assign that proxy to the job step.

Note You must create a credential before you create a proxy if one is not already available.

Figure 3-21 shows the New Proxy Account dialog box, in which you specify the settings for a new proxy and some essential subsystems.

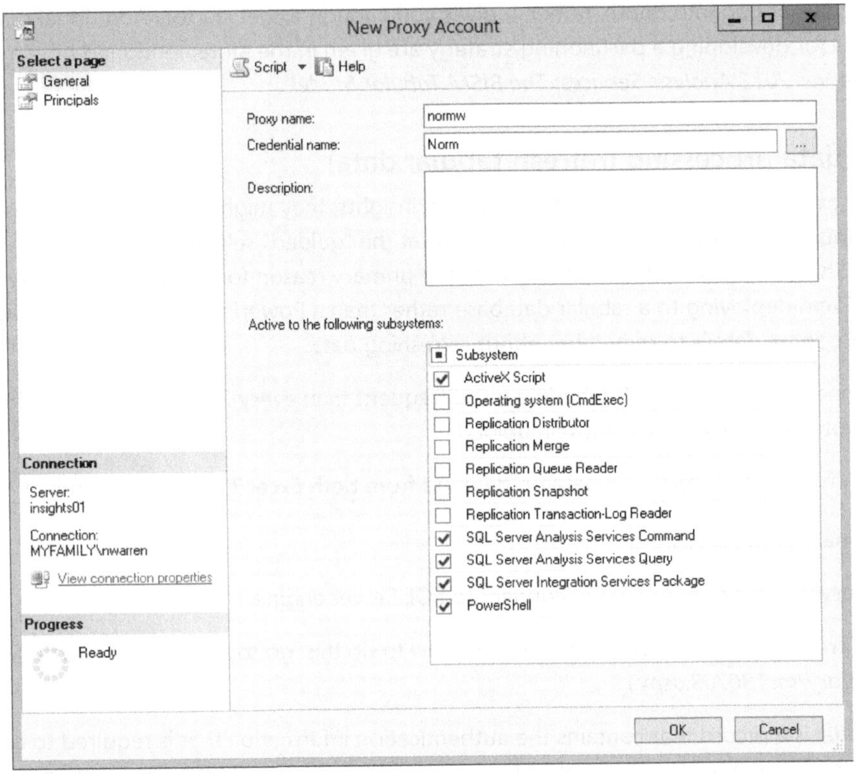

FIGURE 3-21 The New Proxy Account dialog box.

Create the XMLA for a new job

1. Log on to the Analysis Services tabular database.

2. Right-click either the table or complete database.

   Figure 3-22 shows only one of the tables selected.

> **Note** You can also choose to process or script only one partition of a table. You want to do this for cases in which you only want the most current data and you have partitioned historical data.

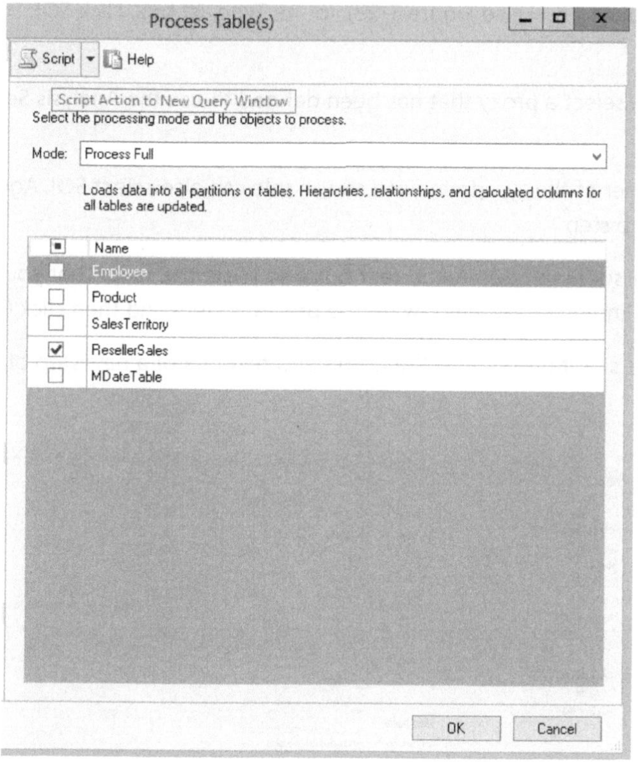

FIGURE 3-22 The Process Table dialog box.

3. On the shortcut menu that appears, click Script to open an new query window.

   The XMLA populates the query window.

4. Select the XMLA script and copy it for the next step.

Create a job to automate data processing

1. In the Object Explorer, click the plus sign to expand the server on which you want to create a SQL Server Agent job.

2. Click the plus sign to expand SQL Server Agent.

3. Right-click the Jobs folder and then, on the shortcut menu that appears, click New Job.

4. In the New Jobs dialog box, click the Steps page and then click New.

5. In the New Job Step dialog box (see Figure 3-23), in the Type list box, click SQL Server Analysis Services Command.

6. In the Run As list box, select a proxy that has been defined to use the Analysis Services Command subsystem.

   A user who is a member of the sysadmin fixed server role can also select SQL Agent Service Account to run this job step.

7. Click to place your cursor in the Command text box and paste the script that you previously copied from the SQL Engine query window (in the previous step) and then click OK.

   Figure 3-23 shows the script pasted into the Command text box of a new step of a job for processing.

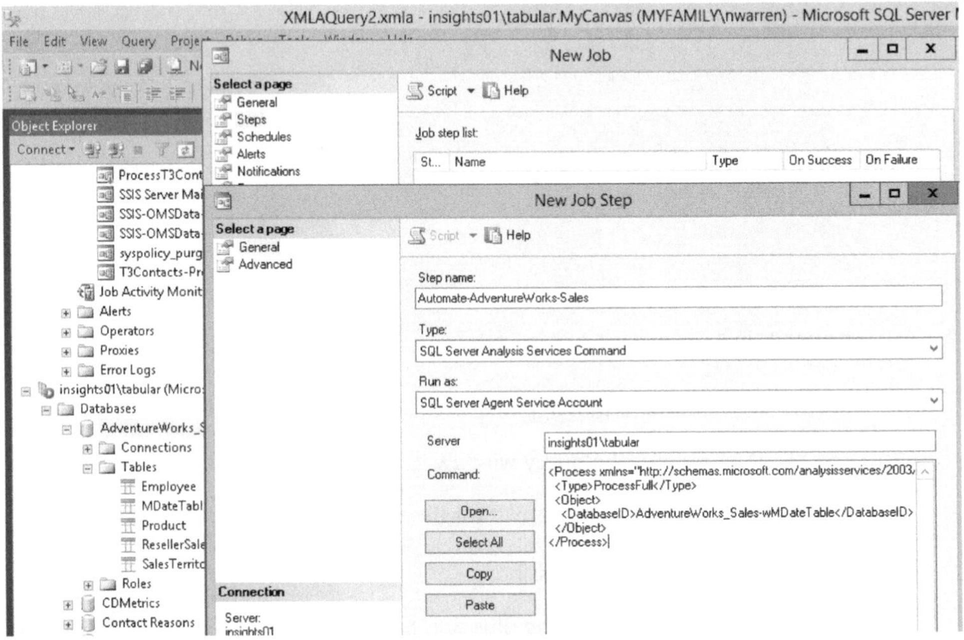

FIGURE 3-23 The New Job dialog box.

8. On the Schedules page, organize schedules for the job.

   Figure 3-24 shows that we want to load our *AdventureWorks* tabular database with fresh data from the *AdventureWorksDW* every hour, starting at midnight and ending at midnight.

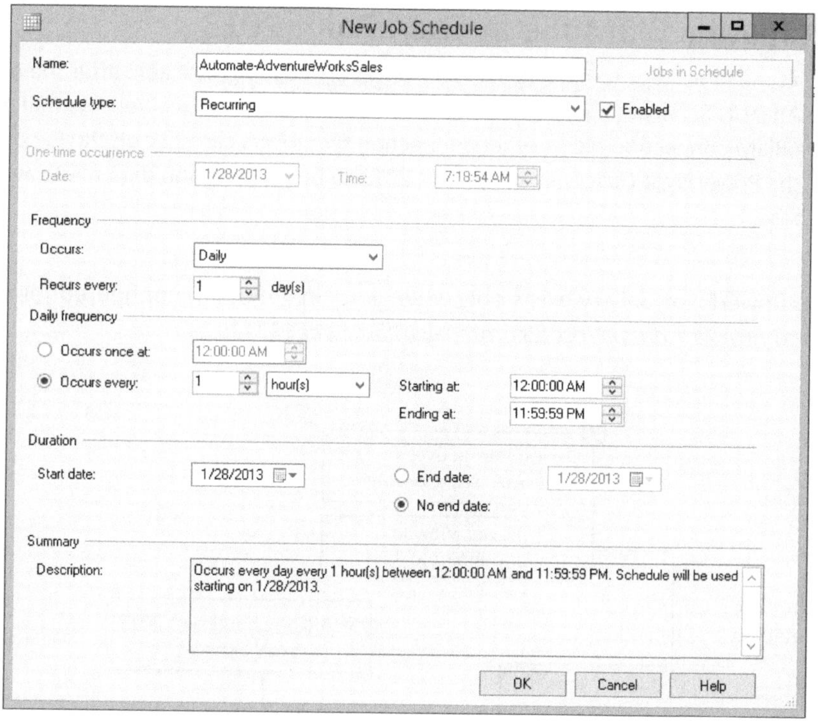

FIGURE 3-24 The New Job Schedule dialog box.

More Info To read more about the available options on this page, see Job Properties / New Job Source, available at *http://msdn.microsoft.com/en-us/library/ms177295.*

9. On the Alerts page, organize the alerts for the job. (For more information on the available options on this page, see Job Properties / New Job (Alerts Page), available at *http://msdn. microsoft.com/en-us/library/ms186556.*)

10. On the Notifications page, set the actions for Microsoft SQL Server Agent to perform when the job completes. (For more information on the available options on this page, see Job Properties / New Job (Notifications Page) , available at *http://msdn.microsoft.com/en-us/ library/ms189685.*)

11. On the Targets page, manage the target servers for the job. (For more information on the available options on this page, see Job Properties / New Job (Targets Page), available at *http://msdn.microsoft.com/en-us/library/ms186886.*)

12. When finished, click OK.

Step 7: Create a BISM file in SharePoint 2013

You are now at the final steps to making self-service report building available after the model is deployed to Analysis Services. Figure 3-25 shows the Power View and Excel reports that you can create from a BISM connection file or other connection files. Users can click on the Excel or Power View icon in the PowerPivot Gallery in SharePoint 2013 to begin using the data made available in the tabular database.

> **Note** The PowerPivot Gallery exists only when your SharePoint is configured for it. To learn more, go to *http://msdn.microsoft.com/en-us/library/ee637430.aspx*.

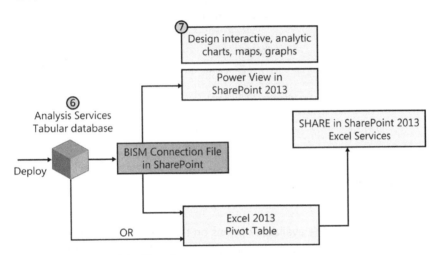

FIGURE 3-25 Step 7 of the lifecycle process.

Before you can create a connection file, you must set up the sites in SharePoint 2013 in which you can create connection files and host reports. This is typically a PowerPivot Gallery, which is like a library in SharePoint (discussed in Chapter 7, "Using PowerPivot for SharePoint 2013").

Adding content types to SharePoint 2013 library

After you have a PowerPivot Gallery, perform the following procedure to add the BISM content type:

1. On the ribbon of your document library, click the Library tab (Figure 3-26).

FIGURE 3-26 The ribbon with the Library Settings button selected.

2. On the Library Settings page, in the General Settings section, click Advanced Settings (Figure 3-27).

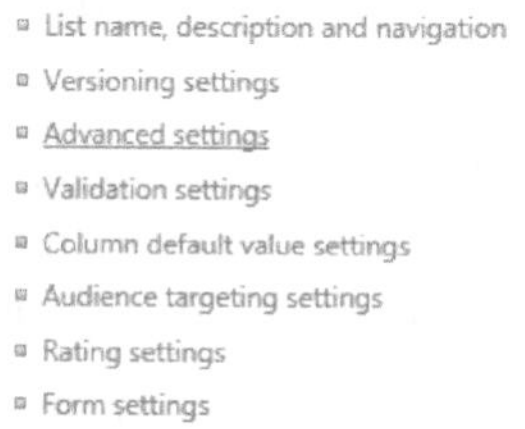

- List name, description and navigation
- Versioning settings
- Advanced settings
- Validation settings
- Column default value settings
- Audience targeting settings
- Rating settings
- Form settings

FIGURE 3-27 SharePoint 2013 Library General Settings.

3. On the Advanced Settings page, click Yes to allow management of content types. Then, scroll to the bottom of the page and click OK (Figure 3-28).

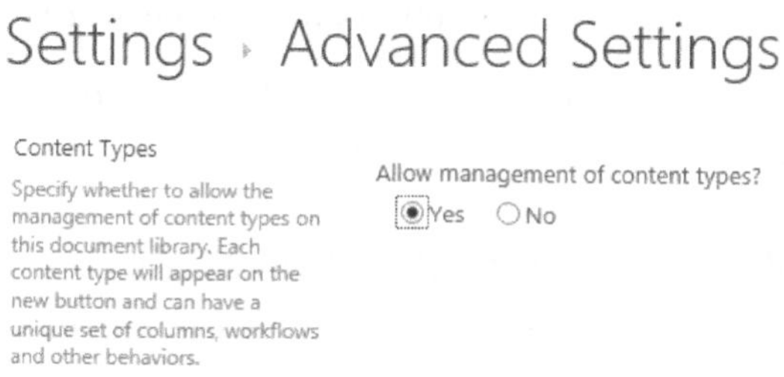

Settings › Advanced Settings

Content Types

Specify whether to allow the management of content types on this document library. Each content type will appear on the new button and can have a unique set of columns, workflows and other behaviors.

Allow management of content types?
⦿ Yes ○ No

FIGURE 3-28 The Advanced Settings page.

You are now in the Library Setting page again.

4. In the Content Types section, click Add From Existing Site Content Types.

5. In the Available Site Content Types list, click BI Semantic Model Connection File (Figure 3-29).

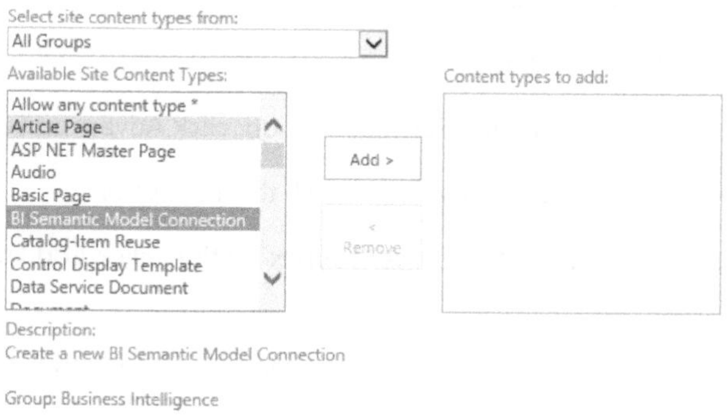

Select site content types from:
All Groups

Available Site Content Types:

Allow any content type *
Article Page
ASP NET Master Page
Audio
Basic Page
BI Semantic Model Connection
Catalog-Item Reuse
Control Display Template
Data Service Document

Content types to add:

Add >

< Remove

Description:
Create a new BI Semantic Model Connection

Group: Business Intelligence

FIGURE 3-29 Settings->Add The Add Content Types PowerPivot Gallery settings page.

Note There are other content types that you might consider selecting such as Report Builder Model or Report and Report Data Source. The PowerPivot Gallery can be a library for several content types that are relevant to your business intelligence needs.

The BISM connection file must have permissions set such that the users that you want to create in Excel 2013 or Power View have SharePoint access to the BISM file and also for the underlying tabular model data. If users get an error, you should check both SharePoint and database (Roles) permissions.

Here are some other methods by which you can connect to back-end data in Analysis Services:

- A user can connect directly to the tabular model from a client application, such as Microsoft Excel or SQL Server Management Studio, by specifying a connection string to Analysis Services.

- A user can connect to Power View or Reporting Services by using a report server data source file (.rsds), and Power View or Reporting Services in turn connects to Analysis Services.

- A user can connect to a middle-tier application, such as an ASP.NET web application, and the middle-tier application in turn connects to Analysis Services.

Creating a BISM connection file to a specific tabular database

After you have added the BI Semantic Model Connection File content type in your PowerPivot Gallery, you are ready to create the BISM connection file.

1. If you don't have a PowerPivot Gallery, create one in SharePoint 2013. In the upper-right corner of the window, click the Settings icon (the small gear graphic). On the menu that appears, click Add An App. Follow the short wizard to complete the procedure.

   If Allow Management Of Content Types is not enabled, you must enable it and add the BI Semantic Model Connection as a content type.

2. In PowerPivot Gallery, click the Library tab

3. In the Settings group, click Library Settings.

4. On the Library Settings page, in the General Settings section, click Advanced Settings.

5. In the Allow Management Of Content Types section, click the Yes option.

6. Go back to the Library Settings page. In the Content Types section, click Add From Existing Site Content Types.

7. In the Available Site Content Types list, click BI Semantic Model Connection File.

Now, when you go to the File tab of the PowerPivot Gallery, you will see the option to add a BISM connection, as shown in Figure 3-30.

FIGURE 3-30 The SharePoint BI Semantic Model Connection content type in the New Document menu in SharePoint 2013.

Now, you are ready for the last step. To provide a connection file from which users can create reports.

Adding a BISM connection file in SharePoint 2013

1. Go to the PowerPivot Gallery and click the Files tab.

2. Click the New Document button. In the list that appears, click BI Semantic Model Connection.

3. Fill out the File Name, Description, Workbook URL or Server Name, and Database, as shown in Figure 3-31.

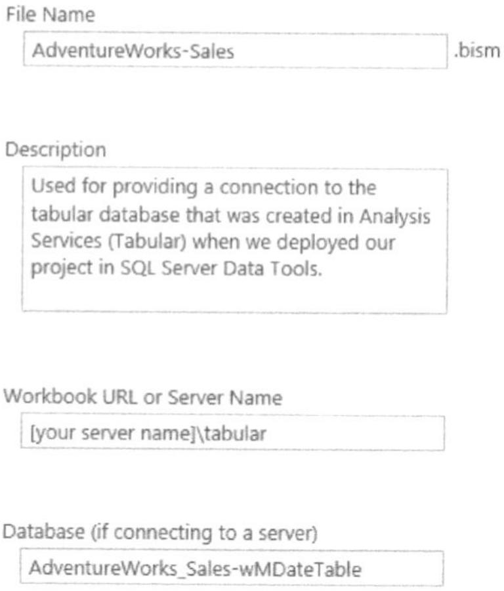

File Name

| AdventureWorks-Sales | .bism |

Description

| Used for providing a connection to the tabular database that was created in Analysis Services (Tabular) when we deployed our project in SQL Server Data Tools. |

Workbook URL or Server Name

| [your server name]\tabular |

Database (if connecting to a server)

| AdventureWorks_Sales-wMDateTable |

FIGURE 3-31 Creating a BISM connective file in SharePoint 2013.

4. Click OK. You should see the PowerPivot Gallery, as shown in Figure 3-32.

FIGURE 3-32 BI Semantic Model Connection.

Summary

This chapter provided an overview of the major steps involved in getting to trusted data by using SQL Server 2012, SQL Server Data Tools, and SharePoint 2013. Keep in mind that ensuring data quality throughout an organization or even in a department is a process rather than a single event or initiative. The process, showing the connection between the BI developer, end-user, IT support roles, and tools, was summarized in Figure 3-1 at the beginning of the chapter.

Creating a repeatable ETL process and getting data from disparate sources to a staging database and then to the data warehouse is a time-consuming process and might be accomplished by another team. This does not stop you or your team from benefiting from data that is not yet stored in the data warehouse and can be explored and used to create proof-of-concepts, prototypes, reports for decisions that must be made more quickly. The tabular tools described in this chapter and book introduce a much faster life-cycle to implementing business intelligence across teams and the organization.

At this point, you should understand the following:

- PowerPivot and Power View in Excel 2013 are excellent places to start for users to begin exploring the data. A little bit of training in either or both of these will go a long way.

- You can formalize what is created in PowerPivot by importing into SQL Server Data Tools, deploying to Analysis Services Tabular, sharing in SharePoint 2013, and automating the processing (or refresh of the tabular databases).

- Many steps are involved in getting to trusted data that BI developers and analysts can use in the authoring tools.

Office 2013 is one of those authoring tools, familiar to many users, which you can count on for surfacing data prepared for business users to consume and from which they can confidently make decisions, analyze, and predict patterns and behavior in business. SharePoint 2013 is the platform that organizes and shares the results of having authored dashboards, reports, charts, graphs, heat maps, and other products of the Microsoft BI stack. Among other things, SharePoint 2013 provides the following:

- Scalability, collaboration, backup and recovery, and disaster recovery capabilities to manage your BI assets created in PowerPivot, Excel, Microsoft Visio, Report Builder, and Performance-Point Dashboard designer.

- To simplify security, user authentication is handled by SharePoint Server 2013.

- Authentication of Services users is validated by the SharePoint Server 2013 authentication provider. Trusted locations can also limit access to content types and files.

Publishing BI assets to SharePoint Server websites is a quick and secure way to share the right data, to the right people, at the right time, helping employees work faster and helping them make better decisions, faster.

CHAPTER 4

Using PowerPivot in Excel 2013

Microsoft Excel is a powerful spreadsheet and data analysis application, with hundreds of capabilities that can help you to organize and make sense of the data and numbers in your life. In this Excel release, a lot has been done to both improve the experience and empower the user when employing it as a business intelligence (BI) tool; for instance, PowerPivot, which was introduced as an add-in for Excel 2010 and now is a native feature in Excel 2013. Among the many self-service BI features, this chapter will focus on the Excel Data Model feature and the PowerPivot in Excel native add-in.

The Data Model

The Data Model is a collection of tables and their relationships that reflect the real-world relationships between business functions and processes; for example, how Products relate to Inventory and Sales. It can be used when you create PivotTables, PivotCharts, and Power View reports (see Chapter 5, "Using Power View in Excel 2013"), depending on how you import the data. The Data Model uses a built-in version of xVelocity, which is an in-memory, column-based version of the Analysis Services engine, similar to what the Vertipaq engine is for the PowerPivot for Excel 2010 Add-in. xVelocity stores data that you import in-memory in a highly efficient, compressed form. It then calculates implicit measures (created by dragging a table field to the values area of a PivotTable) and explicit measures (created by using Data Analysis Expressions [DAX] functions). We can create the Data Model by using one or more tables. Another key characteristic of the Data Model is its ability to consume large amounts of data.

Excel 2013 can act as a starting point or as a central hub for tabular BI development, as described in Chapter 3, "The lifecycle of a business intelligence implementation." For example, the business analyst can create simple analytical models that can gradually be used beyond just oneself. It can be uploaded into SharePoint so that others can use it, and if it becomes broadly used, it can evolve into a full BI application. For instance, the Excel workbook can be used as a starting point for modeling in the SQL Server Data Tools (SSDT) and be imported and deployed into an Analysis Services server. This was already possible in Excel with PowerPivot for Excel 2010. However, for simple models, there is no need to use PowerPivot. Also, Excel 2013 makes it possible for you to build Power View reports that can be stored centrally in SharePoint. Figure 4-1 shows the high-level relationship of BI components in Excel 2010, and Figure 4-2 shows how they are related in Excel 2013.

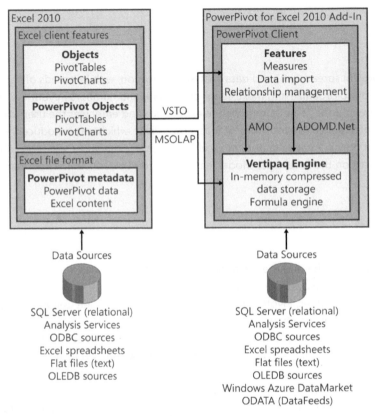

FIGURE 4-1 The Excel 2010 BI architecture.

The main changes in Figure 4-2 as compared to Figure 4-1 are the built-in xVelocity engine migration for the PowerPivot add-in to Excel (the Data Model), and the introduction of Power View Add-in. In summary, with the new Excel architecture, the user can create and interact with data models by using the xVeloxity engine, and the PowerPivot Add-in makes it possible for the user to create richer, more complex reports, use DAX to work with data, create KPIs, and manage the Data Model.

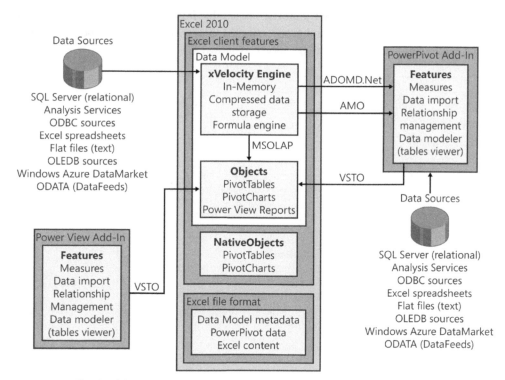

FIGURE 4-2 The Excel 2013 BI architecture.

Creating the Data Model

We need to revisit some of the questions posed at the beginning of this chapter. The first one being, how do we create a Data Model?

There isn't a unique way in Excel 2013 for creating a Data Model right out of the box without enabling and opening the PowerPivot window. There are various dialog boxes in Excel with which you can add data to the Data Model by selecting the appropriate check box. For a given workbook, the first time you use a dialog with this check box selected, Excel creates the Data Model. We will first look at the Import Data dialog box because this is the most common way of adding data to the Data Model.

Let's first see what happens when we import a single table from a Microsoft SQL Server database. On the Data tab, in the Get External Data group, click the Other Sources button and then, in the drop-down list that appears, click From SQL Server, as shown in Figure 4-3.

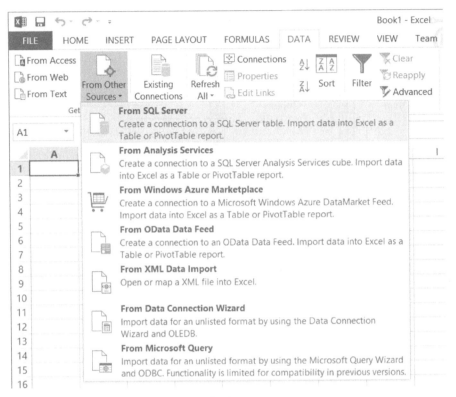

FIGURE 4-3 Importing from a SQL Server database.

The Data Connection Wizard opens. On the Connect To Database Server page, in the Server Name text box, type the server name and instance of the SQL Server that you want to access, choose the authentication method (see Figure 4-4), and then click Next. On the Select Database And Table page of the wizard, in the Database name drop-down list, choose the database from which you want to import the data. For now, use the sample *AdventureWorks* database, as shown in Figure 4-5, and then click Next.

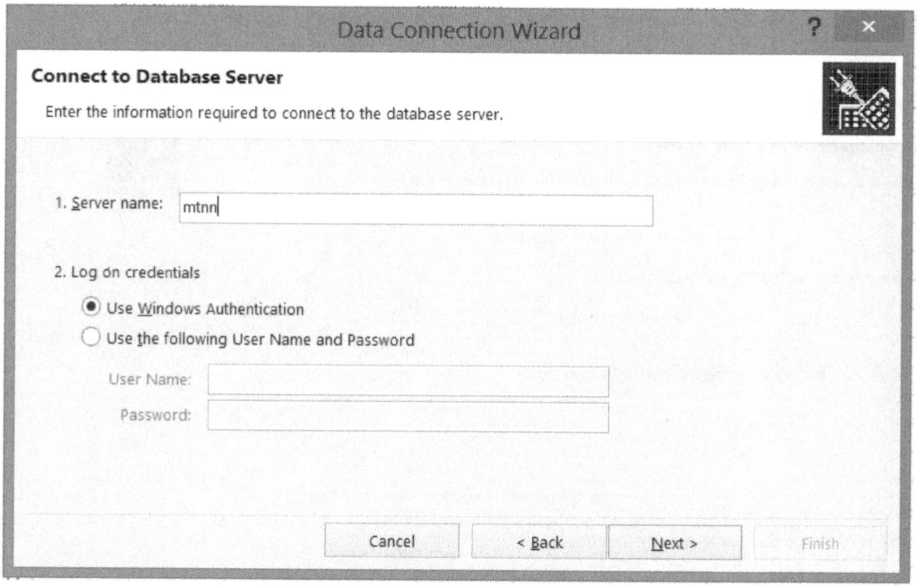

FIGURE 4-4 The first page of the Data Connection Wizard.

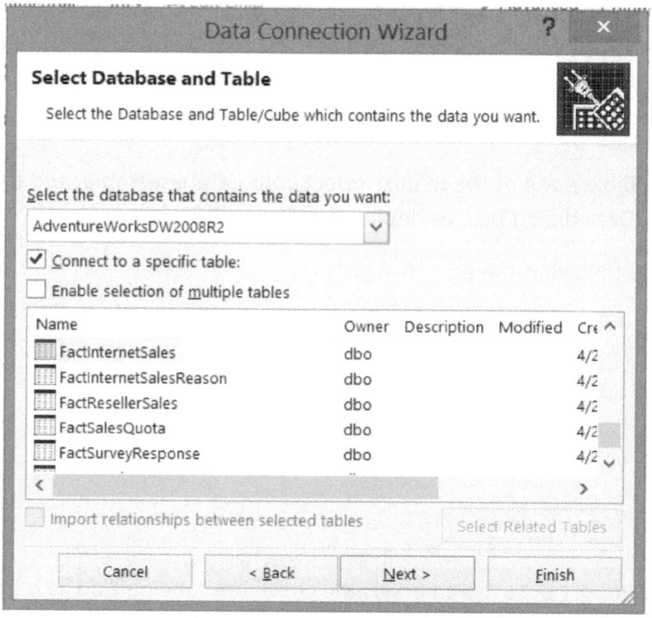

FIGURE 4-5 The second page of the Data Connection Wizard.

Click Finish to save the data connection information, as shown in Figure 4-6.

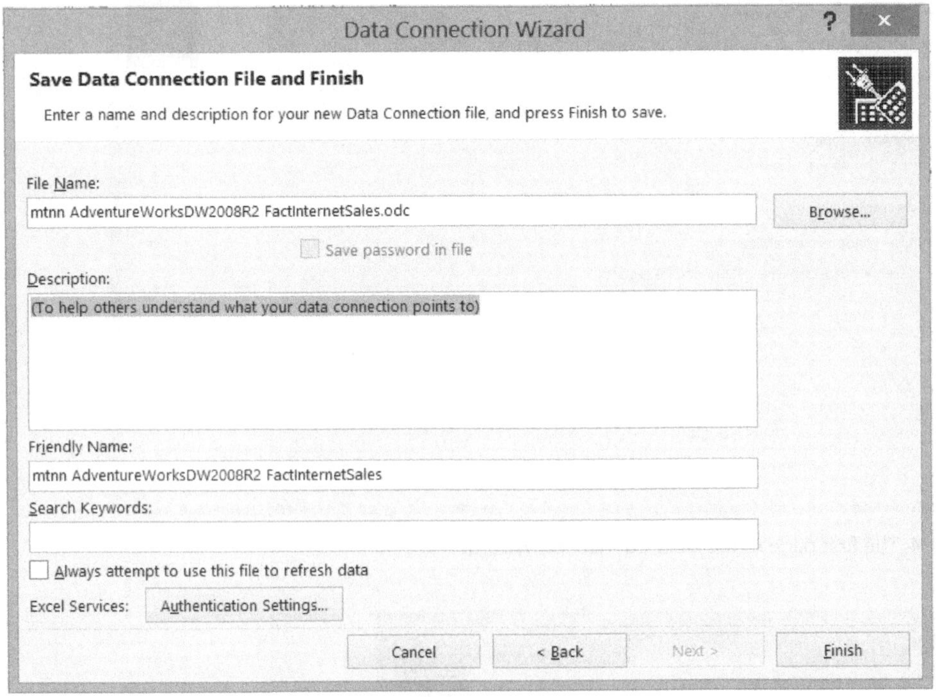

FIGURE 4-6 Saving the connection information.

Back in the Select Database And Table page of the wizard, select your database, table, and then click Next. Excel displays the Import Data dialog box, as depicted in Figure 4-7.

The examples in this book use the following tables:

- DimDate

- DimEmployee

- DimSalesTerritory

- DimProduct

- FactResellerSales

A new element in the Excel 2013 Import Data dialog box is the check box labeled Add This Data To The Data Model. If you *do not* select this check box, Excel will not create a Data Model. There won't be any xVelocity engine, which means, for example, no compression and no in-memory performance gain. It also means that you cannot create a Power View report. You will be able to create PivotTables and PivotCharts, though. If you create a PivotTable report, Excel will create a *classical* or *native* PivotTable. The native PivotTable (or PivotChart) is limited to using a single table, it has limited data handling, and it has limited calculated field functionality. In other words, a classical PivotTable/PivotChart is one that we have been creating in earlier versions of Excel.

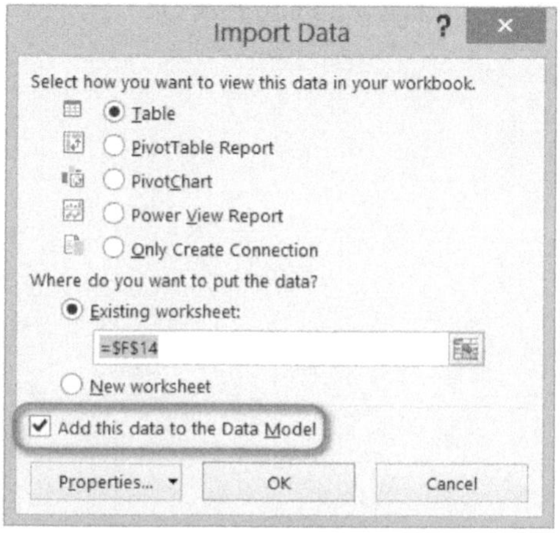

FIGURE 4-7 The Import Data dialog box.

Another way to create a Data Model is by selecting multiple tables. On the Select Database And Table page of the wizard, select the Enable Selection Of Multiple Tables check box (see Figure 4-8). Choose a table, click Select Related Tables, which instructs the xVelocity engine to find tables that have relationships with the one you've selected, and then click Finish.

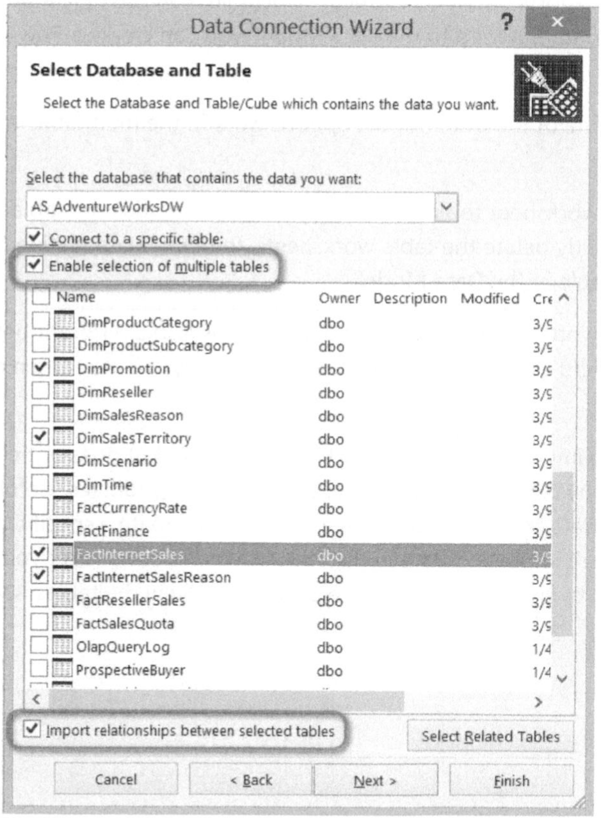

FIGURE 4-8 Selecting multiple tables from a database.

Figure 4-9 shows the Import Data dialog box that Excel displays after you click OK.

FIGURE 4-9 Import Data dialog box after multiple tables were selected.

Figure 4-9 demonstrates that when you select more than one table to import, the Add This Data To The Data Model check box is disabled, and the tables are added to the Data Model in the xVelocity engine. This behavior is logical because reports based on classical PivotTables can use only a single table. Moreover, because the imported data is added to the Data Model, you can create a Power View report.

It's interesting to understand how some of the other report options work in the multitable import scenario:

- **Table**   Excel creates a separate worksheet to hold each table, and it also adds the tables to the Data Model. If you subsequently delete the table worksheets, the table data (defined by the connection) will still be available in the Data Model.

- **PivotChart**   Excel creates the PivotChart without a PivotTable. This is also a different behavior from PowerPivot for Excel 2010 Add-In, for which a PivotTable was always created when creating a PivotChart.

- **Only Create Connection**   Excel imports the tables into the Data Model but does not create any specific report. There are many reasons why you would choose this option. It's useful if, for instance, you plan to import data from multiple sources before you create a specific type of report (as you would if you were importing data in the PowerPivot window). After you import data into the Data Model by using this option, the only way to view the tables is via the PowerPivot 2013 window.

Internally, Excel holds a connection to the external data source, in this case to the Adventure Works sample database, and another to the recently created Data Model. Figure 4-10 shows the Workbook Connections dialog box that Excel displays by clicking the Data tab and then clicking the Connections button. The internal name for the Data Model is ThisWorkbookDataModel.

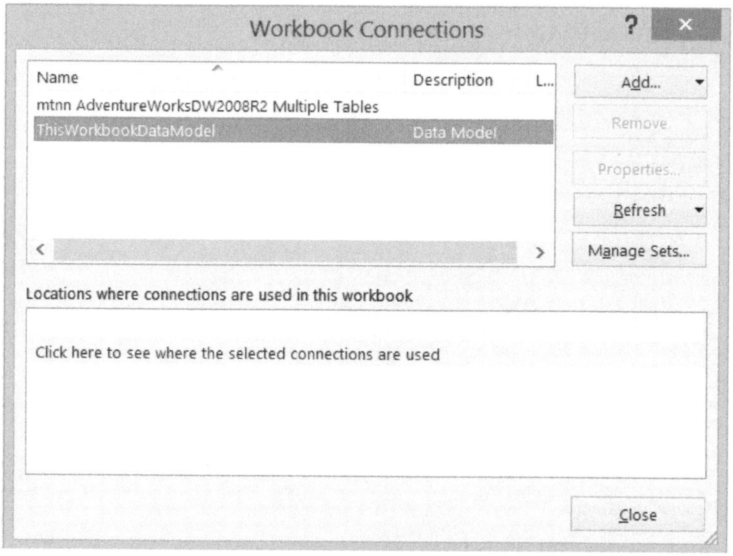

FIGURE 4-10 The Workbook Connections dialog box showing the Data Model connection name.

Let's examine the internal Data Model name (ThisWorkbookDataModel) for a minute. The name implies that a Workbook contains only one data model. For PowerPivot users, this should not be surprising, because in the Excel 2010 PowerPivot Add-in, we can only use one instance of xVelocity in a workbook.

Another way to see the name is through formula autocomplete, using a cube function (for more information, see *http://office.microsoft.com/en-us/excel-help/cube-functions-reference-HA010083026.aspx*). In Figure 4-11, for example, we can see the name displayed after typing the opening quotation for the connection argument.

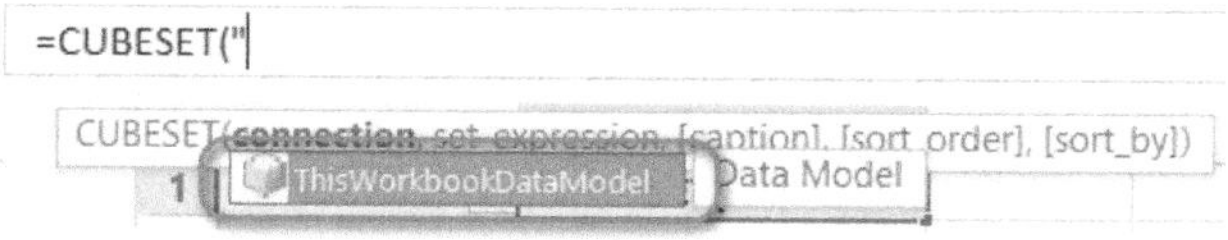

FIGURE 4-11 The Data Model name listed for the connection argument.

Also new to Excel 2013 is support for two more data sources (see Figure 4-12): Windows Azure Marketplace and OData data feed.

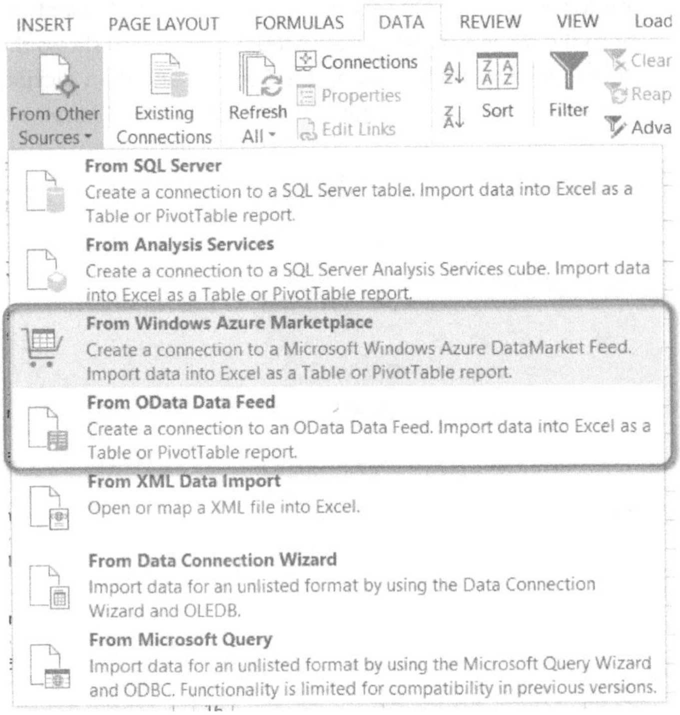

FIGURE 4-12 The two new, supported data sources in Excel 2013.

Those new data sources were already available from the PowerPivot Add-In, but now, they are available from Excel 2013. As Chapter 1, "Business intelligence in SharePoint," describes, you can use the OData feature to bring SharePoint list data into Excel by way of exporting an OData feed on the ribbon of the list properties. This becomes extremely useful as more and more data is stored in the form of lists in SharePoint.

Let's try importing data from an open OData data source from the web. On the ribbon, click the Data tab. In the Get External Data group, click the From Other Sources button and then, in the drop-down list that appears, click From OData Data Feed. In the Data Connection Wizard (see Figure 4-13), in the Link Or File text box, enter the location of the data feed, click the Use The Sign-In Information For The Person Opening This File option, and then click Next.

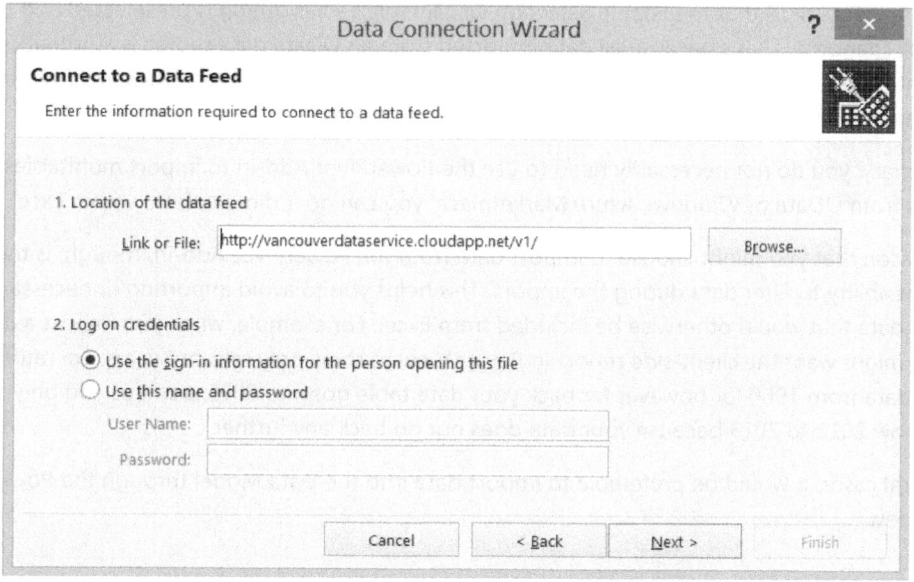

FIGURE 4-13 Use the Data Connection Wizard to import data from an OData data source.

On the Select Tables page of the wizard, we selected a single table to import, as shown in Figure 4-14.

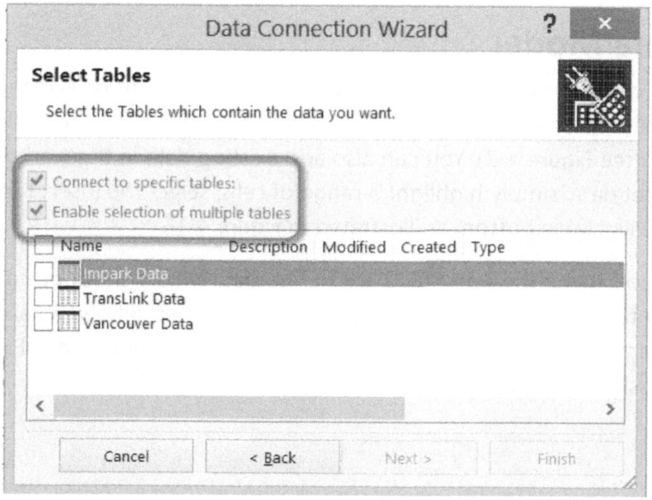

FIGURE 4-14 Selecting tables from an OData source.

Notice in Figure 4-14 that the Enable Selection Of Multiple Tables option is preselected and that you cannot change it. That's because all data imported from an OData data source is automatically inserted into a Data Model. This means that you can choose as many tables as you want. The same behavior applies for data that you import from the Azure Marketplace.

In summary, you do not necessarily need to use the PowerPivot Add-in to import multitables or data feeds from OData or Windows Azure Marketplace; you can do it directly from within Excel 2013.

One reason that you might choose to import data from the PowerPivot Add-in, though, is the PowerPivot ability to filter data during the import. This helps you to avoid importing unnecessary or unwanted data that would otherwise be included from Excel. For example, when you import a date table, you might want the client-side report in Power View to show only relevant years. So, rather than including data from 1960 (or however far back your date table goes) to 2025, perhaps you only want a slicer to show 2012 to 2013 because your data does not go back any further.

In several cases, it would be preferable to import data into the Data Model through the Power-Pivot Window.

> **More Info** You can find a good source of extra information on how to create a memory-efficient Data Model at *http://office.microsoft.com/en-us/excel-help/create-a-memory-efficient-data-model-using-excel-2013-and-the-powerpivot-add-in-HA103981538.aspx*.

Adding data to the Data Model

After creating the Data Model, you can add new data to it in a variety of ways. The most evident method is to add the data during import. To do so, in the Import Data dialog box, select the Add This Data To The Data Model check box (see Figure 4-7). You can also add existing data in the workbook to the Data Model. To add worksheet data, simply highlight a range of cells, select the Insert tab and then, in the Tables group, click the PivotTable button, as illustrated in Figure 4-15.

In the Create PivotTable dialog box, select the Add This Data To The Data Model check box and click OK. The range will appear as a table in the PivotTable field list. If you haven't defined a name for the range, Excel uses the generic name "Range." If you don't add the data to the Data Model, Excel creates a classic PivotTable, or a classic PivotTable with a PivotChart.

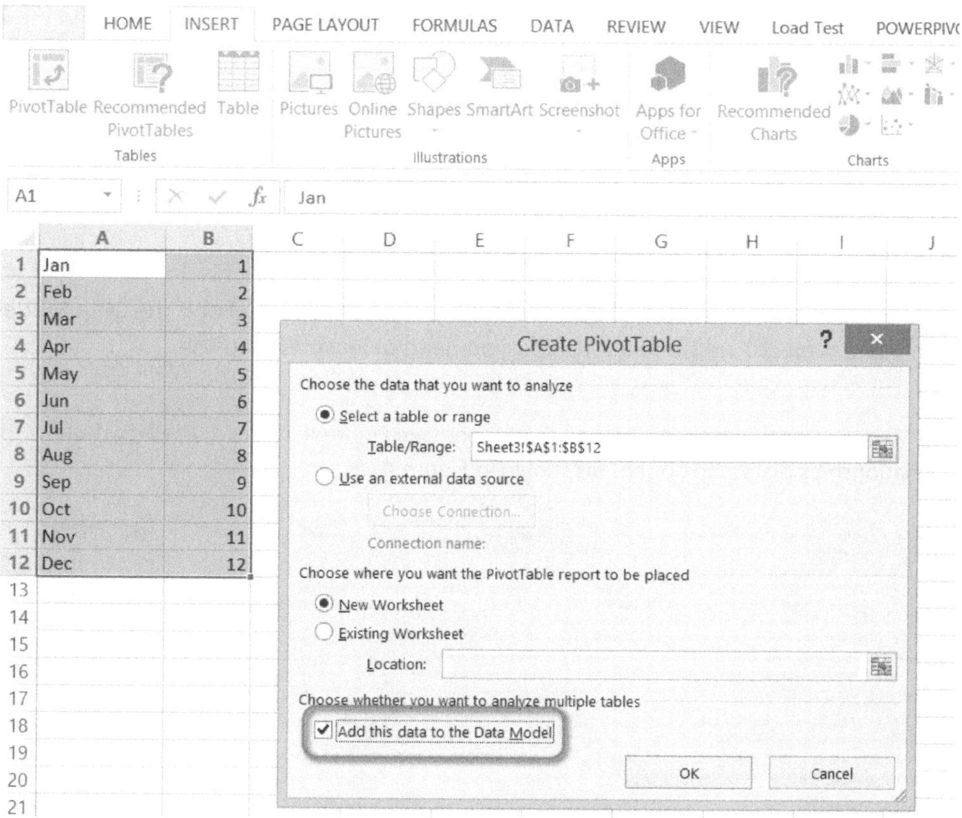

FIGURE 4-15 Adding data to the Data Model from a range selection.

Creating table relationships by using the Data Model

After you create a Data Model in a workbook, you can create, view, or modify relationships between tables. A relationship is a connection between two tables of data, based on one or more columns in each table (for more information on relationships, go to *http://technet.microsoft.com/en-us/library/gg399148.aspx*). When you import multiple tables from the *same* relational data source, Excel detects primary and foreign key relationships and, by default, creates the relationships automatically.

Regardless of whether you import relationships, you can create or modify relationships at any time. To do so, on the Data tab, in the Data Tools group, click the Relationships button, as shown in Figure 4-16.

DATA
REVIEW
VIEW
Load Test
POWERPIVOT
Team
Sort
Filter
Clear
Reapply
Advanced
Sort & Filter
Text to Columns
Flash Fill
Remove Duplicates
Data Validation
Consolidate
What-If Analysis
Relationships
Data Tools

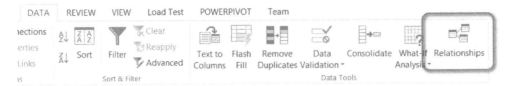

FIGURE 4-16 The Relationships button on the Data tab.

> **Note** The Relationships button is disabled if there is no Data Model or if the Data Model has only one table (to create relationships, you need at least two tables).

In the Manage Relationships dialog box that opens (see Figure 4-17), click the New button. The Create Relationships dialog box opens, as shown in Figure 4-18.

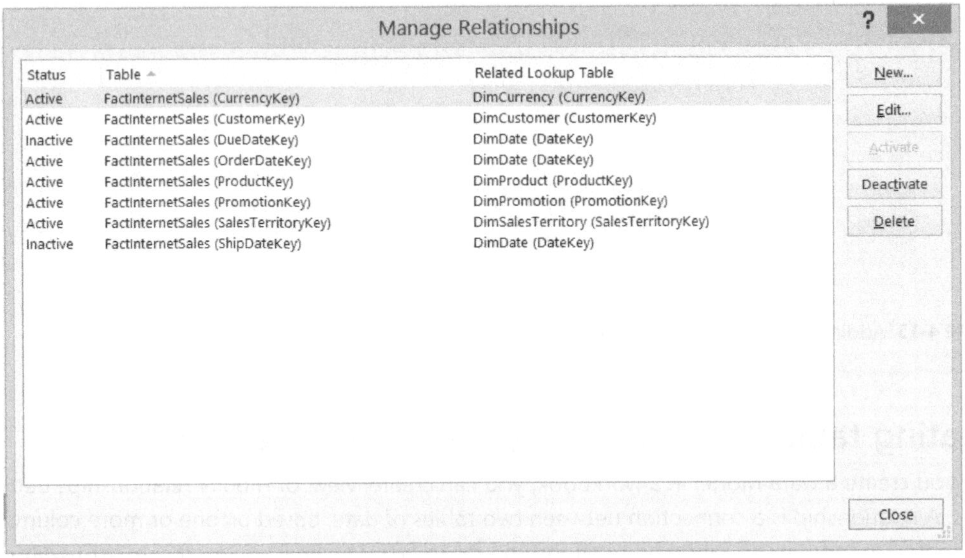
Manage Relationships
Status
Table
Related Lookup Table
Active FactInternetSales (CurrencyKey) DimCurrency (CurrencyKey)
Active FactInternetSales (CustomerKey) DimCustomer (CustomerKey)
Inactive FactInternetSales (DueDateKey) DimDate (DateKey)
Active FactInternetSales (OrderDateKey) DimDate (DateKey)
Active FactInternetSales (ProductKey) DimProduct (ProductKey)
Active FactInternetSales (PromotionKey) DimPromotion (PromotionKey)
Active FactInternetSales (SalesTerritoryKey) DimSalesTerritory (SalesTerritoryKey)
Inactive FactInternetSales (ShipDateKey) DimDate (DateKey)
New...
Edit...
Activate
Deactivate
Delete
Close

FIGURE 4-17 The Data Model Manage Relationships dialog box.

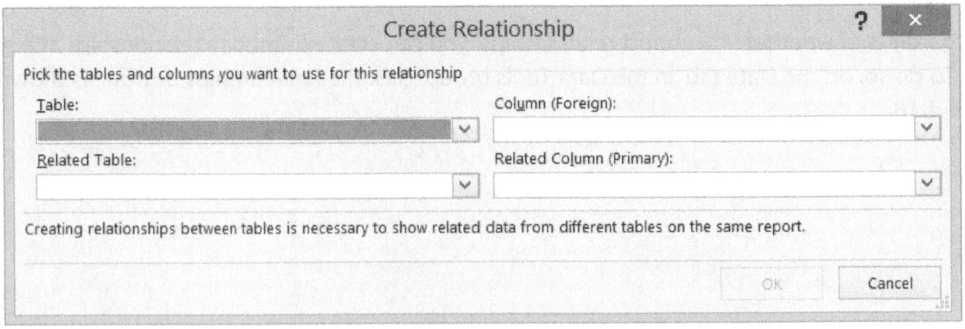
Create Relationship
Pick the tables and columns you want to use for this relationship
Table:
Column (Foreign):
Related Table:
Related Column (Primary):
Creating relationships between tables is necessary to show related data from different tables on the same report.
OK
Cancel

FIGURE 4-18 The Data Model Create Relationship dialog box.

The Manage Relationships and the Create Relationship dialog boxes are similar to the corresponding dialog boxes in previous versions of PowerPivot.

Working with the Data Model

After you create the Data Model in a workbook and have related tables, you can create PivotTables, PivotCharts, and Power View reports. Power View is a new Excel 2013 add-in that you use to analyze data visually. (For more information about Power View, see Chapter 5.) PivotTables and PivotCharts that you create in the Data Model have the following advantages over classic PivotTables and PivotCharts:

- You can work with considerably more data. You can import and work with hundreds of millions of rows thanks to the compression algorithms used by the Data Model's xVelocity engine.

- You can work with multiple tables and easily import, create, and manage relationships between tables.

- PivotCharts that you create with the Data Model do *not* require a corresponding PivotTable.

Regardless of whether you use PivotTables and PivotCharts with Data Models or the classic Excel PivotTables and PivotCharts, you can create implicit measures, apply custom calculations, use slicers, and use a Timeline (new to Excel 2013). However, you can *substantially* extend the analysis capabilities of Data Model–based PivotTables and PivotCharts by using PowerPivot.

PowerPivot 2013

Up to this point, you've already seen that you can do many things with Excel 2013 right out of the box when creating simple reports by using the Data Model. But, to create richer, more complex reports, KPIs, hierarchies, perspectives, to use DAX to work with data, or even to view or delete a table, you need the PowerPivot Add-in.

> **More Info** The subjects of data modeling and DAX with Excel 2013 and PowerPivot are large topics, deserving books of their own. A full explanation is beyond the scope of this book, but you can find a more complete and in-depth view of DAX and PowerPivot for Excel features in *Microsoft Excel 2013: Building Models with PowerPivot* (2013, Microsoft Press), by Alberto Ferrari and Marco Russo.

PowerPivot comes with Excel 2013. Unlike the add-in for Excel 2010, you no longer need to download anything. PowerPivot 2013 provides essentially the same functionality as the 2010 version, although a few things have changed in the user interface.

PowerPivot 2013 is not enabled by default. To enable it, click the File tab to display the Backstage view and then click the Options tab, as illustrated in Figure 4-19.

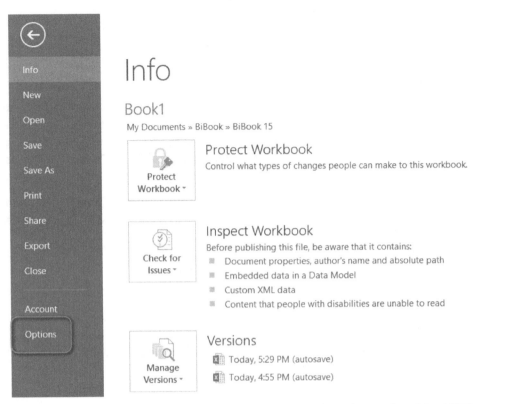

FIGURE 4-19 To enable PowerPivot 2013, click the Options tab in the Backstage view of Excel 2013.

In the Excel Options dialog box that opens, click Add-Ins. In the Manage drop-down list, select COM Add-Ins and click Go, as shown in Figure 4-20.

In the COM Add-Ins dialog box, select the check box labeled Microsoft Office PowerPivot for Excel 2013, as depicted in Figure 4-21.

In PowerPivot for Excel 2013, you can create *calculated fields*. In previous versions of PowerPivot, you created *measures*. Practically speaking, they're the same thing. Excel used the term calculated fields long before PowerPivot even existed, and measures is a term from multidimensional databases. The change in the name makes sense for Excel users.

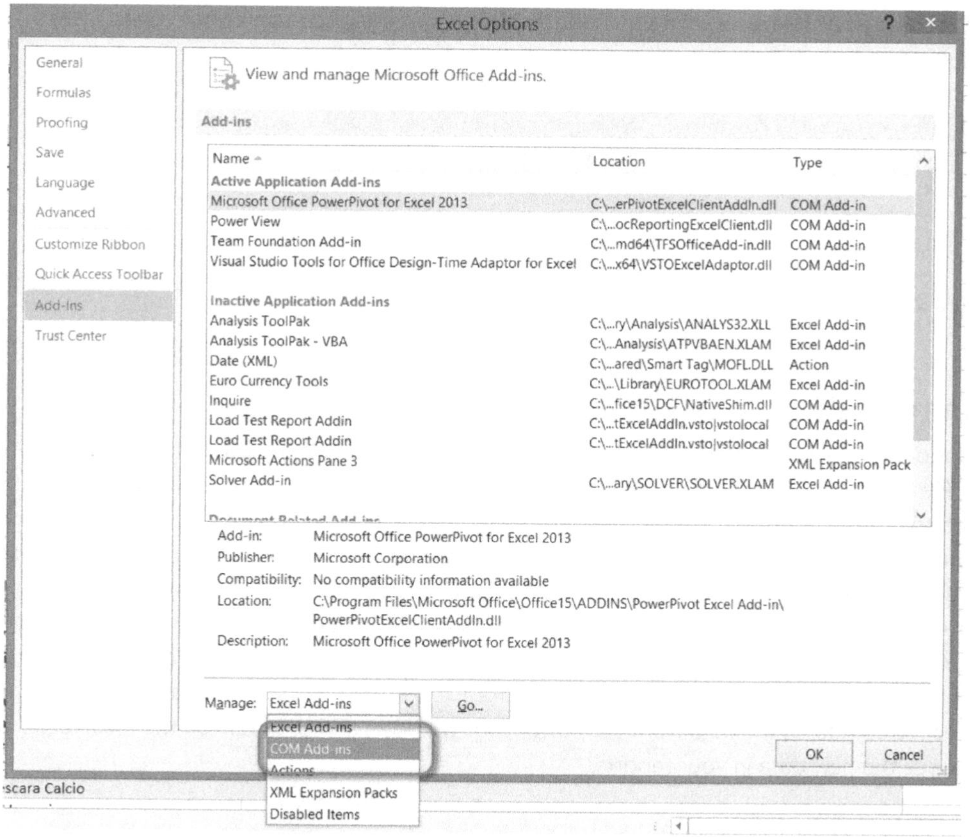

FIGURE 4-20 The Excel 2013 Add-Ins tab in the Excel Options dialog box.

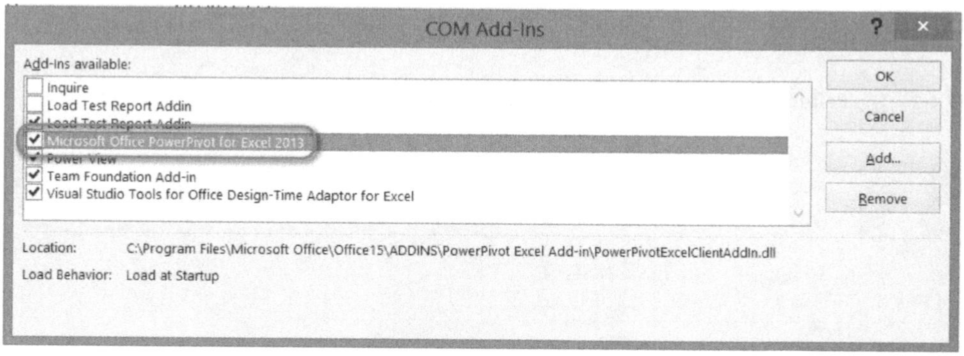

FIGURE 4-21 Enabling PowerPivot for Excel 2013 Add-In.

The contents of the PowerPivot 2013 ribbon has been rearranged somewhat, as shown in Figure 4-22.

FIGURE 4-22 The Excel 2013 PowerPivot tab.

Data refresh

Perhaps one of the most significant advantages of the internal xVelocity Data Model engine over the PowerPivot for Excel 2010 Add-in involves data refresh. When you refresh data in Excel 2013, any calculated columns and other metadata changes that you make in PowerPivot, are immediately reflected in any underlying dependent report that you create in Excel. For instance, if you click the Refresh button in the PowerPivot for Excel window (see Figure 4-23), or the Refresh button on the Data tab (Figure 4-24), the Data Model will fetch data from the underlying data sources, refresh the data in the Data Model, and then the new data will automatically be reflected in any PivotTable you might have that references the related tables. In PowerPivot for Excel 2010, this used to be a two-step process. You needed to refresh the data from the PowerPivot windows and then refresh the PivotTables to be able to see the new data in your reports.

FIGURE 4-23 The Refresh button in the PowerPivot for Excel 2013 window.

FIGURE 4-24 The Refresh button on the ribbon in Excel 2013.

Compatibility issues

With the introduction of Data Models, an Excel 2013 workbook is incompatible with any previous Microsoft Office products (Excel 2010, SharePoint 2010, and so on). If you want to see it for yourself, you can take a look inside the Excel file. To analyze the content of the Excel file, you can rename it to add the .zip extension. Then, you will be able to browse through the .xlsx file structure. Looking into the .xlsx file organization, you will notice the reason behind the incompatibility is that in Excel 2013 .xlsx files, the data from the Data Model is stored in the *item.data* file, which is found in the xl/model folder, whereas previously, in Excel 2010 with the PowerPivot Add-in, the data was stored in the customData folder. If you attempt to open an Excel 2013 file in an Excel 2010 client, it will attempt to extract data from a customData folder and return an error. Figure 4-25 shows the Excel 2013 file structure, wherein you can observe that the Excel 2010 customData folder is replaced by a model folder.

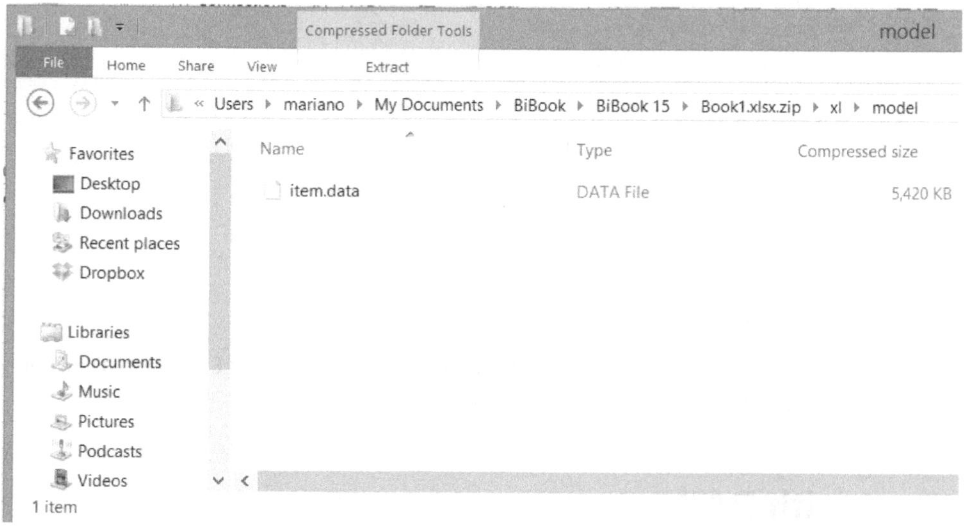

FIGURE 4-25 The item.data file for Excel 2013 now resides in the xl/model folder.

Excel 2013 can open Excel 2010 workbooks that contain PowerPivot models. However, it will not be able to refresh the data in the Excel 2010 workbook. Excel will display the message shown in Figure 4-26.

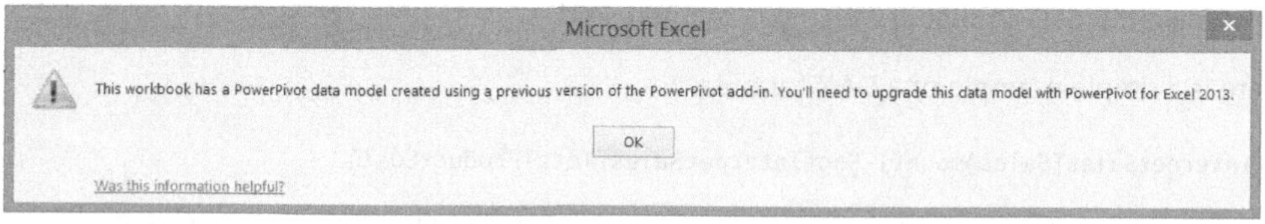

FIGURE 4-26 The warning message that appears when attempting to refresh old Excel workbooks.

To upgrade the 2010 workbook to work in Excel 2013 by using the Data Model, you need to use the PowerPivot Add-in. This is covered in the next section. Okay, there's nothing alarming about the message. You get a similar message when opening a PowerPivot v1 workbook in a PowerPivot v2 environment. However, the message is misleading because the data is *not* upgraded after you click OK to dismiss the dialog. Click Refresh again; the message reappears. What is going on? It's nothing more than Excel displaying an inappropriate message in the current context—an issue that should be fixed. If you have PowerPivot installed and click Manage on the PowerPivot tab, Excel displays the message in Figure 4-26, but this time after you click OK, you see the confirmation message shown in Figure 4-27. The difference now is that although Excel displays the same message as the refresh attempt, the message is shown in a context in which the update can be done.

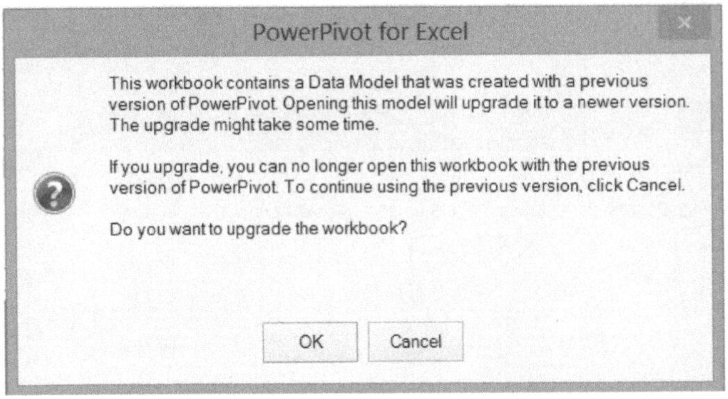

FIGURE 4-27 The unsupported data update confirmation message box.

And now, after clicking OK, the data is truly updated. The message that Excel displays when you attempt to refresh the incompatible workbook should be more instructive.

Calculations with DAX

DAX formulas are designed to be as similar as possible to Excel formulas. Just as in Excel, all DAX formulas begin with an assignment operator, such as an equals sign (=), but DAX works with tables (as in a database) rather than with cells arranged in a tabular fashion. The main difference between Excel formulas and DAX formulas is that DAX never uses cell coordinates (B2, C3, and so on). Also, DAX does not work with cell ranges. To work with ranges, you can use DAX functions to apply filters to narrow down the data to that in which you're interested.

Here is a simple example of a DAX formula:

```
=FactInternetSales[SalesAmount]-FactInternetSales[TotalProductCost]
```

This calculation defines the Margin column in the sample workbook by subtracting the TotaProductlCost column from the SalesAmount column, which yields a profit-margin value.

PowerPivot evaluates the DAX expression for each row of the FactInternetSales table and populates the FactInternetSales [Margin] column with the result, as shown in Figure 4-28.

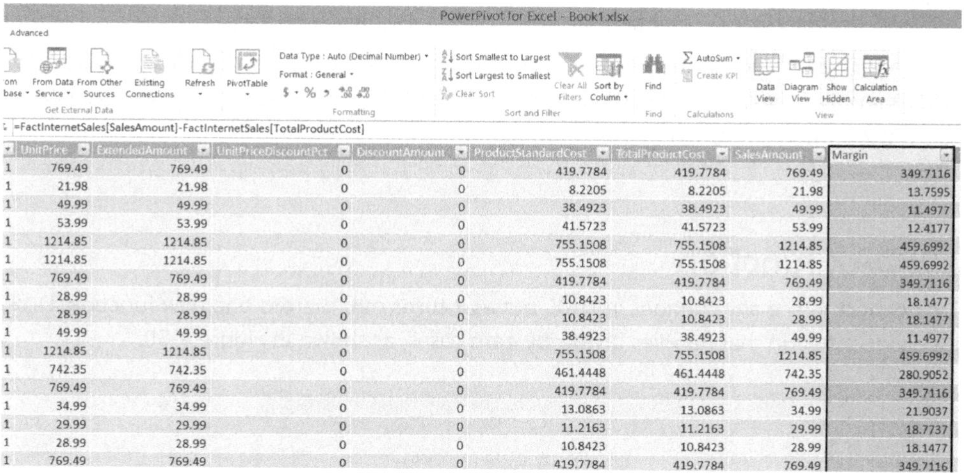

FIGURE 4-28 A simple DAX calculation.

Here's a slightly more complex DAX formula:

```
=SUMX(RELATEDTABLE(FactSales),FactSales[SalesAmount])
```

Here, the DAX expression calculates a value for each row by scanning the rows in the FactSales table for the current row (from the DimProduct table). In other words, this DAX formula filters the FactSales table that corresponds to the product of the current row and aggregates the SalesAmount value, as shown in Figure 4-29.

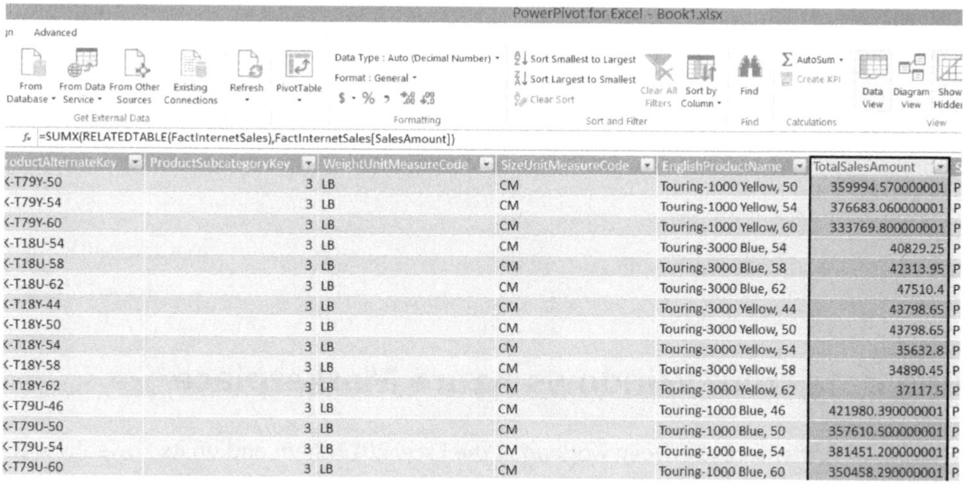

FIGURE 4-29 Applying a more complex DAX formula.

More Info Appendix B, "Microsoft and "Big Data"," provides a list of all available DAX functions along with a short description of each. For more information about DAX, see the white paper *Data Analysis Expressions in PowerPivot for Excel 2010* and sample workbook available for download at *http://www.microsoft.com/downloads/en/details.aspx?displaylang =en&FamilyID=1ae63bfb-c303-44e3-ae44-7413d499495d*. Another good resource on DAX is *http://www.mssqlgirl.com/tag/bism-tabular-model.*

A new DAX function

We didn't expect to see any changes in DAX, but as it turns out, there is one new function: DIVIDE. This is a divide function that handles divide-by-zero cases, as shown in Figure 4-30.

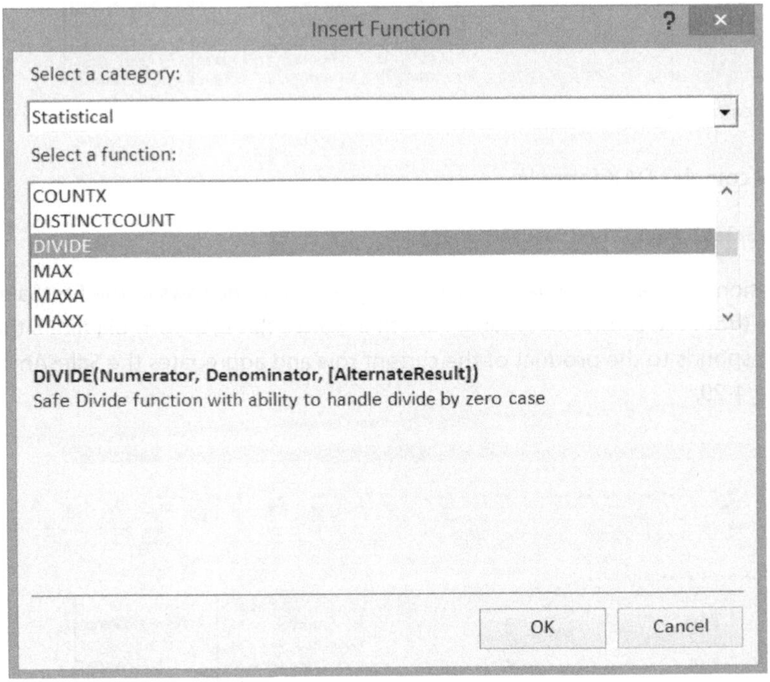

FIGURE 4-30 The new DAX DIVIDE function.

Importing data from Windows Azure Marketplace

One of the major differences between working in the Excel 2013 client and on its PowerPivot windows is the Import Data Wizard. Most of them are very similar in content and form, but some are very different. This is especially true when importing data from Windows Azure Marketplace, for which the user experience is far better from than that of the PowerPivot window.

Figure 4-31 shows the Excel 2013 Data Connection Wizard. You need to know upfront the URL for the service from which you want to retrieve data. The wizard pages that follow are similar to importing data from other sources (see Figure 4-14, for example).

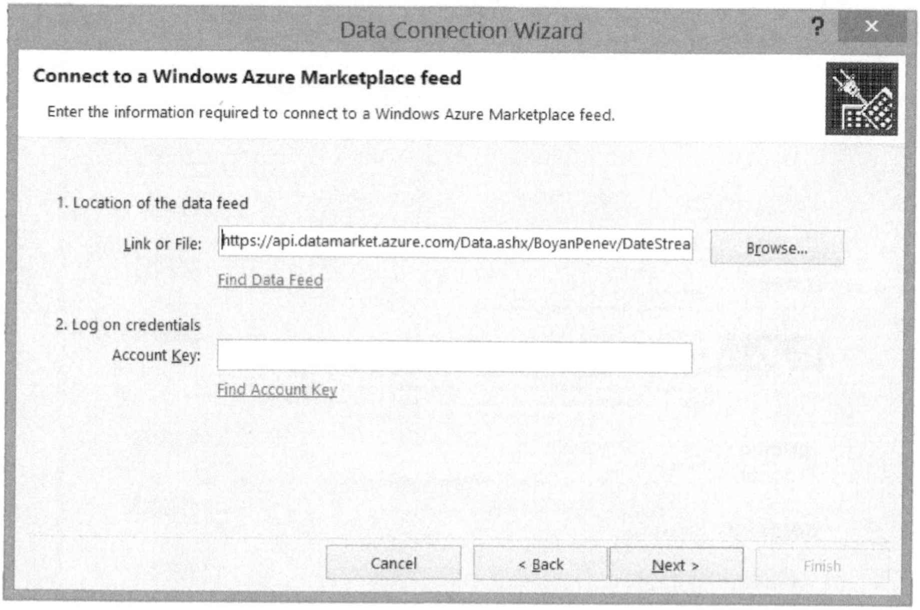

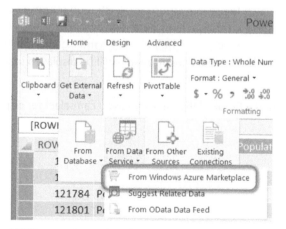

FIGURE 4-31 Importing data from the Windows Azure Marketplace using Excel 2013.

Alternatively, and preferably, you can import data from the PowerPivot windows. Click Get External Data, point to From Data Service, and then click From Windows Azure Marketplace, as shown in Figure 4-32.

FIGURE 4-32 Importing data from the Windows Azure Marketplace using PowerPivot.

From the Table Import Wizard pages, you can browse through or search the Windows Azure Marketplace and you can sign in (or create a new account), as demonstrated in Figure 4-33.

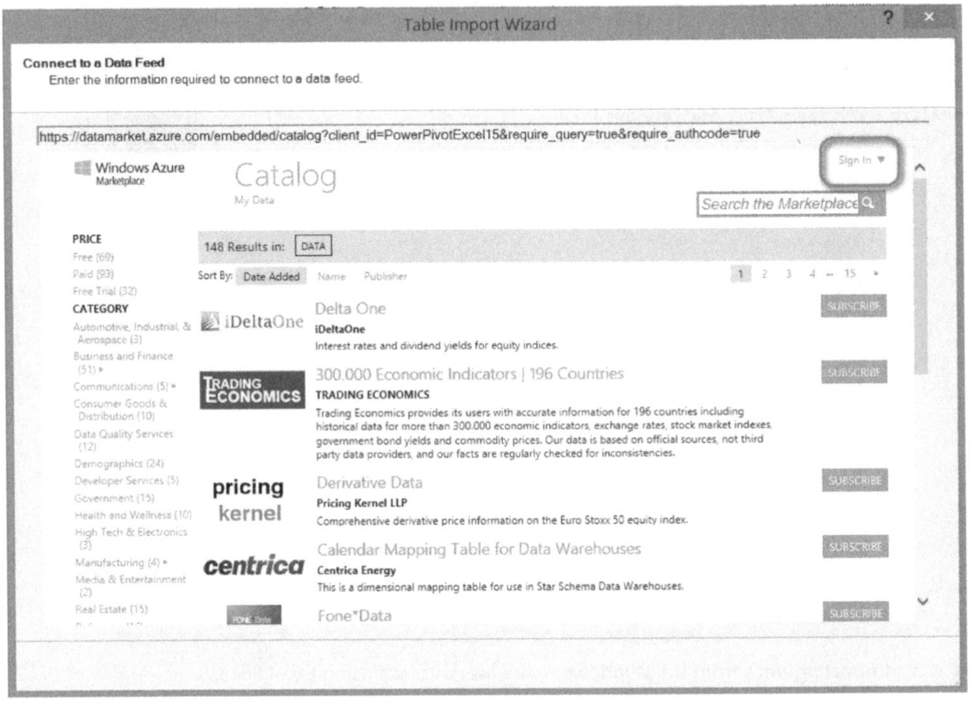

FIGURE 4-33 The Table Import Wizard for the Windows Azure Marketplace.

If you have already subscribed to the data feed that you want to import, click the My Data link and select the feed. If you have not yet subscribed to the feed that you need, you can type an appropriate search string to display a list of feeds that match the search string. For illustration purposes, let's search for "datestream". DateStream is a free, unlimited transactions data feed available at the Windows Azure MarketPlace that provides dates to make it easier to build business intelligence applications in PowerPivot. After you subscribe to and select a feed, a default table will be displayed in the window, as shown in Figure 4-34.

Note that on the bottom of the window there is a list of all the tables that you can select for display, as illustrated in Figure 4-35.

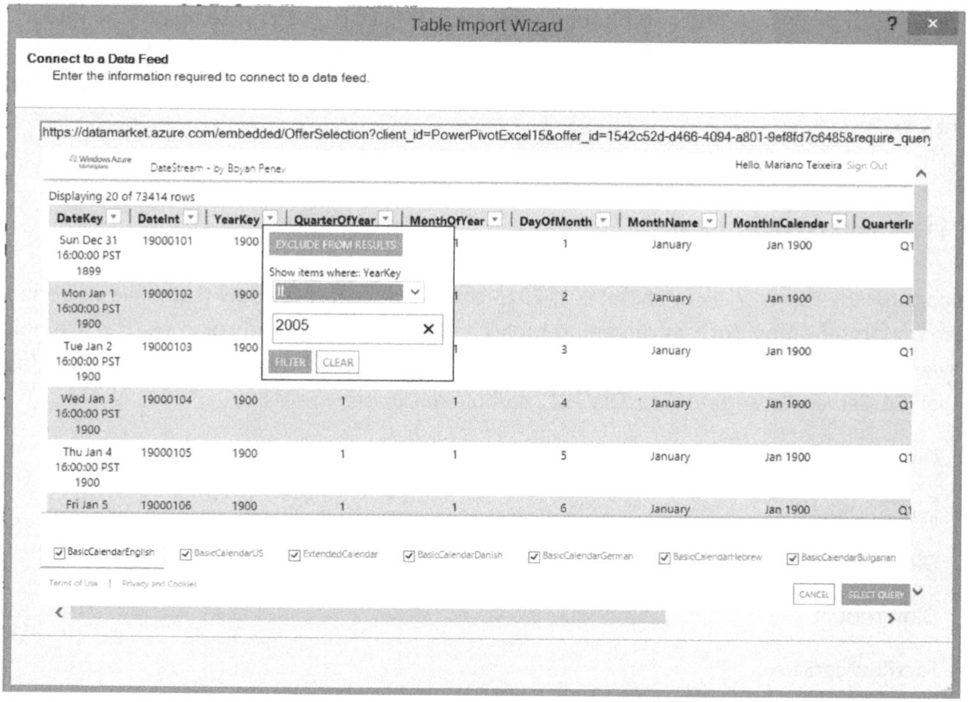

FIGURE 4-34 Browsing through the data from the feed.

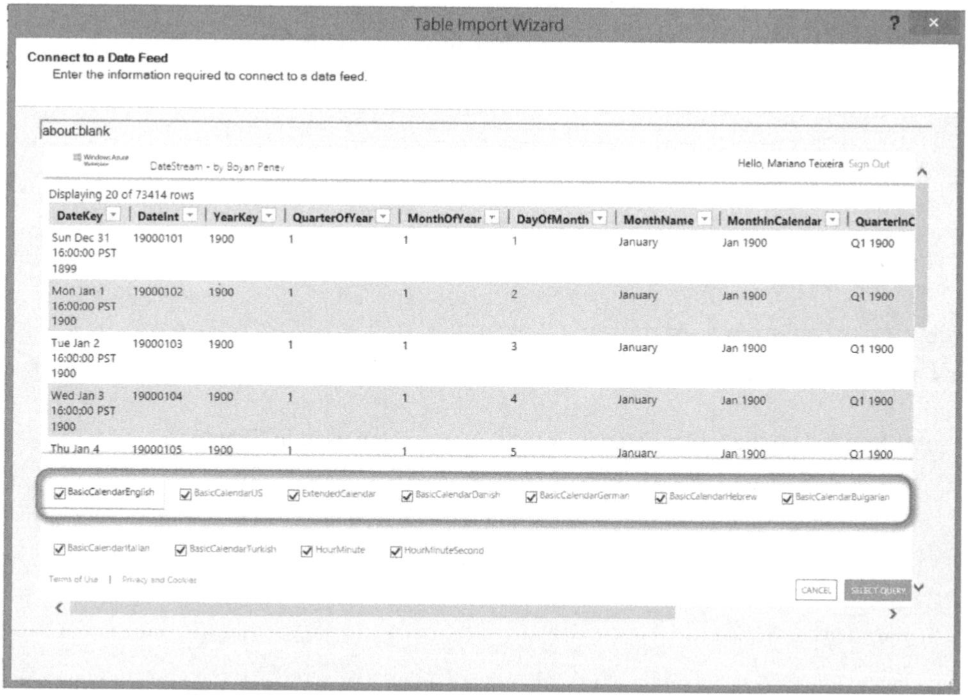

FIGURE 4-35 A list of tables for selecting and prefiltering.

After you complete selecting and filtering tables, click SELECT QUERY. The rest of the import wizard is identical to that of the corresponding PowerPivot 2010 wizard. In this much better user experience, you can seamlessly import the tables into PowerPivot without having to type a service URL and account key.

Paving the ground

To prepare for the Power View in SharePoint 2013 chapter, there were a few things we've done to improve the presentation, such as renaming tables and adding calculated columns. The examples in the Power View chapter rely on an Excel 2013 Data Model based on data from the following tables from the SQL Server *AdventureWorksDW2012* sample database:

- DimDate

- DimEmployee

- DimSalesTerritory

- DimProduct

- FactResellerSales

You can reproduce the importing of these tables following the instructions in the section "Creating the Data Model," earlier in this chapter. Also, we've renamed tables to remove Dim/Fact prefix and added spaces to break into two words. In the PowerPivot window, you can rename a table by right-clicking the table's tab at the bottom of the window, as shown in the Figure 4-36.

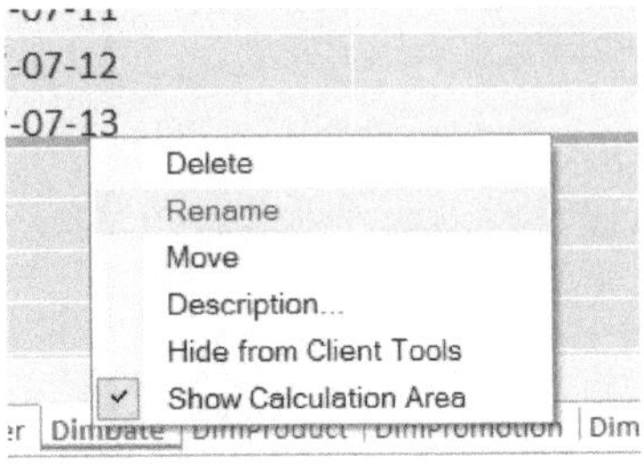

FIGURE 4-36 Renaming a table.

The outcome will be the tables listed in Table 4-1, which are used in Chapter 5.

TABLE 4-1 Changing tables names

Was	Now is
DimDate	Date
DimEmployee	Employee
DimSalesTerritory	Sales Territory
DimProduct	Product
DimResellerSales	Reseller Sales

Updated Date table:

- Row Identifier: FullDateAlternateKey

- Default Label: FullDateAlternateKey

- Marked as Date Table

- Changed data type on FullDateAlternateKey to Date and set format to mm/dd/yyyy EnglishMonthName - sort by MonthNumber

- CalendarYear - changed to Text data type

    Updated Sales Territory:

- Row identifier: SalesTerritoryKey

- Keep unique rows: SalesTerritoryKey

- Default label: SalesTerritoryRegion

- Created hierarchy - SalesTerritoryGroup, SalesTerritoryCountry, SalesTerritoryRegion

Updated Reseller Sales:

- Added calculated field: Reseller Sales YTD:=TOTALYTD(sum([SalesAmount]), 'Date'[FullDateAlternateKey])

Updated Product:

- Row identifier: ProductKey

- Default label: EnglishProductName

- Default image: LargePhoto

- Default Field Set: EnglishProductName, Color, ListPrice

- Added calculated field: Reseller Margin:=(sum('Reseller Sales'[SalesAmount]) - sum('Reseller Sales'[TotalProductCost])) / sum('Reseller Sales'[SalesAmount])

Updated Employee:

- Added calculated column called Employee Name: =[FirstName] & " " & [LastName]

- Row identifier: EmployeeKey

- Keep Unique Rows: EmployeeKey

- Default label: EmployeeName

- Default Image: EmployeePhoto

Summary

In this chapter, we introduced Excel 2013 as a BI tool, highlighting the new Data Model and PowerPivot Add-in. This is just an introductory chapter. Entire books can be written just to cover this topic, let alone all Excel 2013 features.

We've shown the new xVelocity engine and the Data Model in Excel 2010, and what you can do with it. You can use it to create simple reports, import data to the Data Model, and create and manage relationships. We also introduced the new features and user experience built in to PowerPivot for Excel 2013.

In the next chapters, you'll learn how to use the data in the workbook's Data Model to build rich reports with Power View and publish and share it in SharePoint 2013.

CHAPTER 5

Using Power View in Excel 2013

Introducing Power View

If you've worked with Power View in its initial release as part of Microsoft SQL Server 2012, you will quickly adapt to the newest version available as part of Microsoft Excel 2013. However, even if you've never worked with Power View, you will find it easy to learn how to use it. In this section, we explain the history of Power View and how the functionality of Power View in Excel compares and contrasts with Power View in SharePoint. We also introduce the improvements added to the product in this latest release.

A brief history

Power View was introduced in SQL Server 2012 as a new ad hoc reporting tool with an emphasis on data visualization and ease of use for nontechnical business users. To use this release, you must install Reporting Services in SharePoint integrated mode as part of a SharePoint Server 2010 farm. Before you can create a report by using the initial release of Power View, you must publish a Data Model, either as a workbook published to PowerPivot for SharePoint or a tabular model to an Analysis Services instance. Another option that is coming soon (but not available as of this writing) is the ability to use an Analysis Services multidimensional cube as a data source. Unlike traditional reporting with Reporting Services, which requires you to design the report layout in one view and then run the report in a separate view, with ad hoc reporting in Power View, you can make changes to the design in a browser-based Microsoft Silverlight application and see the results instantly in the same view. However, you cannot make changes to the underlying model.

With the release of Excel 2013, Power View is now also available as an add-in component of Excel. This add-in version is known as Power View in Excel to distinguish it from Power View in SharePoint. Like the SharePoint version, Power View in Excel requires you to install Silverlight on the client computer.

Comparing editions of Power View

Power View in Excel is very similar to Power View in SharePoint. With both products, you can create reports to visualize data from a model. However, the reports are not interchangeable. You use Power View in Excel to create a report that resides only within an Excel workbook. That is, you cannot detach the report from the workbook and share it with others separately. However, you can upload the workbook to SharePoint (on-premises or Microsoft Office 365) where others can view it online or download it to their own computer for editing, if they have the appropriate permissions, of course. If the workbook is less than 5 MB, you can save it to a SkyDrive folder for others to download. SkyDrive does not support online viewing of Power View sheets in a workbook.

By contrast, you use Power View in SharePoint to create a file with a .rdlx extension that you can store in a SharePoint document library. This file is a stand-alone report that can be viewed and edited only online. After opening a Power View in SharePoint report, you can export it to Microsoft PowerPivot to create an interactive set of slides for data exploration during a presentation, which is a feature not supported in Power View in Excel.

Another difference between the two editions is the source of the data to visualize. Power View in SharePoint requires you to access an existing model, whether that model is stored in a PowerPivot for SharePoint workbook or in a tabular instance of Analysis Services. Furthermore, all views in a Power View in SharePoint report must use the same data source, whereas each Power View sheet in an Excel workbook can use a different Data Model in Excel as a source. In fact, Power View in Excel can use a simple Excel Data Model (described in Chapter 4, "Using PowerPivot in Excel 2013") as one of its data sources, which is not a supported source for Power View in SharePoint.

If you want to share Power View in Excel views with others who do not have access to Excel, you can save the workbook as a PDF document. You don't have this option with Power View in SharePoint, although that version does give you the ability to export the views as a set of Microsoft PowerPoint slides. As an added feature, the export retains the connection to the data model and makes it possible to interact fully with the Power View visualizations as long as the user's computer can connect to the SharePoint server that is hosting the source reports.

What's new in Power View

Regardless of whether you use Power View in Excel or Power View in SharePoint, there are a variety of enhancements in the latest edition. There are more visualizations to choose from, additional options for formatting your reports, support for key performance indicators, and a better exploration experience through drilling into details.

More visualizations

Power View includes the following two new types of visualizations that you can use to develop new insights about your data:

- **Pie Chart**   A pie chart is useful for comparing a limited number of categories. Power View now includes a pie chart visualization. Like other visualizations, it supports the highlighting feature to help you see how much a selected value in one chart contributes to each pie slice value, as shown in Figure 5-1. You can also double-click a slice to drill to another level if you configure multiple levels in the field layout for the pie chart.

FIGURE 5-1 You can use highlighting and drill to multiple levels in a pie chart.

- **Map** You can use a map to display variable-sized bubbles representing data values by location, or categorize the values to display the bubbles as pie charts by location, as shown in Figure 5-2. Just like working with an online Bing map, you can use zoom and pan controls to adjust the resolution and center point of the map in your Power View sheet. In addition, you can use the highlighting and drill features in a map.

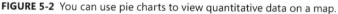

FIGURE 5-2 You can use pie charts to view quantitative data on a map.

> **Note** The map visualization relies on Bing map tiles and therefore requires Internet connectivity.

Additional formatting options

One of the benefits of using Power View for ad hoc reporting is that you can focus your attention on the data, not the appearance. Power View automatically prepares the presentation and applies formatting to produce attractive visualizations. However, if you prefer greater control over formatting, you can take advantage of the following new features:

- **Themes**   The first release of Power View had only eight themes for you to use to set color palettes for charts. Now, Power View offers 39 more themes that not only affect color palettes but also fonts and background colors.

- **Fonts**   You can also set font style and text size independent of a selected theme. These settings affect all text in the current view, however, and cannot be set separately for individual elements.

- **Backgrounds**   Another new formatting option is the ability to set the background of each view. Rather than use the default white background, you can choose from among various shades of gray, with or without a gradient. Or, you can use your own image as a background, instead. After adding the image to the view, you can adjust its position by stretching it to fit the view, generating multiple tiles, or centering the image. You can also adjust the level of transparency for the image.

Key performance indicators

You can use key performance indicators (KPIs) to visualize the comparison of actual results to specified goals, as shown in Figure 5-3. As long as your data model includes calculated fields (explained in Chapter 4), you can create KPIs as needed directly within Power View by selecting the calculated field to use as a base and defining the target as another calculated field or an absolute value. You also specify the status thresholds to use and assign the icons to display for each threshold as an indicator of bad, poor, or good performance.

CalendarYear	ProductLine	SalesAmount	Reseller Margin Status
2005	M	$4,920,358.19	○
	R	$3,093,899.30	●
	S	$51,177.81	○
	Total	$8,065,435.31	●
2006		$85,604.46	●
	M	$10,957,635.83	●
	R	$12,600,361.96	●
	S	$500,827.41	●
	Total	$24,144,429.65	●

FIGURE 5-3 You can display KPIs as a visual indicator of progress toward goals.

New drill functionality

A common feature of business intelligence (BI) tools is the ability to drill from summary data to detail data. Power View now supports this ability to drill by making it possible for you to use a hierarchy built into your data source or by enabling you to create a hierarchy specifically for a visualization. With a hierarchy in place, you can drill from one level to another in a matrix, bar chart, column chart, pie chart, or map. When you drill to a new level, Power View applies a filter to the chart, as shown in Figure 5-4.

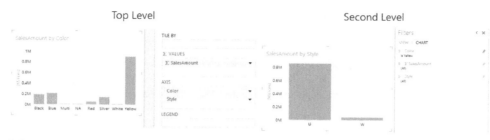

Top Level   Second Level

FIGURE 5-4 You can create a hierarchy to drill from summary data to detail data.

Using Power View

Power View is one of many tools available in the Microsoft BI stack for deriving insights from your data. Although it has many features that are well suited for ad hoc reporting and analysis, it also has some limitations that prevent it from being the only tool you will ever use for reporting.

When do you use Power View?

Power View is a great choice for users who are not professional report developers, because it hides the complexities of report development and makes it possible for users to quickly and easily explore data. You can use Power View for any of the following scenarios:

- You want to create an interactive report to find patterns and explore relationships in your data, regardless of source.

- You want to explore millions of rows of data that are not already available from a data warehouse or structured data model.

- You want to explore changes in data over time through the use of animated scatter charts.

- You want to dynamically drill from summary data to detail data by using hierarchies that are predefined in your data model or by using levels that you create at design time.

- You want to explore analytical data based on location, regardless of whether the location data has been geocoded.

If you decide Power View is the best tool for the task at hand, you must then decide whether to use Power View in Excel or Power View in SharePoint. Table 5-1 highlights the differences between these two tools to help you choose the correct version.

TABLE 5-1 A comparison of Power View versions

Power View in Excel	Power View in SharePoint
Requires Excel 2013 and Silverlight installed on computer	Requires supported browser and Silverlight installed on computer
Uses Excel Data Model or PowerPivot in Excel model as data source	Uses PowerPivot in SharePoint model or Analysis Services tabular model as data source
Supports multiple views based on different Data Models	Supports multiple views based on a single Data Model
Provides no support for duplicating a view	Supports duplication of a view
Provides no support for export to PowerPoint	Supports export of views to PowerPoint
Does not display thumbnail images of views for workbooks published to a PowerPivot gallery	Displays thumbnail images of view for reports published to a PowerPivot gallery

When do you avoid using Power View?

The existence of multiple tools in the Microsoft BI stack reflects the reality that different tools serve different purposes. As wonderful as Power View is, there are scenarios for which it is not the best choice. In Chapter 2, "Planning for business intelligence adoption," we provide an overview of the available user tools to help you make the appropriate selection. In this section, let's consider the situations for which you should consider a tool other than Power View:

- You want to present information that conforms to specific formatting or pagination guidelines, or you want to make it possible for users to export the report to alternate formats such as Excel workbooks or PDF files. In this case, you should use Reporting Services.

- You want to distribute information to a wide audience by using subscriptions. Again, Reporting Services supports this requirement.

- You want to control the user's navigation path from one section of a report to another or from one report to another. You can develop reports in Reporting Services and use actions to support this type of navigation.

- You want users to be able to construct reports or dashboards from prebuilt components. For this functionality, you can create and publish report parts in Reporting Services or PerformancePoint components such as scorecards, indicators, charts, and grids for use in SharePoint.

- You want to explore data that contains many-to-many relationships, such as you might find with bank accounts that have multiple owners or sales transactions for which multiple salespeople receive credit.

Setting up Power View

If you decide that Power View is the right choice, you will need to set up your environment correctly to use it. If you are using only Power View in Excel, you will, of course, need to install Excel 2013. In addition, you will need to install Silverlight. If Silverlight is not installed, you'll see a warning message the first time that you try to insert a Power View sheet into your workbook. Fortunately, the message includes a link that you can use to download Silverlight to make it easy to get set up properly.

Creating visualizations

In this section, we step through the process of creating several different types of visualizations to introduce you to the key features of Power View. You learn how to add a Power View sheet to your Excel workbook and then how to add a table as a starting point for any visualization. As we lead you through the creation of visualizations, we explain important techniques for interacting with visualizations that are typically applicable to more than one type of visualization.

Getting started

Before you can create visualizations, you must first create a Data Model and then insert a Power View sheet into an Excel workbook.

Creating a Data Model

Although in Power View you can add a Power View sheet to your Excel workbook, you won't be able to do anything besides selecting a theme or adding a background image. To create any of the visualizations, you need to first prepare your data by creating a data model as we describe in Chapter 4. At minimum, you can create a table of data manually in an Excel workbook and then select the range of cells in the table to add to a Data Model. However, you can also import from an external source or even integrate data from multiple sources to produce a data model.

> **Note** To reproduce the visualizations we describe in this chapter, you can download a sample workbook that contains a data model based on tables from *AdventureWorksDW2012* to use as a starting point. To create this workbook, we imported the database tables and then used PowerPivot in Excel to enhance the Data Model to support reporting with Power View in Excel.

Inserting a Power View Sheet

After a Data Model is added to the Excel workbook, you must add a new sheet to the workbook to contain the Power View visualizations. To do this, on the ribbon, on the Insert tab, click the Power View button (located near the center of the ribbon), as shown in Figure 5-5.

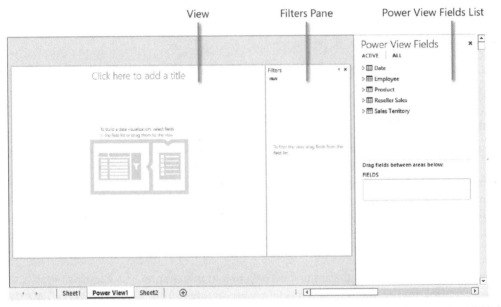

FIGURE 5-5 You use the Insert tab on the Excel ribbon to create a new Power View sheet.

The new Power View sheet appears in the workbook (see Figure 5-6) and consists of the following three areas:

- A blank view to use as a design surface to create one or more data visualizations.

- A Filters pane to which you optionally add fields to define filter conditions for all visualizations in a view or for a selected visualization.

- A Power View Fields list that initially displays the tables in the data model. You expand a table in this list to view the available fields and then select fields to add to a visualization.

FIGURE 5-6 A new Power View sheet contains three sections: View, Filters pane, and Power View Fields list.

> **Note** You can use the commands in the Get Data From External Data Sources group on the Data tab on the ribbon to retrieve data as a model of external data to use as a source for Power View. In the Import Data dialog box, you have the option to select Power View Report.

Creating a table

A table is the simplest form of visualization available in Power View. It is also the starting point for creating any other type of visualization. To create a table in the view, you can use fields from any data table in the Power View Fields list, as long as a relationship exists between the data tables containing the selected fields. After creating the table, you can change the table contents by values in any column in either ascending or descending order. Additionally, you can move the table to a different location in the current view.

Adding fields to a table

Let's create a table to display sales amount values by sales territory group.

1. In the Power View Fields list, expand the Sales Territory table and select the SalesTerritoryGroup check box.

   A table containing a single column of distinct values for the selected field displays in the view, as shown in Figure 5-7.

   SalesTerritoryGroup
   Europe
   NA
   North America
   Pacific

   FIGURE 5-7 You can select a field to display a column of values in a table.

2. In the Power View Fields list, expand the Reseller Sales table and select the SalesAmount check box.

3. Another column appears in the table, as shown in Figure 5-8. Because *SalesAmount* is a number, Power View automatically groups by sales territory group, calculates the sum of sales for each sales territory group, and adds a total row to the table. Power View performs this automatic aggregation for both decimal and whole number data types. Notice that NA no longer appears in the table because it has no related sales.

SalesTerritoryGroup	SalesAmount
Europe	$10,870,534.80
North America	$67,985,726.81
Pacific	$1,594,335.38
Total	$80,450,596.98

   FIGURE 5-8 Power automatically performs grouping of string data and aggregation of numeric data.

4. In the Power View Fields list, point to SalesAmount, click the arrow that appears to the right of the field name, and then select Add To Table, as shown in Figure 5-9. As an alternative, you can also drag SalesAmount into the Fields box in the layout section that appears below the Power View Fields list.

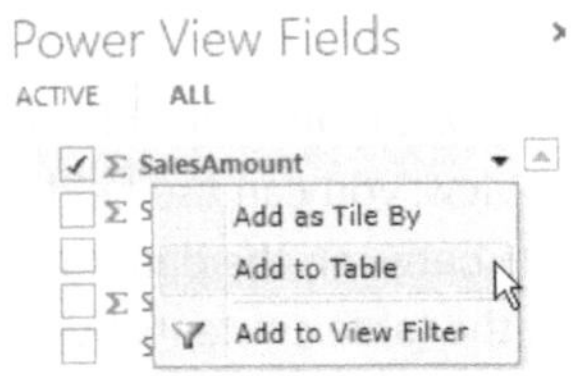

FIGURE 5-9 You can use a field's context menu to add it to the layout.

5. You can change the default aggregation behavior in the layout section by clicking the arrow next to the field name and then, on the menu that appears, click a different aggregation type, as shown in Figure 5-10:

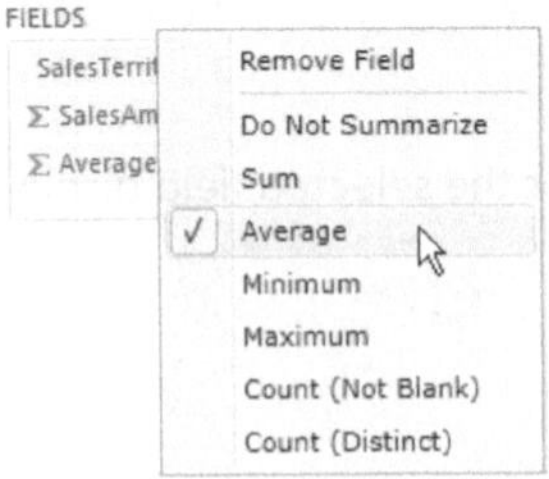

FIGURE 5-10 You can use a numeric field's context menu to select an alternate aggregation type.

> **Tip** If you want to add more fields to the table later, click the table first and then repeat the preceding steps.

Sorting a table

By default, the table sorts data in each column alphabetically in ascending order, starting with the leftmost column. You can override the default sort order by clicking the column header to set an ascending sort for the selected column. A second click of the column header toggles the sort order back to descending, as shown by the arrow next to column header in Figure 5-11.

SalesTerritoryGroup	SalesAmount	Average of SalesAmount
North America	$67,985,726.81	$1,352.87
Europe	$10,870,534.80	$1,222.92
Pacific	$1,594,335.38	$930.73
Total	**$80,450,596.98**	**$1,322.00**

FIGURE 5-11 You can click a column header to change the sort direction.

Resizing and moving a table

You can also add another table to the view by clicking any blank area of the view or dragging a field to a blank area. The number of tables that can fit in a single view depends on the height and width of each table, which you can adjust by pointing to the table border and, when the mouse pointer turns into a double-headed arrow, dragging the border to increase or decrease the table size. Power View will add horizontal or vertical scroll bars to the table if the amount of data cannot display fully in the newly allocated size. Because the Power View sheet size is fixed, you must add another sheet to your workbook if you want to create more tables or other data visualizations.

You can also move a table to a new location in the view. First, click the table to display the borders. When the mouse pointer turns into a hand, drag the table to another area of the view. You can move it to a blank area of the view or place it on top of another data visualization. You can even copy or move it to another Power View sheet, but you must use the Cut, Copy, or Paste buttons on the Power View tab on the ribbon to do that.

Creating a matrix

Whereas you use a table to aggregate numeric values as row groups, you use a matrix when you want to aggregate by both row and column groups. You use the layout section below the Power View Fields list to define the fields to group as rows or as columns as well as the values to aggregate. Optionally, you can configure a matrix to use a hierarchy so that you can drill from one level to another as you explore your data.

Converting a table to a matrix

As with any visualization, you can start a new matrix by creating a table and then use a command on the ribbon to convert it to a matrix. As an alternative, if you already have another type of visualization in the view that you want to replace, you can select it and convert it to a matrix in the same way. Let's copy the table in the view and convert it to a matrix.

1. In the View section, click the table. On the ribbon, on the View tab, click the Copy button. Click a blank area of the View and then, back on the ribbon, click the Paste button.

   Power View adds the matrix to the right of the existing table if sufficient space exists for the second table in this area. Otherwise, Power View adds it to the lower-left area of the View.

2. Click the new table, point to one of its borders, and then drag the new table to the area below the first table, as shown in Figure 5-12:

FIGURE 5-12 You can drag a table to a new location after pointing to one of its borders.

3. With the new table still selected, on the Design tab, click the Table button and then, on the menu that appears, click Matrix, as shown in Figure 5-13:

FIGURE 5-13 Choose one of the options from the menu for the Table button to select a different type of visualization.

Defining the matrix layout

Although the appearance of the matrix in the View section matches the table immediately after the conversion, the structure of the visualization changes. Now, let's configure the matrix to display sales amount values by sales territory group on rows and by color on columns.

1. Remove the *Average of Sales Amount* field from the matrix by clicking the arrow that appears next to the name in the layout section below the Power View Field list and selecting Remove Field.

2. In the Power View Field list, click All to display all tables in the model, expand the Product table, and then drag *Color* to the Columns box, as shown in Figure 5-14:

Drag fields between areas below:

TILE BY

Σ VALUES

Σ SalesAmount ▼

ROWS

SalesTerritoryGroup ▼

COLUMNS

Color ▼

FIGURE 5-14 You add a field to the Columns box in the layout to define the structure for a matrix.

3. Drag the right edge of the matrix to the right to see more columns, as shown in Figure 5-15. Power View adds a total row for each column and row group. Because the full width of the matrix is greater than the width of the View section, you must use the horizontal scroll bar to view the totals for the row groups. You can choose to display totals for row groups only, column groups only, or neither row groups nor column groups by selecting the desired option in the menu that displays when you click the Totals button on the Design tab on the ribbon.

SalesTerritoryGroup	Black	Blue	Multi	NA	Red	Silver	Silver/Black	White
Europe	$3,132,766.72	$2,181,507.01	$82,749.70	$128,791.01	$870,143.07	$1,496,998.47	$26,013.05	$1,879.36
North America	$26,153,472.55	$4,366,419.09	$450,487.99	$512,555.02	$13,001,464.77	$13,077,463.42	$119,768.48	$22,759.45
Pacific	$111,472.83	$775,828.59	$9,321.82	$22,841.18	$1,952.44	$89,488.98	$1,702.39	
Total	$29,397,712.10	$7,323,754.69	$542,559.51	$664,187.22	$13,873,560.28	$14,663,950.87	$147,483.91	$24,638.81

FIGURE 5-15 A matrix displays values in rows and columns.

> **Tip** If the Design tab on the ribbon is not visible, click the matrix to activate it.

Adding hierarchies to the matrix

Regardless of whether your data model contains a hierarchy, you can define multiple fields to use as separate levels for rows or columns in a matrix. Initially, the fields display as separate rows or columns in the matrix, but you can switch the display of the matrix to show only one level at a time. To see how this works, let's modify the matrix to use the Data Model's built-in hierarchy for territories on rows and a custom hierarchy of color and style on columns.

1. Click the matrix to ensure it is selected and then remove the *SalesTerritoryGroup* field from the Rows box. Next, in the Sales Territory table, select the Territories check box.

    The three fields that are part of this hierarchy now display in the Rows box and appear in the matrix: *SalesTerritoryGroup*, *SalesTerritoryCountry*, and *SalesTerritoryRegion*.

2. In the Power View Field list, locate the *Style* field in the Product table, drag it to the Columns box, and then drop it below the *Color* field.

3. On the Design tab, click Show Levels and then, on the menu that appears, click the Rows – Enable Drill Down One Level At A Time command, as shown in Figure 5-16:

FIGURE 5-16 You use the menu for the Show Levels button to enable drilling.

> **Note** You can use the techniques described in steps 2 and 3 to work with hierarchies in bar charts, column charts, pie charts, and maps, but only the matrix visualization requires you to specify whether to show one level at a time.

4. Click Show Levels again, but this time select Columns – Enable Drill Down One Level At A Time.

    The matrix now appears as it did before you added the hierarchies to rows and columns.

5. In the matrix, double-click Europe to drill to the country level and then double-click Black to drill to the style level, as shown in Figure 5-17. Notice the arrow that displays on the first row. Click this arrow to return to the previous level.

SalesTerritoryCountry	M	U	W	Total
France	$62,362.25	$5,975.00	$1,326,593.65	$31,270.63	$1,426,201.53
Germany	$14,982.31		$191,438.56	$7,027.46	$213,448.33
United Kingdom	$58,064.71	$3,887.35	$1,402,466.73	$28,698.06	$1,493,116.86
Total	$135,409.27	$9,862.36	$2,920,498.94	$66,996.15	$3,132,766.72

FIGURE 5-17 You can use the arrow that displays in the visualization to return to the previous level after drilling.

Creating a chart

Often, patterns in your data are easier to see when you present that data chart form. After creating a table or matrix, you can use the tools on the Design tab to convert it to one of the following chart types:

- Stacked bar

- 100% stacked bar

- Clustered bar

- Stacked column

- 100% stacked column

- Clustered column

- Line

- Scatter

- Pie

Adding a clustered bar chart

The process of working with column, bar, and line charts is similar. Let's create a clustered bar chart to learn the basic steps.

1. In the View section, click the matrix. On the ribbon, on the Power View tab, click the Copy button. Click a blank area of the View section and then, on the ribbon, click the Paste button. If necessary, drag the new matrix to the area below the first matrix.

2. Remove the *Style* field from the Columns box by dragging it back to the Power View Fields list.

3. With the new matrix still selected, on the Design tab, click the Bar Chart button and then, on the menu that appears, click Clustered Bar. Resize the width of the chart to fully display the legend, as shown in Figure 5-18:

FIGURE 5-18 You can easily change a matrix into a clustered bar chart.

Notice the arrangement of fields in the layout section for the chart, as shown in Figure 5-19. You can change the appearance of the chart by replacing fields in the Values, Axis, or Legend boxes. You can add multiple fields to the Values box, but at that point the Legend box is disabled. You cannot add a separate field to the Legend box because the legend in the chart can display only colors representing each field in the Values box.

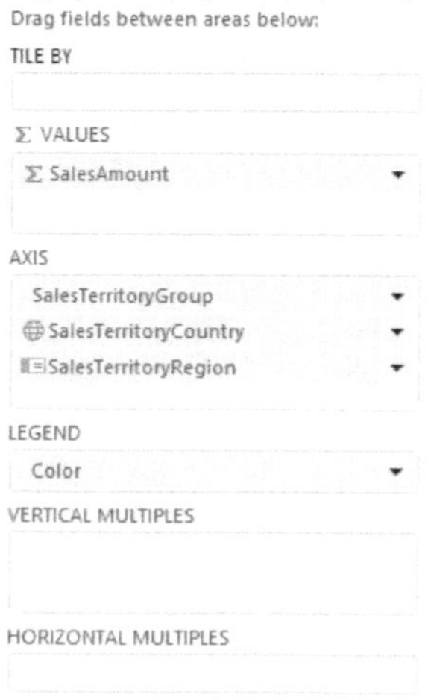

Drag fields between areas below:

TILE BY

Σ VALUES

Σ SalesAmount ▼

AXIS

SalesTerritoryGroup ▼
⊕ SalesTerritoryCountry ▼
⫩ SalesTerritoryRegion ▼

LEGEND

Color ▼

VERTICAL MULTIPLES

HORIZONTAL MULTIPLES

FIGURE 5-19 You can arrange fields in the layout section to control the appearance of your visualization.

Configuring multiples

When working with any chart type (or even a map), you can create a grid layout to display the same visualization with different data points. Let's modify the bar chart to display as horizontal multiples by sales territory group.

1. In the View section, click the bar chart and then drag *Color* from the Legend box to the Axis box in the layout section.

2. Remove the *SalesTerritoryGroup* and *SalesTerritoryRegion* fields from the Axis box.

3. Drag *SalesTerritoryCountry* from the Power View Field list to the Horizontal Multiples box. One bar chart displays for each country, as shown in Figure 5-20. You must use the horizontal scroll bar to view the additional countries not currently visible.

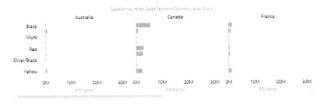

FIGURE 5-20 You can repeat a chart as a set of multiples.

> **Tip** Notice that there are more horizontal bars than labels in the vertical axis. You can re-size, reposition, or even remove other visualizations in the view so that you can add more height to the chart for better visibility of the labels. Another option is to cut or copy your chart to another page.

To view your bar chart multiples in a larger format, let's move it to another sheet.

4. Click the bar chart and then, on the Power View tab, click the Copy button.

5. Again, on the Power View tab, click the Insert button. On the menu that appears, click Power View to insert a new sheet and then click the Paste button.

6. Resize the bar chart so that it fills the view.

7. Drag the SalesTerritoryCountry field to the Vertical Multiples box.

Power View adjusts the layout to display multiples in multiple rows and columns, as shown in Figure 5-21:

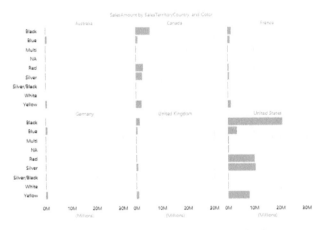

FIGURE 5-21 You can repeat a chart as a set of multiples.

Tip You can use the Grid Height and Grid Width buttons on the Layout tab to select the number of rows and columns for the multiples grid. If the overall size of the visualization cannot display the entire grid, you can use a scroll bar to view the remaining rows or columns.

Interacting with a scatter chart

You can explore relationships between two numeric values when you use a scatter chart. Furthermore, you can animate the scatter chart by adding a field to the Play Axis. For example, you can use a data field in the Play Axis to observe changes in the chart over periods of time. At minimum, you use two values in the scatter chart: one for the horizontal or X axis, and the other for the vertical or Y axis. You must also define a field to use as a category (in the Details box of the layout section) for grouping and aggregating the X and Y values. With this minimal layout, your scatter chart will display points representing coordinates for each distinct value for the category, as shown in Figure 5-22, but the chart does not label each coordinate. You can hover the mouse pointer over the point to see the details displayed as a ToolTip, which is also shown in Figure 5-22.

SalesAmount, and OrderQuantity by Sales

SalesTerritoryGroup: Europe
SalesAmount: $5,632,816.55
OrderQuantity: 19,255

FIGURE 5-22 You can use a scatter chart to display values as coordinates on the X and Y axis.

For deeper analysis, you can add a third value to create a bubble chart for which the size of the bubble reflects the proportional difference in values for each category. Another option, whether you use a scatter chart or a bubble chart, is the use of color to group related categories. And finally, you can add a field to the Play Axis area of the layout section to add animation to the visualization. Let's set up a scatter chart to see the relationship between sales amounts, year-to-date sales, and margins for sales territories over time.

1. Add another Power View sheet to your report and then create a table using the following fields from the Sales Territory table in the model: *SalesTerritoryCountry* and *SalesTerritoryGroup*.

2. Add the following fields from the Reseller Sales table: *Reseller Sales YTD* and *SalesAmount*. The *Reseller Sales YTD* column is empty because the table does not yet contain a date-time data type that this calculation requires to return a value.

3. Add the *Reseller Margin* field from the Product table and the *EnglishMonthName* field from the Date table to complete the table in the view.

4. On the Design tab, click Other Chart and then, on the menu that appears, click Scatter to convert the table into the scatter chart visualization. If necessary, rearrange the fields in the layout section, as shown in Figure 5-23.

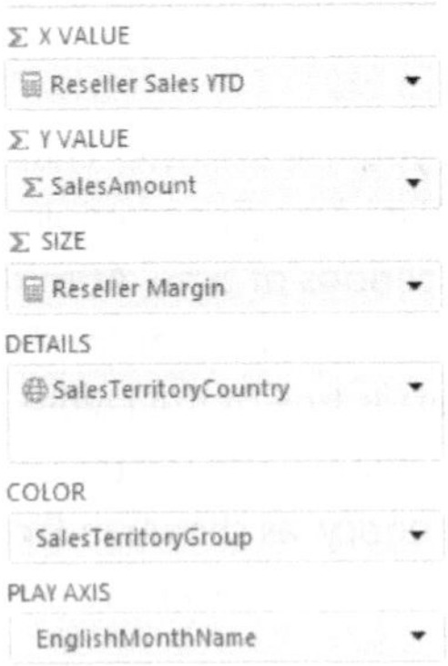

Σ X VALUE
Reseller Sales YTD

Σ Y VALUE
Σ SalesAmount

Σ SIZE
Reseller Margin

DETAILS
SalesTerritoryCountry

COLOR
SalesTerritoryGroup

PLAY AXIS
EnglishMonthName

FIGURE 5-23 You can build a more complex scatter chart by assigning fields to the X Value, Y Value, Size Details, Color, and Play Axis boxes in the layout section.

5. Resize the scatter chart so that it fills the view.

6. Before you can view bubbles in the chart, you must filter the view to display a specific year. To do this, drag *CalendarYear* from the Date table into the Filters pane to the right of the view and select a year, such as 2006, as shown in Figure 5-24.

FIGURE 5-24 You can add a field to the Filters pane to filter visualizations in the current view.

Note Notice that the Filters pane offers you the choice of View or Chart in this step. When you filter the view, your filter criteria apply to all visualizations on the sheet, whereas criteria for a chart filter apply only to the selected chart. Refer to the "Using the Filter pane" section later in this chapter to learn more.

7. Click the play button to the left of the play axis to watch the visualization change for each month.

    As another option, you can drag the slider on the play axis to move forward and backward within a specific time range or to select a specific point in time. A watermark displays in the scatter chart to denote the current item in the play axis, as shown in Figure 5-25.

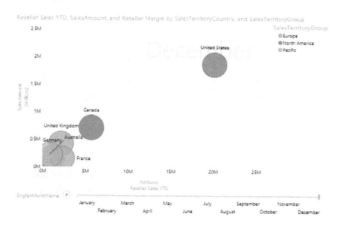

FIGURE 5-25 You can set the slider of the play axis to a specific point in time.

8. You can track the path of a particular bubble for each value in the play axis by clicking it. In addition, you can hover your cursor over a bubble to see the corresponding values display as a ToolTip, as shown in Figure 5-26.

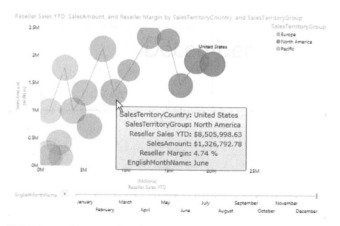

FIGURE 5-26 You can view the path of a specific bubble for the range of time represented on the play axis.

Creating a map

The map visualization is new to Power View and provides a way to put data into context by including a location. In many cases, you do not have to perform any additional steps to geocode your location data to map it correctly. That is, if your Data Model does not already include longitude and latitude fields, Power View connects to Bing to automatically detect the correct spatial locations. However, if you do have latitude and longitude available, you can also use these fields to build maps with greater precision.

> **Tip** If your data contains values that could be detected as distinct values but should be treated separately—such as Springfield, which is a city in both Illinois and Missouri—you should create a calculated field in your model to concatenate columns and ensure accuracy.

Converting a table to a map

To learn how to work with a map, let's create a map to display relative sales by country. Because the countries in the data set are spread around the world, let's also use the multiples feature to view countries by sales territory group.

1. Add another Power View sheet to your report and then create a table using the *SalesTerritoryGroup* and *SalesTerritoryCountry* fields from the Sales Territory table and the *SalesAmount* field from the Reseller Sales table. Be sure to add the fields in the order listed to produce the correct results in the map.

2. On the Design tab, click Map.

3. Click Enable Content to allow Power View to securely connect to Bing and send data for geocoding.

4. Resize the map to better see the visualization.

5. In the layout section, drag the *SalesTerritoryGroup* field to the Vertical Multiples box to create separate versions of the map for each sales territory group, as shown in Figure 5-27:

FIGURE 5-27 You can repeat a map as a set of multiples.

Tip To display pie charts on your map instead of bubbles, add a field to the Color box to categorize the Size value. For example, in the preceding chart, Power View determines the size of the bubble by using the SalesAmount field. You can add the Style field to the Color box to create a pie chart for each country that displays the breakdown of sales by style.

Drilling to details

Rather than use multiples to focus on a particular sales territory group, you can use hierarchies in a map and drill from sales territory group to country.

1. In the layout section of the map visualization, drag the *SalesTerritoryGroup* field to the Locations box and drop it above the *SalesTerritoryCountry* field.

2. In the map, double-click the bubble in Europe to drill to the country details, as shown in Figure 5-28.

FIGURE 5-28 You can double-click a bubble on a map to drill to another level of detail.

3. To return the map to its previous state, click the Drill Up button that appears above the upper-right corner of the map, as shown in Figure 5-29.

FIGURE 5-29 A Drill Up button displays in the upper-right corner of a map after you drill to a lower level of a hierarchy.

Note The Drill Up button also appears in this location when you drill to detail in a chart.

Creating cards

Yet another type of visualization is a list of cards. Each card is a group of fields that you define. If the card includes the default label and default image fields (as defined in the Data Model), the default label displays in the card with a larger font than the other text fields, and the default image displays larger than other images that you include in the card, if any. The layout section for a card is similar to the one for a table, having only a Tile By and Fields area.

Converting a table to cards

Whereas charts and maps require numeric fields, the card visualization uses any type of field. In the following example, we use a combination of field types to produce a card for employees: text, numeric, and image.

1. Click the View section anywhere other than the map to start a new table. Add the following fields from the Employee table: *EmployeeName*, *EmployeePhoto*, *Phone*, *Title*, and *SalesAmount*.

2. On the Design tab, click Table and then, on the menu that appears, click Card to convert the table. A scroll bar appears if there are more cards than currently visible. Notice the size of the employee name text relative to other text in the card shown in Figure 5-30. Notice also that the field name appears below each value for all other non-image fields in the card.

FIGURE 5-30 You can arrange any type of field in a card visualization.

Restructuring cards

As you work with a visualization, you might decide to reorder the fields or adjust its size. Power View makes it easy to make changes to the structure of the visualization and immediately see the results in the view.

1. In the layout section for the cards, rearrange the fields to how they appear in Figure 5-31.

    Notice the employee photo does not change location in the card. The default image always displays on the left side of the card, regardless of its position in the list of fields.

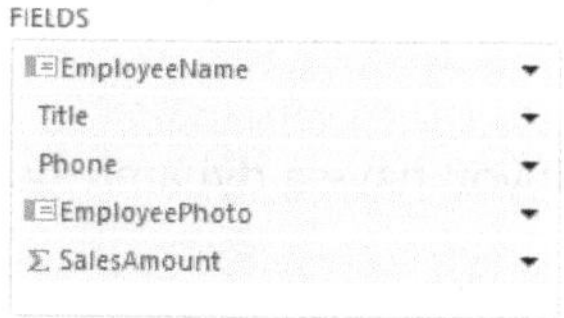

FIELDS
- EmployeeName
- Title
- Phone
- EmployeePhoto
- Σ SalesAmount

FIGURE 5-31 The arrangement of fields in the layout section controls the card visualization, except that the default image always appears on the left side of the card, regardless of its position in the list of fields.

2. Drag the right border of the cards so that the fields display in a single row, as shown in Figure 5-32.

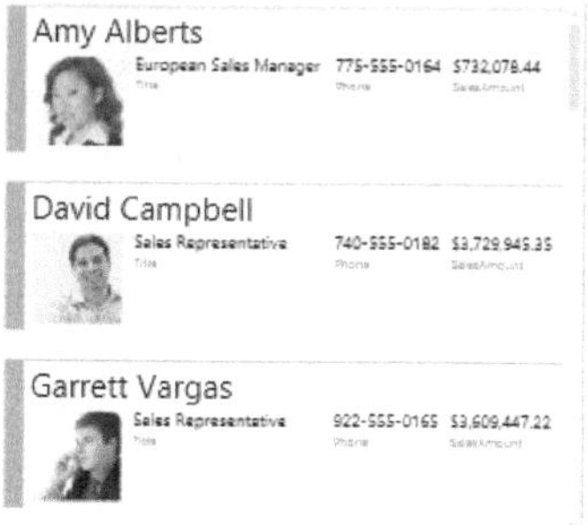

Amy Alberts
European Sales Manager 775-555-0164 $732,078.44
Title   Phone   SalesAmount

David Campbell
Sales Representative   740-555-0182 $3,729,945.35
Title   Phone   SalesAmount

Garrett Vargas
Sales Representative   922-555-0165 $3,609,447.22
Title   Phone   SalesAmount

FIGURE 5-32 You can resize the card visualization to display fields in a single row.

Using KPIs

A popular reason to use BI is to monitor progress toward goals by displaying an icon to represent the current state as positive, neutral, or negative. As we explained earlier in the "What's new" section, you can create KPIs in Power View if your Data Model includes calculated fields. Another option is to use KPIs that are already defined in a PowerPivot model.

> **Note** If you are using Power View in SharePoint, you can also use KPIs defined in an Analysis Services tabular instance.

Defining KPIs

If your data model already includes calculated fields, you can easily add KPIs to display in a table or matrix. Let's add a KPI to compare actual reseller sales margins to a fixed goal of 15 percent.

1. On the PowerPivot tab, click KPIs and then, on the menu that appears, click New KPI.

2. In the Key Performance Indicator (KPI) dialog box, in the KPI Base Field (Value) list box select Reseller Margin. Only calculated fields display in this list.

3. Select the Absolute Value option and then, in the Absolute Value box, type **0.15**.

> **Note** You can choose to use a calculated field, instead, if you have a dynamic goal defined in your Data Model.

4. You can use the slider to establish status thresholds that Power View uses to determine the color to assign to the KPI's icon. For greater precision, you can type values into the box that appears above each threshold. For this KPI, type **0.05** for the red threshold and **0.1** for the yellow threshold, as shown in Figure 5-33. Keep the remaining defaults and click OK to save the KPI.

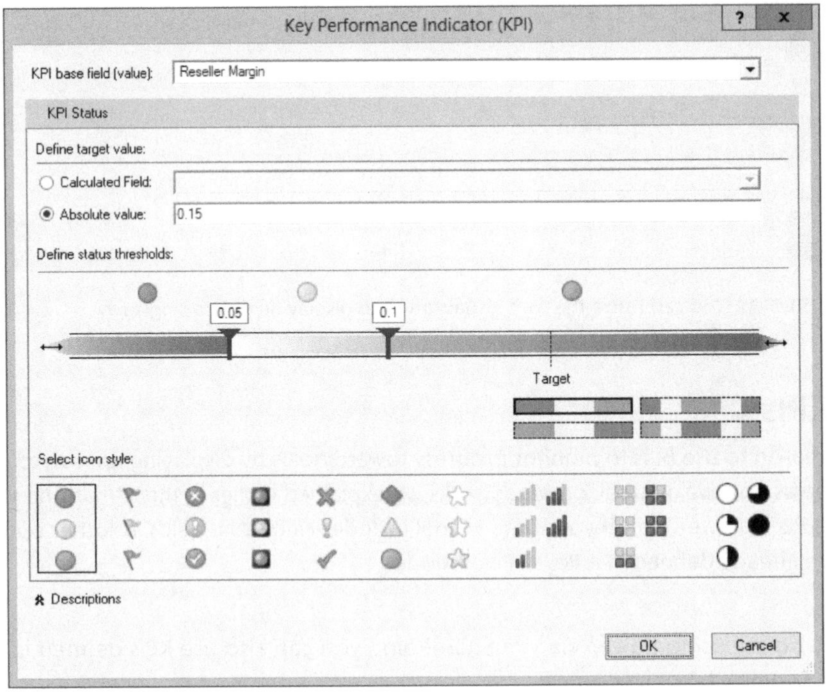

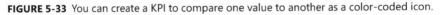

FIGURE 5-33 You can create a KPI to compare one value to another as a color-coded icon.

> **Note** Saving the KPI updates the model and makes it available to all Power View sheets in your workbook.

Visualizing KPIs

Regardless of whether you add KPIs explicitly for use in Power View or they exist already in the Data Model, you can add the value or goal to any visualization. However, because the status displays as an icon, you can only add it to a table, matrix, or card. Let's create a table to display the Reseller Margin KPI by calendar year and style.

1. Add another Power View sheet to your report and then create a table using the *CalendarYear* field from the Date table, the *Style* field from the Product table, and the *SalesAmount* field from the Reseller Sales table.

2. On the Design tab, click Table and then, on the menu that appears, click Matrix to convert the table to a matrix and automatically add totals for each year.

3. Locate the Reseller Margin KPI in the Product table and expand it to select the *Status* field, as shown in Figure 5-34. Although we are adding only the *Status* field to the matrix, we have the option to include the other fields associated with the KPI.

FIGURE 5-34 You select the Status field of a KPI to add an icon to a table or matrix.

4. Drag the right border of the matrix to view all the columns.

Filtering data

After you place one or more visualizations in a view, you can apply different types of filters as another option for exploring data. If you have multiple visualizations in the same view, an effective technique is to use highlighting to emphasize the contribution of a selected item to an overall value. You can also use a slicer or a tiles container as a way to restrict the data that displays in visualizations. Yet another approach is to add fields to the Filters pane to apply filters to all visualizations in the current view or only to a specific visualization. An advantage of using the Filters pane is the ability to create complete conditions.

Highlighting data

When you have multiple visualizations in the same view, you can see the relationships that exist in the data by using highlighting. You can select an item in a visualization to see Power View highlight all related values in the other visualizations (see Figure 5-35). In this example, the selection of Europe in the line chart's legend at the lower right of the view activates highlighting in the other visualizations. For example, in the column chart in the upper right of the view, the original values continue to display with a dimmer color, but the values representing Europe's contribution to the original values display. Similarly, the bubbles in the map related to Europe are highlighted. In the card visualization, a filter applies to show only those employees having sales in Europe. When you click the same item a second time, Power View clears the highlighting.

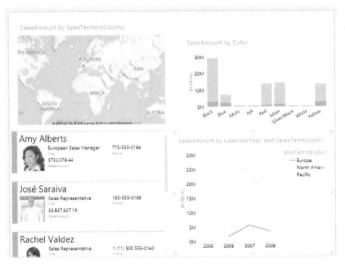

FIGURE 5-35 You can click a value in a chart or a legend item to filter all visualizations in the same view.

Adding a slicer

If you want to entirely eliminate unrelated values from your visualizations, you can add a slicer to the view for filtering. You start by creating a single-column table by using either a string or image field and then you convert it to a slicer by using the Slicer button on the Design tab on the ribbon. You can then click an item in the slicer to filter all visualizations and related slicers in the view (see Figure 5-36). When you want to filter by using several items in the slicer, press and hold the Ctrl key as you select each item in the slicer. When you're ready to restore the original unfiltered view, click the Clear Filter icon that displays in the upper-right corner of the slicer.

FIGURE 5-36 You can use a slicer to filter visualizations and other slicers in the same view.

Filtering by using tiles

Sometimes, you might not want to filter every visualization in the view. In that case, you create a tiles container into which you place the visualizations to be filtered. You can place any type of visualization inside a tiles container except a scatter chart or a chart for which you have configured multiples.

Adding tiles to a visualization

To get started, click on a visualization to display its layout section and then drag the field to use for filtering to the Tile By box. Although a field with an image data type is shown in Figure 5-37, you can use a field that contains a string value, instead. Each tile represents a distinct value for the field in the Tile By box. Unlike a slicer, you can click only one tile at a time, which Power View then uses to filter each visualization in the tiles container. You can identify the current tile selection by the border around the image or the darker font when using a string field as a tile.

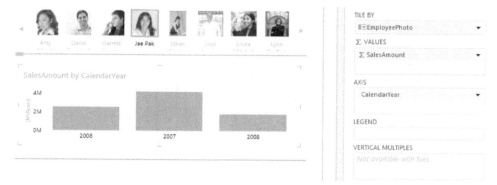

FIGURE 5-37 You can use a tiles container to filter a visualization.

By default, Power View uses the Tab Strip when you first add a tile field to a visualization. You can click Tile Type on the Design tab to switch to Tile Flow, as shown in Figure 5-38. In the Tile Flow mode, the tiles display along the bottom edge of the container. Additionally, the current selection appears in the center of the strip and is slightly larger than the other tile items.

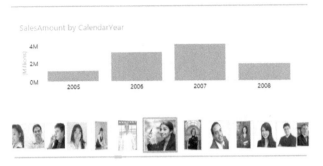

FIGURE 5-38 You can display tiles in Tile Flow mode at the bottom of the tiles container.

Adding a second visualization to a tiles container

You can expand the size of the tiles container in the same way that you resize a visualization. Click it to reveal its borders and then drag one of the edges to increase the size of the container. You can resize a tiles container to add one or more visualizations to it. That way, you can filter multiple visualizations with a single tile selection, as demonstrated in Figure 5-39. Any visualization outside the tiles container is unaffected by the tile selection.

FIGURE 5-39 You can place multiple visualizations inside the same tiles container.

Using the Filter pane

You can also apply multiple filters to all visualizations or selected visualizations by defining filter conditions in the Filter pane. When no visualizations are selected in the View section, the conditions you add apply to all of them. Otherwise, if you select a visualization first, you can then click the visualization label (such as Table or Chart) in the Filters pane to configure filters for that visualization only.

Creating a basic filter

A basic filter is one you create by dragging a field to the Filters area and then specifying a value for the field. If the field has a string or date data type, you select one or more check boxes corresponding to the filter conditions that you want to set. To the right of each check box, you can see a count of records in the table corresponding to that value (see Figure 5-40). If the field has a numeric data type, you use a slider to set a minimum and maximum value instead. Click the field name in the Filters pane to toggle the view of available lists between collapsed and expanded.

FIGURE 5-40 You can select specific values or numeric ranges when creating a basic filter.

When a field has a long list of values, a vertical scroll bar displays to help you quickly scroll through the list to find a specific value. Another option is to use the search box to filter the list of values, as shown in Figure 5-41.

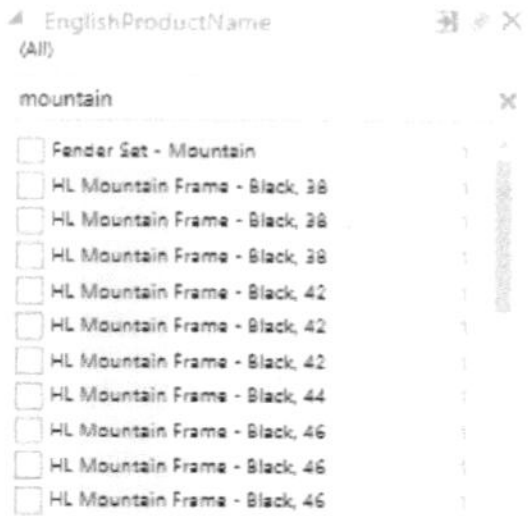

FIGURE 5-41 You can filter the list of available values by using a search condition.

> **Tip** You can remove the effect of a filter while retaining the option to use the filter again later by clicking the Clear Filter button, which is the second button in the toolbar that appears to the right of the field name. To permanently remove the filter, click the third button, Delete Filter.

Creating an advanced filter

Rather than select a single string or date value or a range of numeric values for a basic filter, you can switch a filter to advanced mode to access more options for specifying filter conditions. To switch to advanced filter mode, click the Advanced Filter Mode button, which is the first one in the toolbar appearing to the right of the field name in the Filters area. The steps you use to set the filter condition depend on the type of field, as follows:

- **String Value**   Use one of the following operators to create a filter based on a partial word, as shown in Figure 5-42: Contains, Does Not Contain, Starts With, Does Not Start With, Is, Is Not, Is Blank, or Is Not Blank.

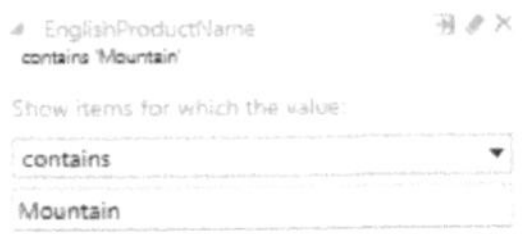

FIGURE 5-42 You can define a filter based on a subset of characters in a string.

- **Numeric Value**   You can use one of the following operators to compare a value in the tabular model to a specified value, as illustrated in Figure 5-43: Is Less Than, Is Less Than Or Equal To, Is Greater Than, Is Greater Than Or Equal To, Is, Is Not, Is Blank, or Is Not Blank.

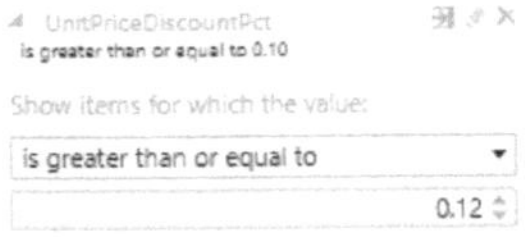

FIGURE 5-43 You can use comparison operators to define a filter on a numeric value.

- **Date Value**   You can use a calendar control (see Figure 5-44), and a drop-down list with 15-minute increments of time to set date and time values in combination with the following operators: Is, Is Not, Is After, Is On Or After, Is Before, Is On Or Before, Is Blank, or Is Not Blank.

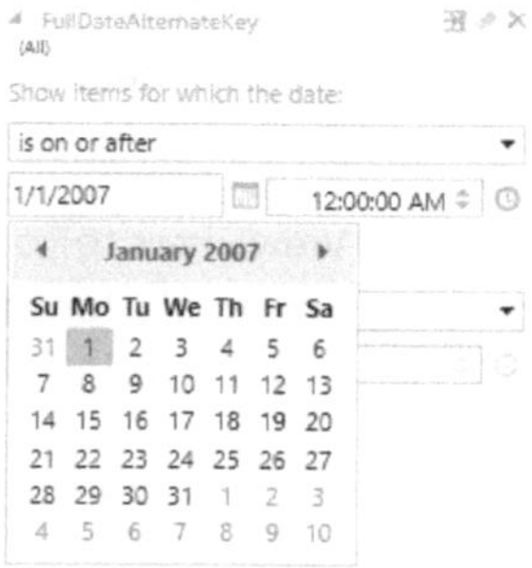

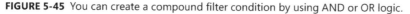

FIGURE 5-44 You can use a calendar control to define a filter for a date/time field.

Whichever type of filter you configure, the view does not update until you click the Apply Filter link. If you like, you can create a compound condition for each filter by using a logical AND or logical OR operator between two conditions, as shown in Figure 5-45.

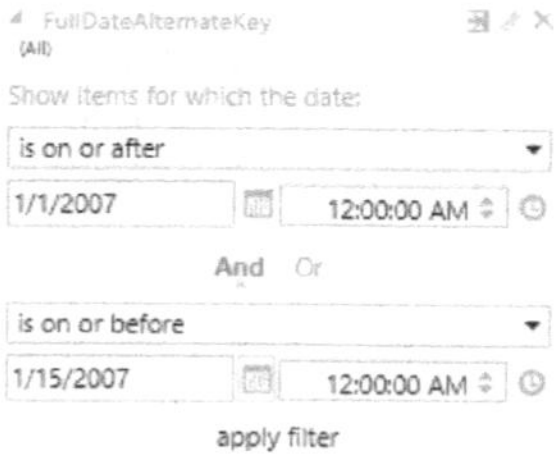

FIGURE 5-45 You can create a compound filter condition by using AND or OR logic.

Saving a Power View workbook

When you finish editing your report, you can save it to review later. You can choose a location, such as SharePoint, Office 365 SharePoint, SkyDrive, or your computer, and then specify a location and file name for your workbook. To get started, click File, and then click Save As. You can save your report by using any of the following locations:

■ **SharePoint Server 2013**   You can save your workbook in any SharePoint document library. However, if you decide to save a workbook to a PowerPivot Gallery, be aware that thumbnail images of the Power View sheets in that workbook will not display. By contrast, the PowerPivot Gallery does display thumbnails for any Power View in SharePoint reports that you save to that location. Other users can view and interact with the workbook from the web browser.

■ **SharePoint Online in Office 365**   You can save your workbook to a folder accessible through SharePoint Online. This environment offers full support for Power View's interactive features to users accessing the workbook with a supported browser.

- **SkyDrive** You can save a Power View workbook to a SkyDrive folder to share it with others. However, anyone accessing from that location must open it in Excel because it cannot be viewed online.

- **Local computer** You can save a workbook containing Power View views to your local computer (or even a network file share) when you are creating workbooks for personal use or when you have no SharePoint environment available for sharing with a group.

Summary

In this chapter, we reviewed the history of Power View and described the new features that make an already great tool for data exploration even better. We also introduced you to the variety of data visualizations available in Power View by showing you how easy it is to set up a new visualization from scratch or converting an existing visualization to an alternate structure. Along the way, we showed you how to work with visualization size and location, how to add interactivity with hierarchies and animated scatter charts, and how to apply various filtering techniques. By now, you should have a better appreciation for how it fits into your BI strategy. Although Power View has many benefits for ad hoc reporting and analysis, there are other tools better suited for other types of tasks that learn about in subsequent chapters.

CHAPTER 6

Business intelligence with Excel Services 2013

Excel Services in SharePoint Server 2013 is a shared service that you can use to publish Excel workbooks on Microsoft SharePoint Server. Using Excel Services in SharePoint, you can manage and secure according to your needs and share the workbooks among SharePoint Server 2013 users, who can open and interact with the workbooks in a browser.

Excel Services's focus is on business intelligence (BI) scenarios. You can create Microsoft Excel workbooks that connect to external data sources, develop reports, and then publish them to a SharePoint document library. When a user opens the workbook from the document library, Excel Services renders it in the browser. To create and edit office documents in the browser, you need the Microsoft Office Web Apps Server 2013. With the Office Web Apps Server, users can view and, depending on the license, edit Office documents, including Excel documents, by using a supported web browser on computers and on various mobile devices, such as Windows Phone–based smartphones, iPhones, and iPads. Because the Office Web Apps Server does not focus on BI scenarios, such as support for data models, we will not cover it in this book. For more information on Office Web Apps, visit *http://technet.microsoft.com/en-us/library/ee855124.aspx*.

Excel Services consists of Excel Calculation Services, the Excel Web Access Web Part, and Excel Web Services for programmatic access. It supports sharing, securing, managing, and using Excel workbooks in a browser by providing the following:

- Global settings for managing workbooks. Use these settings for security, load balancing, session management, memory utilization, workbook caches, and external data connections.

- Trusted file locations. With trusted file locations, you can define which document libraries are trusted by Excel Services. They also make it possible for you to perform session management, and configure workbook size, calculation behavior, and external data settings of workbooks stored in those locations.

- An extensive list of trusted data providers for connecting to your data, plus the ability to add your own trusted data provider.

- Trusted data connection libraries. Use these to define which data connection libraries in your farm are trusted by Excel Services.

- The ability to add your own user-defined function assemblies.

- The ability to configure a Data Model Server. By doing so, you can interact with workbooks with data model.

Table 6-1 looks at three specific scenarios, which can help you understand how best to take advantage of Excel Services.

TABLE 6-1 Three scenarios for using Excel Services

Sharing workbooks	Users can save Excel 2013 workbooks to a SharePoint Server document library so that other users can have a managed and secure way to access it. When the user opens with workbook in the browser, Excel Services loads the workbook, refreshes the external data if it is necessary, calculates it if it is necessary, and then sends the resulting output view back through the browser. A user can interact with workbook's data by sorting, filtering, expanding, or collapsing PivotTables, and by passing in parameters. This provides the ability to perform analysis on published workbooks.
Extensibility	Besides a browser-based interface with the server, Excel Services provides a web service–based interface so that a published workbook can be accessed programmatically by any application that uses web services. Web service applications can change values, calculate the workbook, and retrieve some or the entire updated workbook by using that interface, according to what security permissions have been set for the published workbook.
Report Building	One of the most useful features of Excel Services is report building. By publishing data-connected workbooks to a SharePoint document library and making them available through Excel Services, you can make reports that you have created in Excel available to others in your organization. Instead of multiple users having separate copies of the workbooks on their computers, the workbooks can be created and changed by a trusted author in a central location that is trusted by Excel Services. The correct version of the worksheet is easier to find, share, and use from Excel, SharePoint Server, and other applications.

A brief history of Excel Services

2007: The introduction of Excel Services

In 2007, Excel Services was introduced as part of Microsoft Office SharePoint Server Enterprise. This initial release of Excel Services was really focused on extending Excel-based BI solutions onto the server and about making managing Excel files easier.

BI functionality

The Excel client added a lot of BI functionality in 2007, such as Online Analytical Processing (OLAP) formulas, structured tables, conditional formatting for creating things like data bars and key performance indicators (KPIs), better PivotTable functionality and more. A significant part of BI is about sharing the insights after they are gathered. Excel Services was the answer to widely sharing those Excel-based BI reports across SharePoint. This is the reason why Excel Services generally did a great job at rendering new Excel file types that were oriented toward BI. In 2007, there were many types of Excel files and objects that Excel Services couldn't calculate or render—it was clearly a subset of Excel functionality and was really about being a good subset with respect to the BI features.

A Web Part—and the ability to view parts of Excel workbook files in a Web Part (for instance, just show a single chart)—also shipped with SharePoint 2007. This made it possible to create dashboard experiences that natively integrated Excel content.

Sharing and managing workbooks

The sharing and managing of Excel files was the other problem Excel Services tackled in 2007. Users could store their Excel files in SharePoint and assign permissions to them, as well, so that the files could be tightly managed and controlled.

When users needed to broadly share the files, they no longer needed to copy and paste content into emails, or send email attachments, or set up a terminal server that people could log on to in order to view the Excel file. They could simply send a link to the file that was published to SharePoint, and people could view the Excel file by using Excel Services in a way that didn't alter the contents of the Excel file. Based on permissions, viewers could open the file directly in Excel to do more advanced analysis or editing, or they could be limited to only the browser-based view.

This way, workbook authors didn't need to worry about showing up at the Friday board meeting greeted by five other people who have five different versions of the file and, by extension, five different versions of the numbers. The "one version of the truth" for the numbers could be contained in a single Excel file in a single place, and yet, a broad audience could view it by using Excel Services.

Extensibility

There was also a simple extensibility story for the 2007 release. Actually, there were two parts to it: a web service and User-Defined Functions.

Excel Web Services

Excel Services could be used as a way to offload Excel calculations to more powerful server hardware. Custom solutions could load those files on the server, set parameters, recalculate them, and get the results back by using Excel Web Services, which is a set of Simple Object Access Protocol (SOAP)–based web services that could be called from any application.

User-Defined Functions

Excel Services also had the ability to take advantage of User-Defined Functions (UDFs). These are simply custom managed code solutions that can be installed on the server and then called from a workbook file just like any function. For example, I could write some custom C# code that returns all the items from a specific SharePoint list. Somebody could use that custom routine from a workbook on the server just like any other function. Thus, instead of typing

```
=SUM(A1, B1)
```

he could type something like the following:

```
=MyCustomSharePointListFunction("http://URLtoMyList")
```

2010: Expanded capabilities

The capabilities of Excel Services were expanded in the 2010 release wave of Office and SharePoint products.

Continued BI support

Excel Services added support for more features that blocked files from loading in the previous release, making it more relevant for more workbook files. It also added support for the new BI functionalities that Excel client 2010 introduced, such as Sparklines, Slicers, and PowerPivot support.

Improved extensibility

The extensibility aspect was also revised in the 2010 release. The existing SOAP-based web service was updated to support the new editing functionality, and the UDFs were still there and still supported. In addition to these, a new object model was added: the ECMAScript object model.

This new object model (using JavaScript or JScript) gave developers the ability to build applications that ran in the browser using a language that is native to most web developers. It can do many of the things the web service does, but it also gives the developer control over basic properties of the workbook (such as whether the toolbar is shown in the UI) as well as capture and respond to basic events. For example, it is fairly easy to write an application with which a user can edit an Excel file in the browser but have various processes kick off, display warnings, and so on as the user enters values in certain cells or selects cells. This is because the developer can listen for and respond to events such as the cell selection event or other events by which you might want to trigger key application behaviors.

Last, but certainly not least, a Representational State Transfer (REST)–based API was added, as well. This makes it possible for users to access parts of the workbook, such as a specific chart, by using a simple URL. This makes it quite easy to embed Excel content in blogs, web pages, or even as refreshable images in applications such as Microsoft PowerPoint.

The world of services

Excel Services was also introduced to the world as a hostable service in the 2010 release. All of SharePoint can be hosted on premises and exposed as a service, and Excel Services supports that. There are separate chapters in this book that discuss hosted cloud-based services, so I won't delve too deeply in it here. But, Excel Services works as part of service-based SharePoint solutions.

Excel Services capabilities are now also available on the Internet, hosted by Microsoft. To try it, simply send an Excel file as an email attachment by using your Hotmail account or upload it to your Microsoft SkyDrive account (*www.skydrive.com*) and click the file to view or edit it. The fundamental technology being used there is Excel Services.

2013: Continued expansion

In the 2013 release wave of Office and SharePoint products, Microsoft expanded the BI capabilities of Excel Services yet further.

Continued BI Support

The 2013 release includes support for data models and greater integration with PowerPivot and Power View. As previously mentioned, SharePoint 2010 introduced the REST API for use in getting and setting information in Excel Workbooks stored in SharePoint document libraries. Excel Services 2013 adds a new way to request data from Excel Services that uses the Open Data Protocol (OData) which you can use to obtain information about Excel Services resources. This new service relies heavily on the existing Excel Services REST API.

Interactive View

Excel Interactive View uses HTML, JavaScript/JScript, and Excel Services to generate Excel table and chart views on the fly, in the browser, from an HTML table hosted on a webpage.

When to use Excel Services

Generally speaking, there can be multiple ways to build a solution with different BI products in the SharePoint ecosystem. This section is intended to give some guidance on when an Excel Services–based solution might be a better fit than some other products.

It's already Excel

Excel is a tool with a rich history, with many existing solutions, and in use at virtually every major business in the world. Excel doesn't require an "authoring" environment or developer tool/environment—it is just Excel. Getting Excel out of a company's system is a tough challenge. It is a tool that people know, often love, and into which they have invested a lot of learning and solution time.

One primary reason to use Excel is that it might already be the tool of choice for many end users of whatever BI solution/system you might be trying to design. Depending on the needs of your users and requirements of the system, often the path of least resistance is to build it by using Excel.

It's fast to create and easy to adopt

Continuing on the theme of the widespread deployment and acceptance of Excel, people already know how to use and likely have solutions already based in it. Prototyping a new BI-based solution is often faster if it is based on Excel Services than some other tool. Why? Because most users don't need to learn anything new.

They don't need to learn a new suite of tools to design a dashboard. A dashboard in Excel is usually the first sheet that has grid lines turned off, the most important charts, data, and PivotTable showing the most important grouping of the results. So, business users, users of the BI system being designed, already know how to create the BI without a bunch of new training time and expense. This means that the overall BI solution designer can focus on putting together the server pieces of the solution, leaving the business logic and visuals to the existing Excel users.

Because it is Excel, as soon as it can be shown that the ability to manage the Excel files exists, many people are likely to try it out. So, it is a great stepping stone to getting richer BI controls and solutions in place. Getting the Excel files working on the server is typically quick and straightforward (often no harder than simply saving them in SharePoint). This makes it a great choice if you are looking for baby steps toward introducing a deeper BI solution later, or if you are looking for a quick prototyping/ proof of concept BI solution.

If users want to extend beyond the reach of just the workbook sheet, there is a Web Part that provides the ability to make more complex dashboards that are more deeply integrated into SharePoint. This can be used from within SharePoint UI, no extra installation or tool is needed.

It is a great ad hoc tool

One of the strengths of Excel is that it is a fantastic tool for doing quick analysis on the fly. It is fairly easy to add a new column to a table for a quick calculation, drill down on a PivotTable to go deeper into the insight, or modify a slicer to change how the data is viewed. This kind of loose, ad hoc data interactivity and exploration is something that works well on Excel Services, too.

Some other BI tools are great, too, but they might not be great at ad hoc exploration. And, if Excel Services doesn't support the full level of ad hoc functionality that the user desires, she can always just click Open In Excel and take the file into the Excel client to do more. This works because Excel Services is loading Excel files natively and there is nothing converted or special about those files—they can be opened on the client or server.

It scales Excel files to many users

Because Excel Services is a true server product, it is can be scaled out to many computers or scaled up to use more resources on a single computer so that it can meet the demands of many users viewing and interacting with workbooks in the system. Thus, if there are some BI reports that are Excel based which need to be shared broadly, Excel Services is a natural choice. This is especially true for cases in which all the people who need to view the data don't have the Excel client installed.

The Data Model in Excel Services

As presented in Chapter 4, "Using PowerPivot in Excel 2013," the Data Model is a collection of tables and their relationships that reflects the real-world business. In the desktop version of Excel, the xVelocity engine is the component that is responsible for handling the Data Model. It runs within the Excel process in Windows. In the server world, this job is the responsibility of one or more SQL Server Analysis Services 2012 SP1 instances. SharePoint 2013 is a game changer compared to the PowerPivot for SharePoint 2010 architecture. At that time, in the 2010 release, the PowerPivot instance of Analysis Services had to be inside the farm, in a SharePoint Application Server. Now, in 2013 release, there is no restriction where the SQL Server Analysis Services in SharePoint Mode instance needs to be, and no one-to-one mapping between SharePoint Application servers and Analysis Services in SharePoint mode instances. This gives more freedom to the SharePoint and Analysis Services administrators to plan for scaling up and out as their farm usage grows. Figure 6-1 shows a high-level Excel Services architecture diagram.

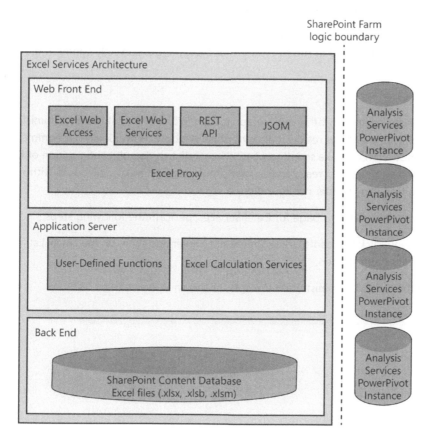

FIGURE 6-1 The Excel Services 2013 architecture.

Configuring the server

This section looks at the high-level security and configuration concerns. It is not meant to be an exhaustive list, but is does focus on the must-know concepts and most common "gotchas" that people encounter when configuring the server.

Installation

There is nothing special or extra to do for Excel Services installation. It is part of the SharePoint installation. If you install the Microsoft SharePoint 2013 Enterprise Edition, Excel Services is installed, as well. If you run the configuration wizard at the end of the installation, Excel Services can be automatically configured, too.

You do need to be aware, however, that if you want the ability to create new Excel files or edit Excel files by using only a browser, you will also need to install the Office Web Applications on top of SharePoint. The Office Web Applications should be installed and configured after the Microsoft Office SharePoint Enterprise Edition is installed and configured.

In the interest of simplicity and for the purposes of this book, it is easiest to allow the SharePoint 2013 post-setup configuration wizard to run to ensure that everything is correctly configured.

Administration

Excel Services is administered like any other service application in SharePoint. It has an administration landing page on which all the settings reside. It also supports Windows PowerShell to accommodate more advanced administration or make scripting possible, as well. In a default configuration of Excel Services, the service should be secure, ready to use, and should support most workbooks without the administrator needing to do any further configuration.

To go to the administration landing page for Excel Services, perform the following steps:

1. On the Start menu, click Microsoft Office SharePoint Server and then, on the Quick Launch bar, click Central Administration.

    This will load the Central Administration Console, as shown in Figure 6-2.

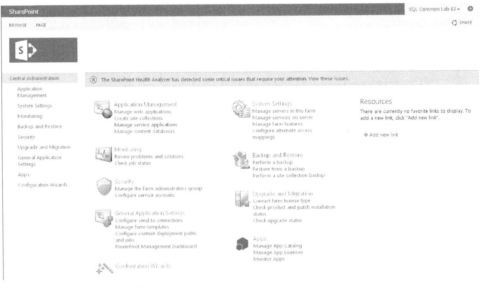

FIGURE 6-2 The Central Administration page.

2. On the Central Administration page, in the Application Management section, click the Manage Service Applications link.

The Service Applications page is the one on which you can manage your service applications. Each service application generally has both a service application and a service application proxy.

With some service applications, you can manage the proxy separate from the service application itself. Excel Services does not. All of the Excel Services management is done from the Service Application page. There is no need to attempt to manage the proxy separately.

Some service applications also support running multiple instances of the service application in the farm. Excel Services is designed to have a single Excel Services application running in the farm. This is because Excel Services only supports working with the default Excel Services proxy of the default proxy group. There are scenarios in which you can have multiple groups defined per web application, but they are beyond the scope of this book. And, for most enterprise deployments, a single Excel Services application is sufficient.

In Figure 6-3, for example, the Excel Services Application Web Service is named ECS Min-Priv. To get to the Excel Services administration page, simply click it.

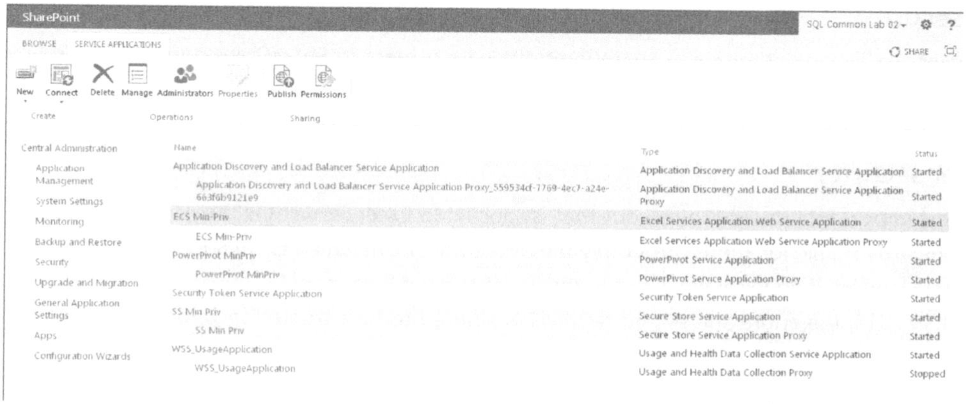

FIGURE 6-3 The Manage Service Applications page.

Figure 6-4 shows the page on which you can configure and manage the major components of Excel Services. Separate pages exist for each set of administrative tasks. Again, things should be generally working for most basic scenarios in a default installation.

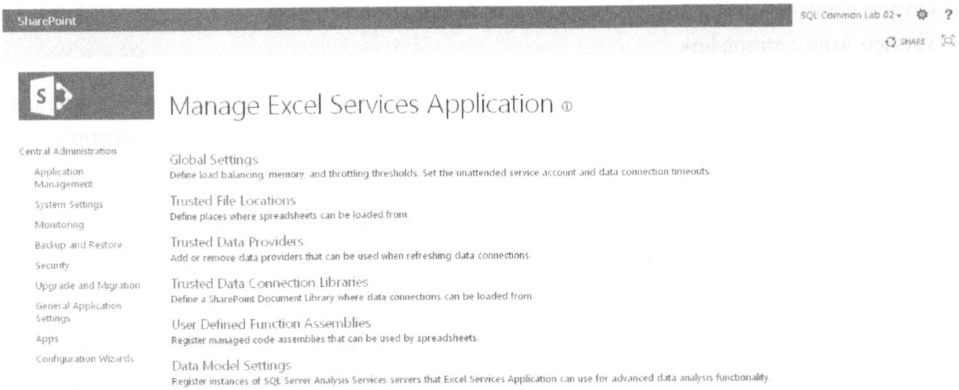

FIGURE 6-4 The Manage Excel Services Application page.

Excel Services security

In this section, you will review a few security topics regarding Excel Services.

File security

Excel files are like any other file in SharePoint; they are subject to SharePoint permissions and security. There is nothing special about them after Excel Services is installed.

Server security

The most important concept to call out that is specific to Excel Services is the notion of trusted file locations. Trusted file locations are simply file directories from which Excel Services will permit Excel files to be loaded. If an Excel file is not in the list of trusted locations, Excel Services will not load it. By default, in 2013, the entire SharePoint farm is considered to be a trusted location. This means that any Excel files from anywhere in SharePoint can be loaded by Excel Services.

When a workbook is loaded on Excel Services, the server forces that workbook to respect settings that are defined for the trusted location from which it was loaded. Trusted locations have many settings available and give the server administrator control over what kinds of operations are allowed and how many server resources can be used by workbooks.

For example, you can define that workbooks loaded from http://portal/teamsiteA cannot be larger than 1 MB and are never allowed to refresh against any data sources. Likewise, workbooks loaded from http://portal/trustedTeamSiteB can load much larger workbooks, up to 20 MB, and are allowed to query data sources.

Note that if workbooks are failing to load or certain operations are failing for those workbooks, one thing to check is that the workbooks are being loaded from a directory that is a trusted location and that the settings for that location permit the types of operations you are trying to perform on the workbook.

To see the trusted location list, go to the Manage Excel Services Application page and click the Trusted File Locations link (see Figure 6-4). Clicking the Trusted File Locations link brings you to a page that lists all locations from which workbooks can be loaded by the Excel Services Application instance, as demonstrated in Figure 6-5.

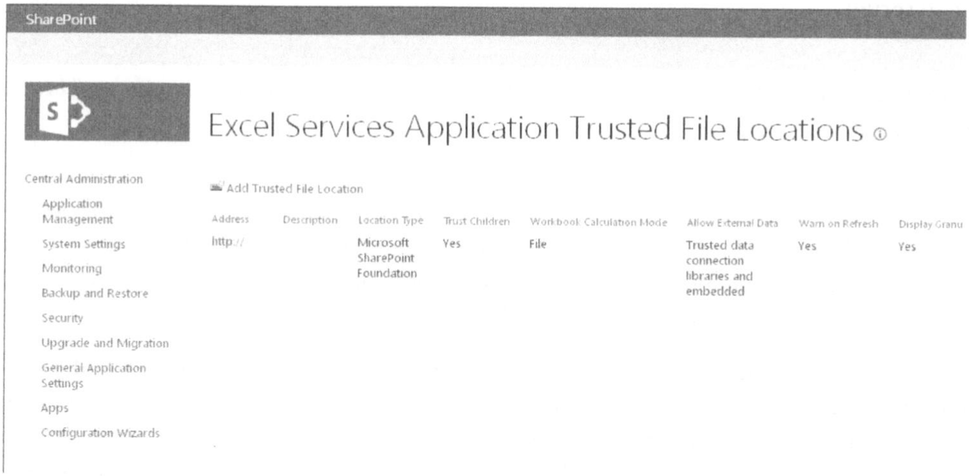

FIGURE 6-5 The Excel Services Trusted File Locations page.

Then, select the trusted location you want to view and click the link to that location. This brings you to a page showing the settings available for that trusted file location, as depicted in Figure 6-6.

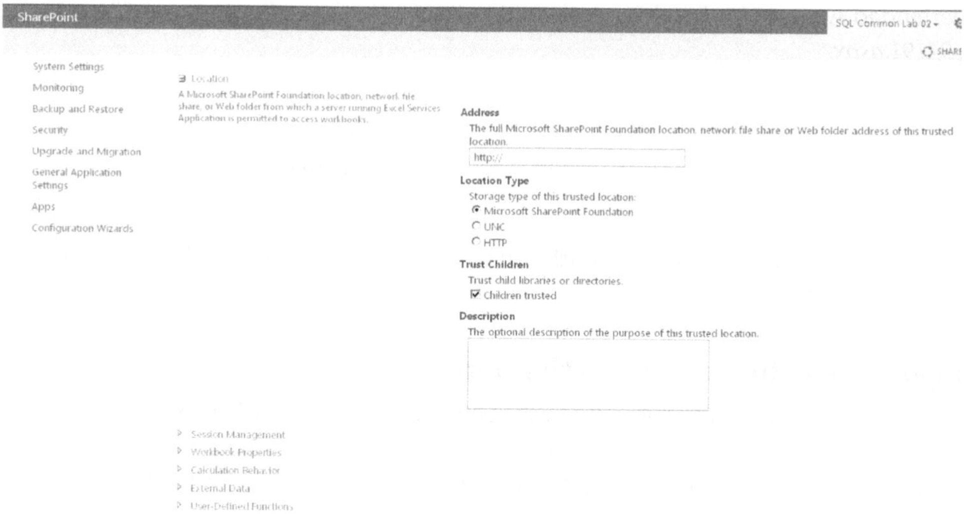

FIGURE 6-6 The configuration page for a trusted file location.

External data configuration

One of the most challenging aspects for administrators is configuring external data for use by Excel Services. Unfortunately, for implementations that aren't single-box, evaluator-style deployments, some amount of configuration is required to make external data connectivity work, especially with regard to security.

 More Info You can read more on this topic at *http://technet.microsoft.com/en-us/library/ hh525341(office.15).aspx.*

This section isn't an exhaustive approach to all external data connectivity. It does, however, provide some simple guidance and links to detailed steps to complete the high-level configuration needed to get going. Also note that much of the configuration work described here can be reused by other service applications such as Visio Services or Performance Point Services.

The simplest way to establish data connectivity on the server is to use a single account to connect to all the data sources. The downside of this is that there won't be any per-user security applied to the data. The single account used for getting data for Excel Services is known as the *Unattended Account*. This is simply a user account that is created for the purpose of read-only access to data sources. The account credentials (user name and password) must be stored in the Secure Store Service (SSS). SSS is another service application, similar to Excel Services, that stores accounts securely.

 More Info You can read an article with details about how to configure SSS and the Unattended Account for Excel Services at *http://technet.microsoft.com/en-us/library/ ff191191.aspx.*

If you want per-user security, the best option is to configure Kerberos in your environment. Kerberos configuration can be complex, and you might not need it if you are satisfied with users having simple read-only access via a single account.

There are other options, as well, by which you can store different credentials used for data refresh for different groups of users.

Configure the authentication in the workbook

In most deployments the workbook author will need to explicitly mark which type of option to use when the file is loaded on Excel Services. If you are using a single-box deployment (and are working from that computer) or you have configured Kerberos, the default settings will suffice and you can skip this section.

To get an existing workbook configured to use the Unattended Account, perform the following procedure:

1. Start the Excel client and open the workbook for which you want to enable data refresh on the server. On the ribbon, click the Data tab. Then, in the Connections group, click the Connections button, as illustrated in Figure 6-7.

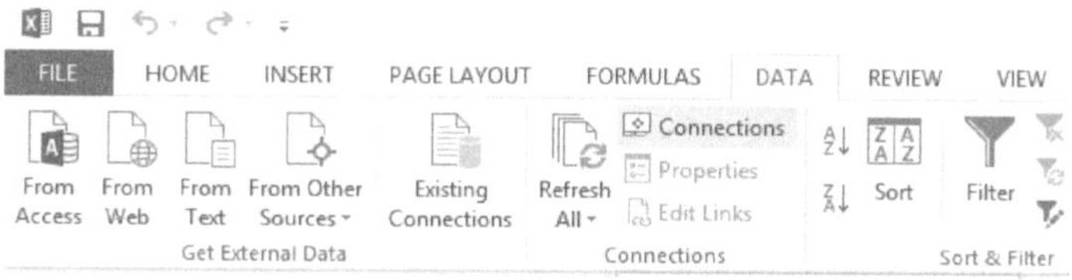

FIGURE 6-7 The Connections option on Excel 2013 Data tab.

The Workbook Connections dialog box opens, as shown in Figure 6-8.

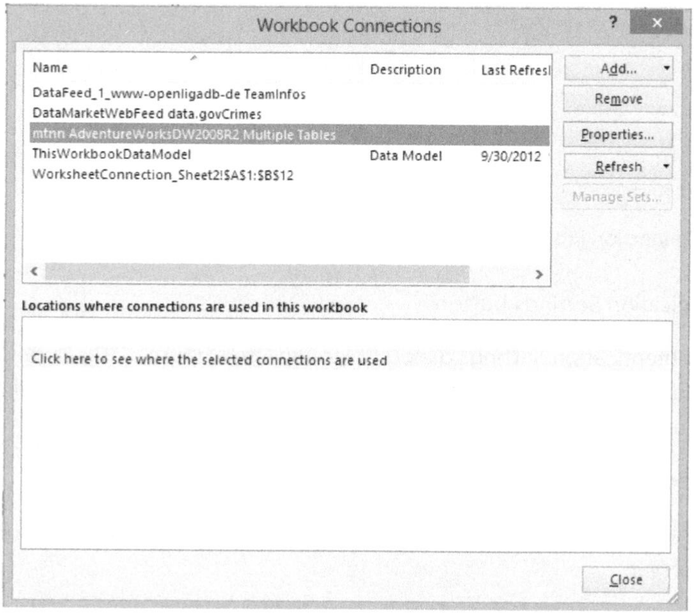

FIGURE 6-8 The Workbook Connections dialog box.

For each connection, you can select the connection and click the Properties button on the left, which opens the Connection Properties dialog box, as illustrated in Figure 6-9.

2. In the Connection Properties dialog box, click the Definition tab.

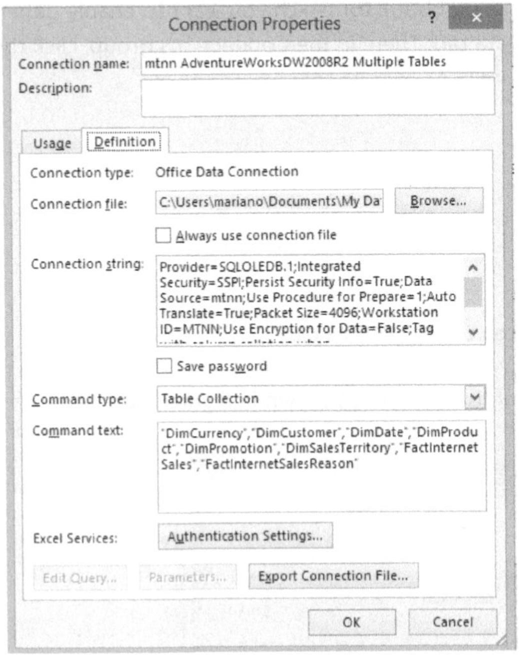

FIGURE 6-9 The Connection Properties dialog box, showing the Definition tab.

3. Click the Authentication Settings button

   Excel Services Authentication Settings dialog box opens (see Figure 6-10), in which you can specify how the data connection should authenticate to be able to connect to the data sources when the workbook is loaded on the server.

4. Choose the correct option based on how your server has been configured.

   In Figure 6-10, the None option has been clicked, which means the Unattended Account will be used on the server.

FIGURE 6-10 The Excel Services Authentication Settings dialog box.

Table 6-2 describes the three options that you can set when the data connection is created; the Authentication Settings button for Excel Services is displayed on the last page of the data connection wizard, for instance.

TABLE 6-2 The authentication settings options

Authentication setting	Description
Use The Authenticated User's Account	This option instructs Excel Services to transform the currently logged-on user's SharePoint security token into a Windows security token. Excel Services uses the Claims to Windows Token Service to carry out the conversion.
Use A Stored Account	This option instructs Excel Services to retrieve the user name and password from a target application in SSS and performs a Windows log on. This target application was previously configured by the SharePoint farm administrator.
None	This is similar to specifying a stored account, except that Excel Services now uses the target application registered under its Unattended Service Account. To specify an Unattended Service Account, in Central Administration, display the Excel Services configuration settings and then, under Global Settings, in the External Data section, register the account credentials. For detailed instructions, see Use Secure Store with SQL Server Authentication (SharePoint Server 2013) at *http://technet.microsoft.com/en-us/library/gg298949(v=office.15).aspx*.

Also note that when someone configures a connection this way, that connection can be shared and reused so that not every user in your organization needs to do this configuration. The best way to do this is to store the .odc connection file to a SharePoint Data Connection library and let your users know to select preconfigured connections from there.

The following links provides more information about external data connectivity and configuration:

- A downloadable document showing more details on configuring Kerberos for Service Applications (like Excel Services) in SharePoint: *http://www.microsoft.com/downloads/en/details.aspx?FamilyID=1a794fb5-77d0-475c-8738-ea04d3de1147&displaylang=en*

- A more basic webpage showing options for configuring Kerberos in SharePoint 2010: *http://technet.microsoft.com/en-us/library/ee806870.aspx*

- Details on how to configure SSS: *http://technet.microsoft.com/en-us/library/ee806866.aspx*

- Specifics of configuring SSS for Excel Services and the Unattended Account: *http://technet.microsoft.com/en-us/library/ff191191.aspx*

Opening an Excel workbook in the browser

In this section, we explore viewing and editing workbooks in the browser.

Viewing workbooks

To use Excel Services, simply navigate to the document library where you saved the file and click the name of the file. Excel Services renders the file in the browser, as demonstrated in Figure 6-11.

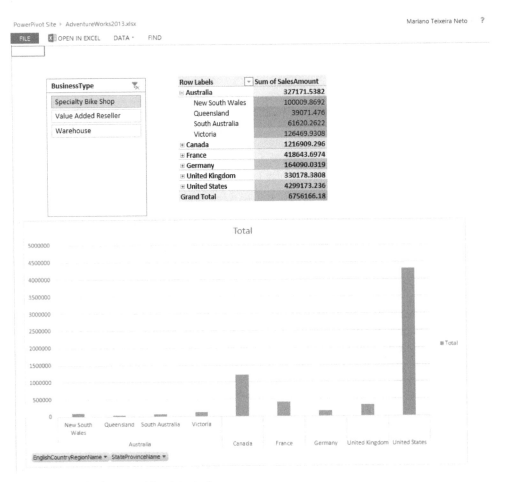

BusinessType 🔽
Specialty Bike Shop
Value Added Reseller
Warehouse

Row Labels 🔽	Sum of SalesAmount
⊟ Australia	327171.5382
New South Wales	100009.8692
Queensland	39071.476
South Australia	61620.2622
Victoria	126469.9308
⊞ Canada	1216909.296
⊞ France	418643.6974
⊞ Germany	164090.0319
⊞ United Kingdom	330178.3808
⊞ United States	4299173.236
Grand Total	6756166.18

FIGURE 6-11 Viewing a workbook in the browser.

Notice the level of visual fidelity that is maintained even though this file is rendered in the browser. Excel Services generally also has complete calculation fidelity (there are some formulas which are deactivated on the server for security reasons because they can expose information about the server environment).

Also note that the workbook is interactive—try interacting with the PivotTable and note that the data refreshes on the server just as it does on the client. Also, try using one of the slicers and note that the entire report is sliced just as it is in Excel client.

Observe that there is a setting to control whether the default click on a document opens the Excel file in the client application or Excel Services. To access it, from the SharePoint document library in the browser, on the ribbon, click the Library tab and then, in the Settings group, click the Library Settings button. On the Library Settings page, click the Advanced Settings link. In the Opening Documents In The Browser section, you can choose whether the document library follows the server policy, opens by using the web browser, or opens by using the client, as shown in Figure 6-12.

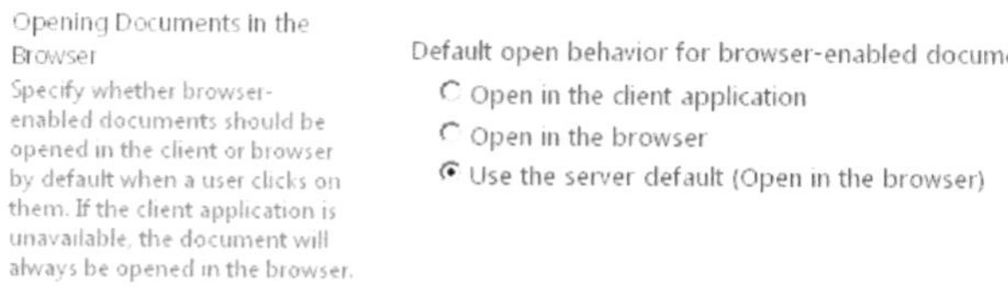

Default open behavior for browser-enabled documents:

- ○ Open in the client application
- ○ Open in the browser
- ◉ Use the server default (Open in the browser)

FIGURE 6-12 Choosing the settings for how to open browser-enabled documents.

Editing workbooks

You can try editing any Excel file that can be viewed in Excel Services. However, editing will only work if you have installed the Office Web Applications product on SharePoint. Without Office Web Applications, you can only edit the PivotTable and PivotChart Fields. Click a PivotTable (or PivotChart) to display the PivotTable Fields, as depicted in Figure 6-13. You can then play around with the available options, which will change the PivotTable and/or PivotCharts.

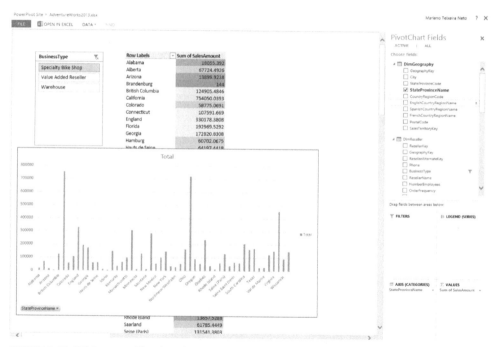

FIGURE 6-13 Editing a workbook in the browser.

Configure a simple Excel dashboard by using Web Parts

Web Parts are logical containers in SharePoint pages that can display content. The Web Part frame-work in SharePoint provides easy drag-and-drop interactivity, settings user interface (UI), and other UI to make configuring pages fairly simple. Web Part pages are generally the backbone of creating a dashboard-like experience in SharePoint. No chapter on BI in Excel Services would be complete without discussing how to use a Web Part to show content from an Excel workbook as part of a SharePoint dashboard.

Create a workbook

The first step is to create a workbook in Excel. You can use the workbook previously created, or you can create any other simple workbook. For this portion, I created a new workbook with the sales amount PivotTable and a simple chart based on that data. After you have created the workbook, save it in the Shared Documents area of the site on which you wish to create the dashboard.

Create the dashboard page

The next step is to create a new page in SharePoint by performing the following procedure:

1. Go to the site that you want to contain your dashboard page. On the Quick Launch bar, click the Site Contents link.

2. At the bottom of the Site Contents page, click the New Subsite link, as illustrated in Figure 6-14.

FIGURE 6-14 The Site Contents page, showing the link to create new subsites.

3. On the Create A Subsite page, type the title and choose the site template (Team Site, for instance), as shown in Figure 6-15.

You must make some choices about the layout of the page, the name of the page, and where the page is stored.

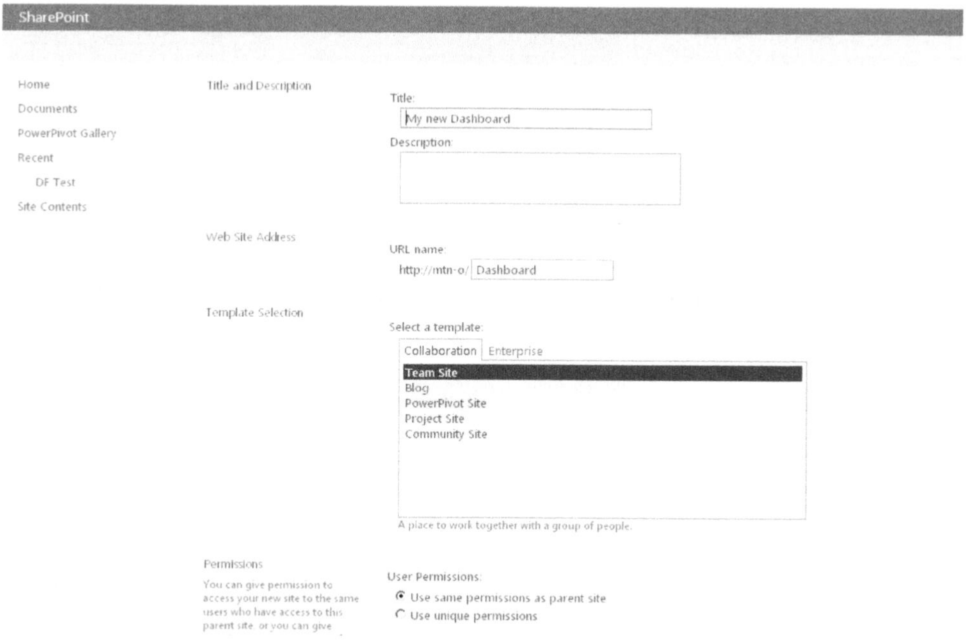

FIGURE 6-15 Creating a new subsite.

In this example, I accepted all the defaults and gave the page the name "My new Dashboard." Feel free to choose different layout options. Each layout option presents different organizations of areas on the page that can contain web parts.

Add the Excel Web Access Web Part

To add a couple of Excel Services Web Parts, perform the following procedure

1. Go to your new dashboard subsite page. In the upper-right corner, to the right of the logged-on user's name, click the Settings button (the small gear icon).

2. On the menu that appears, click Edit Page, as shown in Figure 6-16.

FIGURE 6-16 Editing the page.

The subsite opens in Edit mode, as illustrated in Figure 6-17. The Format Text tab is selected by default.

FIGURE 6-17 The dashboard page in Edit mode.

3. Pick the zone in which you want to insert the Web Part and then, on the ribbon, click the Insert tab.

4. Click the Web Part icon, as shown in Figure 6-18.

This expands the top of the page, from which you can choose the Web Part to add.

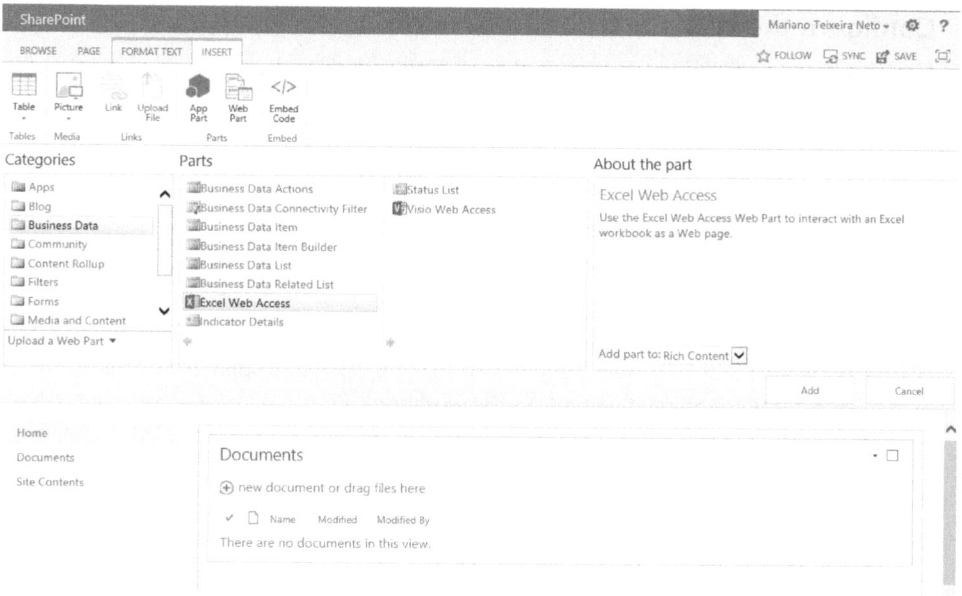

FIGURE 6-18 Inserting an Excel Web Access Web Part.

5. In the Categories pane, click Business Data, choose Excel Web Access from the Parts pane, and then click the Add button to add it to the page in the zone you previously selected.

You should now have an empty Excel Web Access Web Part on the page. This Web Part can be used to load and display Excel workbooks via Excel Services, as illustrated in Figure 6-19.

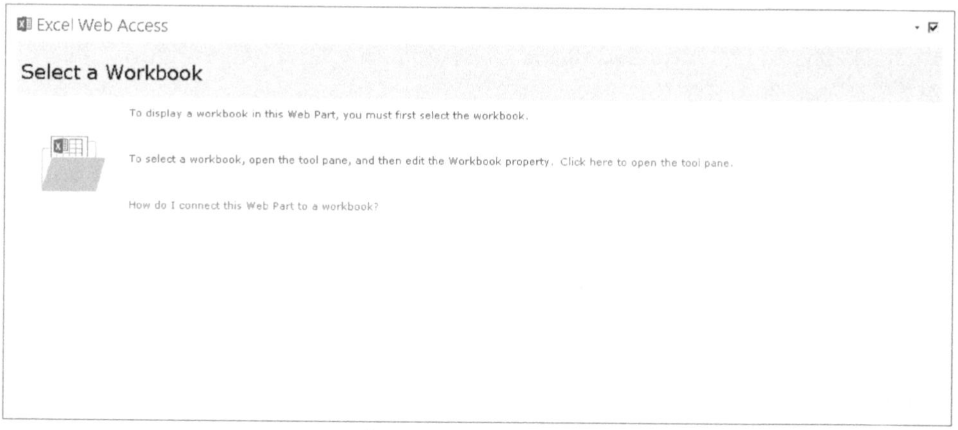

FIGURE 6-19 The Excel Web Access Web Part.

Configure the Web Part

Now, it's time to configure the Web Part to display a workbook.

1. Click the link labeled Click Here To Open The Tool Pane.

   This expands the Tool pane for the Web Part, displaying all the configuration options.

   First, we need to give the Web Part a workbook to display.

2. In the Workbook Display section, click the blue button to browse for a workbook to display.

   A webpage dialog box opens in which you can navigate within SharePoint to pick a workbook. Use that UI to select the workbook you want to display from Shared Documents, or just directly type the relative path to the workbook.

   You should end up with a URL populated to the workbook you want to display, as demonstrated in Figure 6-20.

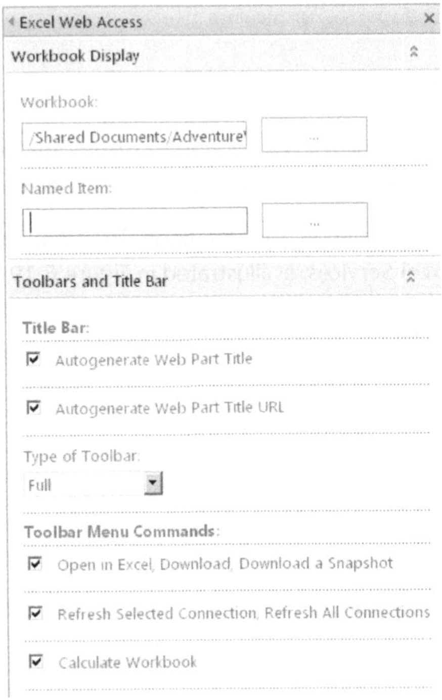

FIGURE 6-20 The Excel Web Access Web Part properties pane.

3. Scroll down to the bottom of the Web Part properties pane and click OK.

   You should now see your workbook displayed in the Web Part, as shown in Figure 6-21.

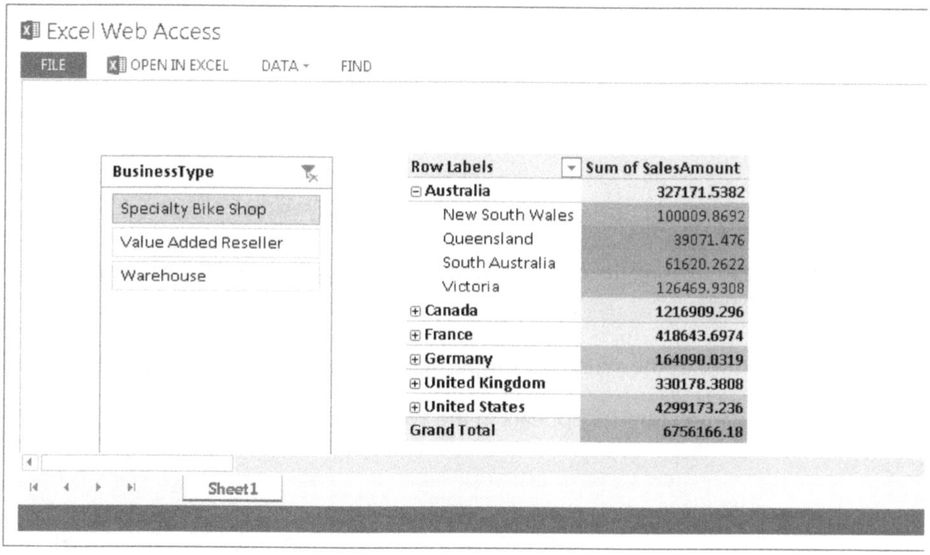

FIGURE 6-21 A workbook in an Excel Web Access Web Part.

Notice how the workbook just looks like an Excel file at this point. You can click the sheet tabs, see the chart, interact with the PivotTable, and so on.

Let's clean up what the Web Part is actually showing and have it shown only the chart.

1. Expand the Web Part properties pane by clicking on the drop-down arrow in the upper-right corner and then, on the menu that appears, clicking Edit Web Part, as shown in Figure 6-22.

FIGURE 6-22 Editing an Excel Web Access web part.

2. In the properties pane, in the Named Item section, type the name of the item that you want to display. In this case, type **Chart 3**, as illustrated in Figure 6-23.

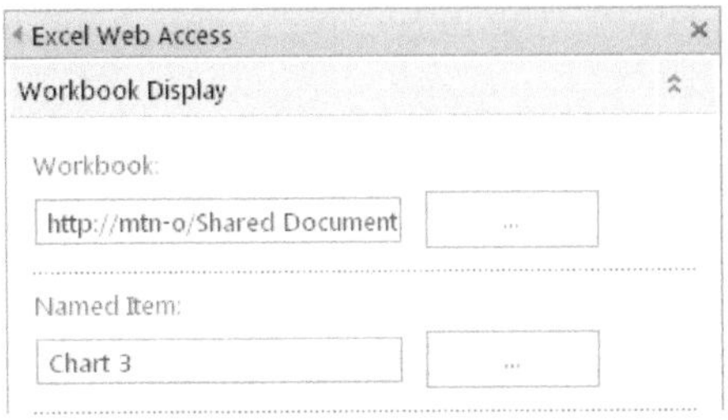

FIGURE 6-23 Choosing the chart named PivotTable2 from the workbook to be displayed in the Excel Web Access web part.

3. At the bottom of the Web Part properties pane, click either OK or Apply.

The chart named Chart 3 appears in the Web Part, as depicted in Figure 6-24.

FIGURE 6-24 The Excel Web Access Web Part displaying a chart.

Note that the Web Part is not displaying this as a spreadsheet; it is displaying each object, one at a time, in the Web Part. If the user viewing the page expands the View drop-down arrow, he will be able to choose any of the other objects in the workbook to display, as shown in Figure 6-25.

FIGURE 6-25 The Excel Web Access named items drop-down menu.

Displaying a single object at a time is known as *Named Item View*. This is typically the view that is used in most Web Parts because most people just want to see the parts of a workbook that are interesting and related in a dashboard. In the publish case, where only certain items were chosen to be displayed, each item is displayed in Named Item View. This is because the workbook author didn't actually choose to display any full sheets. You can read more on publishing to SharePoint at *http://office.microsoft.com/en-us/sharepoint-help/share-workbooks-using-excel-services-HA102772301.aspx*.

So, for the case in which the author only chose to show a set of items from the workbook, the Web Part shows whichever is the first item in the workbook (sorted alphabetically) without the need to specify the name of an item in the Named Item Web Part property. You can always specify which item the Web Part should show via the Named Item property, though.

Set other Web Part properties

Open the Web Part properties pane again. Note that there are many properties that affect how the workbook is displayed. I won't go through all of them here, but there are properties to control settings such as whether the toolbar is shown, what commands are on the toolbar if it is shown, whether the Named Item drop-down list is displayed, as well as what types of interactivity are allowed in the Web Part (sorting, filtering, recalculation, and so on).

For now, let's turn the toolbar off. In the Type Of Toolbar section, choose None from the list. Then, scroll down and expand the Appearance section. Note the presence of some width and height controls. These controls will be used frequently by those adjusting dashboards with many objects on the page to get the right look and feel. You will need to adjust these to make the Web Part fit the Excel content displayed in them in a way that doesn't show unnecessary scrollbars. Now, click OK to close the Web Part properties pane.

Add more Web Parts and finish

Repeat the steps in the previous section but this time set the Named Item to Pivottable1 (this will display the PivotTable you created). In the Excel client, you can see the name of each item on the ribbon for that item. Feel free to add any other Web Parts to the page, as well.

Now, on the ribbon, click the Save button. Until this point, the Web Part page has been shown in Edit mode. This mode shows all the various zones, the drop-down arrows to launch edit menus, editing ribbons, and so on. Clicking Save shows the Web Part page as visitors to the site see it, as demonstrated in Figure 6-26.

In the example from this section, I have two Web Parts on the page: one showing a chart, and the other showing a PivotTable. They both come from the same workbook. However, you might notice that when you drill down on the PivotTable, the chart does not update. This is because each Web Part loads its own copy of the workbook; that is, it gets its own session on the server. Each session is completely separate, and changes from one don't affect the other. This is the reason why there can be a single Web Part page viewed by many users at the same time and an individual user's filters, sorts, drills, and so on are only seen by that user.

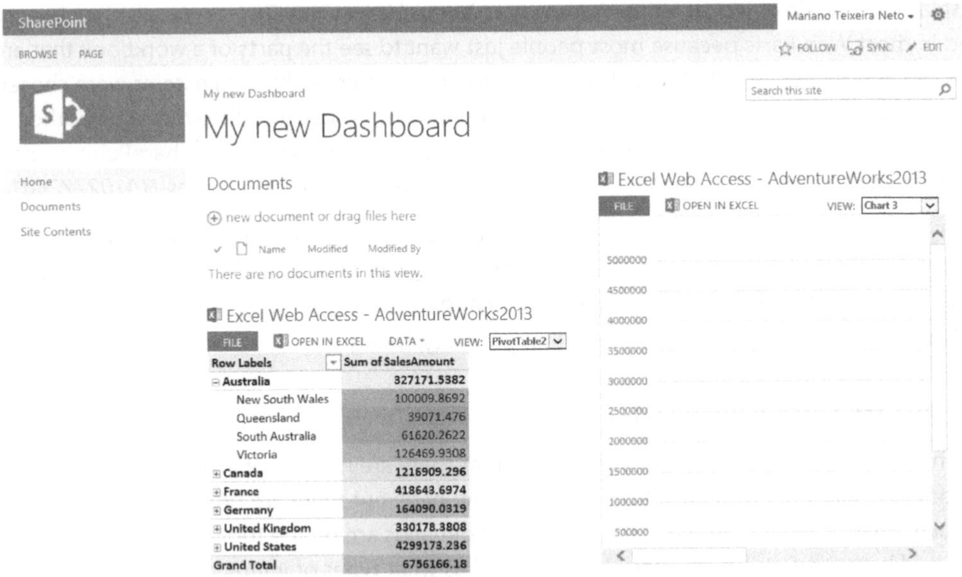

FIGURE 6-26 A page with two Excel Web Access Web Parts.

If you want the Web Parts to interact with one another, you connect them to some other Web Parts on the page, such as one of the SharePoint filter Web Parts. In this case, changing a Web Part that is connected to another Web Part causes both Web Parts to update. Setting up Web Part communication is beyond the scope of this chapter.

Extending Excel Services

As you are designing a BI solution, inevitably you will run into places where the functionality that came with the product isn't enough, and you might want to do something that is custom to your particular needs. This is where extensibility comes in—extending the product into new scenarios and functionality to meet a custom set of scenarios. This section provides a high-level overview of the extensibility mechanisms available for Excel Services. It is not intended to be a one-stop shop for details on any specific extensibility mechanism. Instead, it provides descriptions of what each approach is, when you might want to use it, and then directs you to online references for more information.

There are four primary ways to extend Excel Services: UDFs, Excel Web Services, JavaScript Object Model, and REST. The following subsections provide an overview of each.

UDFs

UDFs are simply managed code assemblies written to perform a specific task, which are deployed to the server. These managed assemblies can be called from a workbook just like any other Excel function. So, they can take a set of parameters from other cells in the workbook and return a single value or an array of values.

UDFs are particularly useful if there are custom, coded, routines you are using to calculate a particular set of values in a particular way. They are also great mechanisms to perform other tasks in the system or in another system. Some examples I have seen of how UDFs have been used include refreshing data from a SharePoint list, writing some custom data values specific to the user viewing the workbook into a data store, retrieving values from a custom data store, performing complex mathematical computations, or parsing data from the web and returning a list of values based on the custom web query.

UDFs aren't a replacement for full Visual Basic for Applications (VBA) solutions or macros; they don't provide any type of object model against a workbook on the server.

 More Info To learn more about UDFs go to *http://msdn.microsoft.com/en-us/library/ ms493934.aspx.*

Excel Web Services

Excel Services provides a SOAP-based web service that allows programmatic access to workbook files loaded on the server. The web service isn't only for use on the "web." You can call it from any application that knows how to call a web service including custom-built client-side applications and other Microsoft applications such as InfoPath.

The web service is a great way to access values from a workbook for cases in which you don't need the Excel UI. With it, you can do things such as set values, recalculate the book, refresh the data, and retrieve the entire workbook or values from certain cells. If the Office Web Applications are installed and Excel Services editing capabilities are enabled, it also allows you to persist values in the workbook.

 More Info To learn more about Excel Web Services, go to *http://msdn.microsoft.com/ en-us/library/ms572330.aspx.*

ECMAScript (JavaScript, JScript) object model

The Excel Services ECMAScript object model is similar to the web services in many ways. It facilitates loading of workbooks, setting values, recalculating and refreshing them, and the ability to retrieve values from the workbook. It also supports a number of things that the web service doesn't, such as displaying the UI and an event model.

It is designed to be run on a page inside a browser as part of a solution where the user is interacting with the core Excel Services UI. It provides events which make it possible for you can programmatically react to things that the user does. For instance, when doing some simple data validation, if a user types in a value that is below 100 in cell A1, you might want to show a pop-up message box with the message, "The value is too low. Enter a value greater than 100." The events that indicate that a cell is being edited or that a value of a cell have changed are fired by Excel Services and your solution can take action on them.

There are also events with which you can determine which cells have been selected. This makes it possible to navigate the Excel Services UI to a different location in the workbook or even have a second window on the page that shows Excel Services UI based on the selection. Solutions with VBA buttons on the first Excel sheet are fairly common. When the user clicks a button on the first sheet, she might be navigated to the correct part of the report. Unfortunately, such solutions don't work on Excel Services, because VBA isn't supported. But, by using the JSOM, such solutions are possible on a webpage.

 More Info To learn more about the Excel Services ECMAScript, go to *http://msdn.microsoft.com/en-us/library/ee556354.aspx*. To learn more about JSON, go to *http://msdn.microsoft.com/en-us/library/bb299886.aspx*.

Excel Services REST

REST is commonly used to retrieve an XML description of a webpage by using only the URL to the webpage. For Excel Services, this means that given a URL to a workbook file, you can access the entire file or parts of the file from anything that knows how to traverse a URL and bring back content.

This is a powerful concept because it makes it possible for users to build effective solutions without actually writing any code. The "code" in this case is just a carefully crafted URL. The URL specifies the path to the workbook, specifies that REST is being used, specifies any values that should be set into certain cells in a workbook, and then specifies what object or values should be retrieved.

REST supports retrieving many types of objects from a workbook (charts, cell values, tables, and so on) and gives you the option to specify what format they should be in (atom, HTML, or an image).

Using REST, it is super simple to embed a chart or table of data based on Excel logic into a blog, webpage, or any other application that can traverse a URL. And, the file itself isn't embedded. The file remains safely stored in SharePoint; Excel Services loads the file, recalculates it to get the latest numbers, and returns only the result to be embedded in the webpage. So, as the file updates, the blog or page gets the latest numbers/image as the page is reloaded.

REST is also a great way to quickly and easily retrieve data from the workbook in atom format for further processing as part of a more advanced solution.

The same concept works for anything that can traverse a URL and bring back data from it, including applications such as Microsoft Word, Microsoft InfoPath, or PowerPoint. Have you ever wondered how to get the Excel chart into a PowerPoint deck and have it refresh dynamically without having to copy the file or embed the full file into PowerPoint? REST is the answer. Leave the file in SharePoint, insert an image into PowerPoint, and then, in PowerPoint, specify that the image is from a Link, provide the REST URL to the chart, and enjoy an image that is refreshed every time the PowerPoint file is opened.

More Info To learn more about the Excel Services REST, go to *http://msdn.microsoft.com/en-us/library/ee556413.aspx*.

Excel Interactive View

Excel Interactive View is a technology that uses HTML, JavaScript, and Excel Services to generate Excel table and chart views on the fly, in the browser, from an HTML table hosted on a webpage. It's a new feature introduced in Excel Services 2013. Using Excel Interactive View, you can take advantage of Excel on any HTML table, on any webpage, in most browsers, without having the Excel client installed. For instance, Figure 6-27 shows a simple HTML table on a webpage.

Item	Movie	Sales Amount
1	New South Wales	100009.8692
2	Queensland	39071.476
3	South Australia	61620.2622
4	Victoria	126469.9308

FIGURE 6-27 A simple HTML table.

It's very simple. To use it, you just need to insert two HTML tags on your webpage. The first tag that you need to insert is a standard HTML <a> tag, which has attributes that you can set to configure the Excel Interactive view.

```
<a href="#" name="MicrosoftExcelButton" data-xl-tableTitle="My interactive view" data-xl-buttonStyle="Standard" data-xl-fileName="Book1" data-xl-attribution="Data provided by My Dashboard" ></a>
```

Just insert the tag above the HTML for the table that has the data that you want to use to create an Excel Interactive View.

The second tag that you need to insert into the HTML of the webpage is a standard HTML <script> tag, which references the JavaScript file that creates the Excel Interactive View.

```
<script type="text/javascript" src="http://r.office.microsoft.com/r/rlidExcelButton?v=1&kip=1"></script>
```

Adding the two HTML tags to the page hosting the table from Figure 6-27 adds a bottom that enables the Excel Interactive View, as shown in Figure 6-28.

Item	Movie	Sales Amount
1	New South Wales	100009.8692
2	Queensland	39071.476
3	South Australia	61620.2622
4	Victoria	126469.9308

FIGURE 6-28 The Excel Interactive View button.

Clicking on the Excel Interactive View button brings you to the Excel Interactive View window, as illustrated in Figure 6-29.

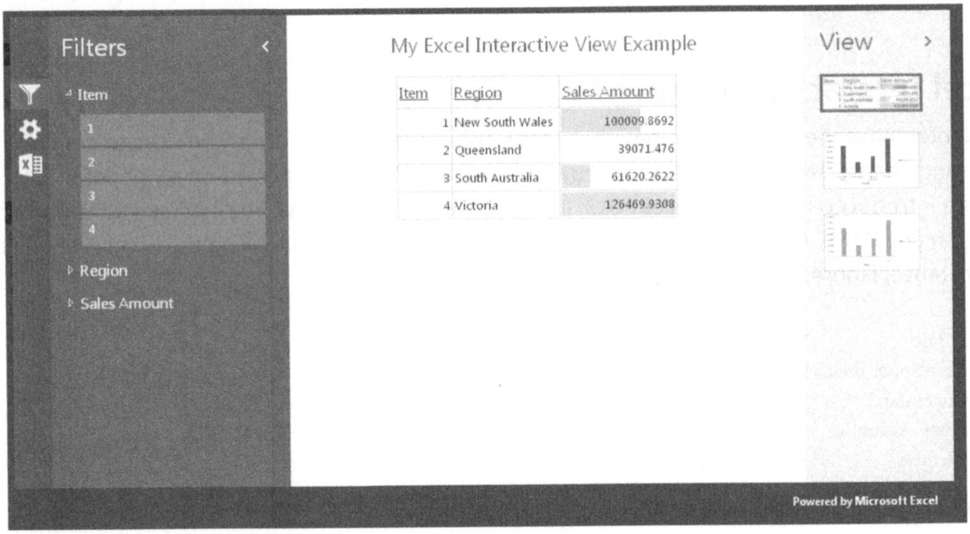

FIGURE 6-29 The Excel Interactive View.

Inside the Excel Interactive View, you have options to filter the view, configure options for the view, open the view in Excel Web App, or download the view as a workbook. In Figure 6-30, for instance, you can change the view to a chart.

More Info You can learn more on Excel Interactive View at *http://msdn.microsoft.com/en-us/library/sharepoint/jj163261(v=office.15).aspx.*

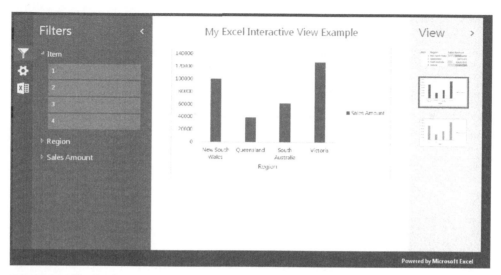

FIGURE 6-30 The Excel Interactive View rendering a chart.

Summary

In this chapter, we reviewed the history of Excel Services 2013 as a BI tool, highlighting its new architecture, introducing the Data Model into the SharePoint environment, and other BI features.

CHAPTER 7

Using PowerPivot for SharePoint 2013

There are many tools that the business user, or the information worker, can reach to, but by far it is Microsoft Excel that is used most often. A great deal of today's business decisions are based on an Excel workbook. However, there are some drawbacks inherent to this approach, and a few caveats must be issued:

- It's fairly common to share those workbooks by email or in a file share. This can potentially raise security issues.

- It's hard to assure that everybody working with a given workbook is using the same version, because access to that workbook is neither monitored nor controlled.

- Refreshing the workbooks with new data can be a lot of work, and potentially, it's a chore that needs to be done frequently.

- Often, the data sources for those workbooks is used without the knowledge IT personnel.

Therefore, a natural yet inevitable mild tension exists between the users (who want to get things done quickly) and the IT department (which wants control). There is nothing wrong with the position of either side. It's just how things are.

To address the needs from the business user's perspective but at the same time not forget about the legitimate concerns of IT, Microsoft developed PowerPivot for Excel, PowerPivot for SharePoint, and Power View. Together, they are Microsoft's core implementation of Self-Service Business Intelligence.

PowerPivot might not solve all the problems, but it is a paradigm-shifter that is bringing business intelligence (BI) to the business analyst. Here are just a few of the benefits that PowerPivot brings to the table:

- **A secure mechanism for sharing the reports**   You can publish the workbook to SharePoint, where it becomes an interactive web application through the Excel Services. Users have to download the workbook; they can open and interact with it in the browser. There is less risk to sensitive data, and when you publish a new version, everyone receives it the next time they visit the site.

- **Scheduled, automatic report refresh**   You can configure the workbooks to be automatically refreshed periodically without human intervention.

- **Transparency for IT**   After the workbook is published to a SharePoint location, everything happens within the realm of IT. IT is able to set the security of the workbooks through Share-Point, learn which data sources are being used by the PowerPivot workbooks, and learn what workbooks are actually being used and by whom. The list goes on and on.

In a few words, PowerPivot for SharePoint 2013 is the integration of the Microsoft SQL Server Analysis Services 2012 SP1 engine with SharePoint 2013. With PowerPivot for SharePoint, the user can securely share, manage, and refresh the workbooks, and IT can securely manage and learn about the workbook's usage.

A brief history

The genesis of PowerPivot derived from two Microsoft internal papers. The first paper was about the concept of a BI *sandbox*, which would be a product that would make the creation of BI applications much easier and in a controlled environment that would include relational databases, multidimensional databases, and a reporting tool. As this first paper gradually shaped PowerPivot from the concept to the product, many of the original ideas changed (originally, Microsoft Access was the client application, not Excel), but many that remained are the soul of PowerPivot.

The second paper was about an in-memory BI engine. The business idea was to take advantage of the market trends in computer hardware (such as decreasing RAM prices, and the increased adoption of multicore processors) that would make an in-memory engine feasible. The in-memory engine described in the second paper would make some of the ideas in the first paper possible.

Both papers were accepted, and a small incubation team was created to explore the concepts further. This incubation team existed during the SQL Server 2008 R2 development wave, writing specifications, plans, code, and tests under the codename *Gemini* for what is now PowerPivot. PowerPivot for Excel 2010 and PowerPivot for SharePoint were released in May, 2010 as part of Microsoft SQL Server 2008 R2.

In the latest release, PowerPivot and Microsoft Office have been drawn into an even closer relationship. As discussed in Chapter 4, "Using PowerPivot in Excel 2013," and Chapter 6, "Business intelligence with Excel Services 2013," PowerPivot and Office are much more integrated. In PowerPivot for SharePoint 2013, there isn't much new exposed functionality, but it was completely redesigned under the hood to make it more reliable and scalable.

When do I use PowerPivot for SharePoint?

After you have created PowerPivot workbooks by using your desktop Excel application, you'll probably want to do the following:

- Refresh workbooks periodically and automatically

- Ensure that all the workbook's users see its most current version

- Turn your workbook into a web BI application, viewing and interacting with it in the browser

- Make your workbook a data source for others

- Have a special SharePoint document library with enhanced functionality and visualization modes, called PowerPivot Gallery

- Empower the IT professionals with tools to assist with the management of the PowerPivot workbooks.

PowerPivot for SharePoint is designed to meet the requirements of all the preceding scenarios, giving you a way to share, refresh, and update workbooks in a secure manner that adheres to IT security policies while providing users with the means to interact with the content of the workbooks from their browsers.

Getting started

This section briefly introduces you to installing PowerPivot for SharePoint 2013.

Installing PowerPivot for SharePoint

An IT professional must perform the installation of PowerPivot for SharePoint because it will require administrative access to servers. It can potentially be a very complex task depending on how your SharePoint farm is configured. Here are a couple of good white papers on how to set up PowerPivot for SharePoint that the IT professionals can review:

- Installing Analysis Services Server in SharePoint Mode for SharePoint 2013:

    http://technet.microsoft.com/en-us/library/jj219067.aspx

- Installing PowerPivot for SharePoint Add-In:

    http://technet.microsoft.com/en-us/library/fe13ce8b-9369-4126-928a-9426f9119424

Publishing to SharePoint

After you create a PowerPivot workbook by using PowerPivot for Excel, you'll likely want to share it with others in your department or organization. Your workbook becomes much more useful when others can use it.

To publish your workbook, perform the following procedure:

1. In Excel, on the ribbon, click the File tab to display the Backstage view.

2. Click the Save As tab, as shown in Figure 7-1.

3. In the Save As section, select Computer and then click the Browse button.

4. Type the URL for the SharePoint site to which you want to upload the workbook and click Save.

If you are publishing to a SharePoint site that has PowerPivot for SharePoint installed, you should publish it to the PowerPivot Gallery. The PowerPivot Gallery is a special PowerPivot-enable SharePoint document library that provides additional functionality beyond what's available in the standard SharePoint 2013 document libraries.

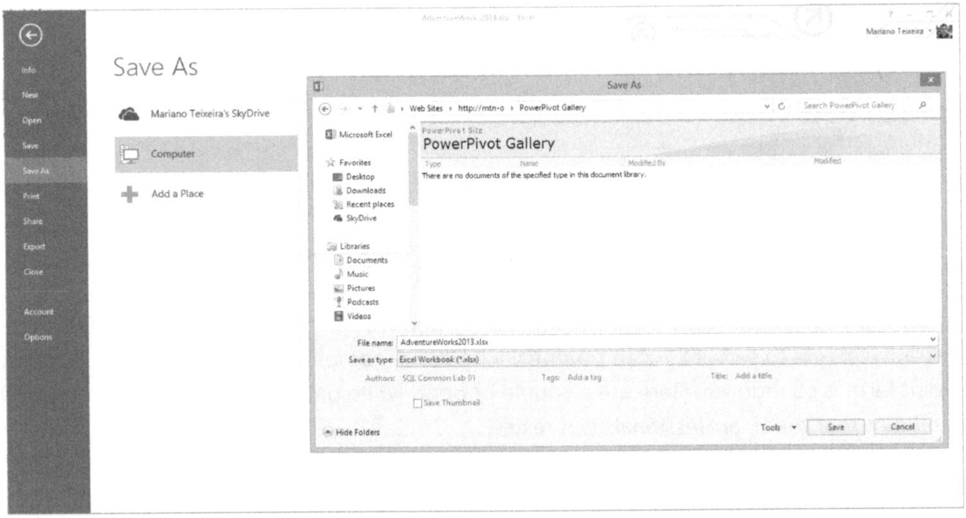

FIGURE 7-1 Publishing a PowerPivot workbook to SharePoint.

The PowerPivot Gallery

The PowerPivot Gallery is a visually rich SharePoint document library that is installed with PowerPivot for SharePoint. Its enhanced visual presentation helps you to better interpret the data in each sheet of a PowerPivot workbook in the Gallery, as demonstrated in Figure 7-2.

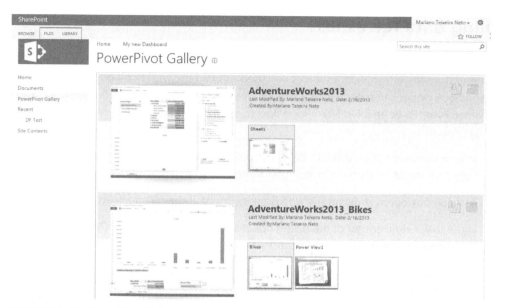

FIGURE 7-2 The PowerPivot Gallery.

Clicking a specific sheet in the PowerPivot workbook opens the workbook in the browser where you can further analyze it, as illustrated in Figure 7-3.

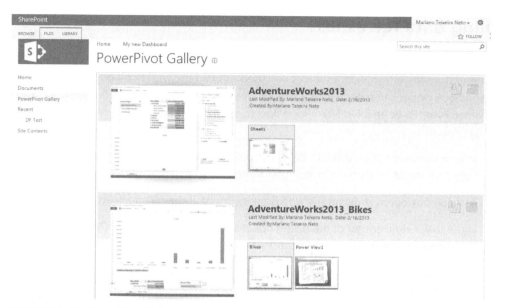

FIGURE 7-3 Analyzing a PowerPivot workbook in the browser.

Scheduling data refreshes

PowerPivot for SharePoint provides a data-refresh feature that can automatically retrieve updated information from the external data sources you used to build the workbook originally. Any Power-Pivot workbook owner can schedule data refresh for workbooks saved to the PowerPivot Gallery or to any other PowerPivot-enabled SharePoint document library. To manage data refresh, perform the following procedure:

1. In your document library, select the workbook for which you want access refresh settings and then click the More Options button (the ellipsis icon).

   A dialog box opens showing the workbook's current authentication settings

2. In the lower-right corner of the dialog box that opens, click the More Options button (again, the ellipsis icon), as depicted in Figure 7-4.

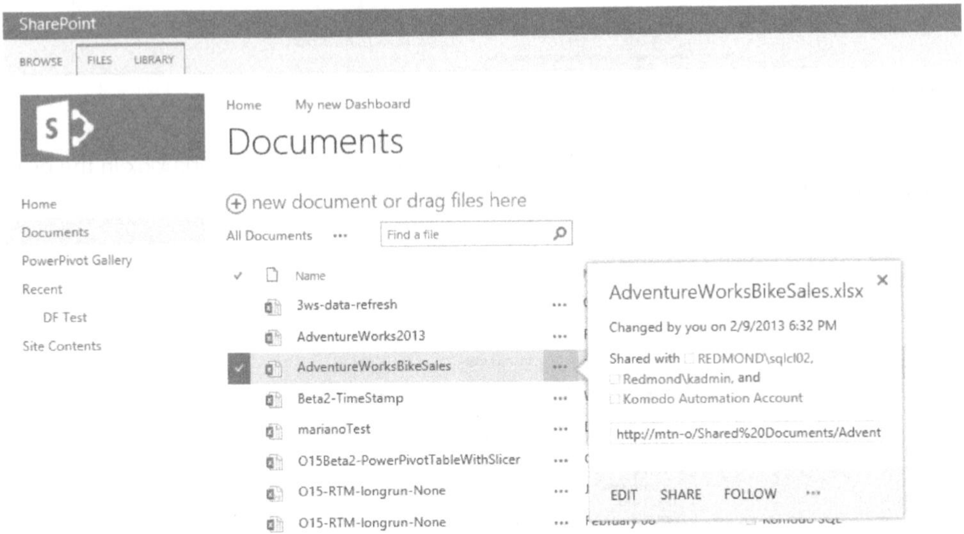

FIGURE 7-4 Accessing the dialog box for a workbook.

3. On the menu that appears, click Manage PowerPivot Data Refresh to schedule a data refresh, as shown in Figure 7-5.

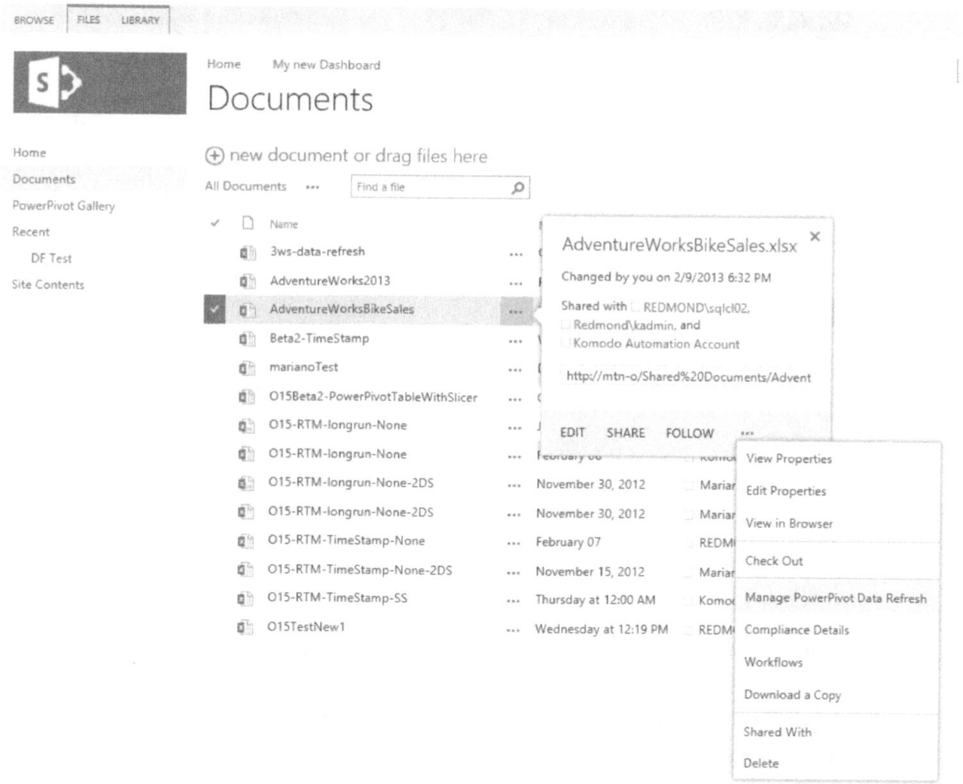

Home   My new Dashboard

Documents

Home

Documents

PowerPivot Gallery

Recent

DF Test

Site Contents

⊕ new document or drag files here

All Documents ··· [Find a file   🔍]

✓	🗋	Name
		3ws-data-refresh
		AdventureWorks2013
✓		AdventureWorksBikeSales
		Beta2-TimeStamp
		marianoTest
		O15Beta2-PowerPivotTableWithSlicer
		O15-RTM-longrun-None
		O15-RTM-longrun-None
		O15-RTM-longrun-None-2DS
		O15-RTM-longrun-None-2DS
		O15-RTM-TimeStamp-None
		O15-RTM-TimeStamp-None-2DS
		O15-RTM-TimeStamp-SS
		O15TestNew1

AdventureWorksBikeSales.xlsx ✕

Changed by you on 2/9/2013 6:32 PM

Shared with   REDMOND\sqlci02,
    Redmond\kadmin, and
    Komodo Automation Account

http://mtn-o/Shared%20Documents/Advent

EDIT   SHARE   FOLLOW   ···

View Properties

Edit Properties

View in Browser

Check Out

Manage PowerPivot Data Refresh

Compliance Details

Workflows

Download a Copy

Shared With

Delete

FIGURE 7-5 Click Manage PowerPivot Data Refresh on the menu.

PowerPivot Gallery offers another way to get to the data refresh feature. To schedule a data refresh through the PowerPivot Gallery, SharePoint users who have Contributor permission can click the Calendar icon shown for each workbook in a PowerPivot Gallery (see Figure 7-6). Note that if the user does not have sufficient privileges on the workbook, the Calendar icon is not available on the page.

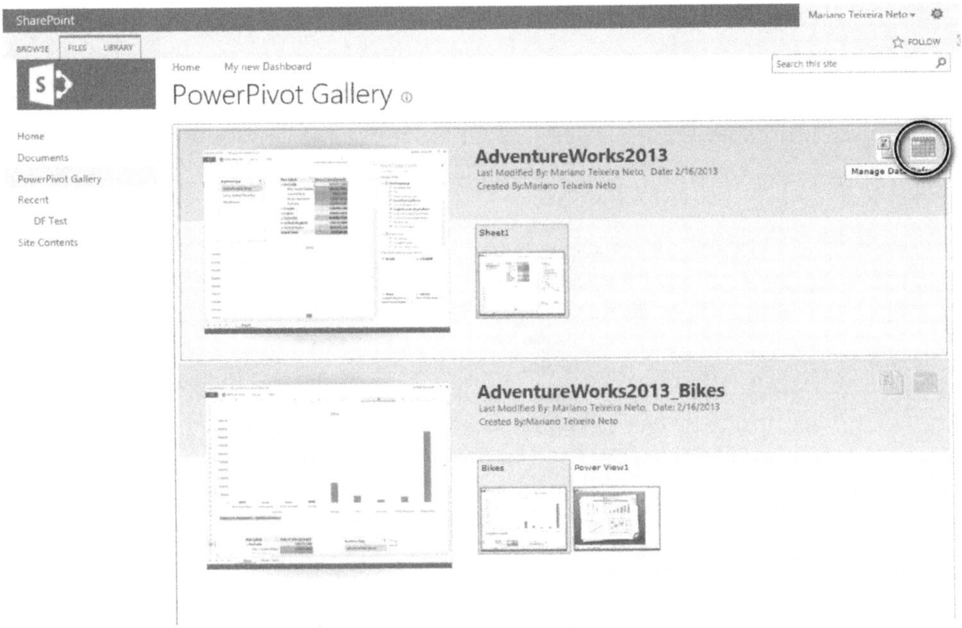

FIGURE 7-6 Accessing PowerPivot Data Refresh from a PowerPivot Gallery by using the Calendar icon.

Regardless of how you get to the Manage Data Refresh page, the details on it are the same. Figure 7-7 shows the initial view of the page.

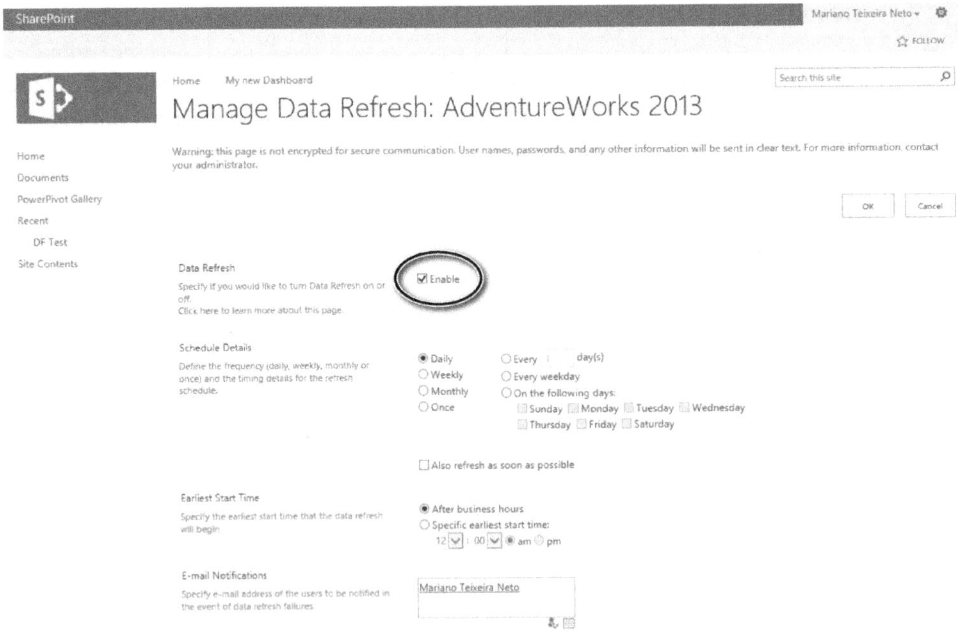

FIGURE 7-7 Enabling Data Refresh in the Manage Data Refresh page.

4. Select the Enable check box to make the page active so that you can fill in the values that you want to use.

The Manage Data Refresh page is organized into six sections. Table 7-1 presents an overview of each section, and detailed descriptions are given in the subsections that follow.

TABLE 7-1 Manage Data Refresh page sections

Section	General description
Data Refresh	Enable or disable a data refresh schedule.
Schedule Details	Define the frequency and timing details of a data refresh.
Earliest Start Time	Specify the earliest start time for a data refresh.
E-mail Notifications	Specify the e-mail address of the users to be notified in the event of data refresh failures.
Credentials	Provide the credentials that will be used to refresh data on your behalf.
Data Sources	Select which data sources should be automatically refreshed. You also use this section to create custom schedules that vary for each data source, or specify different authentication methods for each data source.

Data Refresh

To enable or disable a data refresh schedule, select or clear the Enable check box on the Manage Data Refresh page. If this check box is selected, you can edit all parts of the data refresh schedule. If the check box is cleared, the page is read-only, and after you click OK, subsequent data refresh operations are disabled for that workbook.

Schedule Details

In the Schedule Details section, you can specify the frequency and timing details of the data refresh. There are four options from which to choose:

- Daily
- Weekly
- Monthly
- Once

With the Daily option (see Figure 7-8), you can schedule data refresh to occur every *n* day(s), every weekday, or on specific days of the week.

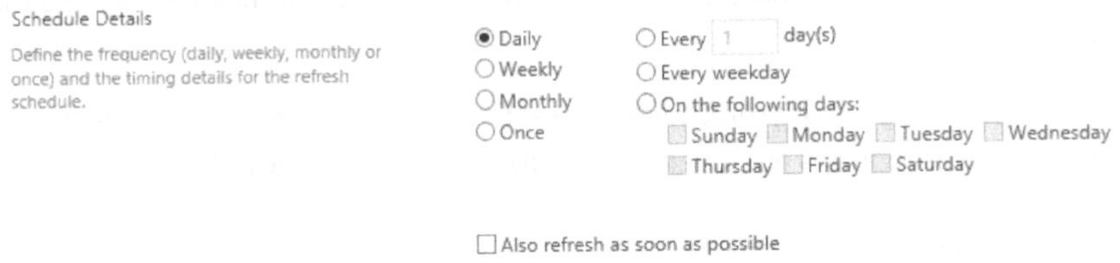

FIGURE 7-8 Daily schedule details options.

If you select the Also Refresh As Soon As Possible check box, data is refreshed as soon as the server can process it. This refresh occurs in addition to the periodic data refresh schedule. This option is available for periodic schedules only (that is, daily, weekly, and monthly schedules). Select this check box if you want to verify that the data refresh will run properly. For example, you might not know whether data credentials are configured correctly. This option provides a way to test the data refresh before its scheduled execution time. In short, checking the Also Refresh As Soon As Possible option refreshes the workbook as soon as possible one time, and then it is refreshed following your periodic schedule specification.

The Weekly option (see Figure 7-9) is for scheduling data refresh on a weekly basis such as every *n* week(s) or on specific days of the week.

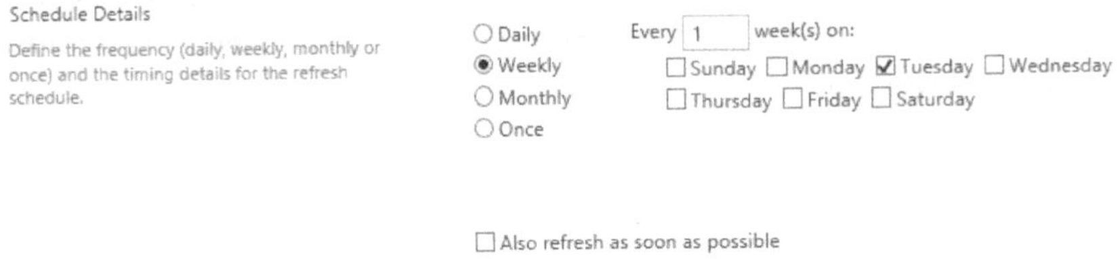

FIGURE 7-9 The Weekly schedule details options.

The Monthly option (see Figure 7-10) schedules data refresh to run on a specific day of the month or on the first, second, third or last specific day of the week every *n* month(s).

FIGURE 7-10 The Monthly schedule details options.

The Once option (see Figure 7-11) is for scheduling a one-time data refresh operation that runs as soon as the server can process the request. After the data refresh is complete, the system disables this schedule. Notice that the Also Refresh As Soon As Possible check box is not available when this option is selected.

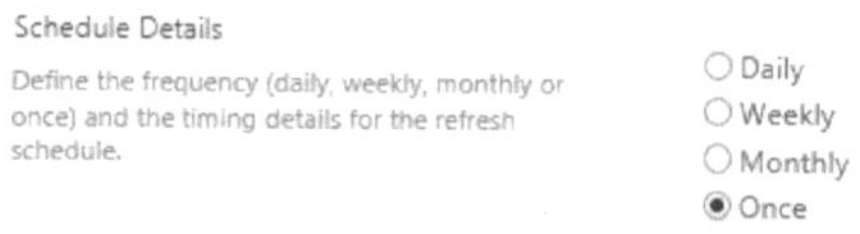

Schedule Details

Define the frequency (daily, weekly, monthly or once) and the timing details for the refresh schedule.

○ Daily
○ Weekly
○ Monthly
◉ Once

FIGURE 7-11 The Once schedule details option.

Earliest Start Time

In the Earliest Start Time section, you specify details regarding when you prefer data refresh to occur (Figure 7-12). You can enter a specific time before which data refresh should not commence, or you can choose to refresh data after business hours. This page does not determine the time at which the data refresh actually starts; instead, the schedule is queued and processed based on available resources. For example, if the server is busy with on-demand queries (which take precedence over data refresh jobs), the server waits to refresh your data until those queries have been processed. You can also choose to run a data-refresh operation after business hours. The administrator of the Power-Pivot Service Application for your organization determines the definition of "business hours."

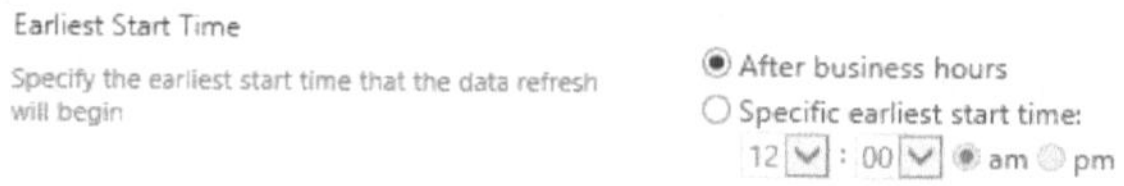

Earliest Start Time

Specify the earliest start time that the data refresh will begin

◉ After business hours
○ Specific earliest start time:
   12 ▾ : 00 ▾ ◉ am ○ pm

FIGURE 7-12 The Earliest Start Time section on the Manage Data Refresh page.

E-mail Notifications

In this section of the Manage Data Refresh page, you can specify email addresses for individuals or groups who should be notified when a data refresh fails (Figure 7-13). You can receive notifications of successful data-refresh operations through the regular SharePoint alerting system for email notification. (The basis of the alert would be a new file added to the target document library.)

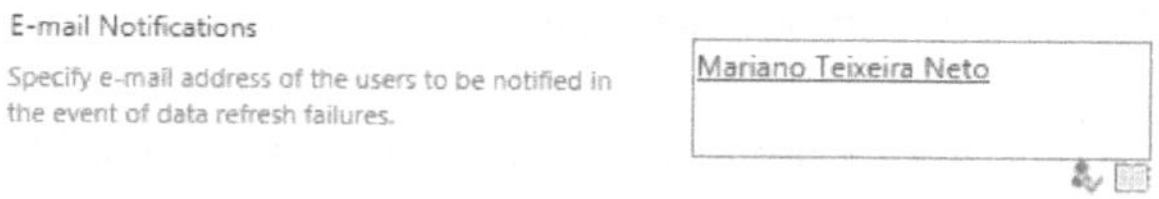

E-mail Notifications

Specify e-mail address of the users to be notified in the event of data refresh failures.

Mariano Teixeira Neto

FIGURE 7-13 The E-mail Notifications section on the Manage Data Refresh page.

Credentials

PowerPivot for SharePoint uses the SharePoint Secure Store Service (SSS) to store any credentials used in data refresh. In the Credentials section of the schedule page, the schedule owner can specify the Windows credentials that are used to refresh data on his behalf. Any data source that uses trusted or integrated security is refreshed by using these credentials. For the data refresh to succeed, the selected credentials must have access to the data sources for the workbook. You can choose from one of the following options (see also Figure 7-14):

■ Use the data refresh account configured by the administrator (this is the service application's unattended data refresh account)

■ Use a specific Windows user name and password

■ Use a predefined SSS target application ID that stores the Windows credentials that you want to use

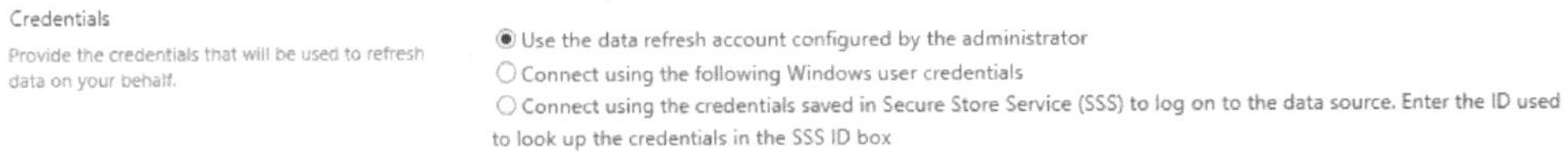

Credentials

Provide the credentials that will be used to refresh data on your behalf.

◉ Use the data refresh account configured by the administrator
○ Connect using the following Windows user credentials
○ Connect using the credentials saved in Secure Store Service (SSS) to log on to the data source. Enter the ID used to look up the credentials in the SSS ID box

FIGURE 7-14 The Credentials options on the Manage Data Refresh page—specifying an account configured by the administrator.

Both the PowerPivot data refresh account and the predefined SSS target application ID must be set up by a SharePoint administrator in Central Administration. Because these credentials are shared among all users, for instance, this option is typically used where additional credentials would be actually used for data access.

A schedule owner can also choose to type the Windows user credentials to be used on the data refresh, as illustrated in Figure 7-15. These credentials are securely stored in the SharePoint SSS.

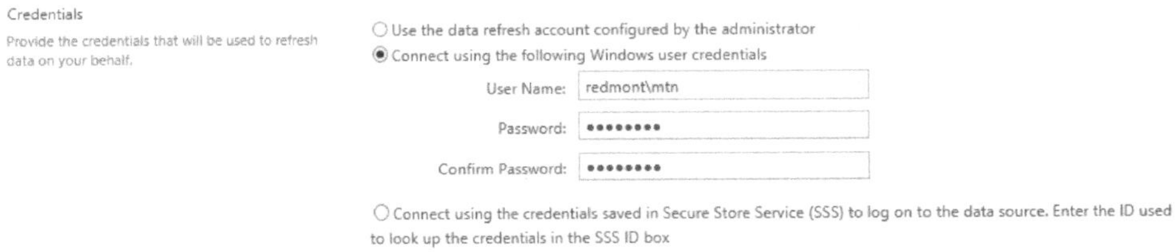

Credentials

Provide the credentials that will be used to refresh data on your behalf.

○ Use the data refresh account configured by the administrator
◉ Connect using the following Windows user credentials

User Name: redmont\mtn
Password: ••••••••
Confirm Password: ••••••••

○ Connect using the credentials saved in Secure Store Service (SSS) to log on to the data source. Enter the ID used to look up the credentials in the SSS ID box

FIGURE 7-15 The Credentials options on the Manage Data Refresh page—specifying Windows user credentials.

With the third option (see Figure 7-16), a schedule owner can specify credentials previously saved in a SSS Target Application ID. To use this option, you must enter the Target Application ID used to look up the credentials in the SSS. The Target Application ID specified must be a group entry, and both the interactive user and the PowerPivot System service account must have read access.

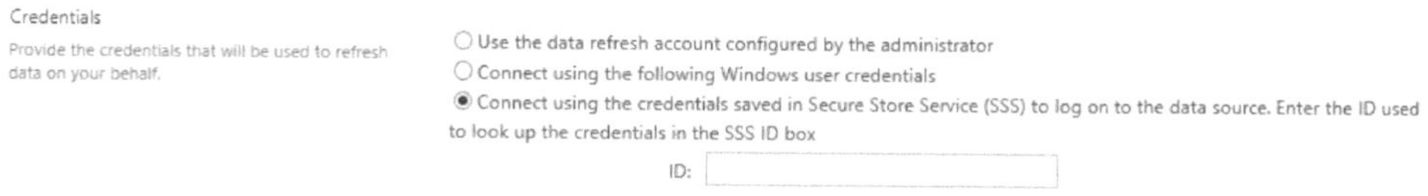

Credentials

Provide the credentials that will be used to refresh data on your behalf.

○ Use the data refresh account configured by the administrator
○ Connect using the following Windows user credentials
◉ Connect using the credentials saved in Secure Store Service (SSS) to log on to the data source. Enter the ID used to look up the credentials in the SSS ID box

ID: [   ]

FIGURE 7-16 The Credentials options on the Manage Data Refresh page—specifying a Target Application ID.

> **Note** Setting up and maintaining SSS is beyond the scope of this book. For more information about it, read the TechNet article at *http://technet.microsoft.com/en-us/library/ee806866.aspx*.

Data Sources

A workbook can have many data sources, each with different characteristics. Figure 7-17 shows that you can choose to create a data refresh schedule by using different settings for each data source, or even disable the data refresh for it (by clearing its corresponding check box). You can have, for instance, one data source scheduled to refresh daily and a second source scheduled monthly.

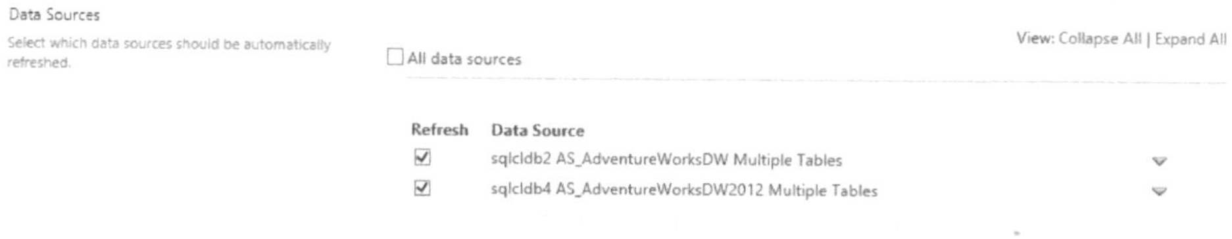

Data Sources

Select which data sources should be automatically refreshed.

☐ All data sources

View: Collapse All | Expand All

Refresh	Data Source	
☑	sqlcldb2 AS_AdventureWorksDW Multiple Tables	⌄
☑	sqlcldb4 AS_AdventureWorksDW2012 Multiple Tables	⌄

FIGURE 7-17 The Data Sources section on the Manage Data Refresh page.

The schedule definition page provides options for choosing the data sources to be refreshed, when to refresh them, and which security options to use for each one. It also provides fields for specifying database credentials or other non-Windows credentials used on the database connection.

You must select at least one data source to save the schedule. The data source's credentials are not used for impersonation but are instead included on the connection string as *UserName* and *Password*. These credentials override those used on the connection string for the original data import.

Figure 7-18 shows that different settings are available for each data source. You can specify a custom schedule data source or use the general schedule specified for the workbook.

> **Note** The only modifiable elements in the connection string are the UserName and Password elements. To edit any of the other elements—for example, to change the source server name—you must download the workbook to your desktop, edit it in Excel 2013, and then republish it to SharePoint.

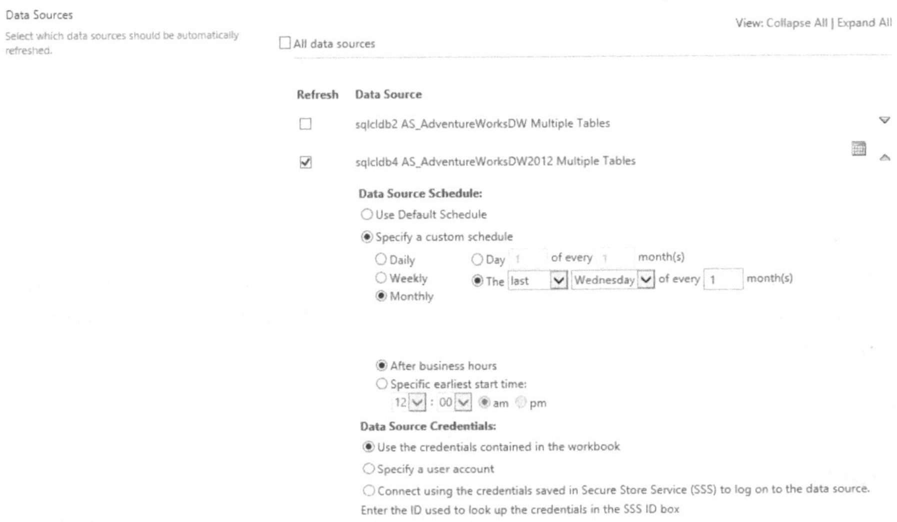
Data Sources
Select which data sources should be automatically refreshed.
View: Collapse All | Expand All
All data sources
Refresh
Data Source
sqlcldb2 AS_AdventureWorksDW Multiple Tables
sqlcldb4 AS_AdventureWorksDW2012 Multiple Tables
Data Source Schedule:
Use Default Schedule
Specify a custom schedule
Daily
Weekly
Monthly
Day
of every
month(s)
The
last
Wednesday
of every
1
month(s)
After business hours
Specific earliest start time:
12
00
am
pm
Data Source Credentials:
Use the credentials contained in the workbook
Specify a user account
Connect using the credentials saved in Secure Store Service (SSS) to log on to the data source.
Enter the ID used to look up the credentials in the SSS ID box

FIGURE 7-18 The Data Sources section, showing schedule and credential details for a data source.

Workbooks as a data source

You can use a workbook hosted in a SharePoint site only if you install PowerPivot for SharePoint 2013. With this feature, you can designate your workbook as a data source for others. For instance, you can create an Excel 2013 workbook (or other tools like Power View, Panorama, ProClarity, and so on) that uses another Excel 2013 workbook that is hosted in SharePoint 2013 with PowerPivot for SharePoint. In the Data Connection Wizard, in the Server Name text box, provide the URL for the workbook in SharePoint, as demonstrated in the Figure 7-19.

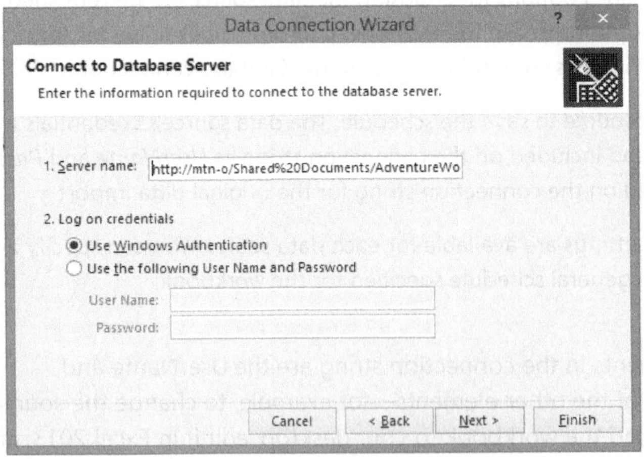
Data Connection Wizard
Connect to Database Server
Enter the information required to connect to the database server.
1. Server name:
http://mtn-o/Shared%20Documents/AdventureWo
2. Log on credentials
Use Windows Authentication
Use the following User Name and Password
User Name:
Password:
Cancel
< Back
Next >
Finish

FIGURE 7-19 Using a workbook as a data source.

In the Log On Credentials section, choose the authentication method (in the example, we use Windows Authentication) and then click Next. On the Select Database And Table page of the wizard, the workbook is shown as a Model of type Cube, as illustrated in Figure 7-20.

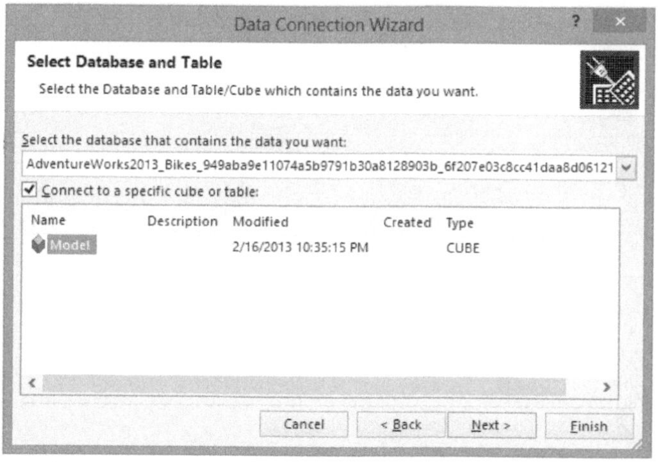

FIGURE 7-20 Selecting the data model from the workbook.

The actions to complete creating a connection to a data source are no different from the actions described in Chapter 4, in the section "Creating the Data Model" (see also Figure 4-5).

Monitoring with PowerPivot for SharePoint

The PowerPivot Management Dashboard provides administrators who are responsible for the server side of PowerPivot with the capabilities they need to understand usage patterns of the PowerPivot workbooks in SharePoint and to take appropriate actions. For example, the growing size of a particular workbook might indicate the need to acquire more memory. You can access the PowerPivot Management Dashboard by going to the SharePoint Central Administration page and then clicking General Application Settings, as depicted in the Figure 7-21.

> **Note** To view some of the Dashboard controls, you need Silverlight installed on the computer on which you are browsing. If you do not have it installed, your browser should prompt you to install it from the web.

FIGURE 7-21 Accessing the PowerPivot Management Dashboard.

Clicking the PowerPivot Management Dashboard link takes you to the Dashboard page, as shown in Figure 7-22.

The PowerPivot Management Dashboard can be broken down into five main areas (Web Parts) Table 7-2 presents an overview of each area, and detailed descriptions are given in the subsections that follow.

TABLE 7-2 The PowerPivot Management Dashboard main areas

Web Part	Description
Infrastructure – Server Health	This section provides information about infrastructure; it shows the CPU and memory usage trends over time. It also contains a histogram of overall query response for the SQL Server Analysis Services in SharePoint mode.
Workbook Activity	This section provides a high-level representation of the number of users, the number of queries sent to a workbook, and the size of the workbook in time.
Actions	An administrator can use this section to configure PowerPivot-specific settings within a SharePoint farm.
Data Refresh	This section provides a breakdown of the recent activities and recent failures for PowerPivot data refresh in SharePoint.
Reports	An administrator can use this section to view the source Excel workbooks and databases used by the PowerPivot Management Dashboard

FIGURE 7-22 The PowerPivot Management Dashboard.

Infrastructure – Server Health

This section of the PowerPivot Management Dashboard provides indicators of the server's health. It does so through the following indicators:

- Query Response Times

- Average Instance CPU

- Average Instance Memory

- Activity

- Performance

Query Response Times

The Query Response Times view is the default view of the Server Health Web Part (see Figure 7-23). The purpose of this chart is to provide a quick overview so that you can determine whether the majority of the queries are running as expected or running too slowly.

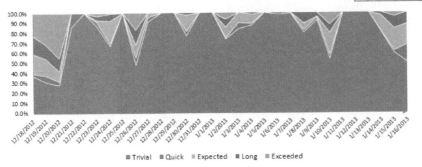

■ Trivial   ■ Quick   ■ Expected   ■ Long   ■ Exceeded

FIGURE 7-23 The Query Response Times view.

When query response time increases, you will want to determine which queries are running slowly, and why.

Table 7-3 summarizes the default query response time definitions. These definitions can be modified by selecting Central Administration | General Application Settings | PowerPivot | Configure Service Application Settings.

TABLE 7-3 Query Response Times category definitions

Category	Definition (in milliseconds)
Trivial	0 < time < 500
Quick	500 < time < 1000
Expected	1000 < time < 3000
Long	3000 < time < 10000
Exceeded	≥10000

Average Instance CPU

Switching to the Average Instance CPU view (see Figure 7-24) in the Server Health Web Part shows the CPU load on the SharePoint Application Server on which PowerPivot is installed.

Figure 7-24 shows that for that SharePoint Application Server, the CPU load is not an issue because, on average, it uses less than 30 percent of the CPU capacity.

Infrastructure - Server Health

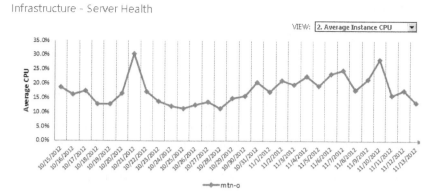

FIGURE 7-24 The Average Instance CPU view.

Average Instance Memory

Memory can become a concern for your environment because the Analysis Services in SharePoint Mode loads the workbook in memory. As the number of users and the size of their workbooks grow, they require an increasing portion of the server's memory. Taking a quick look at the Average Instance Memory view, you can easily see when more memory is being used over time, as demonstrated in Figure 7-25.

Infrastructure - Server Health

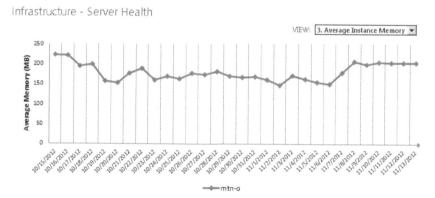

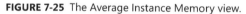

FIGURE 7-25 The Average Instance Memory view.

Activity and Performance

Although you can toggle between the Infrastructure – Server Health Activity and Performance views, you can get an even better view of this data by using the Workbook Activity And Server Health reports directly. To do that, click in either the Workbook Activity or the Server Health workbook located in the Reports area of the PowerPivot Management Dashboard (refer to Figure 7-22).

Workbook Activity

This area comprises two parts: a Chart and a List.

Chart

This Chart Web Part is a Silverlight control that displays a bubble chart. Figure 7-26 shows that the chart's axes represent the number of users and the number of queries sent to a workbook. A sliding bar indicates the date. As you move the pointer over each bubble, the name of the workbook it corresponds to and the number of users that are connected are displayed, along with the number of queries sent to the workbook. In addition, as you move the date sliding bar, it shows animation on bubble size, which represents how the size of the workbook is growing over time.

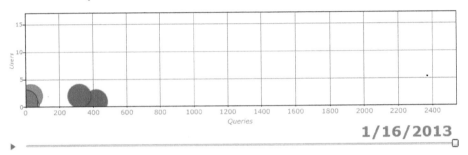

FIGURE 7-26 The Workbook Activity – Chart.

List

The Workbook Activity – List section provides a quick way to view the current activity attributes (workbook name, number of queries, users, and size) of the server, as demonstrated in Figure 7-27.

Workbook Activity - List

Workbook	Users↓	Queries	Size (Mb)
bugbashwb.xlsx	16	3076	18070.75
bugbashwb - Test.xlsx	5	93	11868.00
CLASS_DEMO_Power_View.xlsx	5	755	7506.00
Last30Days.xlsx	4	668	1817439.85
dbmodel.xlsx	4	1387	1452190.43
PPivotWorkbook_ScrumReport_Draft.xlsx	4	86	1416.00
Contoso Retail Workbook.xlsx	4	184	162234.00
Random Test Selection Probabilities Report.xlsx	4	729	312.00
Last30Days0.2.1.xlsx	3	0	30702.00
Last30Days0.2.xlsx	3	0	1818278.84

1 2

FIGURE 7-27 The Workbook Activity – List.

Data Refresh

The PowerPivot scheduled data-refresh mechanism has many activities that run in the background. In the PowerPivot Management Dashboard, you can find a section dedicated to reporting the recent data refresh–related activities in the environment.

Recent Activity

As the name suggests, this Web Part informs the data-refresh activity in this environment. It reports the most recent PowerPivot workbook data refreshes along with the time that it completed the refresh and its duration, as shown in Figure 7-28.

Data Refresh - Recent Activity

	Workbook	End Time	Duration (seconds)
✓	http://picassoapps/Shared%20Documents/AdventureWorks2013_Bikes2.xlsx	2/16/2013 11:16:37 PM	37
!	http://picassoapps/Shared%20Documents/AdventureWorks2013_Bikes.xlsx	2/16/2013 11:11:02 PM	2
!	http://picassoapps/Shared%20Documents/CityCrime.xlsx	2/16/2013 8:01:02 PM	0
!	http://picassoapps/PowerPivot%20Gallery/BI%20ES/Last30Days.xlsx	2/16/2013 8:01:02 PM	2
!	http://picassoapps/PowerPivot%20Gallery/dbmodel.xlsx	2/16/2013 8:00:01 PM	0
!	http://picassoapps/Shared%20Documents/CLASS_DEMO_Power_View.xlsx	2/16/2013 9:15:12 AM	12
!	http://picassoapps/PowerPivot%20Gallery/BI%20ES/Last30Days0.5.xlsx	2/16/2013 9:02:00 AM	0
!	http://picassoapps/PowerPivot%20Gallery/BI%20ES/Last30Days.xlsx	2/16/2013 9:01:43 AM	0
✓	http://picassoapps/PowerPivot%20Gallery/VSTS_NPD_M3_Backlog_SQL.xlsx	2/16/2013 9:01:25 AM	25
✓	http://picassoapps/PowerPivot%20Gallery/VSTS_NPD_M3_Backlog_SQL.xlsx	2/16/2013 9:00:11 AM	11

1 2 3 4 5 6 7 8 9 10

FIGURE 7-28 The Data refresh – Recent Activity Web Part.

Clicking one of the workbooks in the Recent Activity report redirects you to that workbook's data refresh history page, on which you can find details related to the failure. Figure 7-29 shows the data refresh history page for the *AdventureWorks2013_Bikes2.xlsx* workbook.

Mariano Teixeira Neto ▾   ⚙   ?

☆ FOLLOW   ⌐⌐

S▷

Home
Data Refresh History: AdventureWorks2013_Bikes2

Home

Documents

PowerPivot Gallery

Site Contents

Schedule Information

Name:	AdventureWorks2013_Bikes2.xlsx
Schedule Last Updated By:	Mariano Teixeira Neto
Schedule Last Updated:	2/17/2013 12:37:25 AM
Current Status:	Succeeded
Last Successful Refresh:	2/17/2013 12:39:50 AM
Next Scheduled Refresh:	2/18/2013 Configure Schedule …

History

	Started	Duration	Comments
⊞ ✓	2/17/2013 12:39:00 AM	00:00:49	
⊞ ◔	2/17/2013 12:36:00 AM	00:00:30	The data refresh job failed to update the PowerPivot workbook because another user modified the file while data refresh was in progress.
⊞ ✓	2/16/2013 11:16:00 PM	00:00:36	

FIGURE 7-29 The Data Refresh History page.

Recent Failures

This Web Part focuses on reporting recent data refresh failures. With this information in hand, you can go back to Recent Activity Web Part and begin investigating the reason why a particular data refresh failed.

Reports

As shown in Figure 7-30, the Reports Web Part contains the Excel workbooks that are the source for the PowerPivot Management Dashboard charts. Clicking one of the workbooks opens that workbook in the browser, and you can identify the charts shown in the PowerPivot Management Dashboard.

Reports

 ⊕ new document or drag files here

Dashboard Report   ⋯

✓	🗋	Name
	📊	Server Health
	📊	Workbook Activity
	📄	PowerPivot Management Data

FIGURE 7-30 The Reports Web Part.

Summary

This chapter briefly introduced you to PowerPivot for SharePoint. It demonstrated how to publish a PowerPivot workbook to SharePoint and how to schedule data refreshes, and it explained how IT professionals can manage PowerPivot for SharePoint by using the PowerPivot Management Dashboard.

To learn more about PowerPivot, you can look for books dedicated to PowerPivot for Excel and to PowerPivot for SharePoint. You can also find more information by referencing the following resources:

- The official MSDN blog at *http://blogs.msdn.com/b/analysisservices/*.

- Rob Collie's blog at *http://www.powerpivotpro.com* (for PowerPivot for Excel). Rob Collie was a Program Manager in the Analysis Services team that worked on PowerPivot for Excel.

- Dave Wickert's blog at *http://www.powerpivotgeek.com* (for PowerPivot for SharePoint). Dave Wickert is a Program Manager on the Analysis Services team, working on PowerPivot for SharePoint.

CHAPTER 8

Using PerformancePoint Services

C hapter 1, "Business intelligence in SharePoint," shows you the basic pattern for creating key
performance indicators (KPIs), which are derived from a company vision, a company strategy, and
measurable objectives. PerformancePoint Services in SharePoint Server 2013 has been a viable business intelligence (BI) tool that complements SharePoint Server 2013. It's a monitoring and analytics
service that helps organizations monitor and analyze their business by providing tools for building
dashboards, scorecards, and KPIs. When set up properly and with access to trusted data (see Chapter
3, "The lifecycle of a business intelligence implementation") and other data sources and reports, these
PerformancePoint components (and others) help you to answer the following questions across an
organization:

- What has happened? (monitoring)

- What is happening? (monitoring)

- Why is it happening? (analysis)

By answering these questions, you and your employees can better predict what will happen, and
make informed business decisions that align with company-wide objectives and strategy. This chapter
provides an introduction to PerformancePoint Services by helping you to create many of the components that it offers, using the tools it provides.

A brief history of PerformancePoint Services

In 2005, Microsoft Office Business Scorecard Manager 2005 was released as a product to help organizations build, manage, and use scorecards and KPIs, and then make it possible for the organization to
use all these components to perform analysis.

The successor to Business Scorecard Manager, PerformancePoint Server 2007, became part of the
Office 2007 system of products and is positioned to be a complete performance management application. With PerformancePoint 2007, you can monitor the progress of KPIs, which are shared as key
goals or drivers of the business.

Microsoft Office PerformancePoint Server was integrated into SharePoint 2010. It is available as part
of the non-free versions of SharePoint Server 2013 and is influential in the marketplace because of its
well-engineered BI options and features.

An overview of PerformancePoint Services components

Before discussing the improvements made in PerformancePoint Services 2013 (in comparison with PerformancePoint 2010), we want to give you a quick tour of the basic elements: data sources, dashboards, scorecards, KPIs, indicators, and reports. Later in the chapter, you'll see more detail about each element.

PerformancePoint stores these elements as content types in SharePoint document libraries and lists. PerformancePoint elements stored in lists comprise dashboards, scorecards, reports, filters, KPIs, and indicators, whereas the elements stored in document libraries are data sources.

The following sections provide a more detailed look at the PerformancePoint elements.

Data sources

Data sources are of paramount importance to data-driven applications. In PerformancePoint, data sources are elements that store the connection information required to access the data that serves as the underlying source for KPIs, analytic charts, and grids. Data sources can also drive dashboard filters.

You should know that Analysis Services (multidimensional and PowerPivot) are "preferred data sources," because this data source type extends what you can do in a PerformancePoint Services dashboard. For example, you can slice and drill down to uncover the underlying data that results in a high-level value. You cannot do this with relational data. However, because this is a dashboard authoring tool, you have several data-source options available.

> **Important** In Dashboard Designer, when you create a data source for an Excel workbook, you actually import that workbook as the data source. PerformancePoint stores an internal copy of the Excel file, so any modifications you make to it are independent of the original file.

Following are the different data sources that you can use:

- Analysis Services-multidimensional (2005, 2008, 2008 R2, or 2012)

- PowerPivot for Excel 2013

- Excel workbook (2007, 2010, or 2013)

- Excel Services (2007, 2010, or 2013)

- SharePoint list (2007, 2010, or 2013)

- SQL Server-relational data (2005, 2008, 2008 R2, or 2012)

- Custom data source

Indicators

PerformancePoint is all about providing visualizations that help decision makers. Indicators are the images that represent the approximate value of a KPI in a scorecard. Typical indicators consist of icons. An example might be a traffic light icon that confers meaning, such as the following:

- Green: On target

- Amber: Needs attention

- Red: Off target

You can also create custom indicators.

KPIs

KPIs are actually the original reason that Microsoft sold a scorecard product (Business Scorecard Manager). Although KPIs can be displayed in stand-alone Web Parts in SharePoint, they become more meaningful in the context of a scorecard. In their simplest form, they are made up of actual, target, and threshold numbers. KPIs in PerformancePoint can be complex, driven by multiple data sources, with multiple thresholds that correspond to multiple levels of achievement or targets. You can also migrate KPIs from a SQL Server Analysis Services cube. You'll learn more about KPIs later in this chapter as part of the hands-on practice.

Recall from Chapter 1 that two of the key elements that make up a KPI are a company strategy and an objective. An example might be:

- **Strategy** Improve satisfaction for customers who own mountain bikes.

- **Objective** Increase repeat business from mountain bike customers by 20 percent.

The KPI is the number of quarterly repeat sales from customers who purchase mountain bikes. The KPI target is a numeric goal or metric, which as described in the preceding objective, aims to increase repeat business in that segment by 20 percent. The next step is to incorporate a data source to compare the desired target with the actual performance to see where the business is in terms of achieving the objective.

Scorecards

A scorecard collects KPIs and objectives to provide a comprehensive view of the health of a department or organization by comparing and evaluating the strategy.

KPIs and related data sources and indicators are the foundation from which scorecards are created. As part of PerformancePoint Services, scorecards can also contain dimensional data elements that provide a hierarchical breakout of the KPIs.

The important point is that Dashboard Designer provides a feature-rich, drag-and-drop interface for designing layout and for previewing scorecards, making the process quick and intuitive.

Reports

In PerformancePoint Services, a report is a reusable element that can take several forms and provide access to interactive and static data through a variety of avenues. Most of the report types offered by PerformancePoint can stand on their own and are not bound to a scorecard or KPI, so they provide something extra to a dashboard. The report types that exist in PerformancePoint are as follows:

- **Analytic chart** This report type displays interactive charts from specified data.

- **Analytic grid** This report type displays figures as a set of rows and columns.

- **Excel Services** Using this report type, you can reference an Excel spreadsheet published in Excel Services so that you can view it in a dashboard.

- **KPI Details** A simple report type that displays the properties of a selected KPI metric in a scorecard. The KPI Details report works as a Web Part that links to a scorecard or individual KPI to show relevant metadata to the end user in SharePoint Server. You can add this Web Part to PerformancePoint dashboards or to any SharePoint Server page.

> **Note** You must first create a scorecard.

- **ProClarity Analytics Server Page** This report type maintains backward compatibility with existing reports created by using Microsoft ProClarity Professional and published to ProClarity Server.

- **Reporting Services** This report type lets you publish an SQL Server Reporting Services (SSRS) report in a dashboard. This might also include Power View reports (see *http://www.sqlmag.com/blog/sql-server-bi-blog-17/business-intelligence/add-power-view-web-report-pps-dashboards-143517*).

- **Strategy map** This report type uses a Microsoft Visio diagram as a template for displaying KPIs in a rich, graphical format. Using a strategy map report, you can display color-coded KPI indicators. You can also show numeric and textual data on a map. The underlying Visio diagram is linked to a scorecard to show at-a-glance organizational performance measures. When you put the four perspectives discussed in Chapter 1 together with a scorecard and strategy map, you get a Balanced Scorecard that captures the four main areas of Business Connectivity Service (BCS): Finance, Operations, Sales, and Human Resources (sometimes referred to as FOSH metrics).

- **Web page** This is a jack-of-all-trades report type. It's a standard ASPX webpage, so you can display data in HTML format. Parameters selected in the connections between other components are passed to a connected component in the Request. Use this report type to show legacy reports that cannot otherwise be integrated into a dashboard.

Context menu features

Each of the following features requires that you configure the KPI row to be set to Source Data.

A Decomposition Tree is a visual method to let you see how underlying data is connected to a particular value. To use it, you click to drill down in a hierarchical fashion from a parent value to its associated child nodes, broken down by dimension. To open the Decomposition Tree, simply click an individual value, such as a point in a line chart or a cell in a grid or scorecard, and then, in the menu that appears, select Decomposition Tree. The Decomposition Tree opens in a new window in which users can drill down and view the derived dimensional data from the SSAS cube.

> **Note** A Decomposition Tree is available in a PerformancePoint dashboard only after it has been deployed to SharePoint Server 2013. Users must also have Microsoft Silverlight 2, 3, 4, or 5 installed on their computers.

Show details is a feature or report view that gives you detailed row-level information for a specific KPI or report derived from Analysis Services. You access this feature by browsing an analytical chart, grid, or scorecard. Static information is displayed for the data, organized in table format. You can use this feature when you see an interesting value and want to see more data that contributes to that value.

Each report type can be configured to provide visualizations and connect to different data sources. For example, you might need to configure filters and parameters, which are interfaces to help you determine what will drive the report behavior.

Dashboards

A dashboard is a collection of one or more scorecard or report elements arranged in a set of webpages, hosted by SharePoint Server and displayed in a web browser. Users who want to view and work with dynamic report or scorecard data do so through the dashboard. The dashboard synchronizes PerformancePoint components so that they work together to control how business data is aggregated and displayed to users. Filters help determine what data is displayed and the context in which report and scorecard data reach the customer.

Figure 8-1 shows the different elements and how they come together to make a PerformancePoint dashboard.

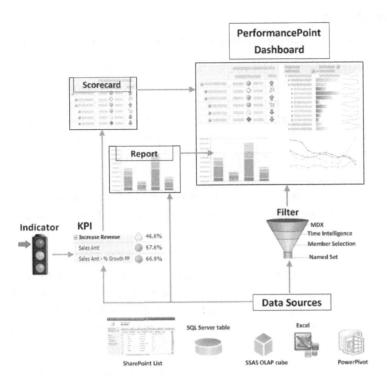

Filters

A filter is a Web Part object with which dashboard users can select a subset of the data rendered on a dashboard. You can apply value-based filters, such as "Top 10" or "is more than," to analytic reports, but you do not create these value-based filters with Dashboard Designer; the filters are automatically available to users when you deploy a dashboard.

When you create a reusable dashboard filter, you must save it to SharePoint Server. Including value-based filters in a dashboard, you give dashboard users the ability to focus on more specific information.

Parts of the Dashboard Designer

Figure 8-2 provides a quick overview of the major features in the dashboard, and the list that follows it describes the numbered elements.

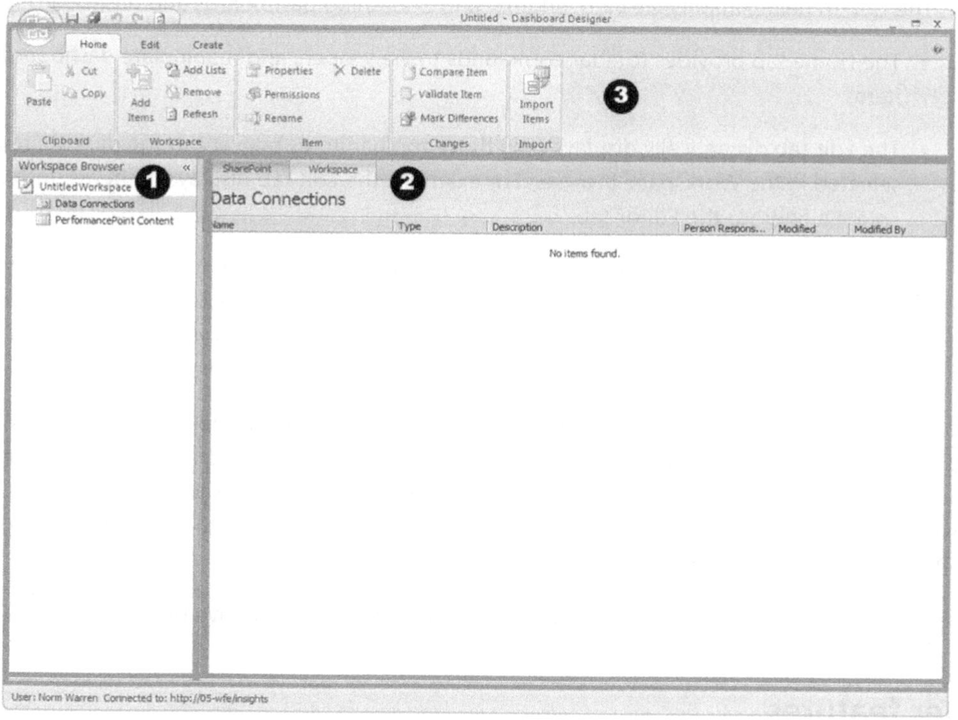

FIGURE 8-2 The Dashboard Designer authoring environment.

1. Use the Workspace Browser to view, open, and save dashboard items and to deploy a dashboard to SharePoint. The Workspace Browser includes two categories: Data Connections and PerformancePoint Content. When you click an item in either category, that item's content appears in the center pane. For example, if you click Data Connections in the Workspace Browser, you see data connection details in the center pane. The ribbon's Edit and Create tabs as well as the Details pane change dynamically to reflect the item selected in the Workspace Browser (Figure 8-3).

FIGURE 8-3 The Workspace Browser.

2. You use the center pane to view and edit data connections and dashboard content. Depending on where the focus is in the Workspace Browser, different tabs are available for the center pane. For example, if you select a Pie Chart, three tabs appear: Design, Query, and Properties. You can also preview dashboard items in the center pane. You might also see the Workspace File appear, which is a PerformancePoint 2010 feature that helps you to locate files saved to your desktop.

3. The ribbon helps simplify viewing, editing, and publishing dashboards and dashboard items.

- The Home tab provides toolbar commands to view, open, and manipulate dashboard items.

- The Edit tab dynamically displays only those toolbar items relevant to the dashboard items selected in the Workspace Browser. For example, the Edit tab displays no items until you create a filter via the Editor tab.

- The Create tab dynamically displays toolbar items relevant to the item that you want to create, such as a KPI, scorecard, dashboard, and so forth. The Details pane appears when you select a dashboard item that shows information about that item. On the File tab, you can view change settings, Save options, and default location for workspace files.

Not numbered in the preceding illustration, the Details pane appears when you select a dashboard item that shows information about that item. You can create and save a workspace file on your computer to view and manage your own reusable dashboard objects. This saves you time because you avoid having to browse through a long list of dashboard objects that others might have saved to SharePoint lists and document libraries.

The Dashboards document library contains only live dashboards that have been deployed.

Other features

Other PerformancePoint features help with the governance and organization of your dashboards.

Dashboard content in SharePoint folders

The following are features for organizing content.

- The Data Connections content library is a container for data sources that you can reuse in dashboard objects. The data connection contains information and security details for each data source.

- The PerformancePoint content list is a SharePoint list that contains scorecards, reports, filters, unpublished dashboards, and other dashboard items that you can organize into folders.

- The Dashboards library contains published dashboards that have been deployed from Dashboard Designer.

Permissions

If you are a site administrator with Full Control permissions, you can control who can view or edit specific dashboard items.

History of dashboard items (versioning)

You can enable version control on SharePoint lists and document libraries that contain your dashboard items. When enabled, if unwanted changes occur, you can revert back to a previous version.

Workspace file

You can create and save a workspace file on your computer to view and manage dashboard objects, which are also reusable. You save time by not browsing a large list of dashboard objects created and saved by others to SharePoint lists and document libraries.

What's new in PerformancePoint Services 2013

SharePoint Services is a service application integrated with SharePoint Server 2013. Additionally, the benefits of document management, backup and restore, and other SharePoint-specific advantages apply to PerformancePoint assets. These include SharePoint features such as a simplified security model, workflow, and more.

What's new for designers

The following are features added to help the designer.

New SharePoint 2013 site themes

PerformancePoint now respects new theming features in SharePoint 2013. The background images from the theme appear behind the elements on your dashboard.

New filter enhancements

PerformancePoint filters boast enhancements, with which you can do the following:

- Show subselections in tree filters by bolding each parent in the hierarchy
- Dynamically size the tree filter height based on the number of visible items in the tree

You can select different tree filter actions by any of the following means:

- Selecting all
- Clearing all
- Resetting to default
- Selecting children
- Getting all filter items (when 5,000 limit is reached)
- Create a filter based on a measure
- See significant performance improvements

New filter search

You can now search filter members. With filter search, you can do the following:

- Search within single and multiselect tree filters

- Search Analysis Services/PowerPivot data sources

- Search Member Selection, MDX Query, and Named Set filters

New BI Center

The BI Center site highlights dashboard components in a clear, simple design such as PowerPivot and Excel Services.

Dashboard Designer on the ribbon

The appearance of the PerformancePoint ribbon tab is based on content type and appears in document libraries where the Web Part Page content type is present. Clicking the Dashboard Designer button launches the click-once application. The icon also appears in lists where any of the PerformancePoint content types have been added. This is so you do not have to launch the designer by navigating to the BI Center.

New for IT professionals

Several features have been developed to simplify administration of PerformancePoint Services.

The *EffectiveUsername* property

You are no longer required to set up Kerberos constrained delegation to use per-user authentication. Per-user authentication enabled on the application settings page adds the *EffectiveUsername* property to the connection string which is then passed to SQL Server Analysis Services (SSAS). The value of the property is the user name of the individual user. When SSAS receives the value, it returns the results of the query.

Custom target applications from secure store

You now have the ability to specify any secure store target application when defining your data source in dashboard designer. You can also use the target application that is auto-generated when you provision the service. In other words, target applications used for Excel Services can also be used for PerformancePoint. This option can be specified for the entire service.

Server-side migration

You can move any or all of your PerformancePoint content from one site or server to another site or server. Enterprise customers can now migrate content, including data sources, between their development, test, and production environments.

When do I use PerformancePoint Services for BI?

Use PerformancePoint Services for creating dashboards, scorecards, KPIs, and various other types of dynamic reports that help deliver a graphical view of performance. Consider the example presented in Chapter 1 of an IT operations scorecard. The scorecard measures database space and other metrics gathered from the Systems Center Operation manager. The dashboard is a point of entry for drill-down analysis to drive agility and alignment across an organization. PerformancePoint Services gives users integrated analytics for monitoring, analyzing, and reporting.

When to use PerformancePoint Services

The following list describes when you can use PerformancePoint Services and Dashboard Designer as an authoring tool:

- When you need to create rich dashboards that convey the right information, aggregating content from multiple sources and displaying it in a web browser in an understandable and collaborative environment. Scorecard and report interactivity lets you analyze up-to-the-minute information and work with the data quickly and easily to identify key opportunities and trends.

- When you want to implement a Balanced Scorecard methodology to measure FOSH metrics.

- When you want to perform root cause analyses, using analytics to examine data while viewing only the most pertinent information by using the new Decomposition Tree.

Available case studies

Although this book covers which tool to use, as described in Chapter 2, "Planning for business intelligence adoption," we suggest that you try to map your particular industry or department's challenges and search for relevant information about how others have resolved those challenges by searching on "Business Intelligence Scenarios" at *http://technet.microsoft.com/en-US/*.

The PerformancePoint Services architecture

Figure 8-4 is a graphical depiction of PerformancePoint Services. It is similar to the diagram in Chapter 1 but focuses on elements specific to Dashboard Designer, the possible data sources for a dashboard, and databases. It also shows that you can export data from a dashboard to an Excel spreadsheet.

The front-end web server runs on Internet Information Services (IIS) and hosts the PerformancePoint Services Web Parts, web services, and the proxy required for communication between the client and the PerformancePoint Services service application.

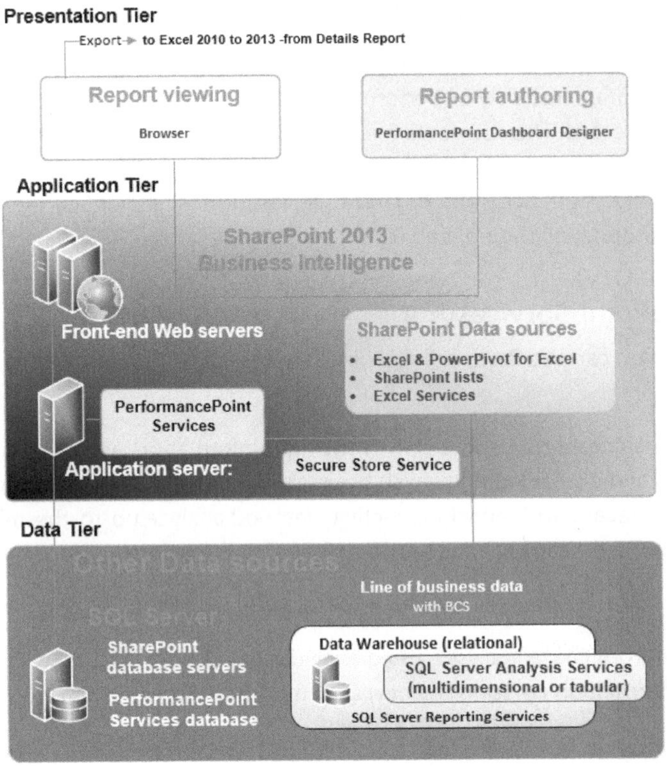

Presentation Tier

Export ➔ to Excel 2010 to 2013 -from Details Report

Report viewing

Browser

Report authoring

PerformancePoint Dashboard Designer

Application Tier

SharePoint 2013
Business Intelligence

Front-end Web servers

SharePoint Data sources
- Excel & PowerPivot for Excel
- SharePoint lists
- Excel Services

PerformancePoint
Services

Application server:

Secure Store Service

Data Tier

Other Data sources
SQL Server

Line of business data
with BCS

SharePoint
database servers

PerformancePoint
Services database

Data Warehouse (relational)

SQL Server Analysis Services
(multidimensional or tabular)

SQL Server Reporting Services

FIGURE 8-4 The PerformancePoint Architecture.

PerformancePoint Services configuration

This chapter doesn't cover setup information (which you can find on TechNet); instead, it contains steps to apply security as well as high-level steps that point you to relevant conceptual documentation. Additionally, these instructions are simplified, because in our configuration, we first ran the Configuration Wizard to establish default service applications for our server. When you do this, the Configuration Wizard creates and starts the PerformancePoint Services service application, which is ready to use after you configure Secure Store Services (SSS) for security. To learn how to set up PerformancePoint Services, go to *http://technet.microsoft.com/en-us/library/ee748644(printer).aspx*.

> **Note** When you run the installation and configuration scripts as described in Appendix A, "Running scripts to set up a demonstration environment," the PerformancePoint Services service application is already running.

PerformancePoint Service Application configured

It is a good idea to ensure that the service application for PerformancePoint Services has been started. You might also want to view the default settings or configure PerformancePoint Services.

To manage PerformancePoint Service Applications in Central Administration, perform the following procedure:

1. In Central Administration, on the Quick Launch bar, click Application Management. Next, click Manage Service Applications and then click PerformancePoint ServiceApps as shown in Figure 8-5.

Note You can also use Windows PowerShell to view running service applications.

2. On the ribbon, in the Operations group, click the Manage button.

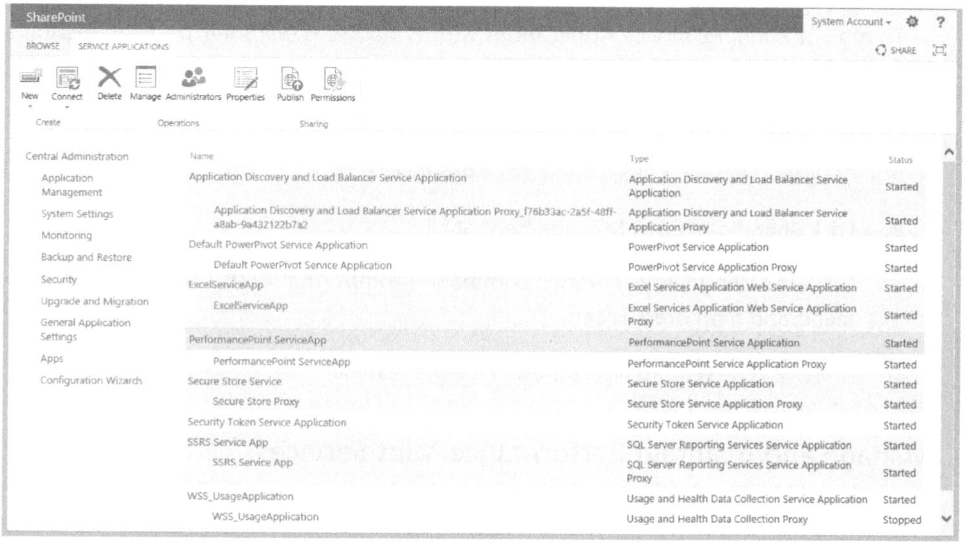

FIGURE 8-5 The PerformancePoint Service Application.

3. In the Manage PerformancePoint Services page (see Figure 8-6), review and observe that you can manage application settings, trusted data source locations, and trusted content locations.

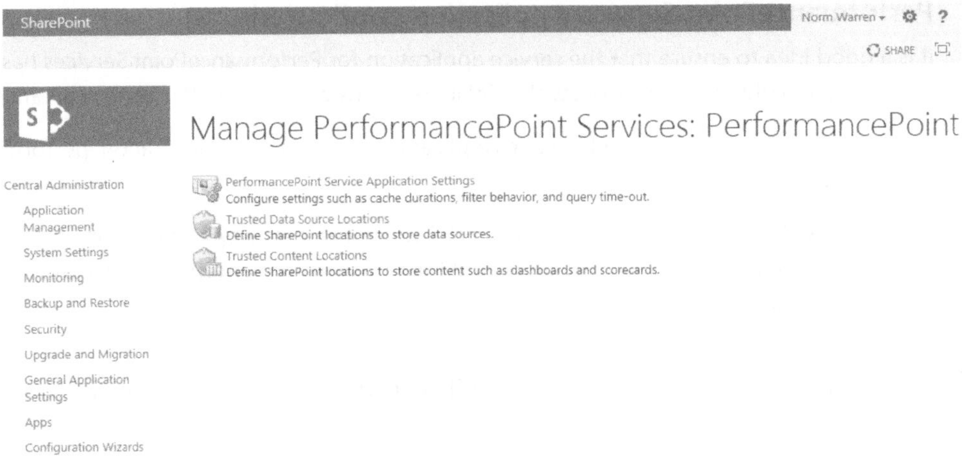

FIGURE 8-6 The management page for the PerformancePoint Services Service Application.

To run List Running Service Applications with Windows PowerShell, perform the following procedure:

1. On the Start menu, click All Programs.

2. Click the Microsoft SharePoint 2013 Products folder.

3. Click SharePoint 2013 Management Shell.

4. From the Windows PowerShell command prompt (that is, PS C:\>), type the following command and then press Enter:

```
PS C:/>Get-SPPerformancePointServiceApplication
```

Manage and maintain PerformancePoint Services

The features that you can manage in a service application for PerformancePoint include the following:

- Use the PerformancePoint Applications Settings to manage configurations that affect performance, security, and data connection refreshes.

> **Note** This is where you configure the Unattended Service Account credentials, which is essential for connecting to external data sources.

- Use Trusted Data Source Locations to restrict access to data sources from PerformancePoint dashboards. You'll see how to configure these in the next section.

Tip Configure trusted data sources to specific sites, particularly when the Unattended Service Account you configure for the data source has access to sensitive information such as financial or personnel data.

- Use Trusted Content Locations to restrict access to PerformancePoint objects, such as KPIs, scorecards, indicators, and reports. You'll see how to configure these in the next section, as well.

Configure security for PerformancePoint

In addition to restricting trusted data source and content lists, you must also configure the SSS.

If you have opened up the Application Settings and see a warning that you do not have the SSS application and Proxy running, you must "generate" a key and then configure an Unattended Service account. The Unattended Service account is an Active Directory domain account that is used for accessing PerformancePoint Services data sources.

Note We specify "for PerformancePoint" in the following procedure because it's important to remember that SSS configuration is performed differently for PerformancePoint than for the other services.

Fortunately, many of the steps are automated for PerformancePoint SSS configuration. You must be a Service Application Administrator for the SSS instance.

To configure SSS for PerformancePoint, follow these steps:

1. In Central Administration, click Manage Service Applications.

2. Click Secure Store Service in the list of service applications.

3. On the Service Applications tab, click Manage.

4. On the Edit tab, click Generate New Key.

Note Steps 4 through 6 are only applicable if secure store is not already configured. If Excel Services or PowerPivot Services are configured, secure store might already be set up, as illustrated in Figure 8-7.

FIGURE 8-7 The SSS Management page.

5. In the dialog box that opens, type a pass phrase that is at least eight characters in length and comprises a minimum of three element types (numbers, letters, and symbols) to make it more secure (example: Strong;54321).

Tip The pass phrase is not stored, so you're responsible for keeping it securely.

6. Click Refresh The Key and then, when prompted, enter the pass phrase you set in Step 5.

To configure the Unattended Service Account, perform the following procedure:

1. In Central Administration, on the Quick Launch bar, click Manage Service Applications.

2. In the list of service applications, click the PerformancePoint Service Application Settings (or whatever you named it if you manually configured it), as demonstrated in Figure 8-8.

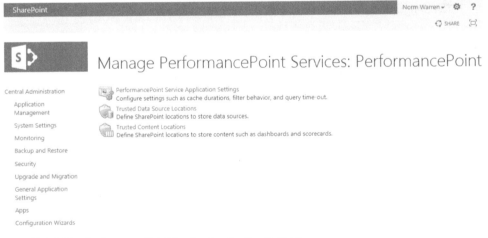

FIGURE 8-8 The PerformancePoint Service Application Settings.

3. In the Unattended Service Account text box (see Figure 8-9), type the account that has access to the data sources that you want available when you create your dashboard and then click OK.

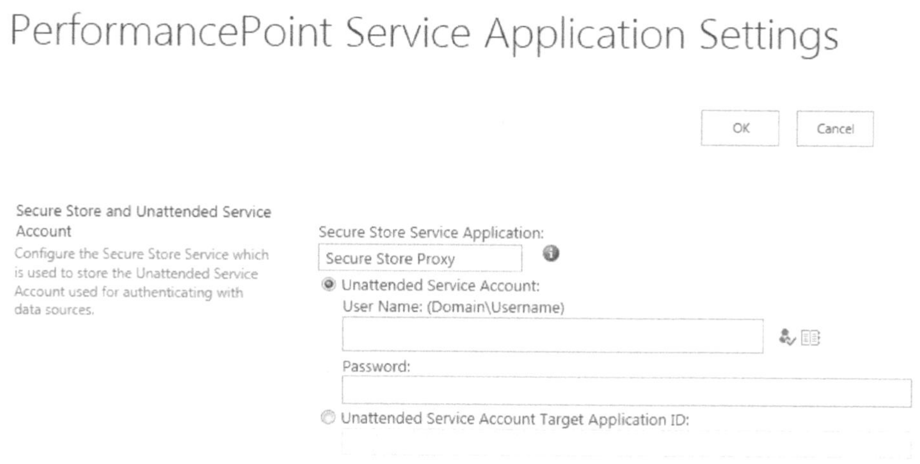

PerformancePoint Service Application Settings

| OK | Cancel |

Secure Store and Unattended Service Account

Configure the Secure Store Service which is used to store the Unattended Service Account used for authenticating with data sources.

Secure Store Service Application:

Secure Store Proxy ⓘ

◉ Unattended Service Account:
 User Name: (Domain\Username)

Password:

◯ Unattended Service Account Target Application ID:

FIGURE 8-9 The PerformancePoint Service Application Settings page.

> **Caution** You should limit the access for the Unattended Service Account to only needed data sources in SQL Server. Also, set this account to read-only access on any data sources so that it has minimum permissions and minimizes vulnerability. You can check the SSS to see that a Target Application for PerformancePoint has been created for you.

Troubleshooting the SQL Server data-source configuration

The following are some things you can do to troubleshoot SQL Server data-source configuration:

- You might need to register the service account to the existing application pool dedicated to PerformancePoint Services.

  You will do this when using an account for the identity of the PerformancePoint service that is different from the identity for the content database(s). This concept also applies to Excel Services and PowerPivot. To do this, use Windows PowerShell (as Administrator) and run the following cmdlets:

```
PS C:\> $w = Get-SPWebApplication(" <your web application> ")

PS C:\> $w.GrantAccessToProcessIdentity(" <insert service account> ")
```

> **Note** This action grants *db_owner* access to the SharePoint content databases.

> **Note** The Windows PowerShell script works on a per–content database basis, so you must run the script for each web application.

- Refresh the SSS key.

- Specify your ADOMD.NET data-provider version. See Kevin Donovan's blog post *http://blogs. msdn.com/b/performancepoint/archive/2012/09/11/specifying-your-adomd-net-data-provider- version.aspx.*

- Follow the instructions in the TechNet documentation for configuring PeformancePoint Services, which you can find at *http://technet.microsoft.com/en-us/library/ee748644(printer).aspx.*

- Check to see if you need to change which ADOMD.NET data provider is used. For more information, go to *http://blogs.msdn.com/b/performancepoint/archive/2012/09/11/specifying-your- adomd-net-data-provider-version.aspx.*

Configure data and content locations

The following procedures show you how to configure trusted data-source and content-source locations.

> **Note** By default, these locations are configured to trust all sites on the farm so that PerformancePoint can work directly upon installation. It is not necessary to configure trusted data-source locations if you don't want to limit access.

To configure a trusted data-source location, follow these steps:

1. In the Central Administration, on the Quick Launch bar, click Manage PerformancePoint Services.

2. In the list of service applications, click Trusted Data Source Locations.

   The Trusted Data Source Locations page opens. Notice that All SharePoint Locations option is selected by default.

3. Click the Only Specific Locations (Current Setting) option and then click Apply, as illustrated in Figure 8-10.

4. Click the Add Trusted Data Source Location link and then, in the Edit dialog box, enter the full web address where you want to store data source connections.

   If necessary, select the type of location and then click OK.

Trusted Data Source Locations

Define SharePoint locations to store data sources.

Trust data sources in:

○ All SharePoint locations

● Only specific locations (current setting)

Apply

📧 Add Trusted Data Source Location

There are no items to show in this view.

FIGURE 8-10 The Trusted Data Source Locations settings page.

To configure a trusted content-source location perform the following procedure:

1. In the Central Administration, on the Quick Launch bar, click Manage PerformancePoint Services.

2. In the list of service applications, click Trusted Content Locations.

   The Trusted Content Locations page opens. Notice that All SharePoint Locations option is selected by default.

3. Click the Only Specific Locations (Current Setting) option and then click Apply, as shown in Figure 8-10.

Trusted Content Locations

Define SharePoint locations to store content such as dashboards and scorecards.

Trust content in:

○ All SharePoint locations

● Only specific locations (current setting)

Apply

📧 Add Trusted Content Location

There are no items to show in this view.

FIGURE 8-11 The Trusted Content Locations page.

4. Click the Add Trusted Data Source Location link and then, in the Edit dialog box, enter the full web address where you want to store data source connections.

5. If necessary, select the type of location and then click OK.

Start PerformancePoint Dashboard Designer

Before you install Dashboard Designer, you should make it available on a site the easy way, by creating a site collection using the BI template.

There are other methods for making PerformancePoint Dashboard Designer available in sites without creating a BI Center site collection. For example, by going to PowerPivot Gallery library settings, you can add a content type called PerformancePoint Data Source, as shown in Figure 8-12. For detailed instructions on how to add a content type, in Chapter 3, read the section "Adding content types to SharePoint 2013 library."

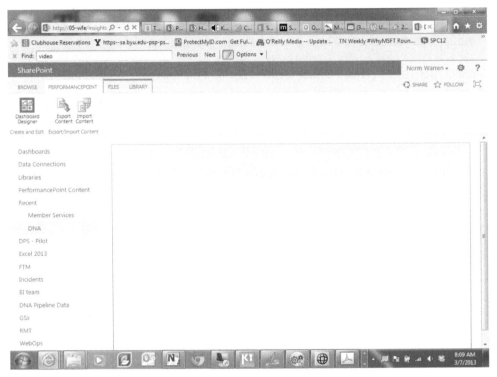

FIGURE 8-12 Adding a PerformancePoint Data Source content type.

After you add the content type, you will see a PerformancePoint tab as an option on the library's ribbon (Figure 8-13).

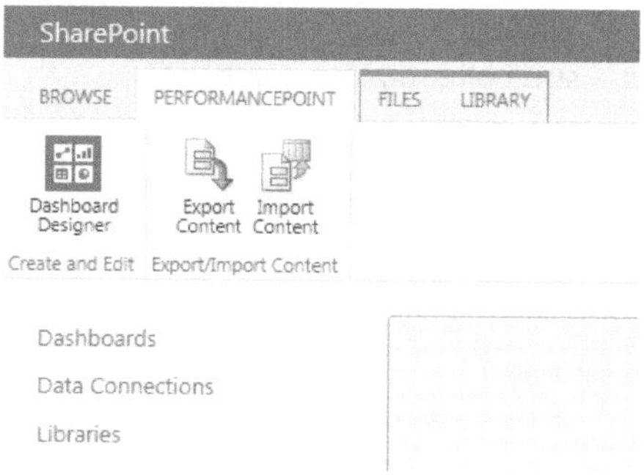

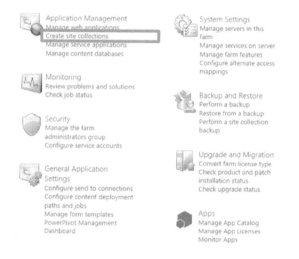

FIGURE 8-13 The PerformancePoint tab on the ribbon for accessing Dashboard Designer.

To deploy the Business Intelligence Center using the template, perform the following procedure:

1. In Central Administration, in the Application Management section, click the Create Site Collections link, as depicted in Figure 8-14.

FIGURE 8-14 Selecting the Create Site Collections link in Central Administration.

2. On the Create Site Collection page (see Figure 8-15), in the Title text box, type **BI Portal**. In the Web Site Address section, choose the URL name and path or create a site at a specific path.

3. In the Select A Template section, click the Enterprise tab and click Business Intelligence Center. Enter user names in the Primary Site Collection Administrator and Secondary Site Collection Administrator text boxes, respectively, and then click OK.

Figure 8-16 shows the site collection that is created.

Note The BI Center site is also available as a site in a site collection or a subsite.

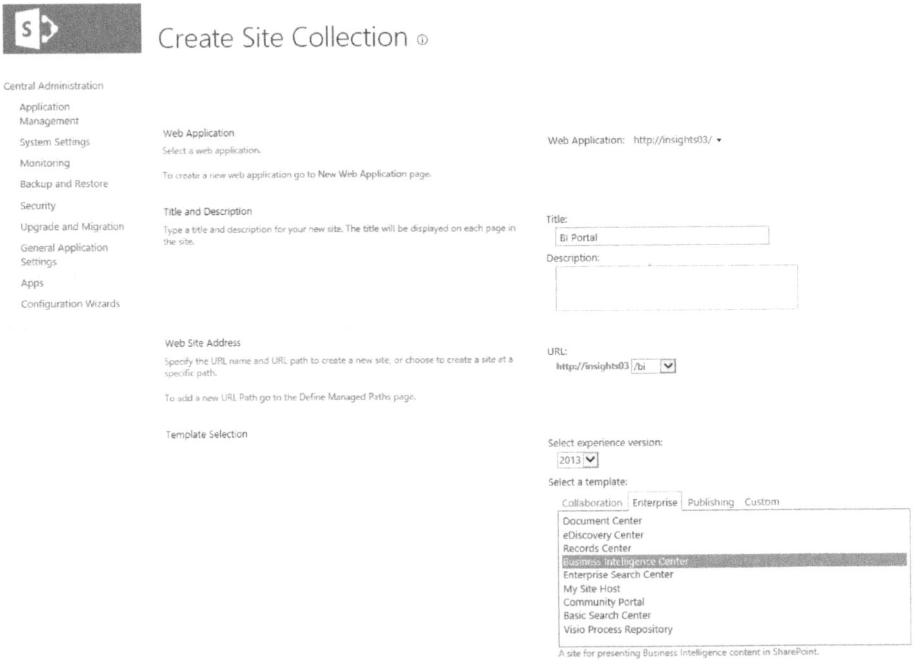

FIGURE 8-15 Creating a Business Intelligence Center site collection in Central Administration.

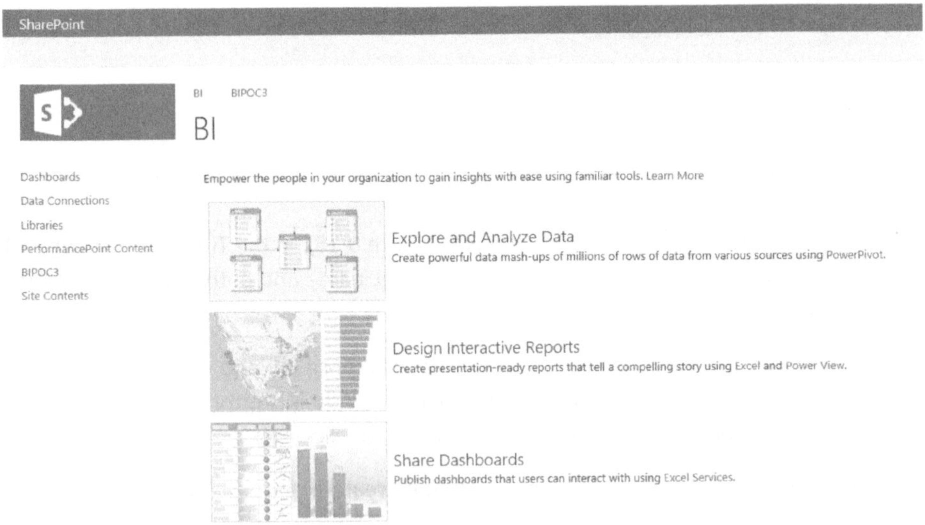

FIGURE 8-16 A SharePoint 2013 Business Intelligence Center site collection.

To start Dashboard Designer, perform the following procedure:

1. Navigate to the Business Intelligence Center site and then, on the Quick Launch bar, click PerformancePoint Content.

2. Choose one of following methods to start Dashboard Designer:

   • On the ribbon, click the PerformancePoint tab and then, in the Create And Edit group, click the Dashboard Designer button (refer back to Figure 8-13)

   • On the ribbon, click the Items tab and then, in the New group, click New Item (Figure 8-17). On the menu that appears, click one of the available templates.

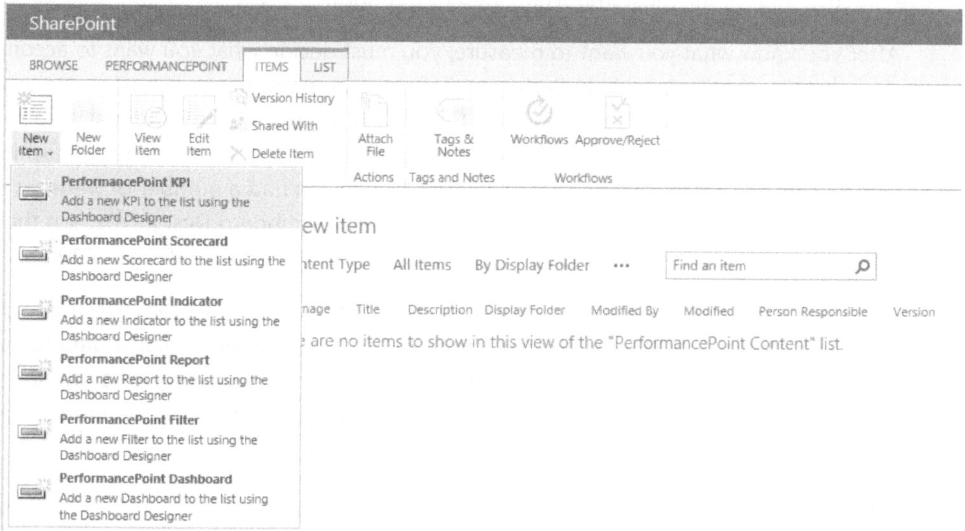

FIGURE 8-17 Selecting a new item in PerformancePoint Content library.

Dashboard Designer opens.

Providing a performance solution

The exercise in this section centers on the sales activities of the Adventure Works Company. This company manufactures and sells products to various global markets via reseller and Internet channels.

The exercise shows you how to produce a dashboard to publish to users on SharePoint Server 2013. The dashboard makes it possible for users to monitor and analyze sales activities and profitability for the company reseller operations.

In the exercise, one KPI is created to support comparisons of sales, sales quotas, and profit margin to a fixed goal of two percent, across several fiscal periods, product categories, subcategories, and sales territory regions.

To support the monitoring requirements, two scorecards are created to produce different perspectives of a single KPI. Three reports are created to support analysis requirements.

These scorecards and reports are then embedded in a dashboard that has filters for slicing data by fiscal periods, product categories, and sales territories. The dashboard is deployed to SharePoint so that it can be viewed and explored by Adventure Works sales management.

Design the KPIs, scorecards, reports, and dashboard

Some or all the documents that this exercise draws from come into play when the Analysis Services Cube is designed and created. As discussed in Chapter 3, getting to trusted data should be an iterative process, and it's the most important step to get right.

After you know what you want to measure, you must decide what you want to accomplish with the functionality that's available in PerformancePoint. You have many ways to create and configure KPIs and scorecards in Dashboard Designer. Consider putting your rating, actual, target, and how these might aggregate in a spreadsheet so that you can review them in prototype fashion, adding the potential users and other stakeholders. Additionally, you can find a number of websites where you can review best practices for dashboard design, such as "Dashboard Design 101," on the UX matters website at *http://www.uxmatters.com/mt/archives/2013/11/dashboard-design-101.php*.

The reports and data sources you choose determine how much you can investigate data and incorporate meaningful visualizations. Consider how you want to filter on available data to give users the right information from which to make decisions. It is also worth reviewing other literature on dashboard design, such as *Information Dashboard Design: The Effective Visual Communication of Data* by Stephen Few (O'Reilly, 2006).

Before continuing, you should be familiar with the following:

- The definition of "business intelligence" (see Chapter 1)
- The "Overview of PerformancePoint Services components" section earlier in this chapter

Dashboard Designer provides a wizard that guides you through the process of importing Analysis Services KPIs into a scorecard. This exercise starts with the KPI because it is the driving element for monitoring, and the cornerstone of any performance management initiative. Even though this exercise shows quite a bit of the best dashboard functionality, PerformancePoint provides much more functionality than we can show you in one chapter.

The following list defines the basic sequence of actions for creating a very simplified dashboard that works with the Analysis Services Cube data source (see Appendix A), an Excel file, and a Visio file, all of which were created in this book:

1. Design your KPIs and Scorecards (already done)

2. Create a data source

3. Create a set of KPIs

4. Create dashboard items (report, scorecard)

5. Create filters to control what data is included

6. Create reports with which the user can perform analysis on the underlying data

7. Assemble the dashboard pages

8. Preview, test, and deploy the dashboard

You can use the procedure in this section to create some data sources for use in your dashboard.

> **Note** Security information for Excel Services is saved in the Trusted Data Connection library.

> **Important** External data sources must reside in the same domain as the SharePoint Server 2013 farm, or authentication will fail. For more information about planning for external data sources, see "Planning considerations for services that access external data sources" at *http://technet.microsoft.com/en-us/library/cc560988.aspx#ConsiderationsForAccessingExternalData*.

> **Tip** Select your authentication method before you type in the server and specify the database.

You must have a data source before you can create PerformancePoint content.

Although the procedure begins on the Create tab, you can also create a PerformancePoint data source from the Data Connections library on the Documents tab. Either way, Dashboard Designer and the Select A Data Source Template open so that you can create the data source.

1. In Dashboard Designer, in the Workspace Browser pane, right-click Data Connections and then, on the shortcut menu that appears, click New Data Source, as demonstrated in Figure 8-18.

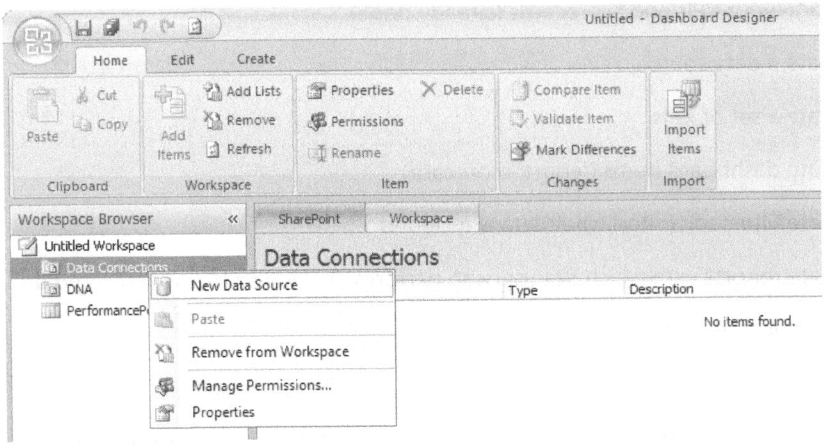

FIGURE 8-18 Creating a new data source for a PerformancePoint Dashboard.

2. In the Select A Data Source dialog box, in the Template section, the Analysis Services is selected by default, as shown in Figure 8-19. Click OK.

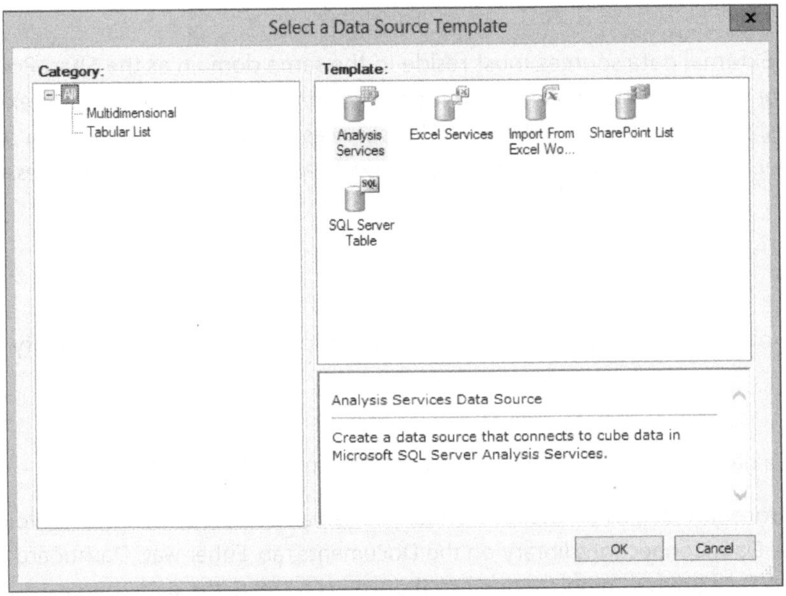

FIGURE 8-19 The Select A Data Source dialog box.

3. In the Workspace Browser, you are given the option to name the data source. Type **AdventureWorks** as its name.

> **Note** How the center pane responds is a function of the data source that you select in the Workspace Browser. In this case, you chose Analysis Services, so the center pane requests specific information for your data source, such as the name of the cube.

4. In the Server text box, type **Adventure Works**. In the Database text box, type **Adventure WOrksDW2012Multidimensional-EE**. In the Cube list box, select Sales. For this demo, keep the default Authentication Unattended Service Account.

The Unattended Service Account is an Active Directory account that is used for accessing PerformancePoint Services data sources. This account is used by PerformancePoint Services on behalf of authorized users to provide access to external data sources for the purposes of creating and using dashboards and other PerformancePoint Services content.

> **Note** The Unattended Service Account is a universal account that provides equal data access to all authorized users. If you need more fine-grained data access, see "Configure Secure Store for use with PerformancePoint Services" at *http://technet.microsoft.com/en-us/library/jj819322.aspx*.

Your information should appear as shown in Figure 8-20.

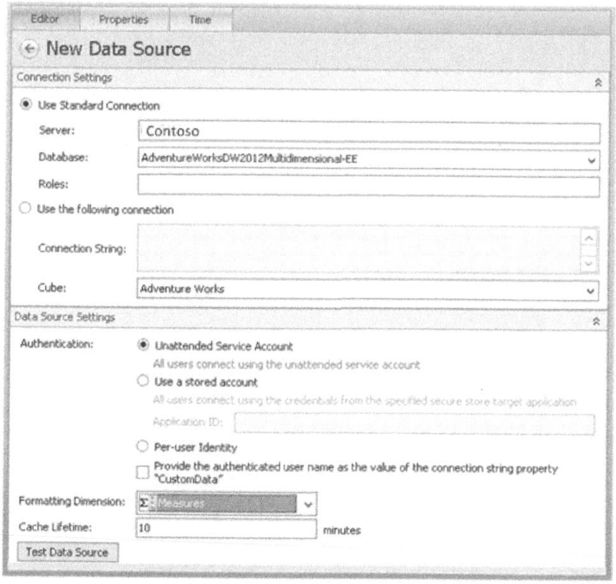

FIGURE 8-20 The New Data Source configuration page.

> **Note** The Unattended Service Account and Provide The Authenticated User Name As A Value Of The Connection String Property "CustomData" in the Connection option shown in Figure 8-20 applies to Analysis Services only. The Per-User Identity option no longer requires the Kerberos protocol if the PerformancePoint Service identity is an admin in SQL Server Analysis Services. Kerberos is still a good choice, though, for applying security to data sources.

Your data source is saved to the Trusted Data Source library without clicking save or OK in the Data Connections library in your BI Center site.

5. Click the Properties Tab and name the data source **AdventureWorks**.

6. On the Time tab (see Figure 8-21), in the Reference Member section, select a member from the dimension that represents the first day of the year, such as January 1, 2011.

   The Time tab is where you configure Time Intelligence before creating a filter that you can use in reports and scorecards. It is worth reviewing to see whether you want to configure your data to use Time Intelligence. For more information, see "Configure data sources to work with Time Intelligence by using Dashboard Designer" at *http://technet.microsoft.com/en-us/library/ff701697.aspx*.

   The Time Dimension list box presents the hierarchies available in the cube, such as Date. Date. Date.Calendar (Year, Week, Day).

7. In the Reference Date section, enter the same date in your regional format so that Performance Point can understand how years are structured in the date dimension.

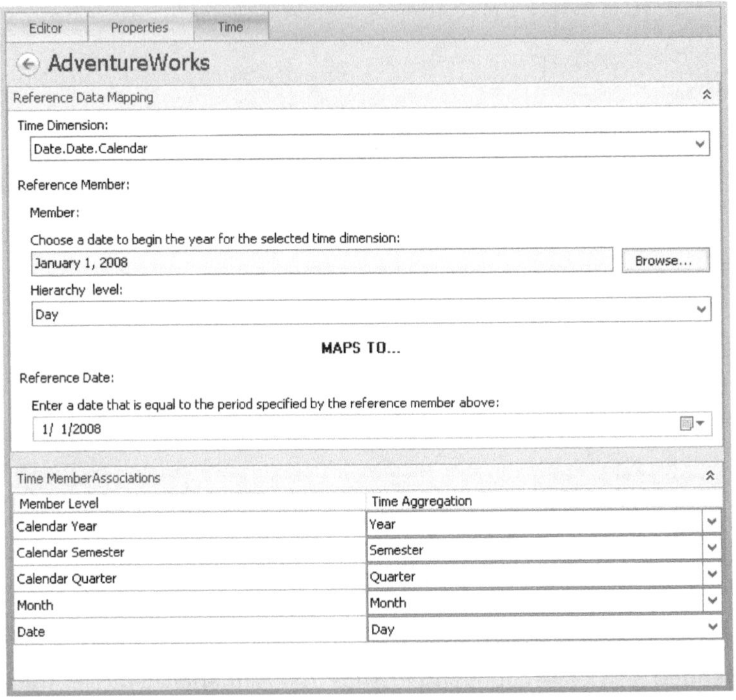

FIGURE 8-21 The Time Intelligence configuration page.

8. Navigate to the Business Intelligence Center and click Data Connections.

   You should see the data connections file saved to the Trusted Data Source library, as illustrated in Figure 8-22.

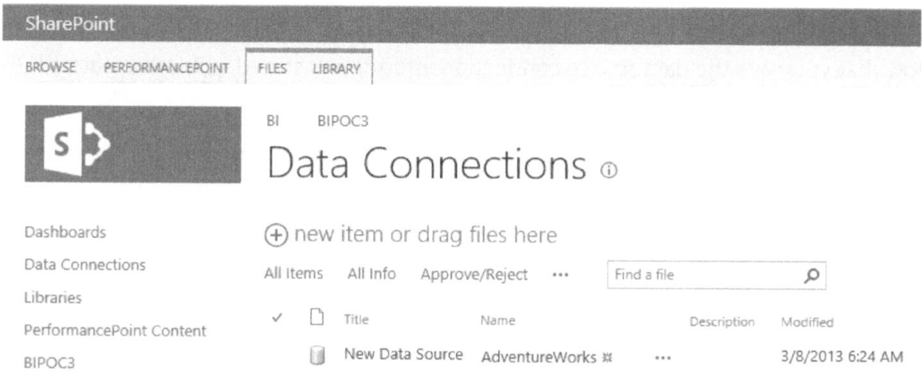

FIGURE 8-22 The SharePoint 2013 Data Connections library.

To save to the workspace and refresh your data sources, perform the following steps:

1. On the Quick Access Toolbar, click the Save button (the diskette icon, as shown in Figure 8-23) to save your dashboard.

> **Note** As you work on objects in the PerformancePoint content, you should regularly click the Save All button (the multi-diskette icon) on the Quick Access Toolbar to save all your files, as shown in Figure 8-23. Also, you have the option of clicking the Refresh icon to refresh your data sources.

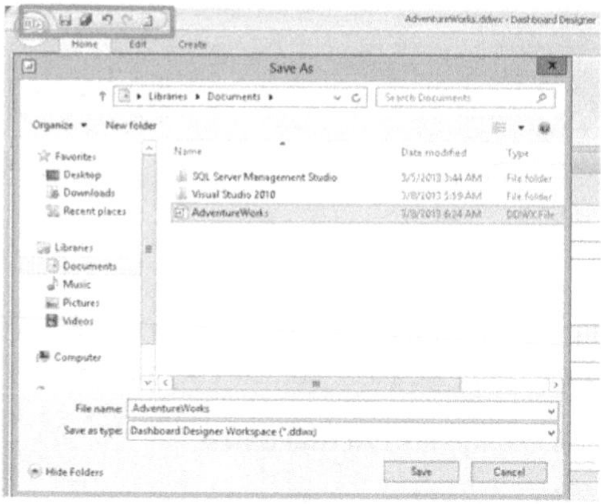

FIGURE 8-23 The Save and Save All buttons on the on the Quick Access Toolbar.

2. In the File Name text box, type **AdventureWorks** and then click Save.

Create KPIs

Now that you have the data source connection information stored, you can create a KPI by performing the following procedure:

1. In the Workspace Browser, right-click PerformancePoint Content. On the shortcut menu that opens, point to New, and then on the submenu that appears click KPI, as depicted in Figure 8-24.

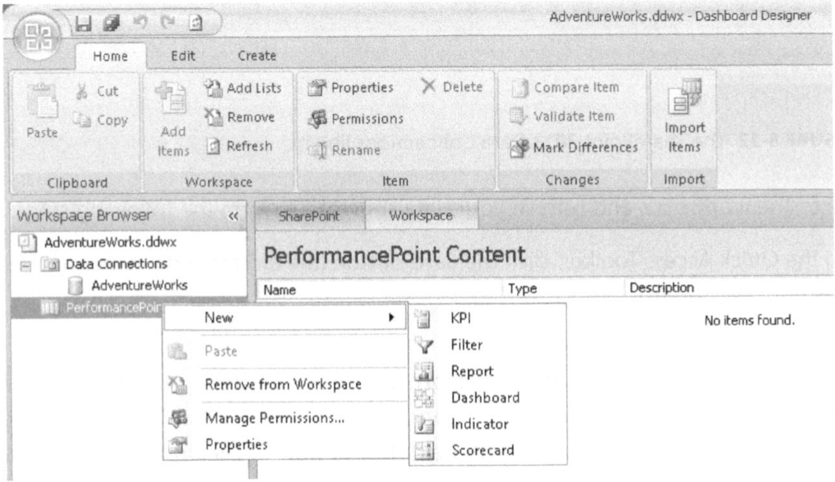

FIGURE 8-24 The first step in creating a KPI.

The Select A KPI dialogue box appears.

2. Click OK to select a blank KPI.

> **Note** Objective KPIs use only the calculated score of a child KPI, in case you want to compare scores of KPIs instead of values.

A blank KPI template opens (see Figure 8-25) with no content or data mappings that include the actual and target metrics for the KPI. Next, you'll customize two metrics.

3. In the Name column, select Actual and change it to **Actual Sales**.

4. Click the cell under Data Mappings for Actual Sales and then click Change Source.

5. In the Select A Data Source dialog box, on the Workspace tab, select the data source that drives the value of the Actual metric.

6. Double-click AdventureWorks, as demonstrated in Figure 8-26.

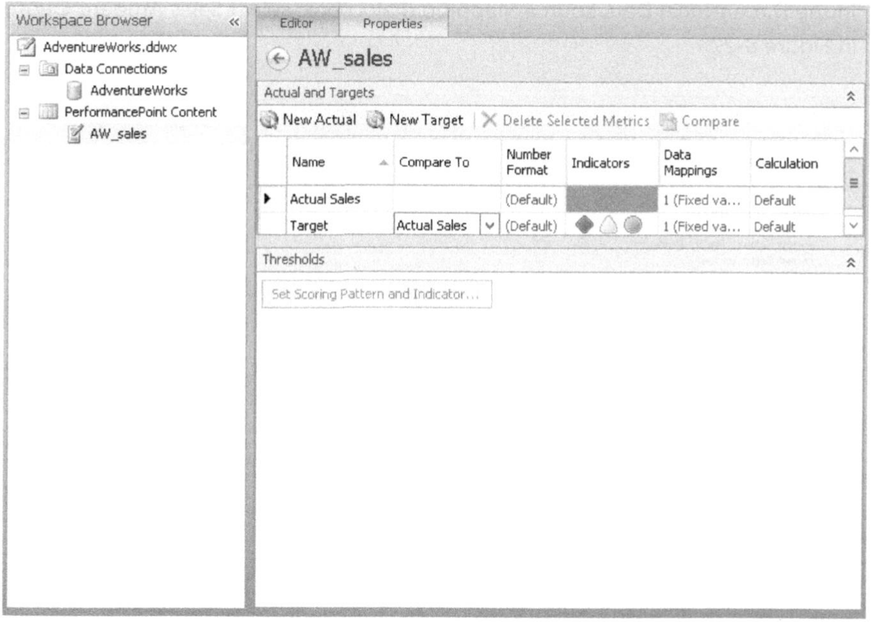

FIGURE 8-25 The PerformancePoint KPI page for configuring metrics.

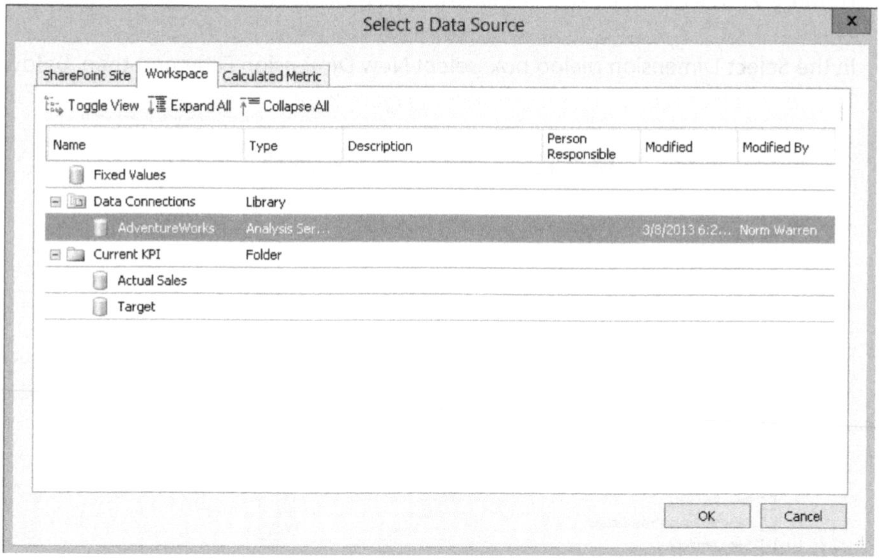

FIGURE 8-26 The Select A Data Source dialog box for KPI.

7. In the Dimensional Data Source Mapping dialog box, select Sales Amount Quota, as depicted in Figure 8-27.

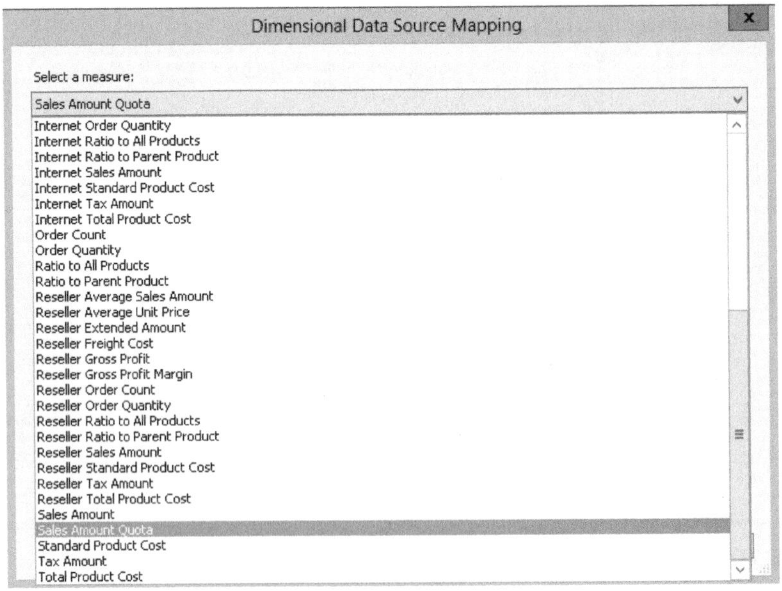

FIGURE 8-27 The Dimensional Data Source Mapping dialog box.

8. In the Select Dimension dialog box, select New Dimension Filter and then, below Sales Territory, select Scenario, as illustrated in Figure 8-28.

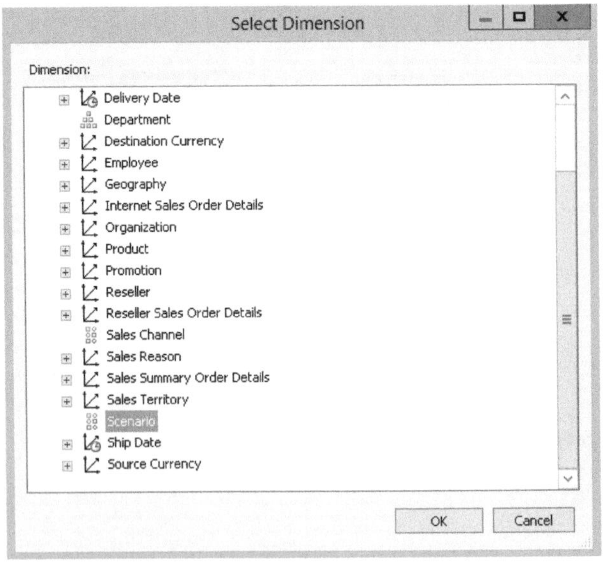

FIGURE 8-28 The Select A Dimension dialog box for KPI.

9. In the Select Members dialog box (see Figure 8-29), select Default Member (All Scenario) to apply the filter on members of the description dimension.

10. Expand All Scenario, select Actual, and then click OK.

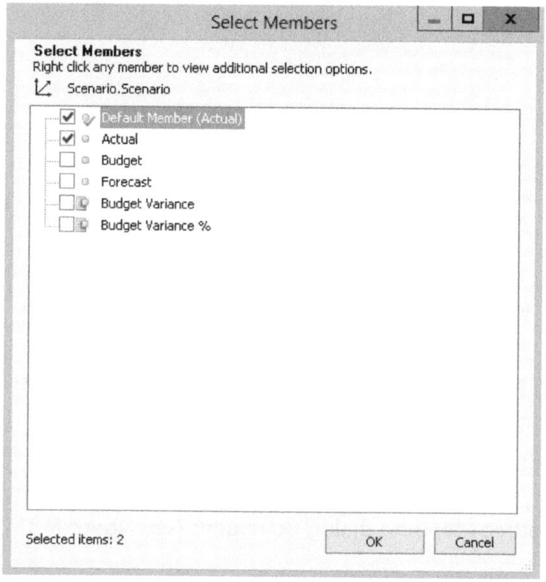

FIGURE 8-29 The Select Members dialog box.

11. Back in the Dimensional Data Source Mapping dialog box, select New Dimension Filter again and then select Sales Territory.TerritoryHierarchy.

12. In the Select Members dialog box (see Figure 8-30), select United Kingdom to select a filter on members of the All Sales Territories dimension.

13. Expand All Sales Territories and select United Kingdom as the dimension member.

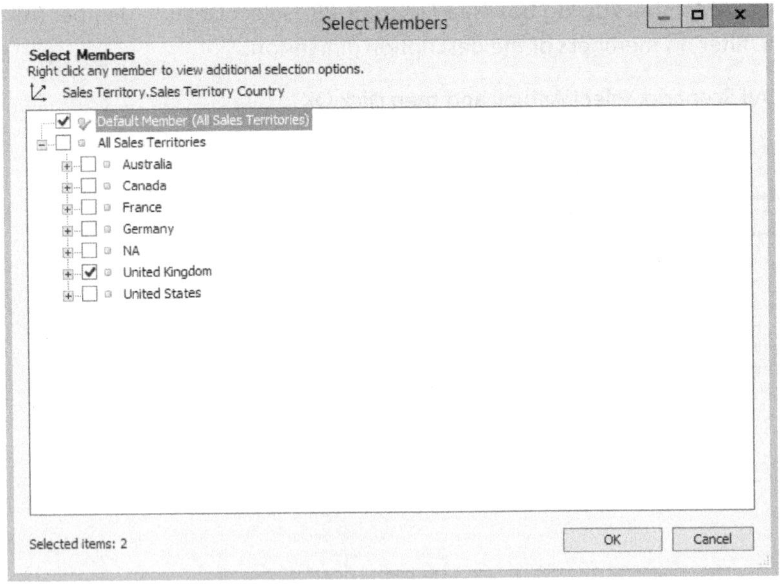

FIGURE 8-30 Selecting Members of Dimension.

14. When the Dimensional Data Source Mapping dialog box opens (see Figure 8-31), click OK.

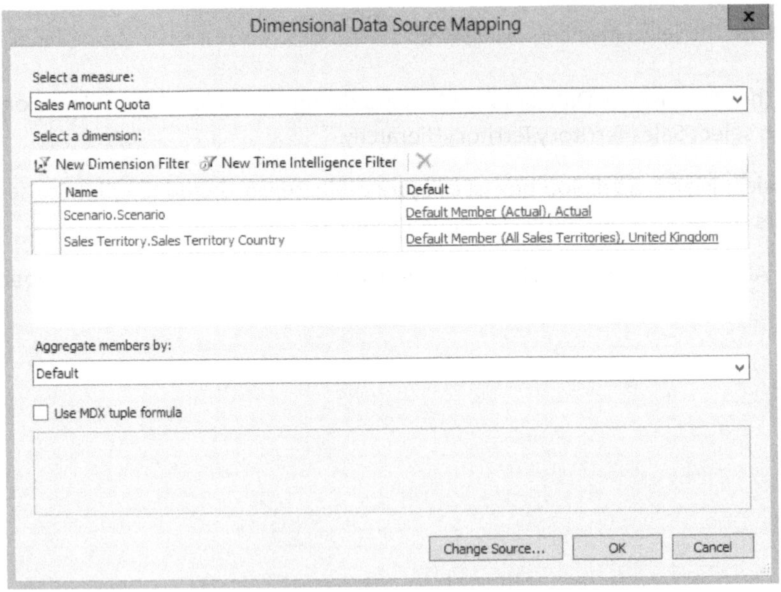

FIGURE 8-31 The Dimensional Data Source Mapping dialog box.

15. In the center pane, with the KPI selected, select Name, Target, and change it to **Forecast Sales**.

16. Repeat Steps 4 through 15 for Forecast Sales, except in Step 10, select Forecast instead of Actual.

17. Click Indicators to see the default. Your KPI should now look as shown in Figure 8-32.

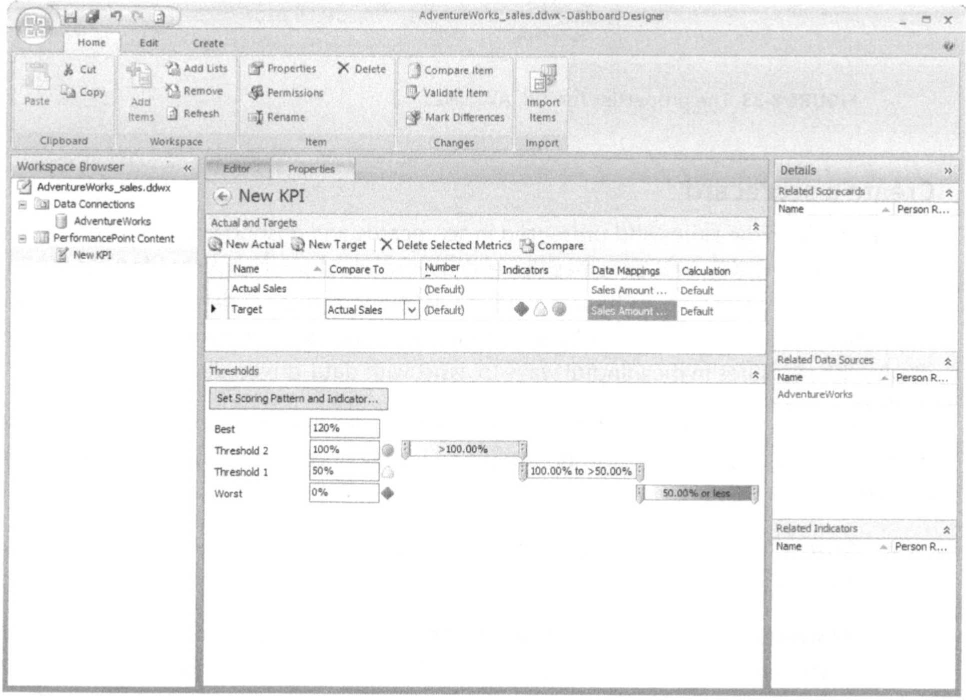

FIGURE 8-32 The indicators for actual and target sales.

Organize the Workspace Browser

As mentioned earlier, the Workspace Browser offers a feature from PerformancePoint Server 2007 by which you can create folders to better organize your PerformancePoint elements.

To create a folder for KPIs, perform the following procedure:

1. In the Workspace Browser, click New KPI, and then, in the center pane, click the Properties tab.

2. In the Display Folder text box, type **KPIs**.

You should now see AW_sales under a folder called KPIs, as depicted in Figure 8-33.

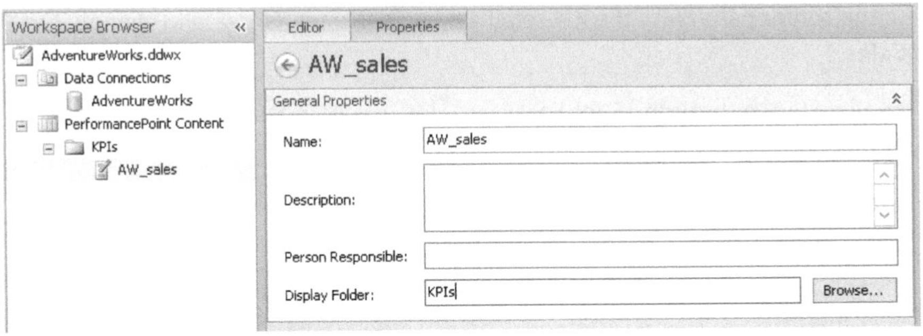

FIGURE 8-33 The properties for KPI, AW_sales.

Create a scorecard

KPIs are built on measures and presented in scorecards and dashboards. The scorecard is the vehicle for indicators and KPIs and becomes the end-user result of the complete lifecycle of a BI solution. That lifecycle is described in Chapter 3, where developers prepare data that can be trusted; put that data into a cube so that the cube becomes the ideal data source for the scorecard; and where KPIs display the measures in meaningful ways to assist with data-driven decision making.

Scoring uses some terms that might be unfamiliar, but they're important as we proceed with configuring our scorecard. The following list provides only brief descriptions of an otherwise complex set of concepts:

- **Score** A calculated value between 0 and 1 that indicates a relative position. 0 is the worst and 1 is the best.

- **Scoring pattern** The language that describes what is good or bad in a score such as "increasing is better" = "a higher value is better." Or, "decreasing is better" = "a lower value is better."

- **Threshold** The minimum value connected to an indicator that produces a change or specified effect to the indicator.

- **Banding** The input type for the threshold boundaries. Some are entered as percent; ages from the target, and others are numeric values with absolute values.

- **Normalize** In KPI hierarchies where there is a parent-child relationship, normalizing describes how scores are combined to represent the parent or rollup score.

> **Important** Your selections for scoring determine how your indicators and visualizations look.

It is worth your time to review other books that can help you understand how a score is calculated by using the band-by value, how to determine the band value, and how to normalize the score. Other material also discusses rollup scoring. The following are some good books on dashboards and scorecards:

- *Strategy Maps: Converting Intangible Assets into Tangible Outcomes* by Kaplan and Norton (Harvard Business School, 2004)

- *The Strategy-Focused Organization: How Balanced Scorecard Companies Thrive in the New Business Environment* also by Kaplan and Norton (Harvard Business School, 2000)

- *Balanced Scorecard Step-by-Step: Maximizing Performance and Maintaining Results* by Paul R. Niven (John Wiley & Sons, 2006)

To set the scoring pattern and indicator for the KPI, perform the following procedure:

1. In the center pane click the default indicators.

   The Thresholds window appears below the Actual Sales and Forecast Sales in Actuals and Targets.

2. Click Set Scoring Pattern to start the Edit Banding Settings Wizard, as illustrated in Figure 8-34.

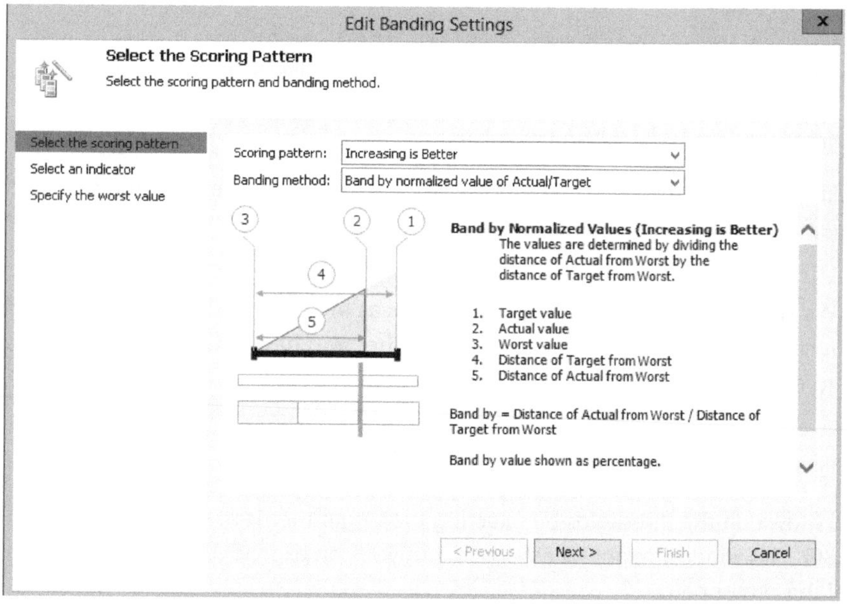

FIGURE 8-34 The Select Scoring Pattern page of the Edit Banding Settings Wizard.

3. Click Next.

The Select An Indicator page appears (see Figure 8-35). Indicators dynamically appear to match the scoring pattern selected in the previous screen.

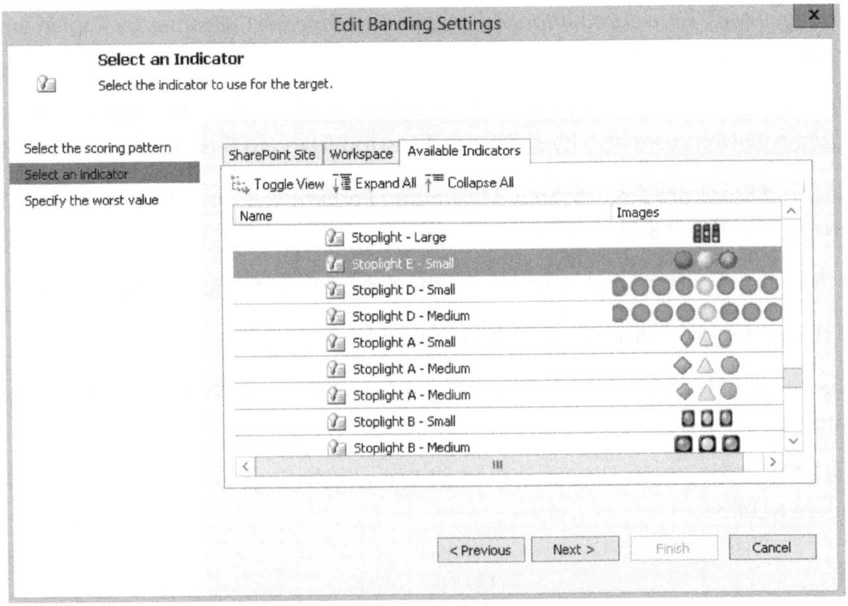

FIGURE 8-35 The Select An Indicator page of the Edit Banding Settings Wizard.

4. Select Stoplight E – Small and click Next.

You now specify the worst value. If the score is below the threshold, the score will be zero. Keep the default in this example.

> **Note** We don't suggest you ever use smiley faces in a real world implementation. We use the stoplight indicators here only to illustrate that you have a wide range of indicators from which to choose.

5. Click Next. Notice how the visualizations have changed.

You can now edit the thresholds by selecting the target metric row that requires editing (see Figure 8-36). This window might be collapsed, but you can expand it by clicking the chevron at the bottom of the center pane.

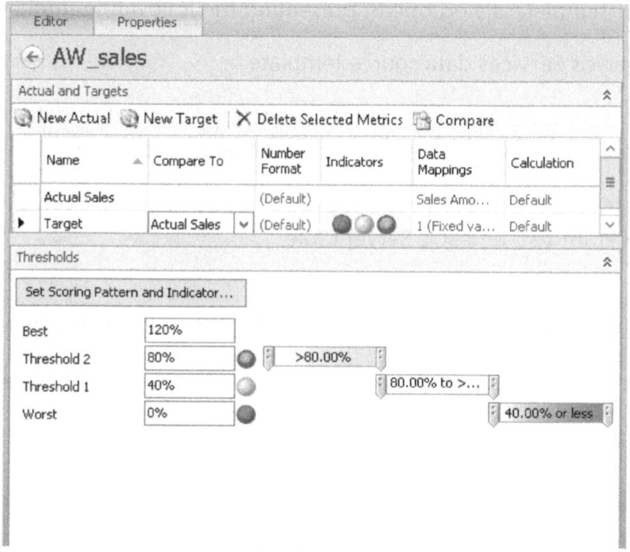

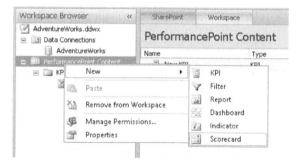

FIGURE 8-36 The scoring pattern of a PerformancePoint KPI, AW_sales.

To create the scorecard, perform the following procedure:

1. In the Workspace Browser, right-click PerformancePoint Content. On the shortcut menu that appears, point to New and then, on the submenu that appears, click Scorecard, as shown in Figure 8-37.

FIGURE 8-37 Create a scorecard from PerformancePoint Content.

The Select A Scorecard Template dialog opens, presenting the following template options:

- **Microsoft** An Analysis Services data source template

- **Standard** A blank Scorecard template without predefined content or data mappings and a Fixed Values Scorecard template where users can define values.

- **Tabular** A template that includes all the options for tabular data sources, such as Excel, ExcelServices, SharePoint List, and SQL Server table.

> **Note** The word "tabular" is used differently here than when discussing Analysis Services tabular data sources.

2. Select Microsoft Analysis Services and click OK.

   A Create An Analysis Services scorecard is selected.

3. Select the AdventureWorks data source and then click Next.

4. Ensure that Create KPIs From SQL Server Analysis Services Measures is selected and click Next.

5. A screen appears, displaying two buttons on the top: Add KPI and Select KPI. Using Add KPI, you can choose an existing KPI from the data source. If there is an existing KPI, you can make more choices such as setting Actual, Band Method, and Targets.

   For this example, select the KPI you created earlier in this chapter.

6. Click Select KPI and then, in the Select A KPI dialog box (see Figure 8-38), click OK.

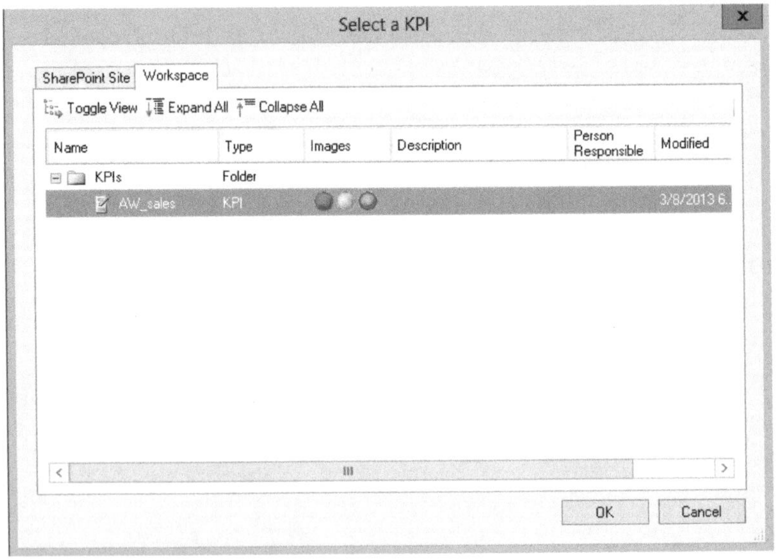

FIGURE 8-38 Select a KPI.

7. Ensure that your KPI is selected and then click Next.

8. The Add Measure Filters dialog box opens. You already filtered data from the Analysis Services cube when you created the KPIs without using this wizard, so just click Next.

9. The same logic applies to the Add Measure Columns dialog box; just click Next.

   Your scorecard now updates to reflect the KPI you created previously. Figure 8-39 shows the items expanded in the Details pane so that you can see the available options. If you had not included the KPI, you could drag it to the center pane.

Figure 8-39 also shows that we used the Workspace feature to create a folder for scorecards by clicking the Properties tab. Finally, notice that the AdventureWorks data source is selected in the lower-right corner.

FIGURE 8-39 The New Scorecard.

10. Save the scorecard and its associated KPI to the server.

    To add dimensions to the scorecard, perform the following procedure:

> **Note** By adding a dimension, you give users the ability to slice KPIs based on different views available through the data source. Specific details might be required to drill down on operational scorecards.

1. Drag the Geography/Hierarchy dimension to just above the AW_sales column of the scorecard, as demonstrated in Figure 8-40.

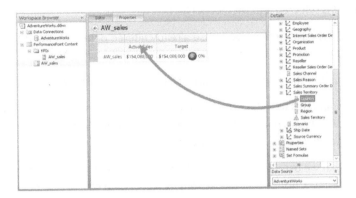

FIGURE 8-40 Drag country to the top of Actual Sales.

The Select Members dialog box appears.

2. Select the check box for United Kingdom.

 Note If you right-click the member you selected, other options appear, as shown in Figure 8-41.

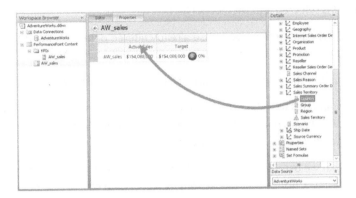

FIGURE 8-41 The Select Members dialog box.

3. Choose Select All Descendants.

Note If you accidently add an unwanted dimension and its members, you can click the Undo button on the Quick Access Toolbar in the upper-left corner of Dashboard Designer.

Important If you're not familiar with multidimensional tools, we highly recommend that you experiment with the user interface by dragging dimensions and selecting members for each value to see the multidimensional views of the Analysis Services data source. Use the Undo button to return to your original state.

4. Perform the same steps listed in Steps 1 and 2, but this time, drag the Forecast Sales column.

   Your KPI in design view (and now with a "dimension") should look as shown in Figure 8-42.

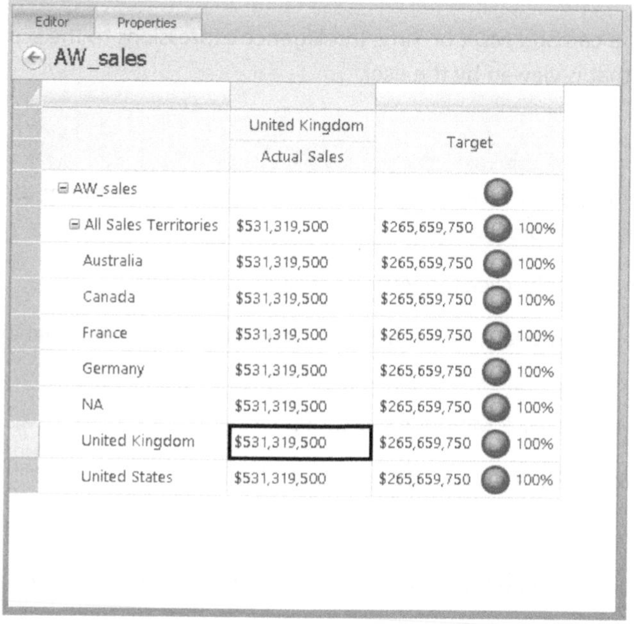

	United Kingdom Actual Sales	Target	
⊟ AW_sales		🔵	
⊟ All Sales Territories	$531,319,500	$265,659,750 🔵	100%
Australia	$531,319,500	$265,659,750 🔵	100%
Canada	$531,319,500	$265,659,750 🔵	100%
France	$531,319,500	$265,659,750 🔵	100%
Germany	$531,319,500	$265,659,750 🔵	100%
NA	$531,319,500	$265,659,750 🔵	100%
United Kingdom	$531,319,500	$265,659,750 🔵	100%
United States	$531,319,500	$265,659,750 🔵	100%

(Editor / Properties tabs, ⊙ AW_sales)

FIGURE 8-42 The results of dragging Territories onto the scorecard.

5. On the Edit tab on the ribbon of Dashboard Designer, click Update to update the scorecard view. Larger scorecards take time to update.

Note The Update and Refresh buttons do different things. Update is unique to scorecards and refreshes only the scorecard. In contrast, Refresh updates the PerformancePoint content and data sources in the Dashboard Designer on your computer.

Notes about the scorecard

At this point, you have created one KPI and one scorecard and associated one dimension with the KPI. You can build more KPIs and add more dimensions to give business users more options for slicing data that they need to view, and much more. Here are a few more scorecard elements that you should explore:

- You can use the Details pane to navigate the elements that you can add to the scorecard, which can dynamically change how your data is visualized.

- You can add metrics on the opposite axes from all KPIs.

- You can use aggregations on the scorecard to make summations of all the metrics. You simply add the aggregation type above the metric column. Aggregations are limited to columns (no row aggregating).

- You can place named sets (from the cube) on a scorecard.

- Using Set Formulas, you can add MDX or Time Intelligence expressions to the scorecard to further filter the data that is viewed by the user.

Creating a filter

You want to include one filter on the dashboard to give users the option to select from other territories. To create one, perform the following procedure:

1. In the Workspace Browser, right-click the PerformancePoint Content.

2. On the shortcut menu that appears, point to Select New. On the submenu that appears, click Filter

3. In the dialog box that opens, click Member Selection.

4. Select the AdventureWorks data source and then click Next.

5. Click Select Dimension.

6. In the Select Dimension dialog box (see Figure 8-43), click Geography.Country Name and then click OK.

7. In the Create A Filter dialog box, click Select Members and then, under Europe, select All Countries.

8. On the Select Display Method page, click List and then click Finish, as shown in Figure 8-44.

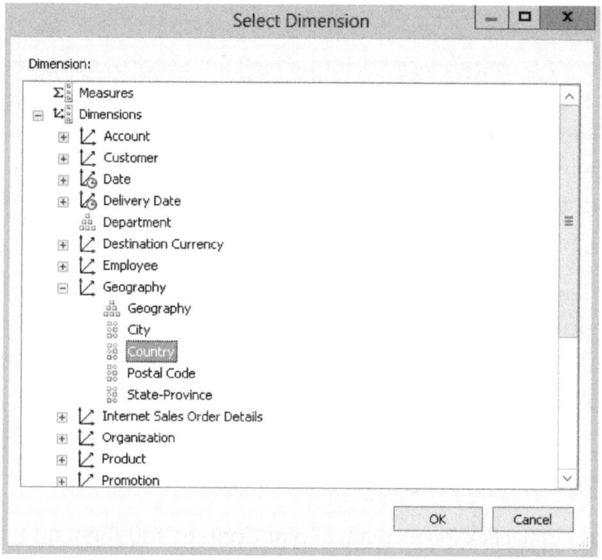

FIGURE 8-43 The Select Dimension dialog box for filter.

> **Note** You have the option of editing the filter.

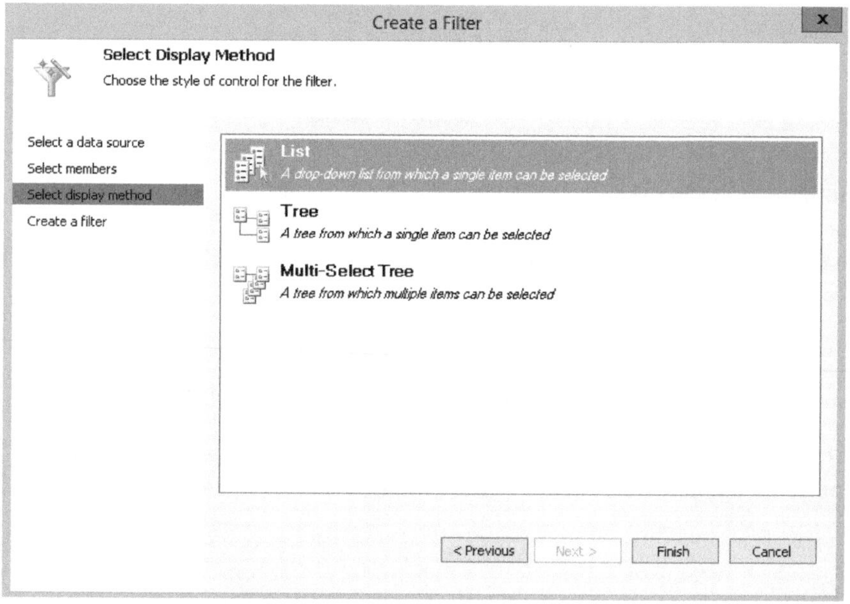

FIGURE 8-44 The Create A Filter Wizard.

Adding a report

As mentioned earlier in the section "An overview of PerformancePoint Services components," there are 10 report types and features that you can use to analyze and investigate data that you monitor by using scorecards and KPIs. The reports help you to create a reporting structure that directs the right data to the decision-makers in the right visualization. For example, an analytic bar chart is useful for comparing groups of members, or you might want to show how sales amounts are distributed across different countries or regions.

We recommend that you review the report types and determine which can best fit your needs for enhancing the scorecard experience. In the following example, it makes sense to include several reports, but we focus on the Analytic chart. The Analytic chart and grid are highly interactive, and you can place them on a webpage; however, the data source must be either PowerPivot or Analysis Services.

To add a bar chart, perform the following procedure:

1. In the Workspace Browser, right-click PerformancePoint Content and then, on the menu that appears, point to New. On the submenu that appears, click Report, as depicted in Figure 8-45.

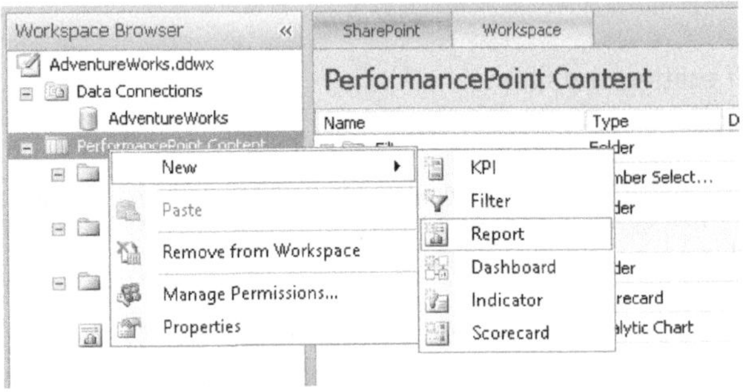

FIGURE 8-45 Adding a bar chart to PerformancePoint content.

2. In the Select A Report Template dialog box (see Figure 8-46), select Analytic Chart and then click OK.

   A wizard opens in which you can select the data source.

3. Select the AdventureWorks Analysis Services data source and click Finish.

   A report authoring environment renders in Dashboard Designer (see Figure 8-47) into which you can drag measures, dimensions, and named sets from the Details pane.

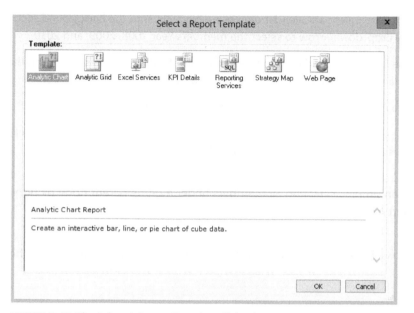

FIGURE 8-46 The Select A Report Template dialog box.

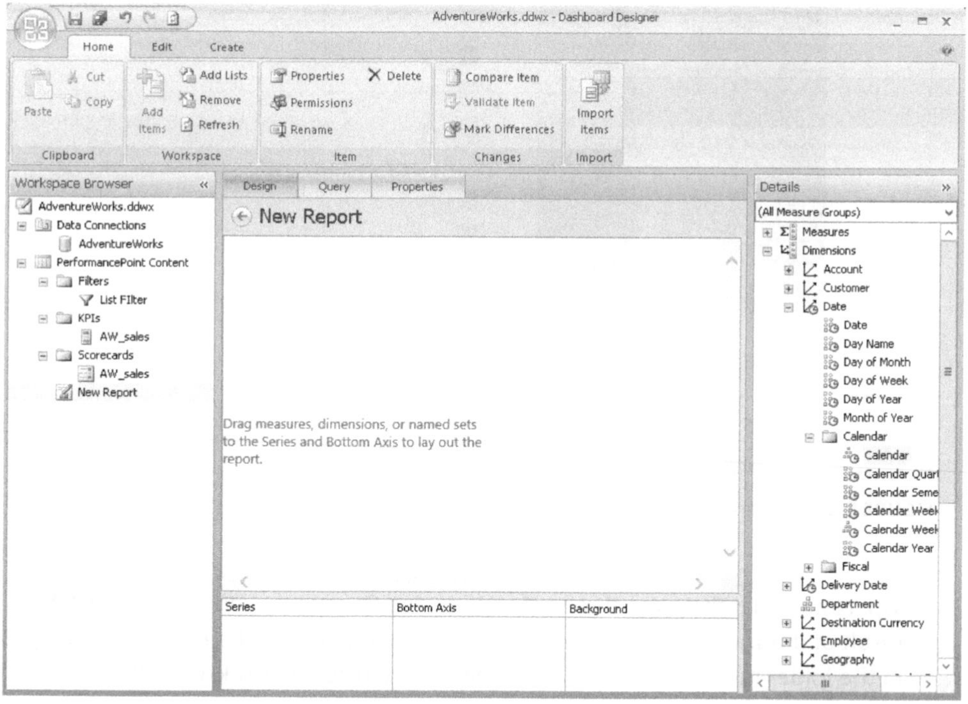

FIGURE 8-47 The New Report page.

4. Drag the Date Calendar:Calendar dimension hierarchy into the Background section and then click the drop-down arrow to select the members Year 2008, 2009, and 2010.

5. Drag the Sales Territory dimension hierarchy into the Background section and then select the Europe dimension hierarchy. (This serves as a background filter for the report.)

6. Drag the Amount measure into the Bottom Axis section.

7. Drag the Geography dimension hierarchy into the Series section and then select dimension members at the country level. Clear All and Europe.

Note You can simplify selecting all members under a single parent node by right-clicking and selecting All Children.

Figure 8-48 shows the result of dragging dimensions and narrowing by selecting members.

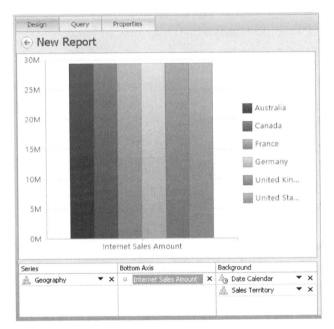

FIGURE 8-48 The Results of new report.

Tip Notice that there are three tabs. Using the Query tab, you can view the MDX query as a result of dragging dimensions and selecting members. On the Properties tab, you can type in the folder name, Reports, to keep things organized in Workspace Browser.

You can enter Data Elements by right-clicking anywhere on the chart. Figure 8-49 shows the result of choosing options for adding a filter, a pivot, changing the report type, and changing the report format.

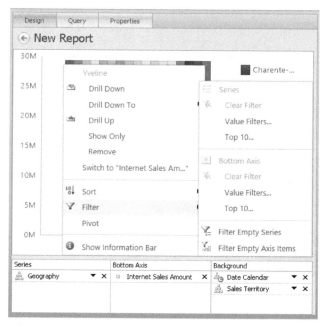

FIGURE 8-49 Adding a filter for new report.

If you click Report Type and then Stacked Chart, the chart updates to visualization depicted in Figure 8-50. Again, it's well worth your time to explore the options to determine the most meaningful visualization for your decision-makers.

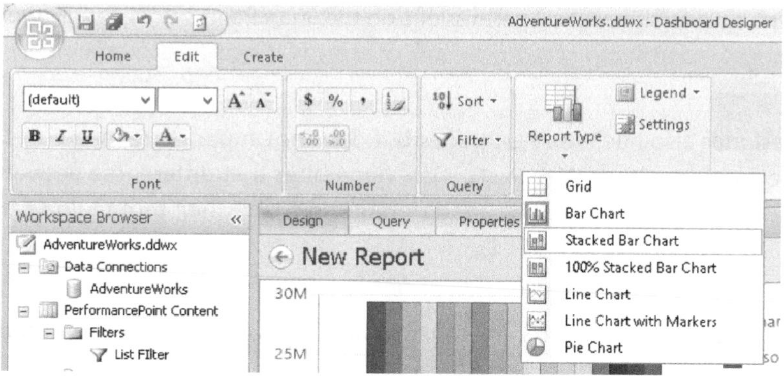

FIGURE 8-50 The list of options to change the Report Type.

If you select Filter and then Top 10, you'll see the Top 10 countries, as shown in Figure 8-51. At the top of the legend, observe the filter icon, which indicates that the report has a filter, and so forth.

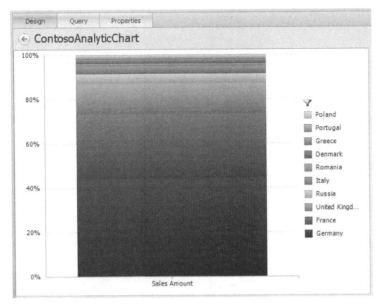

FIGURE 8-51 A Stacked Bar Chart with Top 10 filter.

Creating a dashboard

You are now ready to create a dashboard, the vehicle you use to show PerformancePoint objects to business users. Dashboards are nothing but PerformancePoint Services Web Parts put together on a Web Part page with connections configured between the parts to create interactivity. Dashboards are ASPX pages. You must have Designer-level permissions on the SharePoint site to deploy the dashboard.

> **Note** SharePoint Designer also has Web Part pages but does not support creating connections between PerformancePoint Web Parts. Also, remember that differences between these authoring tools can be confusing; they are different tools, and their terminology and concepts vary.

You can use the following exercise to put Web Parts together and then configure the connections. Web Part connections include:

- Get Value From
- Send Values To

- Source Value

- Connect To

To create a dashboard, perform the following procedure:

1. In the Workspace Browser, right-click PerformancePoint Content and then, on the menu that appears, point to New. On the submenu that appears, click Dashboard.

2. In the Select A Dashboard Page Template dialog box (see Figure 8-52), select Header, 2 Columns. (You can modify this later, after you create the dashboard.)

   The zones mentioned at the bottom of this dialog box define how you can position scorecards, reports, and filters on the dashboard.

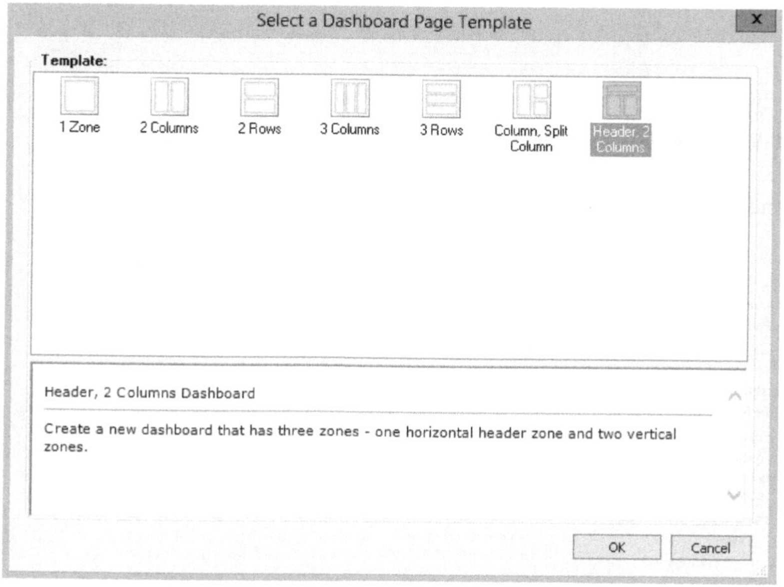

FIGURE 8-52 The Select A Dashboard Page Template dialog box.

3. In the center pane of the Dashboard Designer (see Figure 8-53), type a name for your dashboard as it is highlighted in the Workspace Browser. You can drag scorecards, reports, and filters from the Details pane.

FIGURE 8-53 The results of selecting a zone template for the dashboard page.

The elements shown in Figure 8-54 are available to create a dashboard.

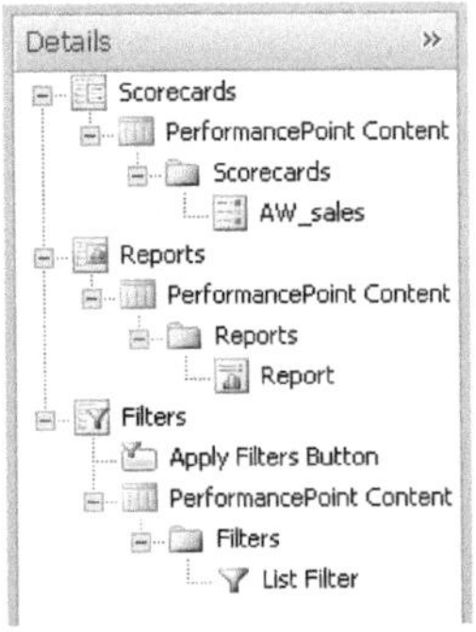

FIGURE 8-54 The dashboard Details pane displays available elements to create a dashboard.

Place a Header on the dashboard by clicking Add in the lower-right corner of the Dashboard Designer. Select the Header item (Figure 8-55). Dashboard Designer automatically adds the Geography.Country filter.

Note that you can also add columns to the zone in the Dashboard page template.

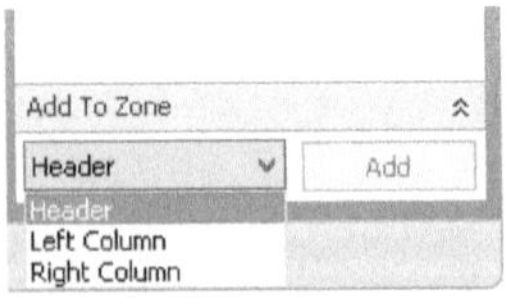

FIGURE 8-55 Adding a Header to a zone.

4. In the Details pane, open the Scorecards node and search until you find the AW_sales scorecard. Drag it onto the Left Column zone (see Figure 8-56).

5. Again, in the Details pane, open the Reports node and look for the AW_sales report. Drag that report onto the Right Column zone.

> **Note** You cannot see the scorecard or chart you created yet. You must deploy the dashboard first.

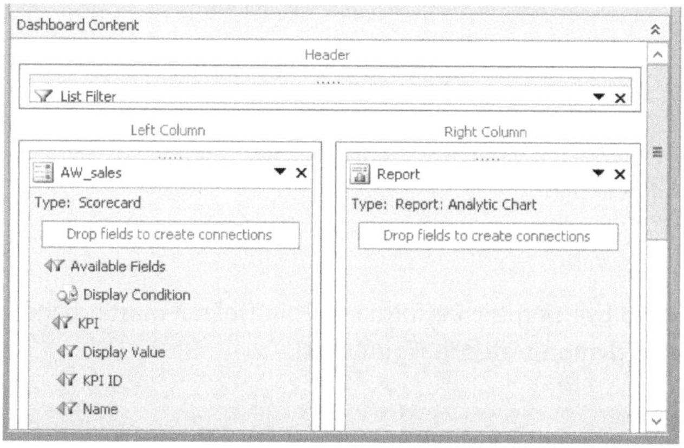

FIGURE 8-56 The Dashboard Content page.

6. In the Workspace Browser, right-click the dashboard and then select Deploy To SharePoint.

7. In the Deploy To dialog box (see Figure 8-57), choose the document library where you want to store this dashboard.

8. Choose the master page that you want to use.

> **Note** You can modify all subsequent deployments for this dashboard by using the dashboard Deployment Properties tab, which is an additional tab next to the Editor tab, to change the target location or master page.

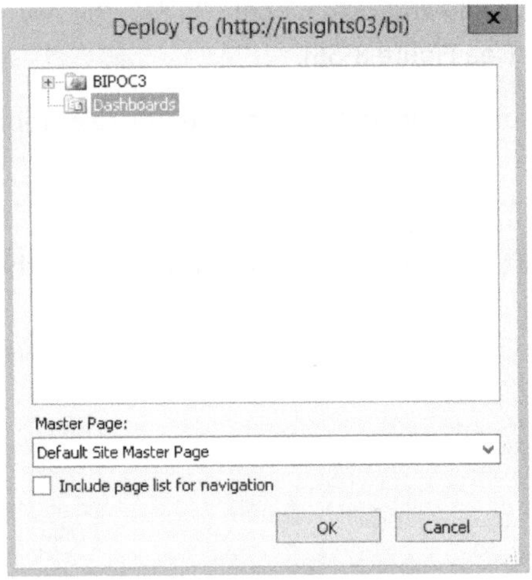

FIGURE 8-57 The Deploy To dialog box.

9. Click OK.

The dashboard is deployed by using the PerformancePointDefault master page, and it fills the entire browser window, as demonstrated in Figure 8-58.

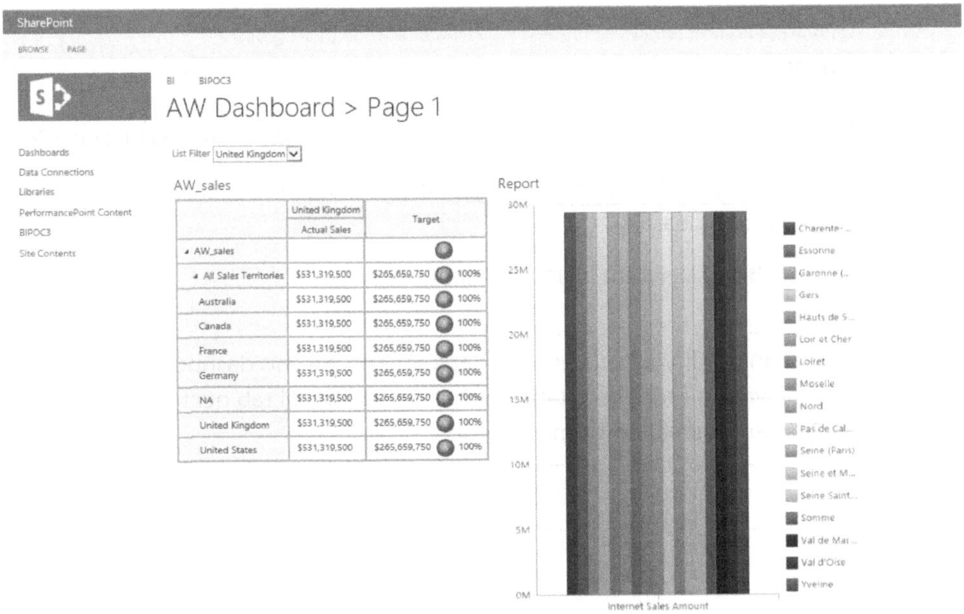

FIGURE 8-58 The deployed dashboard page in SharePoint 2013.

Other options in Dashboard Designer

In addition to the procedures you've seen in this chapter, you can also do the following:

- Add another page or existing dashboard by using the Editor tab when the focus is on your dashboard in Workspace Browser. By doing this, you can separate and organize content by region, product, and so forth. Additionally, it is easy to help users navigate between pages on the Properties tab.

- Modify the filters you created so that users can filter on information they see.

Summary

This chapter provided a taste of the rich functionality available in Dashboard Designer. In this chapter, you explored PerformancePoint Services to understand the following:

- The components and architecture of PerformancePoint, including what's new.

- How to configure security for a data source.

- How to author and publish a dashboard to SharePoint 2013 by using Dashboard Designer.

Along the way, the various sources for more information should give you steppingstones to more information about the concepts presented here. Finally, it's worth noting (again) that PerformancePoint is far too complex to cover fully in a single chapter, so you should plan to spend some time exploring the various features and options to gain a full sense of what's possible.

CHAPTER 9

Using Visio and Visio Services

You've probably used Microsoft Visio to create flowcharts, perhaps network diagrams, maybe an org chart, or a floor plan. But, should Visio be an integral part of your business intelligence (BI) solutions? The goal of this chapter is to provide a "yes" answer to that question by showing you examples of the value that Visio offers, both by itself, and when it's integrated with the products described in other chapters in this book.

Background

The Visio application achieved its twentieth birthday in 2012. The three founders of the company designed the software so that users could build two-dimensional business and technical drawings. What was revolutionary at the time was the building block approach: you weren't required to draw everything from scratch. Instead, Visio provided libraries of predesigned shapes that you could use to build your diagram.

In early 2000 Microsoft acquired what was at the time called Visio Corporation, and in 2001 it released the first Microsoft-branded version of the product, Microsoft Visio 2000. Since then, Microsoft has released year-designated versions of Visio in 2002, 2003, 2007, 2010; the most recent offering is Visio 2013. Most of the Microsoft releases have included both Standard and Professional editions. Visio 2010 was the lone exception—it also included a Premium edition. However, Visio 2013 returns to offering just Standard and Professional.

> **More Info** John Marshall, the first Visio MVP, maintains the historical chronology of Visio on his website at *http://visio.mvps.org*.

Along its evolutionary path, Visio acquired fairly significant data handling capabilities, which are often unused or underutilized in many Visio diagrams. It is those data-handling facilities, however, combined with the graphical power of Visio, that make it such a strong contender for creating dashboards and other BI tools. In this chapter, you will learn how to deploy data-rich Visio diagrams in conjunction with Visio Services in SharePoint 2013.

What's new in Visio 2013

Visio 2013 is packaged in two editions, Standard and Professional. You need the Professional edition for nearly all of the features described in this chapter. New and enhanced features in Visio 2013 include the following:

- **Integration with the cloud**   The Open, Save, and Save As pages in the Visio 2013 Backstage view provide easy access to your SkyDrive account as well as to Microsoft SharePoint and SharePoint Online.

- **Improved integration with SharePoint**   Visio 2010 introduced the ability to save refreshable webpages to Visio Services on SharePoint, but it required saving the Visio drawing in a special file format. In contrast, Visio Services in SharePoint 2013 can open and display Visio files directly, using almost any web browser.

- **Improved integration with other products via SharePoint**   SharePoint webpages can serve as the integration point between Visio and other BI applications. As an example, you might build a BI solution by using a Visio diagram in a Web Part that exchanges data with Excel Services Web Parts and Performance Point Web Parts.

- **SharePoint Workflow integration**   Visio 2013 supports the Microsoft .NET 4.0 workflows that are supported in SharePoint 2013. In addition, SharePoint Designer 2013 can open and manipulate Visio 2013 .vsdx files directly. Consequently, you can use Visio's visual workflow design features to create workflows in both Visio and SharePoint Designer and then execute them with SharePoint Workflow.

- **Coauthoring**   Multiple authors can edit the same Visio 2013 document simultaneously when the document is stored on SkyDrive, SharePoint, or SharePoint Online in Microsoft Office 365. As authors make changes, shapes are flagged to show that edits are in progress, and each author can see presence and contact information for other authors who are editing the same document.

- **Commenting**   When Visio diagrams are stored in SharePoint or SharePoint Online, multiple people can read and add comments to a diagram by using a web browser—you don't even need Visio.

- **Professional appearance**   Visio 2013 themes have been dramatically enhanced, making it easier than ever to produce eye-catching yet professional-looking diagrams. In addition, themes have been supplemented with predesigned visual variants with which you can add your personal touch. Further, you can apply effects such as reflection, glow, and bevel to one or more shapes to provide additional emphasis.

- **Updated, modern shapes**   Hundreds of shapes have been completely redesigned for Visio 2013 to make your diagrams look fresh and modern. You will find new shapes in the stencils used in many templates, including SharePoint Workflow, Business Process Model and Notation (BPMN), Unified Modeling Language (UML) diagrams, organization charts (which now support bulk import of photographs), and network diagrams.

- **Enhanced template and shape search**   It's easier in Visio 2013 to locate the right template to begin a new diagram or to find exactly the right shape to enhance your diagram. Search results are sorted and filtered more effectively and duplicate results are eliminated.

- **Enhanced touch support**   Visio 2013 recognizes a greater array of gestures and touch for easier use on touch-enabled devices.

- **New file format**   All previous versions of Visio stored drawings in a proprietary file format. Visio 2013 joins other members of the Microsoft Office family in using the Open Packaging Convention, an XML-based format. The new .vsdx file format makes the contents of Visio drawings more accessible to other applications for a variety of purposes, including integration with SharePoint.

Six reasons to include Visio 2013 in your BI suite

Visio 2007 introduced several key BI features, including the ability to link shapes to one or more external data sources with just a few mouse clicks. Visio 2007 also introduced data graphics, a set of features designed to make data visible via text callouts, icons, and shape color. In addition, the 2007 release continued to provide the long-standing feature to build a website from a Visio diagram.

Visio 2010 introduced the ability to validate diagrams against one or more sets of business rules and continued the BI trend by integrating with SharePoint in a way that made it possible for users without Visio to view diagrams in their web browsers. Even better, the browser view was dynamic—the drawing updated automatically when the Visio document or its underlying data changed.

The features from previous Visio versions, combined with the new features described in the preceding section, provide six compelling reasons to include Visio 2013 in your SharePoint business intelligence scenario.

1. Dynamic data connections

2. Data visualization

3. Real-time collaboration

4. Diagram validation

5. Instant websites

6. Dynamic diagram rendering via SharePoint

You will learn more about each of these reasons in the following six sections.

Linking to data

Prior to Visio 2007, it was possible to link Visio shapes to external data, but it required a reasonable amount of technical knowledge and frequently required programming skills, as well. Visio 2007 eliminated those requirements with a new data-linking facility. The Professional edition of Visio 2013 extends the data-linking feature to let you create refreshable connections to data stored in Excel Services, SharePoint lists, external SharePoint lists accessible via Microsoft Business Connectivity Services (BCS), SQL Server databases, and almost any Open Database Connectivity (ODBC) or Object Linking and Embedding (OLEDB) data source.

In general, there are two steps involved in data linking.

1. Linking a diagram to one or more external data sources.

2. Linking individual shapes to specific data records.

Later in this chapter, you will walk through the steps involved in linking to external data, but for now, Figure 9-1 displays the result: an External Data window showing one row for each database record or row.

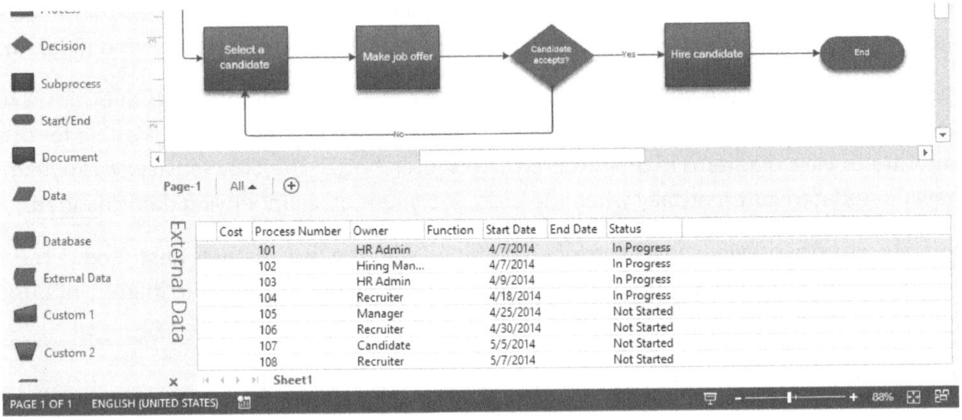

FIGURE 9-1 The External Data window, below the Visio drawing window.

After linking each data row to a shape on the drawing page, the External Data window reflects the data-to-shape link by displaying a link icon at the left end of each row in the External Data window, as shown in Figure 9-2.

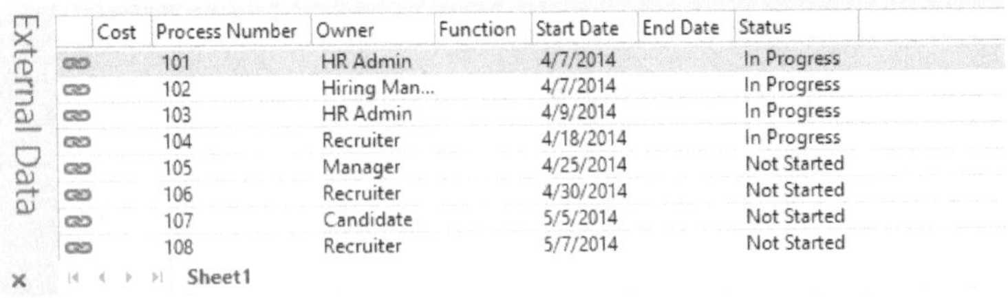

FIGURE 9-2 The link symbols at the left end of each data row.

After completing both steps, you can use various Visio techniques and features to take advantage of that data, including using the visualization techniques described in the next section. And, because the data link is dynamic, as the data in the external data source changes, you can refresh your diagram so that it always reflects the latest information.

Visualizing data

Visio 2007 introduced a very compelling feature that can be used to create dashboards and other BI user interface (UI) designs. Although the idea behind *data graphics* is simple—to annotate shapes on the drawing page with text callouts, icons, or colors based on the data inside the shapes—the potential provided by data graphics is enormous because each data graphic is generated dynamically. If the data in a shape changes, the graphic is updated automatically.

The data-graphic feature is even more powerful when you combine it with the data-linking capability described in the preceding section. In the linked scenario, a data change in a SQL database is refreshed into a Visio diagram, which causes an icon on a Visio shape to change color, or the needle in a speedometer to move, or the height of a bar graph to change. Your Visio diagram becomes a near–real-time reflection of your organization's data.

Each pair of images, shown in Figures 9-3 and 9-4, presents two views of a portion of a diagram. In the basic view on the left, the arrangement of the shapes certainly tells part of a story, and each shape displays a description or name. On the right, however, the same diagram conveys data graphically and moves beyond simply being a diagram to communicating valuable information at a glance.

Figure 9-3 shows several servers in a network diagram.

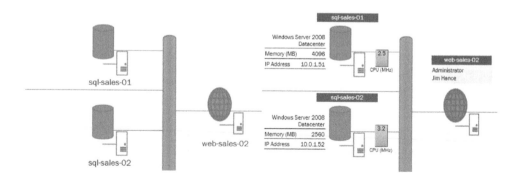

FIGURE 9-3 Two views of a network diagram, without and with Visio data graphics.

Figure 9-4 demonstrates the added value of displaying shape content visually in a process map.

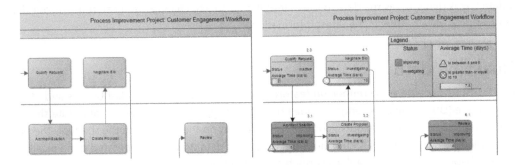

FIGURE 9-4 Two views of a process diagram, without and with Visio data graphics.

Collaborating to create the best result

Running any organization requires collaboration, and the combination of Visio 2013 and Visio Services provides the ideal communication vehicle for coauthoring and commenting on business diagrams.

Visio 2013 further enhances diagram collaboration by providing presence indicators. If you are using the Visio client software and you hover over the user's name or photo in the Comments pane (described in the section "Commenting") or over any of the simultaneous editing icons (described in the section "Coauthoring"), Visio produces a pop-up message box. The box includes the user's name and title and a set of icons indicating whether the user is available via email, instant messaging, or telephone.

> **Note** Some presence indicators appear only if you have Microsoft Lync installed on your computer.

Commenting

A team comprised of both Visio users and people who don't have Visio can comment on the same diagram simultaneously. In Figure 9-5, a Visio user has opened the Comments pane, which shows a pair of comments. The first comment was entered by the Visio user and the second was typed into Internet Explorer by a user logged on to Office 365.

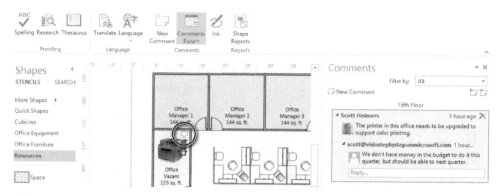

FIGURE 9-5 A Visio 2013 diagram showing the Comments pane and a comment balloon above a printer shape.

Figure 9-6 shows the same diagram, with the same comments, but in this image, the diagram is being viewed with Internet Explorer via Visio Services.

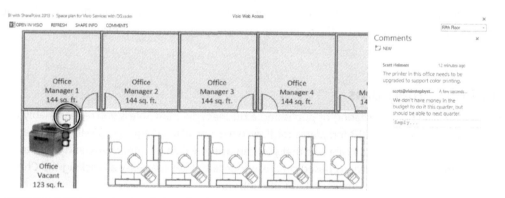

FIGURE 9-6 Visio Services rendering of a Comments pane.

Coauthoring

Visio 2013 coauthoring facilitates multiple people working on a diagram simultaneously. Shapes are not locked while they are being edited, so two people can both be changing attributes or data in the same shape. Visio provides presence indicators so that you know whether someone is working on the same shape, and if two people do happen to change the same shape attribute, the last change wins.

In Figure 9-7, the image on the left shows a user changing shape data for the printer in the Chicago conference room. The image on the right shows a different user running Visio on another computer; in this copy of Visio, the printer in the Chicago conference room displays the "No" symbol (a red circle with a backslash in it) in the upper right of the shape, and pop-up text warns that the shape is being edited by another user.

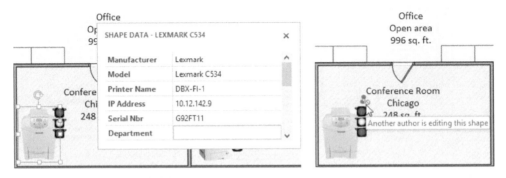

FIGURE 9-7 Two Visio users simultaneously editing the same diagram.

> **Tip** Although you can save a macro-enabled Visio diagram (.vsdm) to SharePoint and open it with a web browser, multiple users cannot work on the diagram simultaneously. You must save the document as a .vsdx file to enable coauthoring or commenting.

Validating diagrams

There is very little point in sharing or publishing a business diagram unless you're reasonably certain that it's correct. The Visio 2013 templates for flowcharts, swimlane diagrams, BPMN, and SharePoint Workflow diagrams all include rule sets that you can use to validate connectivity and other aspects of a diagram. Validating drawings based on these four templates is as easy as clicking the Check Diagram button located on the Process tab on the ribbon.

Figure 9-8 shows the Check Diagram button along with the Issues window that appears when a diagram contains errors. The flowchart shown in the figure is missing several shapes and it contains other errors, as well. Clicking any violation in the Issues window highlights the offending shapes, when appropriate.

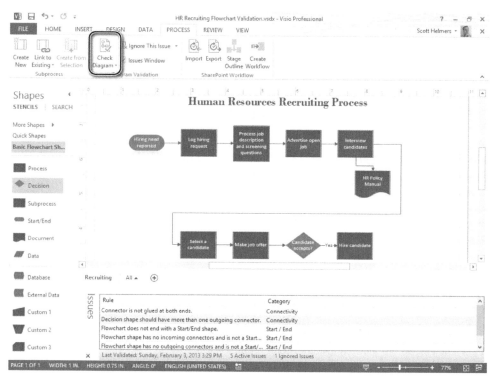

FIGURE 9-8 The Process tab on the Visio 2013 ribbon.

In addition to using or editing preconfigured rule sets, you can also create your own. The latter option is particularly exciting for BI applications because it means that you can build business rules into your diagrams, thereby ensuring that data values, shape arrangement, connectivity, or almost any other characteristic of your diagram is valid before you publish it.

A Visio rule can check a diagram for very simple or very complex conditions. For example, a rule developer might create a rule to answer any of the following questions:

- Are there any unconnected shapes on the page?

- Is there a key performance indicator (KPI) for every key step in this process?

- Does every manager in this organization chart have at least three direct reports?

- Does every server in the network topology diagram have an IP address in the correct range for this company?

These are just representative questions. Visio rules are sufficiently flexible that the real question becomes, "What problem do you need to solve?"

Unfortunately, editing or creating your own rules is not easy because the Visio UI does not include any features for that purpose. However, long-time Visio MVP David Parker has written a book on the subject called *Microsoft Visio 2010: Business Process Diagramming and Validation* (Packt Publishing, 2010), and he offers a free software download called Rules Tools that fills the gap.

> **More Info** Information about David Parker's book and the download links for his Rules Tools add-in are located at *http://www.visiorules.com*.

When you install David's Rules Tools, an additional group of buttons appears on the Process tab on the ribbon, as shown in Figure 9-9.

FIGURE 9-9 The Process tab showing the Rules Tools group.

> **More Info** You can read Scott Helmers' review of David's book at *http://bit.ly/Am7Hvk*.

After you have created your own rules, you can attach them to any diagram. Figure 9-10 shows the list of rules to check for a diagram that contains the built-in Flowchart rules plus a custom rule set.

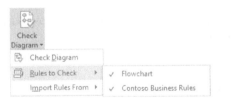

FIGURE 9-10 The Visio submenu menu showing two rule sets.

Saving as a website

In the section that follows this one, you will learn about a technique for creating dynamically updated websites that was introduced in Visio 2010. However, long before that capability existed, Visio offered an option to create a static website from a Visio diagram, and that feature is still useful today. It doesn't offer viewer commenting and automatic updates when the underlying diagram changes, but it does offer read-only viewing of Visio diagrams for people who don't have Visio.

When you save a diagram as a website, the webpages can be viewed with nothing more than Microsoft Internet Explorer. An ActiveX control that runs in Internet Explorer provides helpful navigation features, shape data visibility, and a full-text search option. All hyperlinks in a Visio diagram—links to other pages in the same or a different Visio diagram; links to external documents and web pages; and links to email addresses—continue to work in the browser rendering of the diagram.

In Figure 9-11, you see a full-screen view of a Visio-generated webpage. The original diagram was created with a Visio add-in called TaskMap (*www.TaskMap.com*) that was designed to simplify the documentation and communication of process information across an organization.

TaskMap Professional makes heavy use of data graphics to present important business data, and you can see that the graphics do appear in the web view in Figure 9-11. For example, the numbers in the yellow triangles on some tasks relate to specific risks in the organization's risk management system. In a similar manner, the green diamonds call out controls that mitigate the identified risks. Other icons convey additional business data and are described in the legend in the upper-right corner of the page.

The navigation section on the left side of the Visio-generated webpage includes four panes:

- **Go To pane**   This is a drop-down table of contents from which users can select any page in a diagram and then click the adjacent arrow to view that page.

- **Pan and Zoom pane**   In this pane, a user can draw a rectangle or click the zoom controls to indicate how much of the page, and which section, should be displayed in the viewing pane.

- **Details pane**   This pane displays the data for a shape when users Ctrl+click that shape.

- **Search pane**   The Search pane shows a hyperlinked list of search results. Clicking a link causes an orange arrow to point to the search result on the page (look in the lower-third of Figure 9-11 for the line pointing to the link titled "Pricing override approved" that corresponds to the marked search result).

Go To Pane

Pan and Zoom Pane

Details Pane

Search Pane

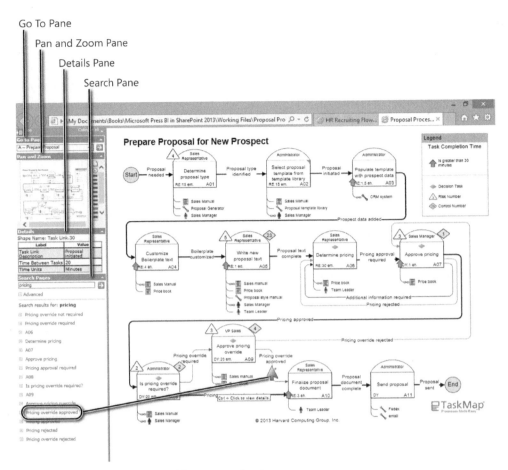

FIGURE 9-11 Data graphics in a Visio-generated webpage.

💡 **Tip** The left-pane navigation, data display, and search features shown in Figure 9-11 are only available when you are using Internet Explorer. Other browsers will display a text-based table of contents but no other features.

Note The Visio Viewer offers another alternative for people who don't have Visio but who need to view Visio diagrams. Unlike the Save As Web Page features described in this chapter, the Visio Viewer can open native Visio diagrams; however, doing so requires that the Viewer is installed on each user's computer. With older versions of Office, the user was required to download the Visio Viewer manually. More recent versions of Office have eliminated the need to download the Viewer by including the software in the release package.

Saving to Visio Services

Visio 2010 introduced features that are a perfect complement to SharePoint for BI, and those features have been enhanced for the 2013 versions of Visio and SharePoint. When using Visio in conjunction with Visio Services in SharePoint, you can create a web rendering of a Visio drawing that has multiple advantages over the Save As Web Page format described in the previous section:

- **Dynamic page rendering**   When either the diagram or the data behind the diagram changes, the web rendering changes automatically.

- **Enhanced ease of use**   Visio Services webpages support familiar UI navigation conventions. For example, you can click and drag to pan around the Visio page and roll the mouse to zoom in and out.

- **Shape data visibility**   Clicking Shape Info at the top of the browser window opens a floating window that displays all data for a selected shape; it also displays any hyperlinks that exist on the selected shape.

- **Offline and online collaboration**   Clicking Comments at the top of the browser window opens a comments pane that not only displays existing comments, but makes it possible for browser users to enter new comments. In addition, if other people are viewing the same page in their web browser or editing it in Visio, all comments are shared and visible by all participants.

- **Browser flexibility**   You can view Visio drawings with Internet Explorer (see Figure 9-12), Mozilla Firefox (Figure 9-13), Google Chrome, and Apple Safari.

In addition to offering enhanced features, saving to Visio Services is simpler in Visio 2013 than it was in 2010. Whereas Visio 2010 required saving in a special intermediate file format, with Visio 2013 you simply save your .vsdx file directly to SharePoint. When a browser user clicks the file in SharePoint, it opens, revealing a view similar to the Internet Explorer 10 screenshot in Figure 9-12, in which the following are visible:

- The Visio diagram with shapes and data graphics

- Shape data for the selected printer located in the San Francisco conference room

- Comments in the Comments pane (more about commenting in the section that follows)

- Simply viewing a Visio diagram via Visio Services is only the beginning of the capabilities offered by Visio and SharePoint. For example, you can embed a Visio diagram in a Web Part, as you'll see later in this chapter. And, that Web Part can exchange data with other Web Parts, whether those parts were created by Visio or other applications, providing even more dynamic BI features.

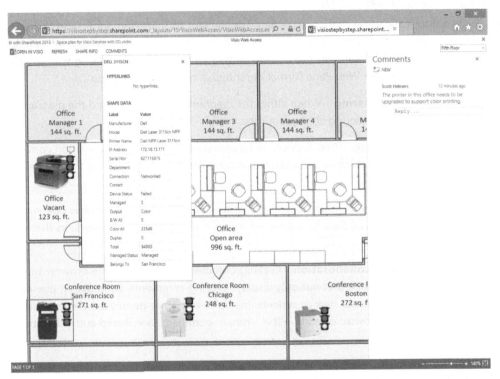

FIGURE 9-12 A Visio 2013 diagram viewed in Internet Explorer 10 via SharePoint 2013 Visio Services.

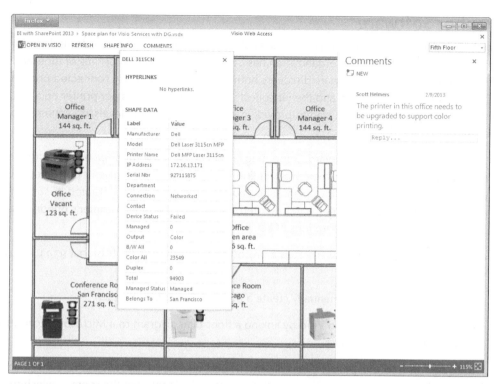

FIGURE 9-13 The same Visio 2013 diagram as in Figure 9-12, but this time viewed in Firefox.

When do I use Visio and Visio Services?

It might sound trite, but the ways in which Visio can be incorporated into BI applications are limited only by your imagination. There is a place for Visio and Visio Services in any situation in which a visual presentation, enhanced by the live display of data in graphical form, can help you achieve your organization's goals. This section includes case studies to describe how several organizations have taken advantage of data-rich diagrams to create BI.

In the first case study, a software vendor was already creating considerable value for their customers. However, the company found that presenting large quantities of statistical data, maintenance information, and live status feedback about thousands of printers was hugely more effective when it added a visual component.

Netaphor Software

Netaphor Software (*www.Netaphor.com*) provides BI solutions for managing a customer's entire inventory of printers, whether the organization has deployed several dozen or tens of thousands of devices. Netaphor's SiteAudit software discovers both networked and locally connected printers without the need for a desktop agent, and then it collects up to 500 data items per printer on a recurring basis. Raw printer data is then analyzed to provide page counts, ink/toner levels, downtime statistics, printer utilization, and much more.

In 2012, Netaphor hired the Harvard Computing Group (*www.HarvardComputing.com*) to assist with adding a visual component to their product line. Netaphor wanted to give its customers the ability to place printer icons onto floor plans, and had two follow-on goals: it wanted its software to capture location data for each printer, and it wanted the spatial view of a customer's printing assets to be augmented by visual representations of key printer data.

Harvard Computing Group (HCG) created a prototype by using Visio Professional so a user could do the following:

- Import a CAD drawing or manually create a building floor plan in Visio.

- Create a printer inventory in Visio by linking a floor plan diagram to a Microsoft Excel workbook containing printer data.

- Drag devices from the printer inventory into rooms on a floor plan. (As they are dropped onto a floor plan, the printer shapes automatically record the identity of the room in which they are placed.)

- Apply Visio data graphics to one device or to a user-selected set of printers to view key operating statistics and errors visually.

Netaphor President and CEO Rakesh Mahajan liked the possibilities inherent in the prototype and hired HCG to build the SiteAudit Visualizer. HCG partnered with Chris Roth (*www.visguy.com*) to design and create the system. The current software features a unique spoke graphic created by Roth that aggregates and visually presents data from a set of user-selected devices.

Figure 9-14 shows a floor plan, a collection of printers, and the visual representation of key device data. Notice that each printer displays a data graphic with two elements: a background color based on the name of the department that owns the printer, and a stacked bar graph showing the ratio of black and white to color print. In addition, two spoke graphics display a visual representation of the aggregate data for the two selected departments' printers.

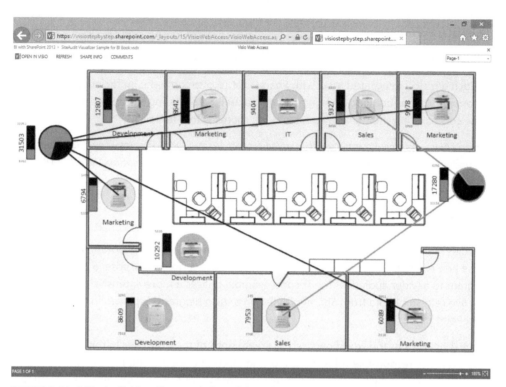

FIGURE 9-14 A SiteAudit Visualizer rendering of the printing assets on a floor in a building.

After demonstrating an early version of the SiteAudit Visualizer to customers in Europe, Mahajan said, "Just seeing the early demonstrations of what Harvard Computing Group created caused us to revise our thinking about how we present large volumes of printer data to our customers. We have traditionally used an Excel-like user interface, but we now strongly prefer the graphical format that Visio provides. It will become the primary interface for our offerings to our clients."

According to Mahajan, SiteAudit Visualizer succeeds because it tells a complex story very simply by taking advantage of data-driven Visio diagrams and data-rich graphics.

Additional case studies

Microsoft has published Visio case studies on the main Visio website, *visio.microsoft.com*. Two that might be of interest to readers of this book are the following:

- VU University Amsterdam integrated Visio with System Center Operations Manager to create a set of intuitive diagrams that are continually refreshed with new data about the state of their global IT infrastructure.

  http://www.microsoft.com/casestudies/Case_Study_Detail.aspx?CaseStudyID=4000011132.

- Giochi Preziosi integrated Visio with SharePoint to overcome the inefficiency that resulted from employees booking meeting rooms manually. Now, using Visio Services webpages on the company intranet, employees can book rooms with a few clicks.

  http://www.microsoft.com/casestudies/Microsoft-Visio/Giochi-Preziosi/Toy-Manufacturer-Conducts-More-Efficient-Meetings-with-Graphical-Booking-Application/710000000465.

Incorporating Visio into a BI solution

The examples in the following section illustrate two different ways to incorporate Visio into a BI solution. In the first example, Visio Services and SharePoint serve a simple purpose: a means to publish a Visio diagram to a wider audience. The second example utilizes a more extensive range of features by including live refresh of data from SharePoint lists in a Visio diagram displayed in multiple Web Parts on a SharePoint page.

Figure 9-15 illustrates the workflow used to create both of the examples in this chapter. The diagram also proposes responsible roles (on top of the tasks) and supporting roles (next to the person icon below the tasks) for each activity. (Chapter 2, "Planning for business intelligence adoption," includes more detailed ideas about which organization roles might be involved in various BI activities.) Each task also displays the required software tools and some tasks include guidelines, as well.

> **Note** The sequence of steps in Figure 9-15 is not absolute. For example, you might choose to link your Visio diagram to data and create data graphics before saving the diagram to SharePoint. Regardless of the sequence you use, be aware of an important restriction if you are linking to Excel workbooks: if you want the data in your diagram to update dynamically based on changes in Excel data, you must store the workbooks to Excel Services on SharePoint *before* you create the data links.

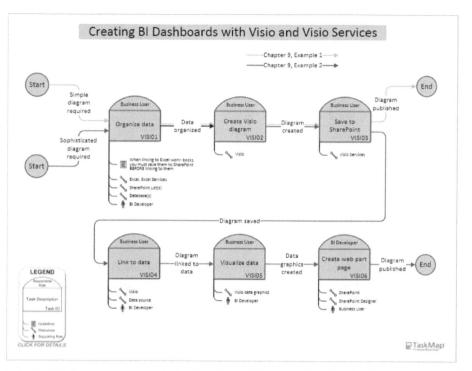

FIGURE 9-15 A process map created with a Visio add-in called TaskMap that illustrates the workflow for creating BI dashboards with Visio.

Visio Services: Example 1

In this example, you will use the Visio Org Chart Wizard and organization data that resides in Excel to generate an org chart. You will also add several data graphics to reflect current performance and training metrics and then publish the resulting diagram to Visio Services.

> **Note** This example uses SharePoint Online that is part of Office 365; however, it will work in essentially the same way using your organization's SharePoint servers.

Organizing the data

The data you will use to create the organization chart for this example resides in Excel and is shown in Figure 9-16. However, as you will notice in step 3 of this exercise, you are not limited to Excel. You can use Microsoft Exchange data as well as other sources to build your chart.

	A	B	C	D	E	F	G	H	I	J
1	Name	Title	Reports To	Employee Number	Extension	Annual Training Completed	Q1	Q2	Q3	Q4
2	Christian Hess	President		367911	101	80				
3	Fabien Hernoux	Vice President	Christian Hess	345180	125	100	80	90	60	100
4	Carole Poland	Manager	Fabien Hernoux	385150	115	50	40	80	70	80
5	Ty Carlson	Manager	Fabien Hernoux	345138	111	40	50	50	45	60
6	Fernando Caro	Accounting Clerk	Carole Poland	345165	120	100				
7	Filip Rehorik	Accounting Clerk	Carole Poland	395177	124	40				
8	Jesper Herp	Accounting Supervisor	Carole Poland	345156	117	60				
9	Oleg Anashkin	Accounting Clerk	Carole Poland	375141	112	80				
10	Geert Camelbeke	Accounting Clerk	Ty Carlson	345171	122	20				
11	Mary Kay Andersen	Accounting Clerk	Ty Carlson	367953	108	80				
12	Jamie Reding	Accounting Supervisor	Ty Carlson	367923	103	40				

FIGURE 9-16 Organization data stored in Excel for building an org chart.

Creating the Visio diagram

To generate the Visio diagram, perform the following procedure:

1. On the ribbon, click the File tab to display the Backstage view (see Figure 9-17), click the New tab and then, in the Business template category, open the Organization Chart Wizard template.

FIGURE 9-17 The Organization Chart Wizard template on the New page of the Visio Backstage view.

2. On the first page of the wizard, indicate whether you already have organization data in a file or database, as shown in Figure 9-18, or whether you want to enter the data via the wizard.

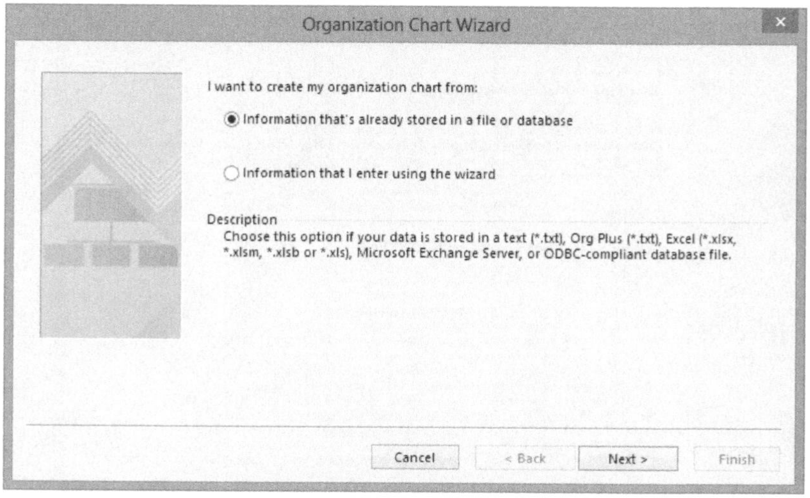

FIGURE 9-18 The first page of the Organization Chart Wizard—choosing how to create the org chart.

3. On the next page, indicate whether your organization data will be read from an Exchange Server directory, a text or Excel file, or an ODBC-compliant data source, and then click Next. For this example, we will use an Excel file, as depicted in Figure 9-19.

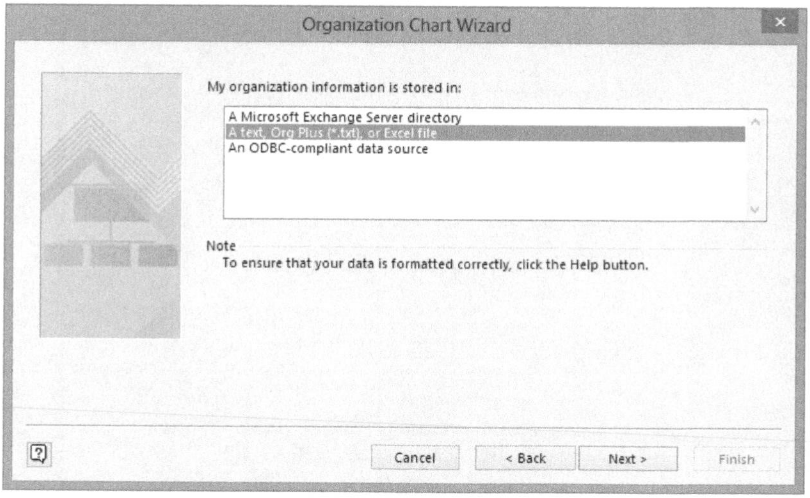

FIGURE 9-19 The second page of the Organization Chart Wizard—selecting the data type.

4. On the next page in the wizard (see Figure 9-20), click the Browse button to navigate to the data source and then click Next.

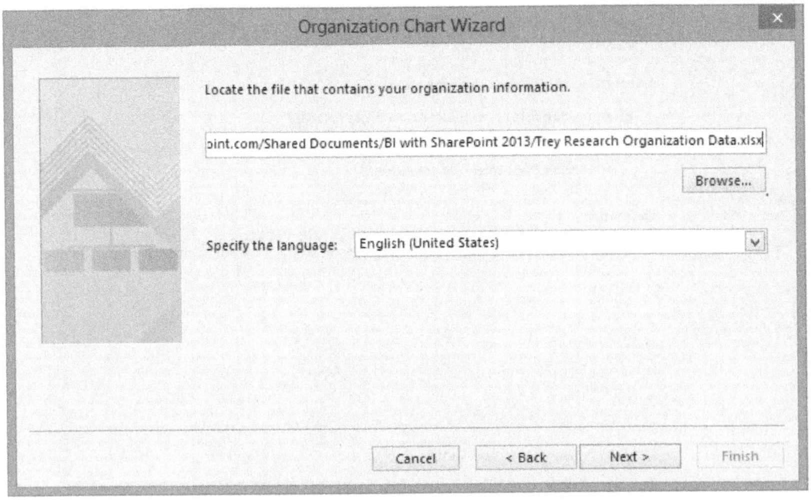

FIGURE 9-20 The third page of the Organization Chart Wizard—selecting the data source.

5. If your organization data already contains columns labeled Name and Reports To, Visio will find them. If not, click the drop-down arrows next to those names, as illustrated in Figure 9-21, select the correct field for each, and then click Next.

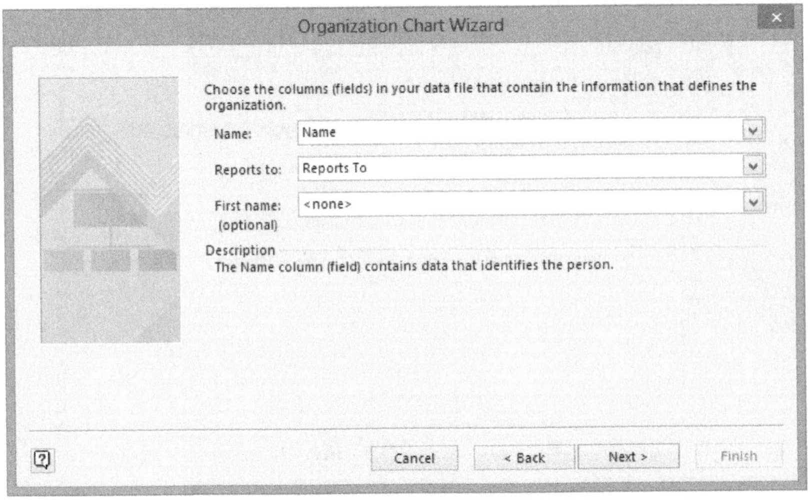

FIGURE 9-21 The fourth page of the Organization Chart Wizard—selecting the data fields for Name and Reports to.

6. Choose which fields that you want to display on each org chart shape (see Figure 9-22) and then click Next.

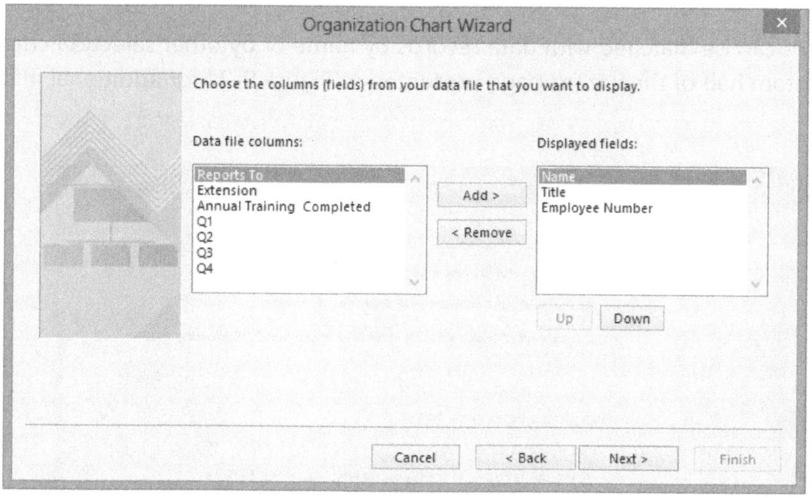

FIGURE 9-22 The fifth page of the Organization Chart Wizard—identifying which field values to display.

7. Choose which fields from your source data that you want to include in the shape data for each org chart shape and then click Next, as demonstrated in Figure 9-23.

Tip It is important to select all fields whose values you might want to analyze, report on, or display using data graphics.

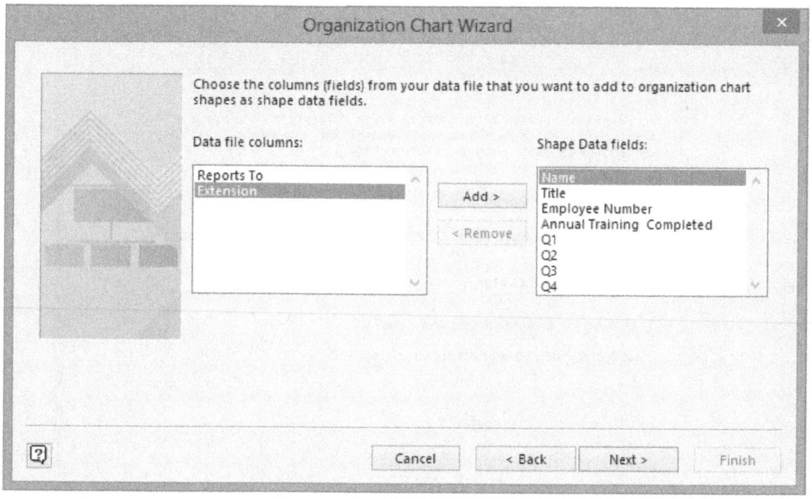

FIGURE 9-23 The sixth page of the Organization Chart Wizard—selecting data fields.

8. If you want to import photos for some or all people in your org chart—a new feature in Visio 2013—browse to the folder containing the photos and then click Next.

Tip Photos can be matched with data records by name or by other selection criteria. Refer to the bottom half of the wizard page presented in Figure 9-24 for additional information.

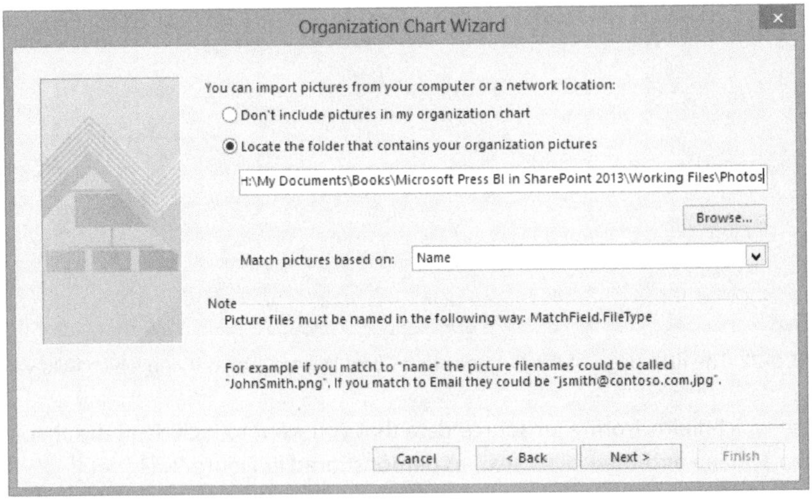

FIGURE 9-24 The seventh page of the Organization Chart Wizard—choose whether to include photos with org chart shapes.

9. Accept the defaults or make changes to the options on the final wizard page and then click Finish, as illustrated in Figure 9-25.

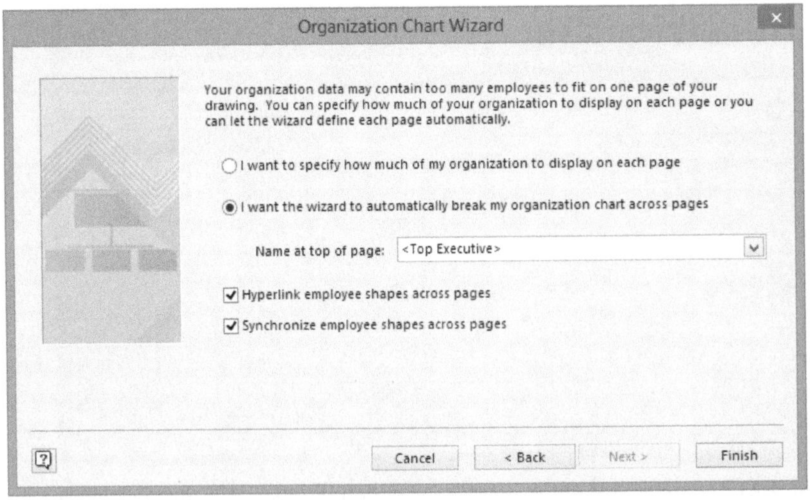

FIGURE 9-25 The final page of the Organization Chart Wizard—specify page layout parameters.

10. Your organization chart appears on one or more drawing pages using a default shape type and layout. You can use the tools on the Org Chart tab shown in Figure 9-26 to change the

shape type, spacing, and layout. The organization chart in Figure 9-28 was customized by using the Belt shape and the Horizontal Stagger layout.

FIGURE 9-26 The Org Chart tab on the Visio 2013 ribbon

You can use the Themes and Variants galleries on the Design tab shown in Figure 9-27 to customize the appearance of the org chart. The organization chart in Figure 9-28 was customized by applying the Whisp theme.

FIGURE 9-27 The Design tab on the Visio 2013 ribbon.

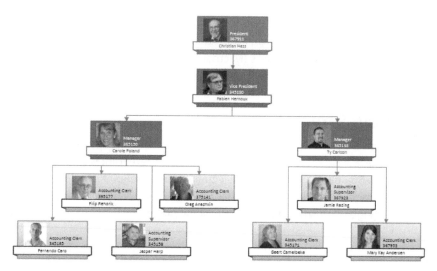

FIGURE 9-28 A Visio org chart.

Visualizing data

It is beyond the scope of this book to provide detailed instructions for creating Visio data graphics. However, Figure 9-29 demonstrates how data visualization in Visio can turn an ordinary org chart into a powerful presentation of organizational data. In the figure, each shape includes a graphic item on its right edge that represents the percentage of required annual training each employee has completed. The Vice President and Manager shapes also include a bar-chart graphic to their left side that depicts performance in each of the four most recent quarters.

FIGURE 9-29 Visio org chart with data graphics and a data-graphics legend.

> **More Info** For additional information about data graphics, refer to Chapter 10 of *Visio 2013 Step by Step* by Scott A. Helmers (Microsoft Press, 2013), which you can also find at *http://www.VisioStepByStep.com*.

Saving to Visio Services

When you've created a Visio diagram that you want to share with other people—especially with people who don't have Visio—saving it to Visio Services on SharePoint is an excellent option. In Visio 2013, saving to SharePoint is as easy as selecting your SharePoint site on the Save As page, and either taking advantage of a recently used folder (refer to Figure 9-30) or using the Browse button at the bottom of the page (not shown) to select another location.

FIGURE 9-30 The upper part of the Save As page in the Visio Backstage view.

Figure 9-31 shows the published org chart with the Shape Data window open on the left side of the page. Users viewing this page have full pan and zoom control along with commenting rights, as described in the section "Saving to Visio Services" earlier in this chapter.

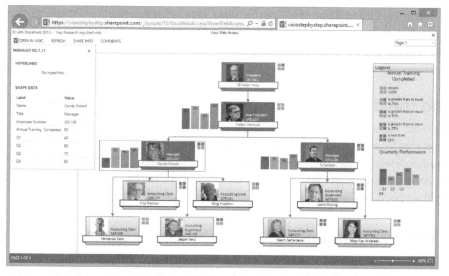

FIGURE 9-31 The Internet Explorer view of the Visio org chart from the previous section via Visio Services.

Visio Services: Example 2

Fashion Station, a fictitious regional clothing store chain, provides the second BI example and includes three primary components:

- A Visio diagram

- Data in SharePoint lists

- A SharePoint page comprising multiple Web Parts

The first page of the Visio diagram contains a regional map with store locations and sales summaries. The store icons on the regional map contain drill-down hyperlinks to store-level sales and inventory diagram pages. Each store page contains a floor plan that includes the locations of merchandise racks. Creative, colorful data graphics enhance the aesthetics of all pages and provide valuable intelligence about store operations. The diagram is linked to two data sources in two different SharePoint lists that contain sales and inventory data.

Finally, a SharePoint page includes multiple Web Parts, each of which presents a different aspect of the Visio diagram or the linked data. When users change data values in either of the SharePoint lists, the changes ripple through the Visio diagram and then appear in the various Web Parts.

Note This example uses SharePoint Online, which is part of Office 365; however, it will work in essentially the same way using your organization's SharePoint servers. It's also useful to know that this example was created without writing any code. You can provide an even richer feature set by utilizing the Visio Services JavaScript Application Programming Interface (API), but as this example illustrates, it isn't necessary to do any programming to add significant value to your organization's data.

Organizing the data

You probably already have the data for your BI application in hand, and there's a very high probability that it's in a form that Visio can use directly. In addition to workbooks stored in Excel Services, you can create refreshable links to data in SharePoint lists, external SharePoint lists accessible via Microsoft BCS, SQL Server databases, and almost any ODBC or OLE DB data source. For this example, the data resides in SharePoint lists.

Creating the Visio diagram

After organizing the data, the next step in building this scenario is to create the Visio diagram for the store chain. You will add the map shapes, place the store shapes onto the map, build the individual store pages, and then add hyperlinks from the store icons to the individual pages. This part of the process should be familiar to anyone who has created any type of hierarchical diagram in Visio, whether it was a network diagram with servers on a topology map linked to the server locations in photo-realistic rack diagrams, a building occupancy plan with a stacking diagram linked to individual floor plans, or a process map with one or more subprocess pages.

The diagram in Figure 9-32 includes a map of the western part of the United States (state map shapes courtesy of *www.visguy.com*) and displays the locations of the six stores in the chain.

FIGURE 9-32 A regional map of six stores in the Fashion Station chain.

Each store layout includes a detailed floor plan created in Visio, as shown in Figure 9-33, which is for the Seattle store. The diagram of the sales floor shows the locations of the merchandise racks.

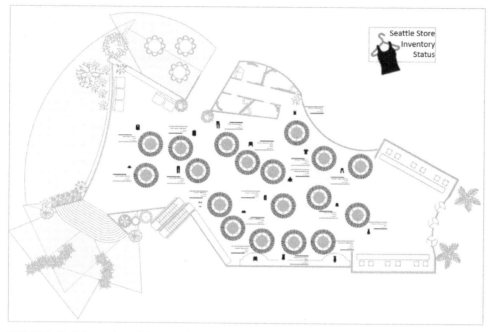

FIGURE 9-33 A floor plan of the Seattle store showing locations of merchandise racks.

At this point, the diagram is a good start but isn't very interesting because it doesn't reflect sales and inventory data. Consequently, we need to publish the diagram to SharePoint and link it to data.

Saving to Visio Services

You can save the diagram to Visio Services by using the same technique described in the section "Saving to Visio Services" in the previous example.

Linking to data

The sales data for the store chain is kept in multiple SharePoint lists. One list aggregates data from all stores, and there is a separate list for each store. To link the Visio diagram to data, perform the following procedure:

1. On the ribbon, click the Data tab and then, in the External Data group, click the Link Data To Shapes button (see Figure 9-34) to open the Data Selector Wizard.

FIGURE 9-34 The Link Data To Shapes button on the Data tab of the Visio ribbon.

2.   On the first page of the Data Selector Wizard, click the Microsoft SharePoint Foundation List
     option and then click Next, as illustrated in Figure 9-35.

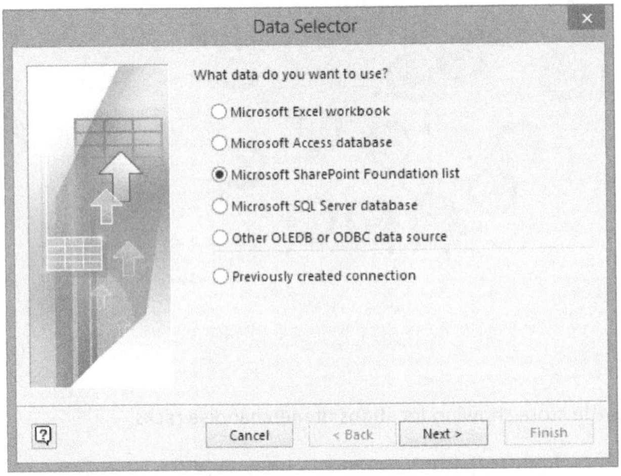

FIGURE 9-35 The first page of the Data Selector Wizard on which you identify your data source type.

3.   On the next page (see Figure 9-36), select the URL for the SharePoint site if it already exists in
     the list. Otherwise, in the Site text box, type or paste the URL and then click Next.

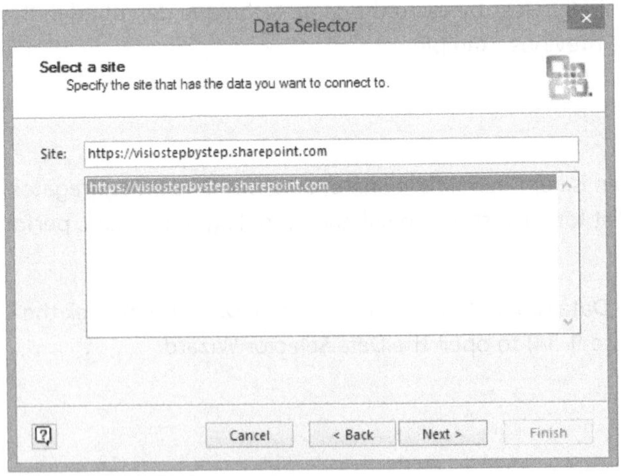

FIGURE 9-36 The second page the Data Selector Wizard—selecting a specific SharePoint site.

4. The wizard displays the names of the SharePoint lists on the site you've chosen (see Figure 9-37). For this exercise, select the Fashion Station -- Overall Sales Data list and then click Next.

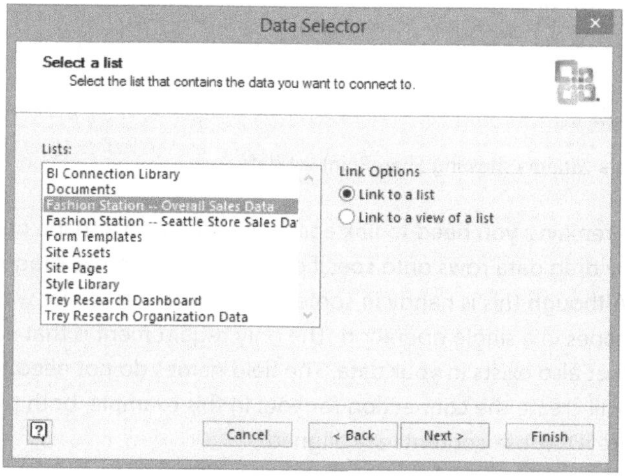

FIGURE 9-37 The third page of the wizard—selecting a SharePoint list.

5. On the final wizard page (see Figure 9-38), click Finish.

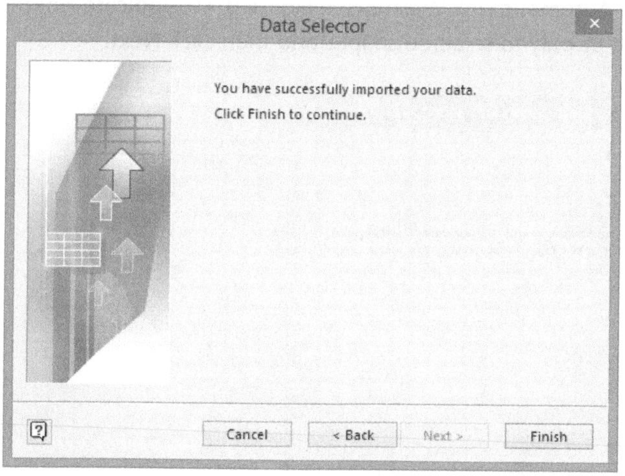

FIGURE 9-38 The final page of the Data Selector Wizard.

You have now linked the diagram to one list and it appears in the External Data window, as shown in Figure 9-39.

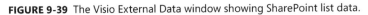

	ID	City	StoreID	State	Employees	SalesGoal	QtySold
	1	Seattle	1	WA	6	300	120
	2	PortLand	2	OR	5	300	72
	3	LA	3	CA	10	300	107
	4	San Diego	4	CA	8	300	83
	5	Boise	5	ID	2	300	117
	6	Las Vegas	6	NV	5	300	252

Fashion Station -- Overall Sales Data

FIGURE 9-39 The Visio External Data window showing SharePoint list data.

However, an important step remains: you need to link each data record to a shape on a drawing page. In Visio, you can manually drag data rows onto specific shapes; for example, drag the Las Vegas row onto the Las Vegas store. Although this is handy in some cases, there is an easier way when you want to link data to multiple shapes in a single operation. The only requirement is that each shape must have a unique identifier that also exists in your data. The field names do not need to match, but if the field values match, Visio will create the connection for you. In this example, both the shapes and the data have a field called Store ID whose contents are aligned.

1. On the Data tab, in the External Data group, click the Automatically Link button. Note: if you only want to link to a specific set of shapes, select them before clicking the Automatically Link button.

2. On the first page of the Automatic Link Wizard (see Figure 9-40), indicate whether you want to link data to all shapes or only to selected shapes and then click Next.

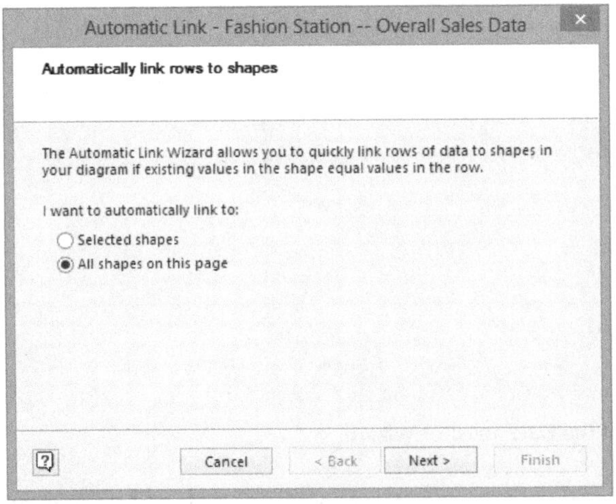

Automatic Link - Fashion Station -- Overall Sales Data ✕

Automatically link rows to shapes

The Automatic Link Wizard allows you to quickly link rows of data to shapes in your diagram if existing values in the shape equal values in the row.

I want to automatically link to:

○ Selected shapes
● All shapes on this page

[Cancel] [< Back] [Next >] [Finish]

FIGURE 9-40 The first page of the Automatic Link Wizard—indicating the shapes to which data should be linked.

3. On the next wizard page, select the data field (or fields) and corresponding shape data fields that contain the unique ID. Figure 9-41 shows that in this example, the field that will be used is called Store ID in both locations. After selecting the fields, click Next.

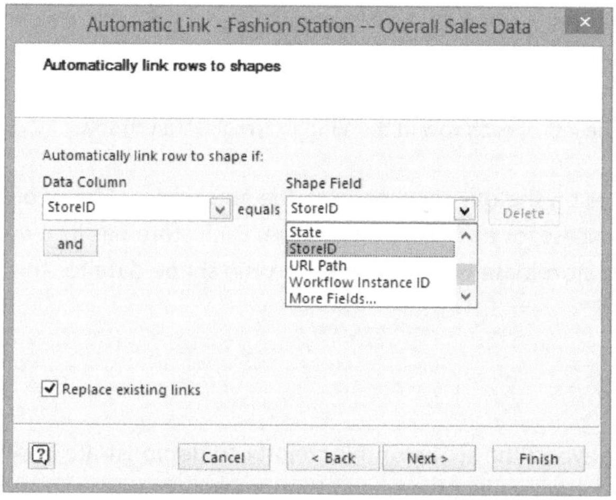

FIGURE 9-41 Identifying how the wizard should match data records to shape data fields.

4. On the summary screen presented in Figure 9-42, click Finish.

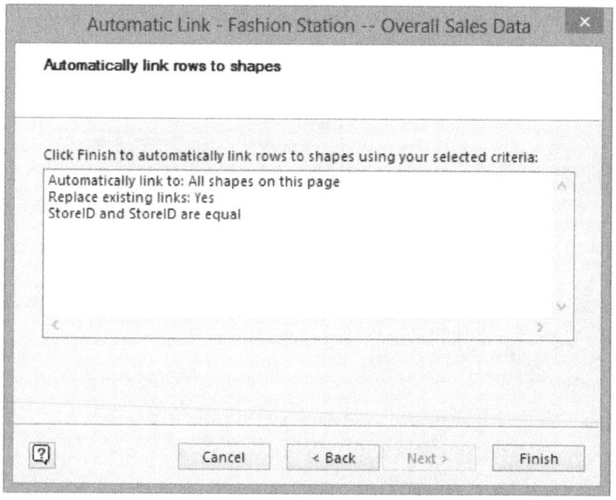

FIGURE 9-42 The summary page of the Automatic Link Wizard.

The link symbols at the left end of each data row in Figure 9-43 indicate that all rows were successfully associated to a store shape.

	ID	City	StoreID	State	Employees	SalesGoal	QtySold
∞	1	Seattle	1	WA	6	300	120
∞	2	PortLand	2	OR	5	300	72
∞	3	LA	3	CA	10	300	107
∞	4	San Diego	4	CA	8	300	83
∞	5	Boise	5	ID	2	300	117
∞	6	Las Vegas	6	NV	5	300	252

◄ ◄ ► ► Fashion Station -- Overall Sales Data

FIGURE 9-43 Link symbols appear to the left of each row in the Visio External Data window.

Now that you've linked the stores on the overview page to the appropriate SharePoint list via the Store ID, you need to repeat the process for each individual store. Each store has its own SharePoint list, and the unique identifier in the store data that matches the Visio shape data for this example is the merchandise Rack ID.

Visualizing data

As with the previous example, it's beyond the scope of this chapter to demonstrate how to create data graphics; however, you can see the results of applying them to the regional map in Figure 9-44. Each store is accompanied by a data graphic that displays the store name and employee count as text callouts. Beneath the text information is a bar graph depicting product quantity sold at each store. In addition, the icon above each store depicts sales per employee by using one of three icons.

The data-graphic legend in the upper-right corner of the page was generated automatically by Visio.

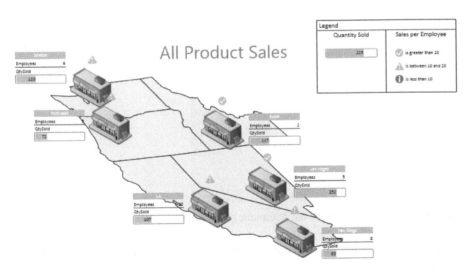

FIGURE 9-44 Each store on the regional map for Fashion Station includes a data graphic depicting critical store information.

Figure 9-45 shows the details for the Boise store.

FIGURE 9-45 A close-up of the Boise store shape and data graphic.

For an excellent example of the value that Visio can bring to your BI applications, compare Figure 9-33 with Figure 9-46: inventory norms and inventory hotspots are immediately apparent, even in a macro-level view. And, because the SharePoint web view makes zooming so easy, you are only a roll of the mouse wheel away from the details, as illustrated in Figure 9-47.

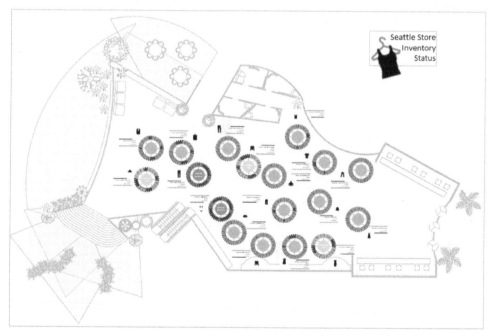

FIGURE 9-46 Each merchandise rack displays inventory status.

The close-up of four merchandise racks in Figure 9-47 illustrates the dynamic way in which sales and inventory data are made available at a glance. Each rack includes the following:

- Markings to indicate sizes of the clothing product

- Hangers that display color when they are full and just the hanger outline when they are empty

- An image of the clothing item

- A callout that displays the product name and number, the quantity sold, and the quantity in stock

- Color coding based on inventory levels.

A note for the technically inclined:

- The callouts for each rack are not data-graphic callouts but were created by using Visio 2013 callouts that are found in the Diagram Parts group on the Insert tab of the Visio ribbon. Several text fields were added to each callout.

- The coloring of the hangers and the appearance of the "Running Low" and "Need to Restock" messages are the result of behavior built into the rack shapes and their components. Each shape or subshape includes ShapeSheet formulae that control the appearance of the shape based on the values of shape data fields.

> **More Info** For information about the Visio ShapeSheet, refer to the Appendix in *Visio 2013 Step by Step* (*http://www.VisioStepByStep.com*).

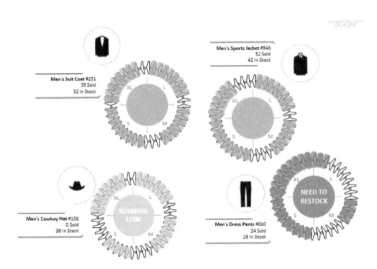

FIGURE 9-47 A close-up of four merchandise racks showing different stock levels; each rack also has a callout that displays the item name, quantity sold and quantity in stock.

Creating a Web Part page

When your diagram is ready to be published you'll need a SharePoint Web Part page. To insert your Visio diagram into a Web Part, open the target SharePoint site and then navigate to, or create, the desired Web Part page. On the ribbon, on the Insert tab, click Web Part, choose the Business Data category, and then select the Visio Web Access part, as depicted in Figure 9-48.

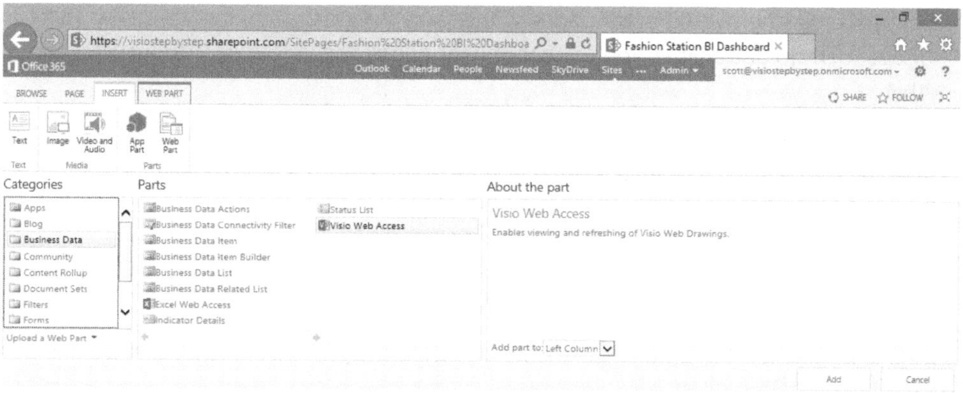

FIGURE 9-48 The Web Part selector for adding a Visio Web Access Web Part.

You can add multiple Visio Web Access Web Parts and mix them with other Web Part types. In Figure 9-49, you can see a simple dashboard that shows page 1 of the Fashion Station diagram in a Web Part on the left, the Seattle store page on the right, and the SharePoint list for the Seattle Store at the top.

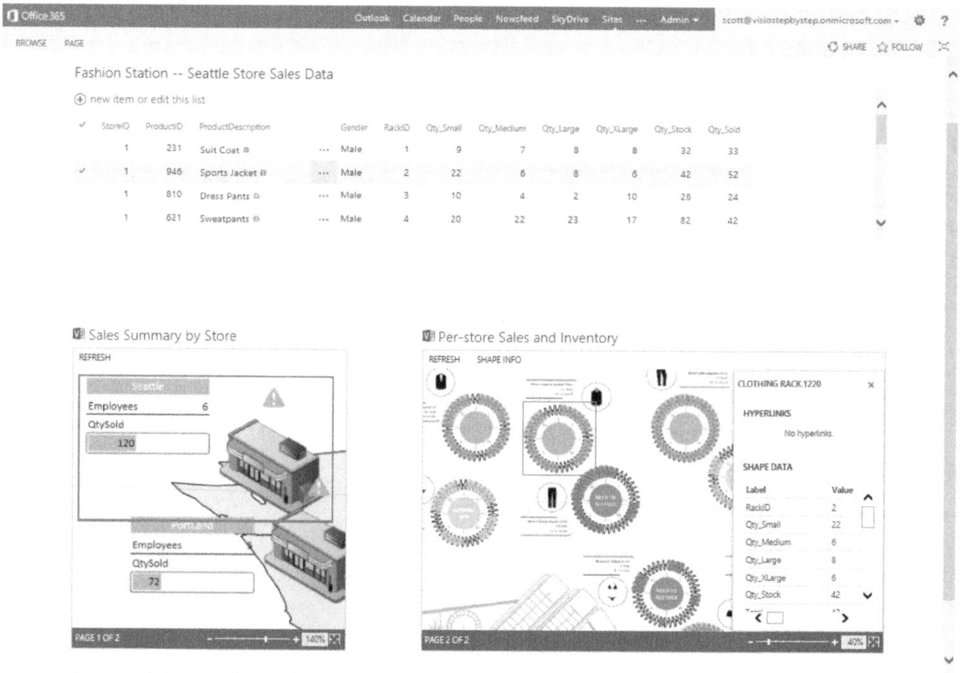

FIGURE 9-49 The Fashion Station BI Dashboard with three Web Parts.

Even on this simple dashboard, there are several features worth mentioning:

- Despite displaying two different pages of the same Visio diagram, the Visio Web Parts are independently controllable; you can zoom in or out in one Web Part without affecting the other.

- Using the Edit Page settings shown in Figure 9-50, the Web Part on the left was configured so that the only control available at the top of the diagram is the Refresh link.

FIGURE 9-50 The Toolbar and User Interface section of the Web Part configuration panel.

- Both the Refresh and Shape Info controls were configured for use in the Web Part on the right. The Shape Info window is open at the right edge of the Web Part and displays data for clothing rack number 2.

Refreshing the diagram when data changes

The two most common ways to refresh a Visio diagram in a Web Part when the underlying data changes are to set a timer in the Web Part configuration, as shown in Figure 9-51, or to click the Refresh button in the Web Part. You can also trigger refresh from code.

Notice also that in the configuration panel in Figure 9-51, you can select which page of the Visio drawing should be opened by default.

Regardless of how the data is refreshed, you can see the results in Figure 9-52. The data for small Sport Jackets on Rack 2 was changed from 22 to 13 in the SharePoint list and the Per-Store Sales And Inventory Web Part reflects the change.

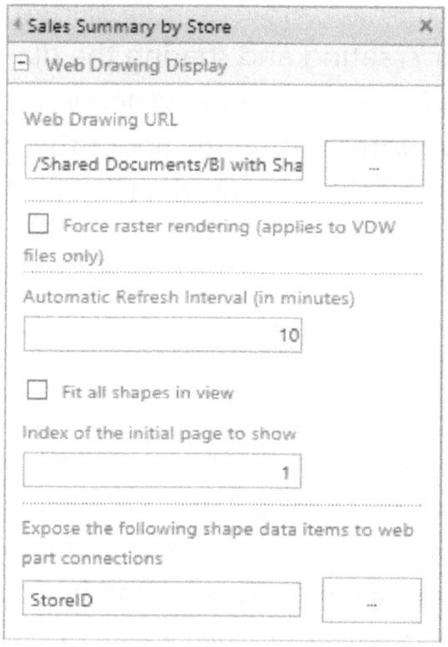

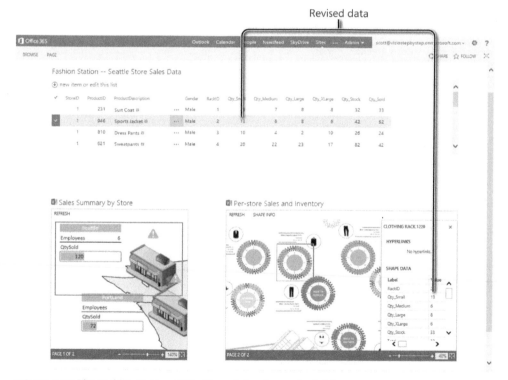

FIGURE 9-51 The Web Drawing Display section of the Web Part configuration panel.

Revised data

FIGURE 9-52 The Fashion Station BI Dashboard showing revised data.

> **More Info** Special thanks to Chris Hopkins at Microsoft for creating and sharing the diagrams and data used for this example. Chris' Visilog, *http://blogs.msdn.com/b/chhopkin*, contains an exceptionally valuable collection of articles. He writes frequently about the integration of Visio with SharePoint and with other parts of the Microsoft product family.

Summary

When you combine a data-connected Visio diagram with data visualization icons and callouts, and then publish the result to a dynamically updated SharePoint page, you have created a powerful BI application. And, you've done it without needing to write a single line of code. You can certainly enhance the features of your Visio-centric BI dashboards with programmed add-ons and functions, but the real story is that you don't need to—you can build innovative, feature-rich webpages by using out-of-the box capabilities.

CHAPTER 10

Bringing it all together

Users in companies and organizations often need to gain insights from data across many different sources. They might need to look at sales data alongside orders data or forecast data. Although the requirement itself seems straightforward, the data often resides in many different places, or the people who analyze the data perform that analysis in different ways, using different products. You don't always have a clear one-size-fits-all answer to the question of which product to use to best visualize a particular data source. You might also need to determine which product to use based on the maturity of an organization, its capabilities, or simply the user's comfort level with the technology.

For example, one user might use Reporting Services to show insights about customer trends, and another might use Excel Services to show how a particular customer segment lines up with cost projections. Management in the organization might actually want to see both analyses alongside one another to help answer a business-critical question. The simplest way to do this would be to allow these products to work in a side-by-side fashion, providing integrated views of the data rather than forcing yet another user to copy each BI report and regenerate it by using a single tool.

One of the strengths of Microsoft SharePoint is that it gives users the ability to bring data and insights from different products together in a holistic way. Whether the data comes from a SQL Server data source, from an Analysis Services cube or Analysis Services tabular model, from within a SharePoint list, from a Microsoft Excel file, or from any one of a number of other places, the Microsoft business intelligence (BI) stack with SharePoint gives you the tools to easily view insights from the various data sources in a single, integrated view. BI developers can choose to use any of the products described in this book because, through SharePoint, all the products can deliver side-by-side analyses to help business users gain deeper insights while still allowing individual users to use the products that make the most sense to them, based on the specific data being used or on their comfort level with a particular product or technology.

Dashboards

The concept of a dashboard is probably very familiar to most readers. At the simplest level, a dashboard brings visualizations of data and status together into a single place so that users can easily—usually at a glance—view how particular business efforts are doing. Dashboards are suitable for many different purposes, including measuring status against goals, monitoring progress, and managing business process. The best dashboards provide a way to take action on the information they show, such as quickly sending an alert or email to the right individual if something needs to be done.

Dashboards can be constructed from many different types of content: charts, icons showing status (usually referred to as key performance indicators [KPIs]), key numbers and statistics, fully interactive reports, tables, or just about any other visualization that shows how well an organization is tracking toward its goals.

You can use all the products discussed in this book to create meaningful views. The previous chapters have provided a good overview of when to use the individual products and how to get started with them. This chapter focuses on what the end user sees. It does this by first walking through some straightforward examples that show how to gather insights created using each product. It then combines those insights onto a single dashboard page so that end users can consume the information easily.

Making dashboards useful

Although it's not within the scope of this chapter to provide all best practices for creating meaningful dashboards, we encourage you to be aware of ways to enhance the end-user experience by reading more. For example, in his article "The Pathetic State of Dashboards" (*http://marksmith. ventanaresearch.com/2012/08/21/the-pathetic-state-of-dashboards/*), Mark Smith gives the following guidance:

- In your dashboard, state who your audience is, what they should understand and interpret from the chart, and describe the chart in the best way possible.

- Try to align the charts to the geographic area of focus, or to the product line of responsibility, or to management KPIs to make them more usable. Provide better role-based dashboards that are generated based on the individual's level of responsibility and the business context.

Remember to use the tools to add annotations and show analysts how to add data interpretations and explanation. Some of the tools to do this include the following:

- To annotate a Power View chart, simply click the Text Box icon on the ribbon and a small box appears which you can move around on the report.

- In PowerPivot and SQL Server Data Tools, you can add a description to a column and also to a table so that when a user's mouse hovers over the table and available dimensions, the description shows in the client tools of either Excel or Power View.

Figure 10-1 shows the shortcut menu that appears when you right-click the column, which includes the option for adding a description.

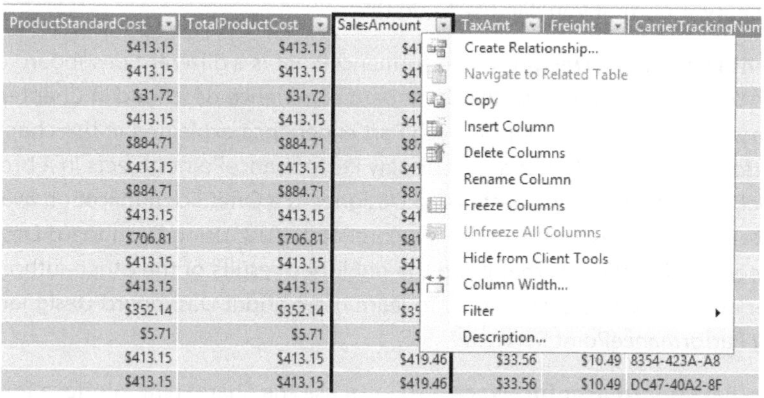

FIGURE 10-1 The method for adding a description to a table.

When you go to the Field List in Power View and hover over the field, you see the description that you created in either PowerPivot or SQL Server Data Tools, as demonstrated in Figure 10-2.

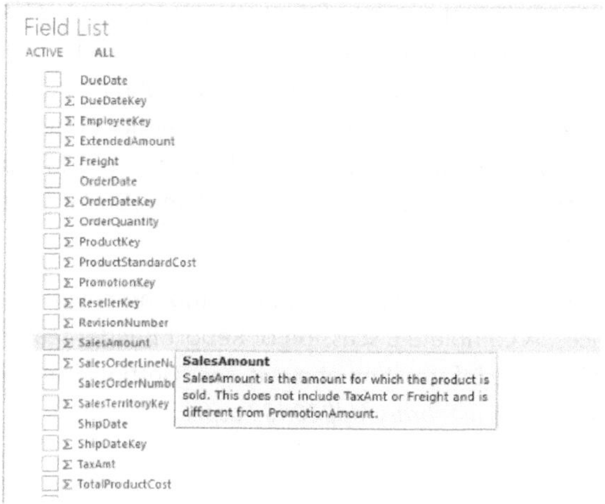

FIGURE 10-2 A description displayed in a ScreenTip in Power View.

Tools in SharePoint for authoring dashboards

Even though you can use each product discussed in this book to create a single, full-page report that functions much like a dashboard, you can also combine views from each product into a single dashboard page.

Here are the three primary tools that you can use to do this:

- **PerformancePoint Dashboard Designer**   PerformancePoint is a different dashboard experience altogether. You should distinguish the dashboard experience described in Chapter 8, "Using PerformancePoint Services," from the Web Part experience explained in this chapter. You can use a PerformancePoint dashboard to display PerformancePoint objects in a browser. The authoring tool, PerformancePoint Dashboard Designer, is a OneClick application available when PerformancePoint Services is configured in SharePoint 2013. Using Dashboard Designer, you can build integrated BI solutions that bring the published results of the other authoring tools together into interactive dashboards. To learn more about Dashboard Designer, see Chapter 8, "Using PerformancePoint Services."

- **SharePoint page/dashboard user interface**   You can use the SharePoint interface for all the other dashboard-building products. For example, using the native SharePoint user interface (UI), you can customize Web Parts, Excel 2013 KPIs, and SharePoint pages to combine insights from such products as Excel Services, Microsoft Visio Services, and more. This chapter discusses the basic elements, such as Web Parts, Web Part pages, filters, and SharePoint KPIs.

- **SharePoint Designer**   Using SharePoint Designer, you can fully customize pages in SharePoint, making it easy to add a custom look and feel while taking advantage of advanced functionality such as configuring custom behaviors for alerts or workflows. SharePoint Designer is the premier tool for creating great no-code customized solutions. It's mentioned here for completeness, but this chapter doesn't cover it in any detail. See the Microsoft product page at *http://sharepoint.microsoft.com/en-us/product/Related-Technologies/Pages/SharePoint-Designer.aspx* for more information about SharePoint Designer.

Report Builder is another available tool for BI developers; it is the report authoring environment for creating reports with SQL Reporting Services. A complete discussion of Report Builder features is beyond the scope for this book, but if you'd like more information about it, see "Getting Started with Report Builder 3.0" at *http://technet.microsoft.com/en-us/library/dd220460.aspx*.

Which dashboard tool should I use?

It is not Microsoft's intention to confuse customers with several different dashboards. Often, the BI tools that you should use depend on the specific problems that you are trying to solve, the BI maturity level of your organization (see Chapter 2, "Planning for business intelligence adoption"), the expertise of the people who build or use the dashboard, and other considerations such as the KPI functionality offered by a SharePoint Web Part dashboard versus a KPI authored in PerformancePoint Dashboard Designer.

Basically, you don't want to use a jackhammer when all you need is a small ping hammer to help users make decisions. The functionality of many of these tools overlaps. You might decide which tool to use based on your familiarity or proficiency with the tool. In any case, the guidelines that follow can be helpful when choosing which dashboard-creation technology to use.

Use PerformancePoint to create comprehensive KPIs, scorecards, reports, filters, and dashboards when you want to do the following:

- You want to include any of the following multidimensional or tabular data sources:

  - SQL Server Analysis Services

  - PowerPivot model

- You want to include tabular data sources such as the following:

  - SharePoint list

  - Excel Services

  - SQL Server table

  - Excel workbook

  - Custom data source

- You need visualizations with which you can drill down, such as decomposition trees to see the underlying data for a particular value.

- You need more advanced KPIs that support the following:

  - Multiple data sources with which KPIs can perform calculations

  - More complex visualizations (such as gauges)

  - A large number of states—this is important when you want to display and communicate the current state of your business as well as its desired future state (or multiple forecasts)

- You want dynamic hierarchies that refresh when the data source is updated.

- You want Time Intelligence features by which you can both filter and create variations on the filter that allow the user to select a single "current date."

- You want to create or include any of the following reports or report features in your dashboard:

> **Note** Some reports or report features are created in Dashboard Designer, whereas others are already created in another BI tool, such as SQL Server Reporting Services. The distinction is discussed in Chapter 8.

- Analytic chart
- Analytic grid
- KPI details
- Show details
- Decomposition tree
- Reporting Services report
- ProClarity Analytics Server Page report

- Use "native" dashboard tools, such as Excel Services, SharePoint dashboard pages, KPIs, and filters, when you want to include any of the following data sources:

- Analysis Services
- PowerPivot
- SQL Server
- Excel workbook
- Visio diagram

- The BI reports or logic are already based in Excel (often the case, given Excel's widespread usage).

- The needs around your KPIs are fairly simple and don't have more than a few states (up to five states).

- You need KPIs on a page or series of pages, have very simple KPI needs, and don't want to spend the time creating and managing more complex solutions such as a PerformancePoint scorecard or workbook file.

- You need to prototype a solution quickly. (For example, experienced Excel users can build a full report faster in Excel, using conditional formatting, and so on.)

- You need a solution that can be manipulated on the fly. (It's easy to edit Excel reports or use the SharePoint UI to tweak dashboard pages with little or no training.)

Dashboard (Web Part) pages in SharePoint

The lightest-weight dashboard authoring tool is a simple web browser that takes advantage of the UI that SharePoint has provided to build dashboard pages that use Web Parts.

Web Parts are logical containers on SharePoint pages that can display content. The Web Part framework in SharePoint provides easy drag-and-drop interactivity, includes a Settings page, and includes other UI features to make configuring pages fairly simple. Web Part pages are generally essential for creating a dashboard-like experience in SharePoint. You would typically use Web Parts when you need to display content from different files or products (such as Excel Services, Visio Services, Reporting Services, and so on) on a page, when you want to display that content side by side with other SharePoint content, or when that content needs to interact with other SharePoint entities on the same page (such as lists or other Web Parts).

PerformancePoint dashboard pages are ordinary Web Part pages that contain various components as connected Web Parts. The Filter, Scorecard, Report, and Stack Web Part are discussed in more detail in the section "Creating a dashboard" in Chapter 8.

To create a dashboard (Web Part) page in SharePoint, perform the following procedure:

1. On your site, on the ribbon, click the Page tab (see Figure 10-3). In the Page Library group, click the View All Pages button.

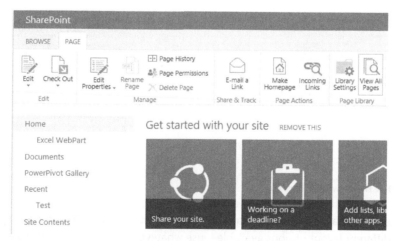

FIGURE 10-3 Description showing in Power View.

2. Select the Files tab and then, in the Ribbon, click the New Document button. On the menu that appears, click the Web Part Page option, as depicted in Figure 10-4.

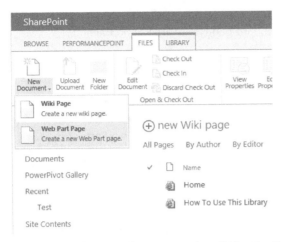

FIGURE 10-4 The menu that appears after clicking the SharePoint 2013 New Document button.

3. Now, you must make some choices. Figure 10-5 illustrates that you need to select your preferred page layout, enter a name for the page, and specify where to store the page.

FIGURE 10-5 The New Web Part Page.

4. Select the zones that you want and name the page **WebPartPage**. Feel free to experiment with the different layout options available—use whatever you find useful. The Save Location is the document library where SharePoint stores your new page.

5. Click Create to display a new blank Web Part page, as depicted in Figure 10-6.

FIGURE 10-6 A new, blank Web Part page.

Using Excel Services in the dashboard (Web Part page)

To make the dashboard more interesting, you can use the next exercise to get some data from an Excel workbook and show it on the page by using the Excel Web Access Web Part. Before you do that, though, you need an Excel workbook.

You can use almost any workbook to do this. The following example walks you through the steps to create a simple workbook that accommodates some of the filters that you can add to the page in later sections of this chapter.

Creating the Excel workbook

The workbook creation process has two parts: First you need to add a PivotTable connected to Online Analytical Processing (OLAP) data in Analysis Services, and then you can generate a chart from that data.

To add a PivotTable to a workbook, perform the following procedure:

1. Open an Excel table with the PivotTable ready by clicking the Excel icon in the upper-right corner of the BI Semantic Model connection we created in Chapter 3, "The lifecycle of a business intelligence implementation," as shown in Figure 10-7.

FIGURE 10-7 BI Semantic Model connection in a SharePoint 2013 PowerPivot Gallery.

2. Scroll through the field list and select the check boxes next to the following PivotTable fields: DimDate: FiscalYear, Measure: Sum of SalesAmount, and DimSalesTerritory: SalesTerritoryCountry.

This adds the primary data to the spreadsheet with which we are working.

3. Drag the SalesTerritoryCountry field from the Rows area to the Filters area, as demonstrated in Figure 10-8 as before-and-after illustrations.

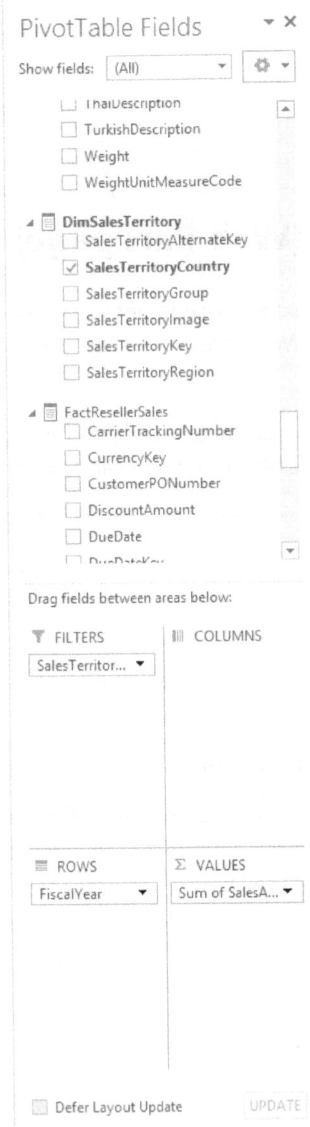

FIGURE 10-8 PivotTable Fields.

You should end up with a PivotTable in your workbook similar to that shown in Figure 10-9.

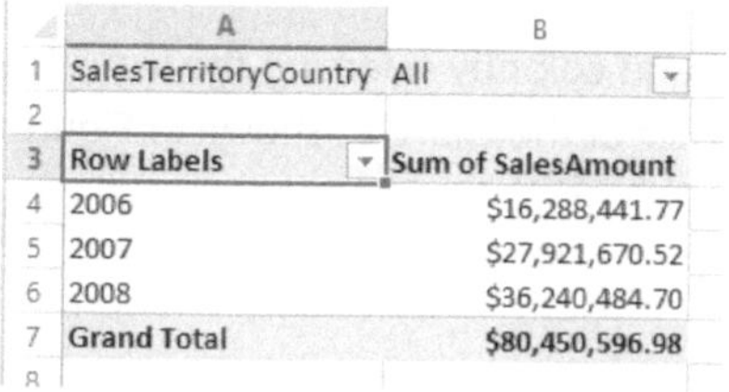

	A	B
1	SalesTerritoryCountry All	
2		
3	Row Labels	Sum of SalesAmount
4	2006	$16,288,441.77
5	2007	$27,921,670.52
6	2008	$36,240,484.70
7	Grand Total	$80,450,596.98

FIGURE 10-9 The result of a table created for SalesTerritoryCOuntry All.

To add a simple chart to the workbook, perform the following procedure:

1. Continuing with the same file you created in the preceding procedure, ensure that your cell selection is located in the PivotTable and then, on the Insert tab, in the Charts group, click Recommended Charts.

2. In the Insert Chart dialog box (see Figure 10-10), select the type of chart that you want to use.

   You can select each to see a preview of it before selecting OK.

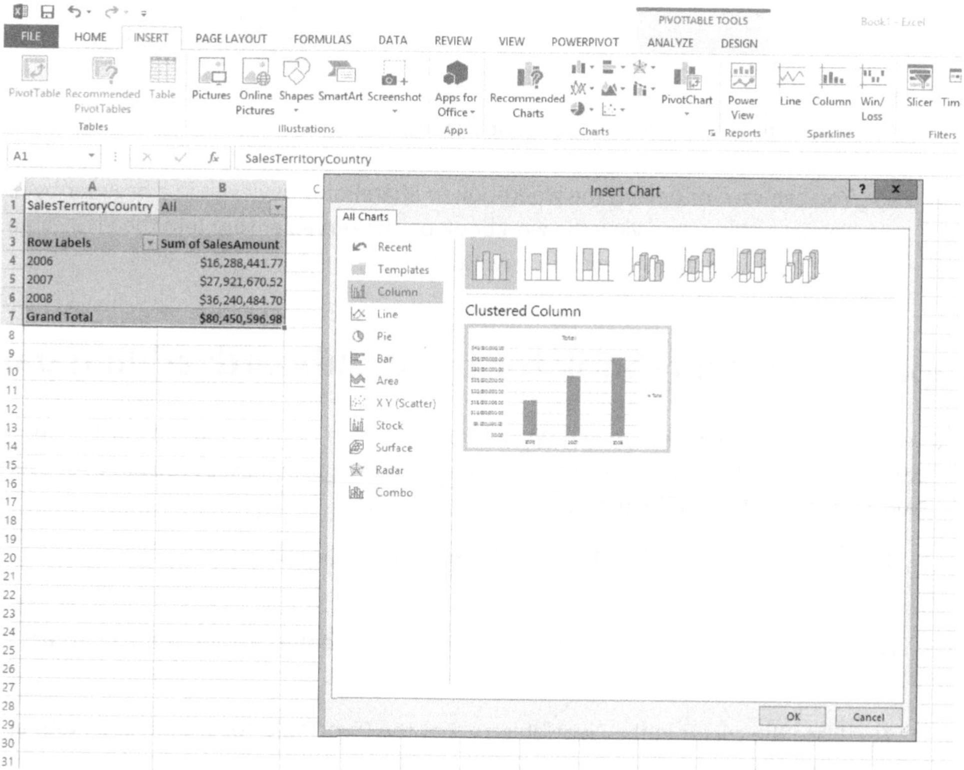

FIGURE 10-10 The Insert Chart dialog box.

3. To format the chart so that it looks a little better in the report, move it and then grab its corner to resize it so that it fits next to your pivot table.

Optionally you can change the chart elements, style, and color by selecting the icons (the plus sign and paint brush) located off the upper-right corner of the chart, as shown in Figure 10-11.

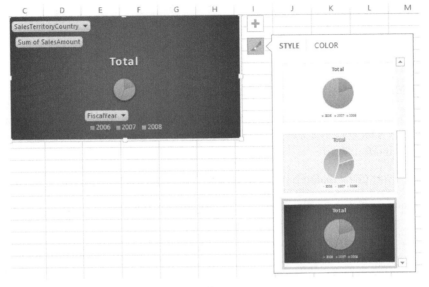

FIGURE 10-11 The SalesTerritoryCountry chart.

4. You can save or upload the workbook to SharePoint to view it in a browser by using Excel Services. When you view the workbook on the server, ensure that the PivotTable refreshes and that all your data connectivity is working.

Preparing the workbook for the dashboard: adding parameters

Because the ultimate goal is to end up with multiple Web Parts on a dashboard page, you want to add a label to each of the PivotTables. This simple mechanism makes it possible for users to choose a PivotTable from the workbook to view in the Web Part.

To specify a workbook PivotTable, perform the following procedure:

 Note This exercise uses the same workbook you created earlier in the chapter.

1. Place the cursor in the PivotTable so that the PivotTable Tools contextual tabs appear on the ribbon.

2. Select the PivotTable Tools|Analyze contextual tab and then, in the PivotTable group, in the PivotTable Name text box, type a name; for this example, type **SumSales**, as demonstrated in Figure 10-12.

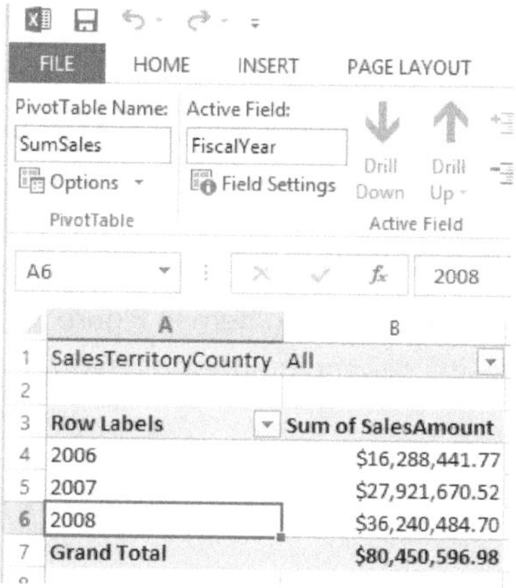

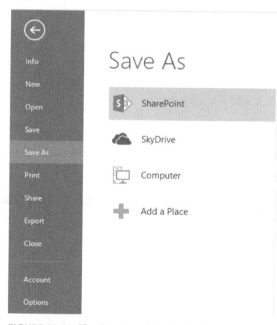

FIGURE 10-12 Adding a PivotTable name.

3. Click the File tab to display the Backstage view. Click the Save As tab and then click SharePoint, as shown in Figure 10-13.

FIGURE 10-13 The Save As tab in the Backstage view for saving an Excel file to SharePoint 2013.

Users can now set values in the DateFilterCell cell by using SharePoint, even if the workbook is in read-only or view-only mode. Changing the cell value triggers a refresh of both the PivotTable and PivotChart. You'll use this parameter later when we associate it with a SharePoint filter.

Showing the workbook in Web Parts

Now, it's time to show the PivotTable and PivotChart in separate Web Parts on the dashboard page. The first step is to add the Excel Web Access Web Parts to the page and configure them.

To add an Excel Web Access Web Part, perform the following procedure:

1. Navigate to the Web Part page that you created earlier, shown here in Figure 10-14. (Remember that it might be in a library of your site, depending on where you saved it.)

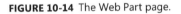

FIGURE 10-14 The Web Part page.

2. In one of the Web part zones, click Add A Web Part.

    The top of the page expands, as demonstrated in Figure 10-15.

3. In the Categories pane, click Business Data and then, in the Parts pane, choose the Excel Web Access Web Part.

FIGURE 10-15 Choosing the Excel Web Access Web Part.

4. Click the Add Part To list box and add the Web Part to the page in the zone you selected previously.

   You should now have an empty Excel Web Access Web Part on the page (see Figure 10-16). You can use this Web Part to load and display Excel workbooks via Excel Services.

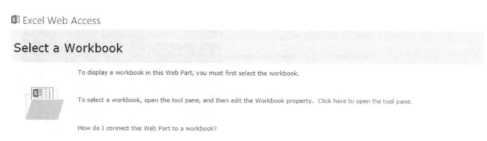

FIGURE 10-16 Select a Workbook to display in the Excel Web Access Web Part.

Now, you can configure the Web Part to display the workbook you created earlier by performing the following procedure:

1. In the Select A Workbook page (refer to Figure 10-16), click the Click Here To Open The Tool Pane link to expand the Properties pane for the Web Part and display all the configuration options.

2. In the Workbook Display section, click the blue button to browse for a workbook to display. A Web Part Properties pane opens, in which you can navigate within SharePoint to pick a workbook. Use that pane to select the workbook you saved in SharePoint from the previous steps or just type the URL to the workbook directly.

   You should end up with a URL for the workbook that you want to display, as shown in Figure 10-17.

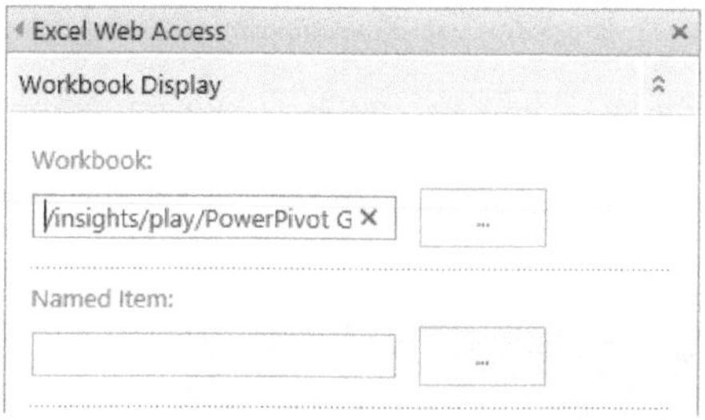

FIGURE 10-17 The Web Part Properties pane.

3. At the bottom of the Web Part Properties pane, click OK.

   You should now see your workbook displayed in the Web Part, as depicted in Figure 10-18.

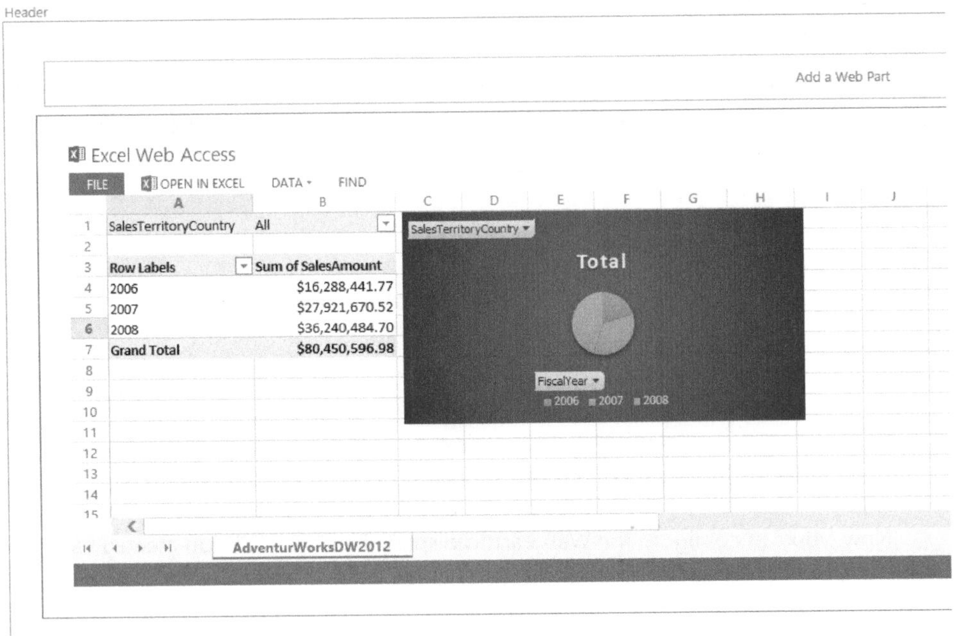

Add a Web Part

FIGURE 10-18 Excel Web Access with SalesTerryitoryCountry PivotChart and graph.

Notice that the workbook looks just like an Excel file at this point. You can click the sheet tabs, see the chart, interact with the PivotTable, and so on.

You can even control what the Web Part shows—for example, you can have it display only the chart.

4. In the upper-right corner, click the drop-down arrow and then, on the menu that appears, click Edit Web Part, as shown in Figure 10-19, to open the Web Part Properties pane.

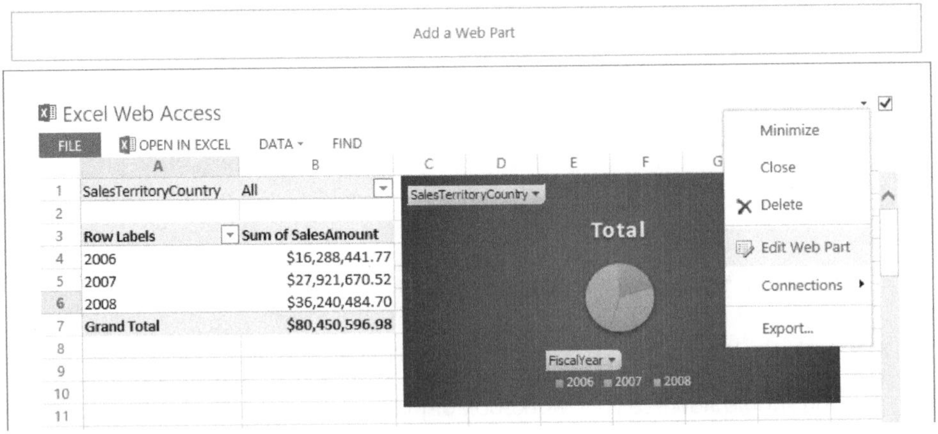

FIGURE 10-19 The Edit Web Part command on the menu.

5. To set the default view for the Web Part, in the Properties pane (see Figure 10-20), in the Named Item text box, type **SumSales**.

    This works only if you have labeled the PivotChart in the previous procuedure.

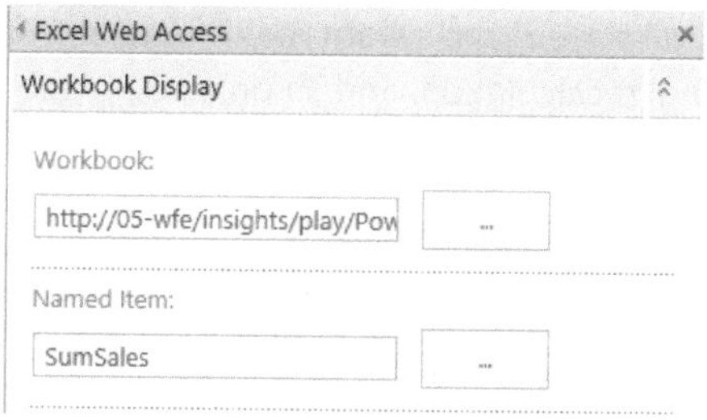

FIGURE 10-20 The Web Part Properties tool pane configuration dialog box.

6. At the bottom of the Web Part Properties pane, click either OK or Apply.

    The Web Part displays the chart named Chart 1, as shown in Figure 10-21.

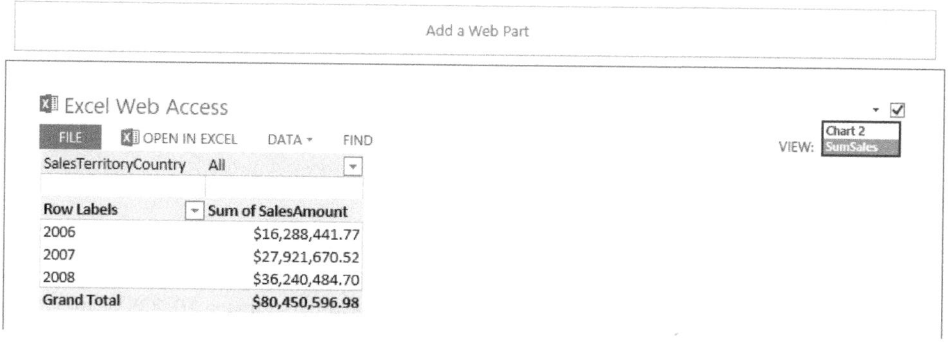

FIGURE 10-21 The Excel Web Access View drop-down list.

Notice that the Web Part no longer displays this page as a spreadsheet. Instead, it displays each item, one at a time, in the Web Part. This viewing mode is referred to as the *Named Item View*. When users expand the View drop-down list, they can choose to display any of the other items in the workbook.

The Named Item View is the view used in most Web Parts because most people just want to see the parts of a workbook that are interesting and related in a dashboard.

Therefore, for the case in which the author chose to show only a set of items from the workbook, the Web Part shows whichever is the first item in the workbook (sorted alphabetically), even if you don't specify the name of an item in the Named Item Web Part Text box. However, you can also specify which item should appear first in the workbook by using the Named Item text box in the Web Part Properties pane.

Setting other Web Part properties

Open the Web Part Properties pane again. Notice that many properties are listed that can affect how the workbook is displayed. You won't explore all the properties here, but generally, you can find properties for controlling whether the toolbar is visible, what commands are on the toolbar (if it is visible), whether the Named Item drop-down list is displayed, and what types of interactivity you want to allow for the Web Part (such as sorting, filtering, recalculation, and so on).

For now, keep the toolbar to Full so that users can immediately open in Excel, refresh data, or use Find. In the Type Of Toolbar section, in the list box, select Full, as illustrated in Figure 10-22.

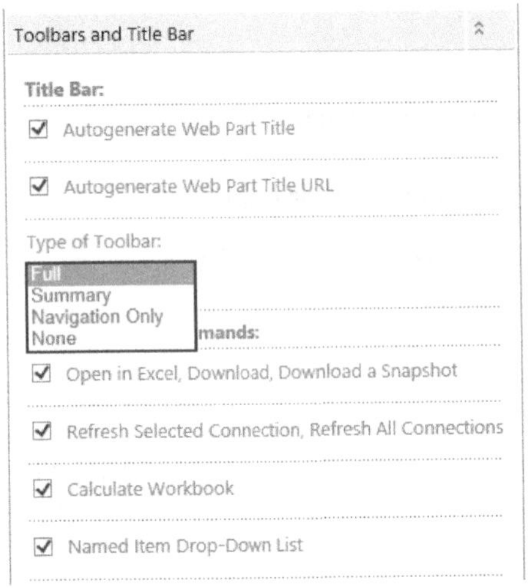

FIGURE 10-22 Configuring the Excel Web Access Web Part toolbar.

Then, scroll down and expand the appearance section (see Figure 10-23). Notice the width and height controls. These controls are used frequently for adjusting dashboards that have many objects on the page, to achieve the right look and feel. You need to adjust these to display the Web Part within the Excel content in a way that doesn't show unnecessary scrollbars. Finally, click OK to close the Web Part Properties pane.

FIGURE 10-23 Configuring the appearance of the Excel Web Access Web Part.

Using the filter added in Excel 2013

In SharePoint 2013, filters no longer need to be added manually; they are part of the user experience in the Web Part in either the chart or the PivotTable, as is demonstrated in Figure 10-24.

Just click SalesTerritoryCountry to see the filter items.

FIGURE 10-24 The Filter dialog box for the Excel Web Access Web Part.

Adding to the dashboard (Web Part page)

You can also add the following Web Parts to your dashboard. Remember that each must be configured on your SharePoint 2013 farm; see Appendix A, "Running scripts to set up a demonstration environment."

Visio Web Access Web Part

Using Visio Services, you can embed Visio Web Drawings in other SharePoint pages. Using the Visio Web Access Web Part, you can embed either static or data-driven Visio Web Drawings in SharePoint pages.

PerformancePoint Web Parts

The following are available PerformancePoint Web Parts.

- **PerformancePoint Filters**   This Web Part displays PerformancePoint filters. Filters can be linked to other Web Parts to provide an interactive dashboard experience. Filter types include lists and trees based on a variety of data sources.

- **PerformancePoint Report**   This displays PerformancePoint reports. Reports can be linked to other Web Parts to create an interactive dashboard experience. Report types include analytic charts and grids, Strategy Maps, Excel Services, Reporting Services, Predictive Trend charts, and webpages.

- **PerformancePoint Scorecard**   This Web Part displays a PerformancePoint scorecard. Scorecards can be linked to other Web Parts such as filters and reports to create an interactive dashboard experience.

- **PerformancePoint Stack Selector**   This displays a PerformancePoint scorecard. Scorecards can be linked to other Web Parts such as filters and reports to create an interactive dashboard experience.

We show how to add a Visio Web Access Part and PerformancePoint Web Part in the book *Business Intelligence In Microsoft SharePoint 2010* (Microsoft Press, 2011).

The Web Part page

As a result of creating the Web Parts without positioning, your page will look similar to that shown in Figure 10-25.

You can see how the Web Parts are interactive when published by clicking Stop Editing on the Page tab. Note in that in the figure, we have selected Denmark to cascade and drill in on the PerformancePoint Scorecard Web Part.

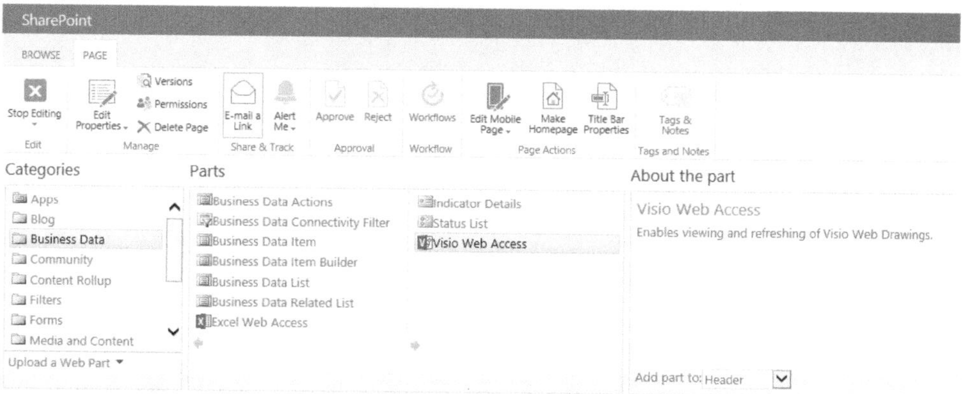

FIGURE 10-25 Web Part Page with Visio, Excel, and PerformancePoint Web Parts.

Summary

This chapter looked at some of the basic features that SharePoint includes for creating dashboards and included step-by-step walkthroughs to help get you started.

Microsoft has many products that can help you achieve great BI. Sometimes, you might want to choose one product instead of another for technical reasons, because of BI maturity, or to meet the comfort level of a particular user. One of the strengths of SharePoint is its ability to store documents related to many BI reports or solutions, and it can also surface BI functionality from many different features and products. So, even if your company discovers insights by using different tools or features, you can use SharePoint to bring them together and enjoy the advantage of using them in a single place. In particular, SharePoint dashboards are extremely useful for bringing all the data and insights together into one place.

Running scripts to set up a demonstration environment

In this appendix, you learn how to run scripts for installing a demonstration environment that includes the following:

- Fictitious CONTOSO\users in Active Directory

- SQL Server 2012 (three instances) and SQL Server Data Tools

- Sample data databases such as the *AdventureWorksDW2012*

- SharePoint 2013

You also learn about the architecture and hardware requirements for setting up a few common scenarios.

Hardware considerations

Your first consideration is a server that will host the tabular model that you want to deploy. It's best if you allocate the hardware budget to good processors and RAM instead of expensive storage. Table A-1 demonstrates the difference between hardware requirements for Tabular and Multidimensional Analysis Services instances.

TABLE A-1 A comparison of hardware needs for Tabular and Multidimensional Analysis Services instances

Feature	Tabular	Multidimensional
RAM	Some (16/32 GB)	A lot (64/128 GB)
RAM Speed	Important	Crucial
Number of cores	4/8/16	4/8/16
Core speed	Less important	Crucial
Disk speed	Less important	NA
SSD disk usage	Recommended	NA
Network speed	Important	Important

The following instruction for determining memory is excerpted from the book *Microsoft SQL Server 2012 Analysis Services: The BISM Tabular Model* (Microsoft Press, 2012).

> As a rule, the memory available for a database should be at least 1.5 times the space required to store the database on disk. Every query can require a temporary peak of memory usage to store partial results required to solve the complete query. Simple queries require minimal memory, but more complex queries might be expensive from this point of view. It is hard to estimate this cost, which also depends on the number of concurrent queries that Analysis Services receives. It is also difficult to provide a guideline for sizing memory, depending on concurrent users, and it is better to follow a heuristic approach, measuring memory consumption in the typical workload you expect to have.

Introducing the scripts

One of the most important steps you can take to show how the client tools such as Microsoft Excel 2013 integrate with Microsoft SharePoint 2013 and Microsoft SQL Server 2012 is to "prop-up" an environment in which you can demonstrate a proof of concept to stakeholders, sponsors, and end users. People must see what can be accomplished when tools and approaches are used to create visualizations and insights which change behavior.

Installing and configuring the software can feel daunting. By providing you the scripts and detailed instruction for a development environment, you will be able to refer back to what is configured and better modify and reuse the scripts for production.

We introduce a tool that installs the scripts for you by unzipping content packs. Content packs are simply the files that are used for running the scripts. In this appendix, we detail what each content pack contains and what it installs.

> **Important** Although we provide some installation and configuration tips, these instructions for running the scripts should not be considerations for setting up critical environments such as something that you would want to use for production. For that, we will provide links for further reading and considerations.

The Windows PowerShell scripts in the each content pack are available for you to review, modify, and use however you wish. We earmark the items that you should consider modifying if you choose to use the Windows PowerShell scripts to install rather than the ContentPack installer.

Table A-2 provides a short description of the content pack and the order in which you will install the Microsoft business intelligence (BI) stack. Details for each are in sections of this chapter.

TABLE A-2 Description of the content pack

Content pack	Description
Active Directory Content Pack Demo 2.0	Adds Active Directory (AD) and fictitious employees including SPAdmin and necessary services accounts for SQL Server and SharePoint configuration
SQL 2012 SP1 Content Pack Demo Build 2.0	Installs three instances of SQL Server in preparation for BI scenarios
Self-Service BI Demo 2.0 Content Pack	Installs sample databases for performing the exercise in this book
SharePoint 2013 Demo Build 2.0	Installs SharePoint 2013

Step 1: Install the Active Directory Demo Build 2.1

The *Application Active Directory Demo Build 2.1* loads a few hundred users, which are used for Social Media, People Search, My Sites, tagging, and blog creation in later service packs. The primary reason this content pack is deployed prior to the others is that it creates the service accounts used in most of the demo builds. This content pack takes about 15 minutes to install. Follow-up tasks and some manual setup steps will take an additional 10 minutes.

Prerequisites

This installable package is built by using the SharePoint Content Pack Installer with Windows Power-Shell on a virtual machine (VM). The instructions assume that you have already successfully created an environment with Windows Server 2012 Guest. The preferred name for the server is DEMO2013a. This document might refer to this machine as "the base VM," "the Contoso server," or "DEMO2013a." See *http://technet.microsoft.com/en-us/library/ee256075(WS.10).aspx*.

You can also use the Active Directory Content Pack within other content packs. Therefore, to maintain the integrity of the Active Directory Content Pack, we advise reverting back to the base image prior to installing additional content packs.

The Active Directory Content Pack has three prerequisites:

- The AD DS Role has been added

- DCPromo has been completed for the Contoso.com Domain

- The server fully qualified domain name (FQDN) is named DEMO2013a.Contoso.com

Software requirements

- Media for Windows Server 2008R2 Sp1 or Windows server 2012. The Server will be required to have installed and configured Active Directory Services so that you can populate AD with users for your walk through of the Hands-on Labs.

- Media for SQL 2012 Evaluation: *http://technet.microsoft.com/en-us/evalcenter/hh225126.aspx*

- Media for SharePoint 2013 Evaluation: *http://technet.microsoft.com/en-us/evalcenter/hh973397.aspx*

- All users of this VM environment must use the password, pass@word1

Hardware requirements

- Minimum 16 GB to 24 GB of RAM for the server DEMO2013a

- Quad-core processor if possible

- 127 GB to 200 GB of available hard disk space

Installing the content pack

To install the content pack, perform the following procedure:

1. In Hyper-V, start the base VM.

2. Log on to the VM as Contoso\Administrator.

3. Download the content pack *ActiveDirectory.zip*.

   The file can be placed on the desktop or in any convenient folder.

4. Open Windows PowerShell and run *Set-ExecutionPolicy RemoteSigned*, type **Y**, and then press Enter.

5. Open Server Manager, enable Remote Desktop, and turn off Internet Explorer enhanced security.

6. Double-click the Firewall Settings, turn Domain off, but leave Public and Private on.

7. If not already done, download the Content Pack Installer executable file (*ContentPackInstaller.exe*) and place it on the desktop.

To complete installation, perform the following procedure:

1. Double-click *ContentPackInstaller.exe* to run it (this will take a few seconds to start).

   If this is the first time the installer has run, you might see the First Time Configuration dialog box; you can accept all default values (Figure A-1).

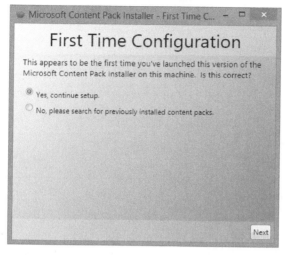

FIGURE A-1 The First Time Configuration dialogue box.

2. Install the Active Directory Content Pack Demo, click the Add A Content Pact tab (see Figure A-2), and then click Browse.

3. Locate the *ActiveDirectory.zip* file, select it, and then click Open.

4. Click Add. When the installer finishes extracting the files (This can take about 10 minutes), continue on to the next step.

5. Click Install and then click OK to accept the default path.

The installation process can take 10 to 15 minutes, and you will not see any feedback indicators other than a flowing progress bar to show that work is being done. For advanced users, there is a log file named *Install-http_intranet_contoso_com-<Date/Time>.log* that is updated with live feedback as the installation progresses; it is located at C:\Content Packs\\SQLServer2012\Packs\Active Directory.

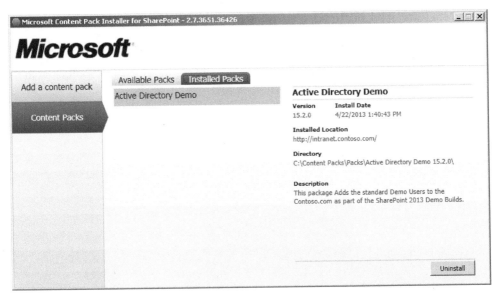

FIGURE A-2 The Content Pack Installer dialog box.

Post installation

At this point, the post-installation document will be opened automatically by the installer for reference.

Step 2: Install the SQL 2012 SP1 Content Pack Demo Build 2.0.0

This section provides instructions on how to install the SQL 2012 SP1 Content Pack Demo Build 2.0.0. Please note that this content pack (and its prerequisite) takes about 40 to 60 minutes to install. Follow-up tasks and some manual setup steps will take an additional 10 minutes.

Contents of SQL 2012 SP1 Content Pack Demo Build 2.0.0

The SQL Server 2012 SP1 Content Pack includes the following four configuration files, which can also be utilized within other content packs.

- **MSSQL.ConfigurationFile** Installs SQL Server Database Engine, SQL Server Agent, REPLICATION, SQL Server Full Text, Data Quality Server, Analysis Services Tabular Mode, Data Quality Client, SQL Server Data Tools (SSDT), connectivity components, Integration Services, backward compatibility components, software development kit, SQL Server Books Online, SQL Server Management Tools Basic & Advanced, SDK for Microsoft SQL Server Native Client, and the Master Data Services

- **MultiDimensional.ConfigurationFile**   Installs SQL Server Database Engine, SQL Server Agent, REPLICATION, SQL Server Full Tex, Data Quality Server, Analysis Services Multidimensional mode, and Native Reporting Services

- **PowerPivot.ConfigurationFile**   Installs Analysis Services PowerPivot Mode calculation engine, preconfigured for in-memory data storage and processing. PowerPivot solution packages, SQL Server Books Online, Database Engine, Configuration Tools, and SQL Server Management Studio

- **RSIntegrated.ConfigurationFile**   Installs Reporting Services for SharePoint Mode and the Reporting Services Add-in for SharePoint Products

The SQL Server 2012 SP1 Content Pack installation instructions assume that the base VM has been modified accordingly with the previously listed prerequisites.

Prerequisites

The prerequisites for this installation are as follows:

- The prerequisites for step 1 are completed.

- The Application Active Directory Demo Build 2.1 described in step 1 has been installed.

- You have a licensed or evaluation version of SQL 2012 SP1 from Microsoft (*http://technet.microsoft.com/en-us/evalcenter/hh225126.aspx*).

- The SQL Server 2012 SP1 ISO should be mounted as drive D.

> **Note** If you mount onto another hard disk, be sure to change the *Install.ps1* script located at C:\Content Packs\Packs\Demo Builds SQL Server 2012 SP! Configuration 2.0.0.

This installable package is built on the *configuration.ini* approach of scripting SQL Server installations. It is assumed that you have already successfully installed Windows Server 2012 and run the Application Active Directory Demo Build 2.1.

> **Note** You might want to use the scripts to install SQL Server 2012 SP1 for a development environment, in which case you will edit the .ini file located in the folder where the ContentPackInstaller places the scripts folder. Typically, the .ini files are placed at C:\Content Packs\Packs\Demo Builds SQL Server 2012 SP1 Configuration 2.0.0\Demo\Scripts. You will likely only change the domain name and service accounts that you use for other installations.

Note All users of this VM environment must use the password, pass@word1.

Installing the content pack

To install the content pack, perform the following procedure:

1. In Hyper-V, start the base VM DEMO2013a.

2. Log on to the VM as Contoso\Administrator.

3. Download the content pack *SQL 2012 SP1 Content Pack Demo Build 2.0.0*.

    The file can be placed on the desktop or in any convenient folder.

4. Right-click *ContentPackInstaller.exe* to run as an Administrator (this will take a few seconds to start).

    If this is the first time the installer has run, you might see the First Time Configuration dialog box; you can accept all default values.

To install the SQL 2012 SP1 Content Pack Demo Build 2.0.0, perform the following procedure:

1. Click the Add a Content Pack tab and then click Browse (see Figure A-3).

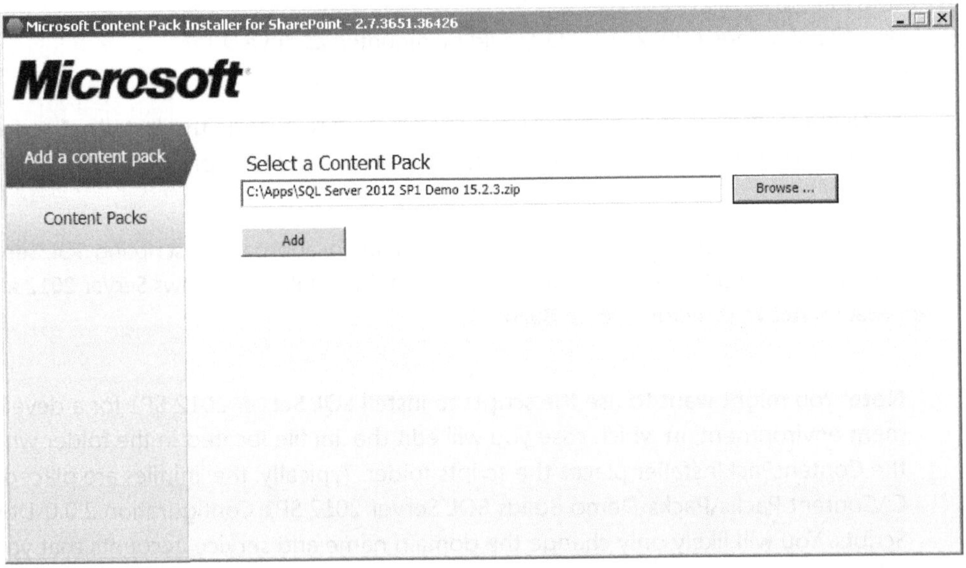

![Microsoft Content Pack Installer for SharePoint - 2.7.3651.36426 dialog box showing the Microsoft logo, an "Add a content pack" tab and "Content Packs" tab on the left, and a "Select a Content Pack" field containing "C:\Apps\SQL Server 2012 SP1 Demo 15.2.3.zip" with a Browse button and an Add button.]

FIGURE A-3 Selecting the SQL Server 2012 SP1 Content Pack in the Content Pack Installer dialog box.

2. Locate the *SQLServer2012SP1.zip* file, select it, and then click Open.

3. Click Add. When the installer finishes extracting the files (this can take about 15 seconds), continue on to the next step.

4. Click Install (Figure A-4).

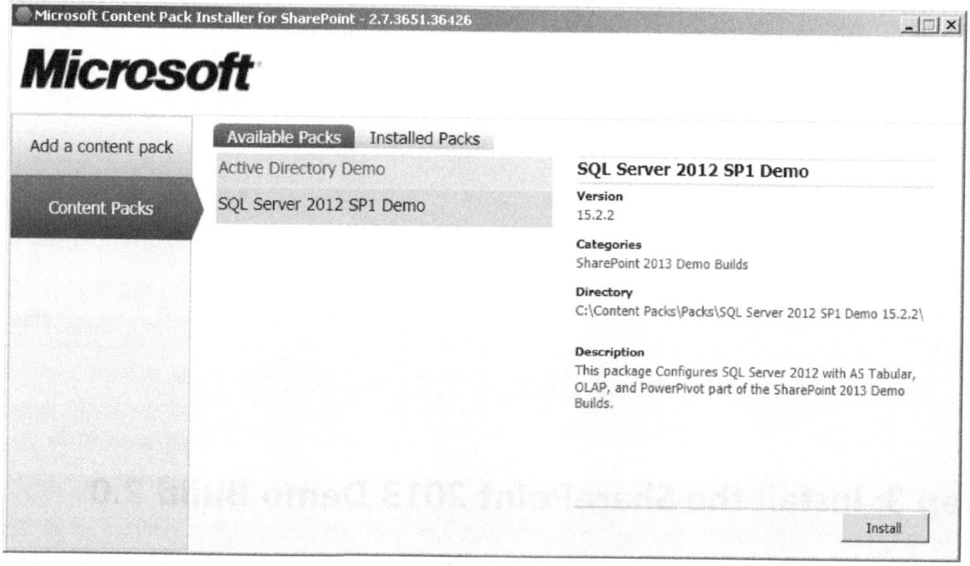

FIGURE A-4 The dialogue box for an installed content pack.

5. Click OK to accept the default path.

The installation process can take 30 to 45 minutes, and you will not see any feedback indicators other than a flowing progress bar to show that work is being done. For advanced users, there is a log file named *Install-http_intranet_contoso_com-<Date/Time>.log* that is updated with live feedback as the installation progresses; it is located at C:\Content Packs\Packs\SQL Server 2012 SP1 Demo 15.2.0, as demonstrated in Figure A-5.

Post installation

At this point, the post-installation document will be opened automatically by the installer for reference.

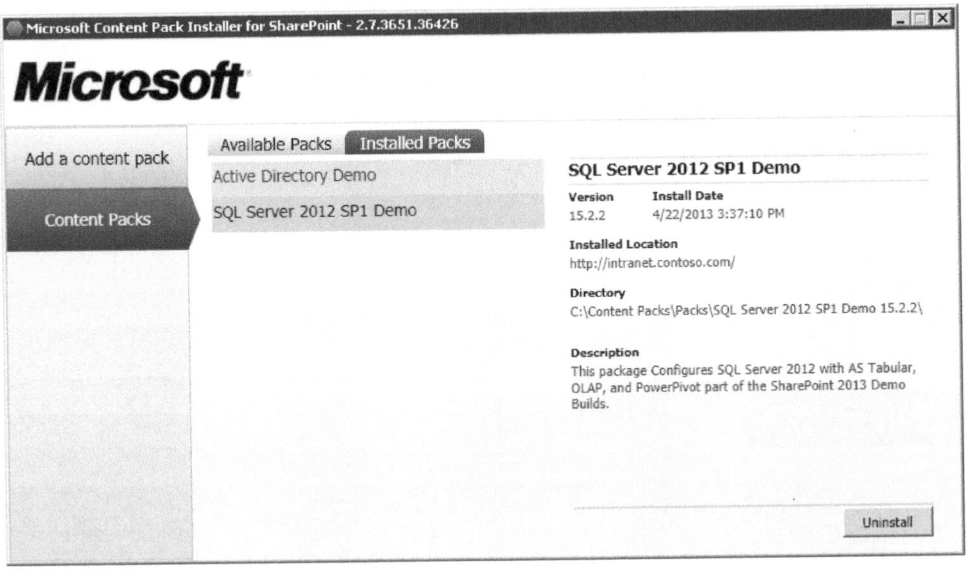

FIGURE A-5 The dialog box shows the successful installation of the content pack.

Step 3: Install the SharePoint 2013 Demo Build 2.0

This section provides instructions on how to install SharePoint Demo Build 2.0 that will configure SharePoint 2013. Please note that this installation takes about 45 minutes to install and about 45 minutes to configure.

Prerequisites

The prerequisites for this installation are as follows:

- The prerequisites for step 1 and 2 are completed

- The Application Active Directory Demo Build 2.1 has been deployed

- The SQL 2012 SP1 Content Pack Demo Build 2.0.0 has been deployed

- All users of this VM environment use the password, pass@word1

Installing the content pack

To install the content package, perform the following procedure:

1. In Hyper-V, start the base VM.

2. Log on to the VM as Contoso\Administrator.

3. If you do not already have the media, download the Evaluation SharePoint 2013 ISO from *http://technet.microsoft.com/en-us/evalcenter/hh973397.aspx* and use the evaluation key NQTMW-K63MQ-39G6H-B2CH9-FRDWJ.

4. Download the content pack *AutoSPInstallerDemo15.2.zip*. Create an Apps Folder on C: (C:\Apps) and extract the content to C:\Apps\AutoSPInstaller15.2.

5. Mount the SharePoint 2013 ISO to your VM.

6. Run the *setup.cmd* from your DEMO2013a VM DVD, install the SharePoint 2013 prerequisites. After the reboot, complete the prerequisite installation, run Setup, and then enter the product key NQTMW-K63MQ-39G6H-B2CH9-FRDWJ to install the SharePoint 2013 binaries.

7. Open Windows PowerShell, run *Set-ExecutionPolicy RemoteSigned*, type **Y**, and then press Enter.

8. Open Server Manager, enable Remote Desktop, and then turn off Internet Explorer Enhanced Security.

9. Double-click the Firewall Settings, turn Domain off, but leave Public and Private on.

10. If not already done, download the Content Pack Installer executable file SharePoint Content Pack Installer v2.7.

To start the SharePoint 2013 configuration, perform the following procedure:

1. Open the folder to which you extracted the AutoSPInstaller.

   C\Apps\AutoSPInstaller15.2\ SP\AutoSpinstaller\AutoSPInstallerLaunch.bat.

2. Right-click the *AutoSPInstallerLaunch.bat* file and then, on the shortcut menu that appears, click Run As Administrator.

Post installations and known issues

The Secure Store will fail to complete as a result of not creating the master key or not starting the Secure Store service. This will cause errors in the Excel Services installation, and PerformancePoint will error out and stop the installation. To fix this, perform the following procedure:

1. Open the SharePoint Central Administration, go to Service Applications, click the Secure Store Service Application, and then create a master key.

2. If you are unable to create a master key, go back to Central Administration, click Services On Server, and then start the Secure Store service

3. Return to the folder where you started *AutoSPInstallerLaunch.bat* and run *AutoSPInstaller.bat* again.

   The Windows PowerShell scripts verify where you left off and complete the configuration.

Step 4: Install the UserProfile Provisioning Demo 2.0

The UserProfile Provisioning Demo Content Pack loads the pictures of a few hundred users. These will be used with Social Media, People Search, My Sites, tagging and blog creation. The primary reason we add this content pack is to enhance the search results and add depth to the demonstration. This content pack takes about 15 minutes to install.

Prerequisites

The prerequisites for this installation are as follows:

- The prerequisites for step 1, 2, and 3 are completed
- The Active Directory Demo 2.0 Content Pack has been deployed
- The SQL 2012 SP1 Content Pack Demo Build 2.0 has been deployed
- The SharePoint 2013 Content Pack Demo Build 2.0 has been deployed

Installing the content pack

1. In Hyper-V, start the base VM.
2. Log on to the VM as Contoso\Administrator.
3. Download the PeoplePack Provision Demo 2.0.
4. Right-click ContentPackInstaller and then, on the shortcut menu that appears, click Run As Administrator,
5. Browse to the folder where you downloaded *PeoplePackDemo.2.0.zip* and then click Add A Content Pack.
6. On the menu, click the PeoplePack – UserProfile Provisioning Demo and then click Install.

Step 5: Install the Self-Service BI Demo 2.0 Content Pack

The Self-Service BI Demo 2.0 Content Pack, in addition to the following databases and models, includes four demo scripts such as the Contoso Oil and Gas Demo, in which you walk through a number of Power View Reports to analyze oil production in different regions of the world. If oil and gas doesn't interest you, maybe Tail Spin Toys or Contoso Auto Sales would be better.

The following are standard versions of the databases and models:

- Databases:
  - *AdventureWorksDW2012*
  - *AutoSalesSourceDW*

- *ContosoEnergyDW*

- *ContosoSchoolsDW*

- *TailspinToys*

■ Models:

  - *AdventureWorksDW2012*

  - AutoSalesModel

  - ContosoEnergyModel

  - ContosoSchoolsModel

  - CustomerProfitability

  - TailspinToysModel

Also included are more than 250 images used in Power View Reports for Auto Sales, School banners, and Tailspin Toys, to name a few.

Prerequisites

The prerequisites for this installation are as follows:

■ Windows Server 2012

■ The Active Directory DS Role for the Contoso.com Domain

■ Active Directory Content Pack Demo 2.0 has been deployed

■ SQL 2012 SP1 Content Pack Demo 2.0 has been deployed

■ SharePoint 2013 DEMO 2 Content Pack has been deployed

■ People Pack version 2.0 has been deployed

All users of this VM environment use the password, pass@word1

Installing the content pack

To install the content pack, perform the following procedure:

1. In Hyper-V, start the base VM.

2. Log on to the VM as Contoso\Administrator.

3. Download the content pack *SelfServiceBIDemo2.0.zip*.

4. If you have not already downloaded the SharePoint Content Pack Installer, download the Content Pack Installer executable file *ContentPackInstaller.exe* and place it on the desktop.

5. Right-click *ContentPackInstaller.exe* and then, on the shortcut menu that appears, click Run As Administrator.

   If this is the first time the installer has run, you might see a First Time Configuration dialog box. If so, accept all default values.

6. Install the Self Service BI Demo Content Pack.

7. Click the Add A Content Pack tab and then click Browse.

8. Locate the *SelfServiceBIDemo2.0.zip* on your desktop, select it, and then click Open.

9. Click Add. (this can take about 10 minutes)

10. After the installer finishes extracting the files, click Install.

11. Click OK to accept the default path.

The installation process can take 15 to 30 minutes, and you will not see any feedback indicators other than a flowing progress bar to show that work is being done. For advanced users, there is a log file named *Install-http_intranet_contoso_com-<Date/Time>.log* that is updated with live feedback as the installation progresses; it is located at C:\Content Packs\Packs\Self-Service BI Demo 2.0.

Post installations/known issues

To configure SQL 2012 RS, run the following three Windows PowerShell Commands:

1. *Install-SPRSService*

2. *Install-SPRSServiceProxy*

3. *get-spserviceinstance -all |where {$_.TypeName -like "SQL Server Reporting*"} | Start-SPService-Instance*

To Configure SQL 2012 SP1 PowerPivot with SharePoint 2013, perform the following procedure:

1. On the Start menu, click All Programs and then click Microsoft SQL Server 2012. Click Configuration Tools and then click PowerPivot For SharePoint 2013 Configuration.

   This tool is listed only when PowerPivot for SharePoint is installed on the local server.

2. Click Configure Or Repair PowerPivot For SharePoint and then click OK.

   The tool runs validation to verify the current state of PowerPivot and what steps are required to complete configuration. Expand the window to full size. You should see a button bar at the bottom of the window that includes Validate, Run, and Exit commands.

3. For the Default Account UserName, type **Contoso\Administrator**.

   This account is used to provision services, including the PowerPivot service application pool. Do not specify a built-in account such as Network Service or Local System. The tool blocks configurations that specify built-in accounts.

4. In the Database Server text box, you can use the SQL Server Database engine that is supported for the SharePoint farm.

5. For the Password, type **Sh@reP0int_ROCKS**.

   If you are creating a new SharePoint farm, the password is used whenever you add a server or application to the SharePoint farm. If the farm already exists, type the applicable password so that you can add a server application to the farm.

6. In the PowerPivot Server For Excel Services text box, type the name of an Analysis Services SharePoint mode server. In a single-server deployment, this is the same as the database server: **LocalHost\POWERPIVOT**.

7. Click Create Site Collection in the left window. Note the Site URL so that you can reference it in later steps. If the SharePoint server is not already configured, the configuration wizard defaults the web application and site collection URLs to the root of http://[ServerName]. To modify the defaults, review the following pages in the left pane: Create Default Web Application and Deploy Web Application Solution.

8. Optionally, review the remaining input values used to complete each action. Click each action in the left pane to see and review the details of the action.

9. Optionally, remove any actions that you do not want to process at this time. For example, if you want to configure Secure Store Service later, click Configure Secure Store Service, and then clear the Include This Action In The Task List check box.

10. Click Validate to determine whether the tool has sufficient information to process the actions in the list. If you see validation errors, click the warnings in the left pane to see details of the validation error. Correct any validation errors and then click Validate again.

11. Click Run to process all of the actions in the task list. Note that Run becomes available after you validate the actions. If Run is not available, click Validate first.

At this point, the post-installation document will be opened automatically by the installer. The installation process can take 90 minutes, and you will not see any feedback indicators other than a flowing progress bar to show that work is being done (Figure A-6). For advanced users, there is a log file named *Install-http_intranet_contoso_com-<Date/Time>.log* that is updated as the installation progresses; it is located at C:\Content Packs\Packs\Self-Service BI Demo 2.0.

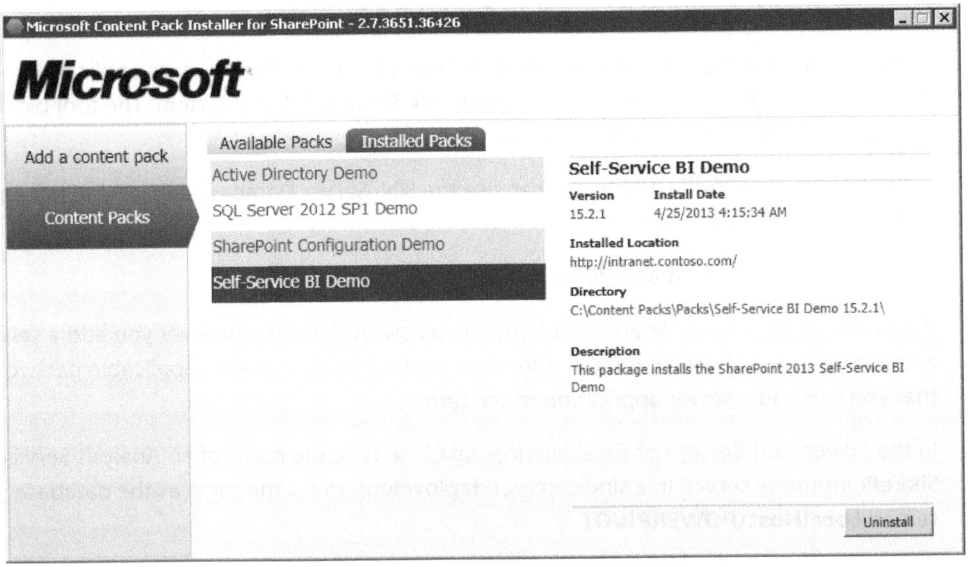

FIGURE A-6 The dialogue box for an installed content pack.

Step 6: Install the Visio Services Demo Content Pack

One of the demonstrations in this Content Pack describes how Visio, SharePoint 2013, and SharePoint Designer 2013 play specific roles in the development process. Visio makes it possible for business analysts to define the process; with SharePoint Designer, skilled users can implement the process. Both Visio and SharePoint Designer feature a complete import/export solution with which users can repeatedly try a process when creating workflows. In this demonstration, Contoso, a fictitious company, is trying to align the right business processes to the right problem.

The Visio Services Demo Content Pack includes the following standard versions of the databases:

- *AdventureWorksIT*

- *DemoDeata*

- *NetworkDB*

- *SCOMR2Simulation*

- *Visio_BI_FoodMart_Data*

- *VisioDemo*

Prerequisites

The Visio Services Demo Content Pack specifies the following prerequisite installations, in the order listed here:

- Windows Server 2012

- The Active Directory DS Role for the Contoso.com Domain

- Active Directory Content Pack Demo 2.0 has been deployed

- SQL 2012 SP1 Content Pack Demo 2.0 has been deployed

- SharePoint 2013 DEMO 2 Content Pack has been deployed

- People Pack version 2.0 has been deployed

- Self Service BI Pack 2.0 has been deployed

All users of this VM environment use the password, pass@word1

Installing the content pack

To install the content pack, perform the following procedure:

1. In Hyper-V, start the base VM.

2. Log on to the VM as Contoso\Administrator.

3. Download the content of *VisioServicesDemo2.0.zip*.

4. If you have not already downloaded the SharePoint Content Pack Installer, download the Content Pack Installer executable file, *ContentPackInstaller.exe*, and place it on the desktop.

5. Right-click *ContentPackInstaller.exe* and then, on the shortcut menu that appears, click Run As Administrator.

    If this is the first time you have run the installer, you might see a First Time Configuration dialog box. If so, accept all default values.

6. Install the Visio Services Demo Content Pack.

7. Click the Add A Content Pack tab and then click Browse.

8. Locate the *VisioServicesDemo2.0.zip* on your desktop, select it, and then click Open.

9. Click Add (this can take about 10 minutes).

10. After the installer finishes extracting the files, click Install.

11. Click OK to accept the default path.

The installation process can take 30 minutes, and you will not see any feedback indicators other than a flowing progress bar to show that work is being done (Figure A-7).

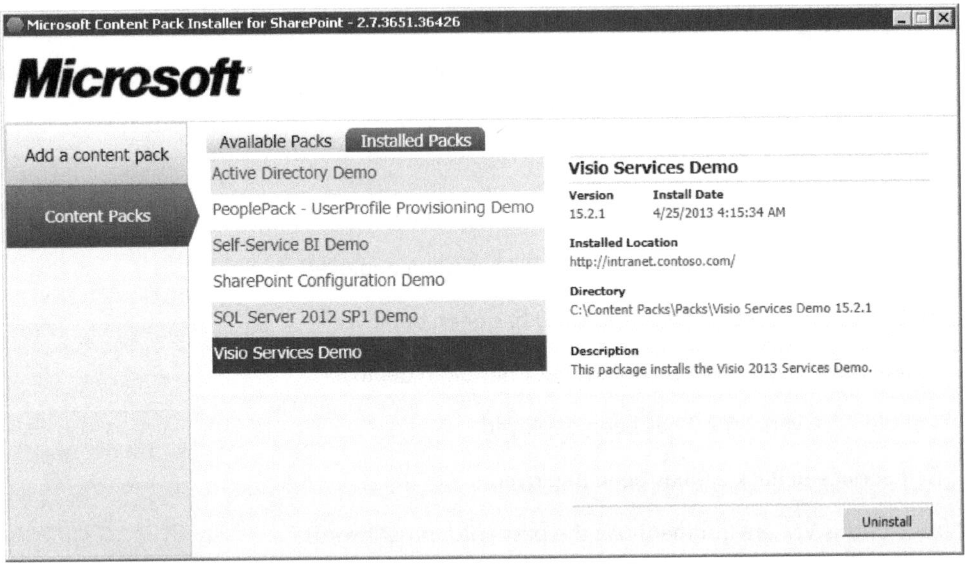

FIGURE A-7 The dialogue box for an installed content pack.

For advanced users, there is a log file named *Install-http_intranet_contoso_com-<Date/Time>.log* that is updated with live feedback as the installation progresses; it is located at C:\Content Packs\Packs\Visio Services Demo 2.0.

At this point, the post-installation document will be opened automatically by the installer for reference. For future reference, the demo script, package installation instructions, and post-installation instructions are located at C:\Demos\VisioServices\Script and Setup Guide\.

Microsoft and "Big Data"

This appendix introduces you to the concept of *Big Data* and the evolving tools that Microsoft and other vendors are using to harness and extract value from large, growing, and increasingly unstructured sources of information. You will begin to see the role the tools discussed in this book play toward getting value from data. We discuss Big Data with respect to Microsoft SharePoint 2013, Microsoft Office 2013, and Microsoft SQL Server 2012, which all play a role in getting value from Big Data investments.

We provide instruction for how Microsoft HDInsight integrates with Hadoop (which we'll introduce and describe a little later in this appendix) to query and visualize data and the difference between open source HDinsights and HDInsightAzure. You will learn how the tools described in this book are relevant to extricating value from disparate and unstructured data sources. It's important to note that it is likely Microsoft will continue to integrate business intelligence (BI) tools with Hadoop.

Chapter 1, "Business intelligence in SharePoint," establishes a clear focus on how we can value and use the data we have. Distilling value from data that is increasing in volume, velocity, and variety will continue to challenge the most capable individuals and computer systems. This appendix introduces tools and concepts that accommodate bigger truckloads of data at the risk of contradicting what was mentioned in the Chapter 1. While reading this appendix (and the book, for that matter), ask yourself how to avoid an endless cycle in which "wisdom" is "lost in knowledge" and "knowledge" is "lost in information." Understanding the tools in this book helps to avoid that dilemma.

> *"Data is changing the definition of computing and business, infusing new layers of experience and understanding into our lives. Data presents fresh opportunities, and the challenge of new technologies and skills. Put bluntly: The future belongs to those who understand how to collect and use their data successfully."* (http://strata.oreilly.com/about)

In addition to using data successfully, Microsoft is trying to put the tools in as many hands as possible for the least cost by using Microsoft Excel. Consider the term "democratization of data." Democratization is a concept Microsoft has always seen as key to its own value proposition. It's based on the idea that new areas of technology, in their early stages, typically are catered to by smaller, pure-play, specialist companies whose products are sometimes quite expensive. In addition, the skills required to take advantage of these technologies are usually in short supply, driving costs up even further. Democratization disrupts this exclusivity with products that are often less expensive, integrate more easily in the corporate data center and, importantly, are accessible to mainstream information workers and developers, using the skills they already have." (*http://www.zdnet.com/microsofts-big-data-strategy-democratize-in-memory-and-the-cloud-7000012223/*)

Note that O'Reilly Media sponsors the Strata conference (*http://strataconf.com*), webcasts, books, and ongoing analysis and coverage, which help give the community a nuts-and-bolts understanding required for building a data-driven business, product, or career. The Strata conference is the leading event for the people and technology driving the data revolution. The home of data science, Strata brings together practitioners, researchers, IT leaders and entrepreneurs to discuss Big Data, Hadoop, analytics, visualization, and data markets.

What is Big Data?

"Big data is data that exceeds the processing capacity of conventional database systems. The data is too big, moves too fast, or doesn't fit the strictures of your database architectures. To gain value from this data, you must choose an alternative way to process it." (http://strata.oreilly.com/2012/01/what-is-big-data.html)

Other characteristics of what can be considered Big Data are the following:

- Hundreds of terabytes, and even into petabytes of data

- Data from financial services, sensors, web logs (data that describes user behavior on the web), social media, and so on

- Processing of data sets too large for transactional databases for which you are analyzing interactions rather than transactions

Cost-effective approaches are working to tame volume, velocity, and variability of massive data.

Volume

Today, everything is either connected to the Internet or someone is in the process of figuring out how to make the connection—from phones to televisions to satellites as well as social networking and cloud data. The amount of machine-generated data available for trend analysis is approaching the exabyte and zetabyte range. A zetabyte is a quantity of information or information storage capacity equal to 1,000,000,000,000,000,000,000 bytes, or about one billion terabytes. As of April 2012, no storage system has achieved one zetabyte of information. Data volume is growing by 10 times every 5 years, According to a recent International Data Corporation (IDC) report, the volume of digital records is forecast to hit 1 to 2 million zetabytes this year, and it is predicted to grow 44 times over the next decade.

IDC reports that 90 percent of the world's data has been created in the last two years. Gartner projects that the volume of information is growing at an annual rate of 59 percent worldwide ("Big Data, the Next Oil?" [*http://www.utopiainc.com/insights/big-data*]).

To put it in plain, unvarnished terms, the volume of data is increasing.

Velocity

Velocity defines how fast data increases and how fast it can be processed. Among other innovations, in-memory and structuring database technologies and developments will continue to stretch data processing limitations in excess of speeds that anyone has ever considered.

One example is happing now. Microsoft unveiled a new in-memory database capability, code named "Hekaton," which is slated to be released with the next major version of SQL Server. Hekaton dramatically improves the throughput and latency of the transaction processing (TP) capabilities of SQL Server.

The speed at which data is being collected and processed is increasing (*http://blogs.technet.com/b/ dataplatforminsider/archive/2012/11/08/breakthrough-performance-with-in-memory-technologies.aspx*).

Variety

Data will always come in a variety of formats. But, when this variety is combined with the ever increasing volumes of data, consuming it becomes more difficult and harder to work with using regular Relational Database (RDB) systems or even data warehouses.

You must accept the messiness of unstructured data instead of treating exactitude as a central priority. You must also trust more in correlations without knowing the casual basis for the predictions. Our understanding will be driven more by the abundance of data rather than hypotheses. Hypothesis that is tested against reality by using a model of underlying causalities is on its way out, replaced by statistical analysis of pure correlations that is devoid of theory. In essence, we look at examining theories less, and we look more to let the data tell a story. (*Big Data: A Revolution That Will Transform How We Live, Work, and Think* by Eamon Dolan [Houghton Mifflin Harcourt, 2013])

Comparing Big Data to electrification

Datafication is another new word that hints at the notion that organizations today are as dependent on their data to operate properly as their ancestor organizations were on electricity. An analogy between datafication and electrification is articulated in the following quote.

> *"The electrification of the nation was the migration toward the democratization of electricity, meaning you had centralized power generation and then a distribution system," said Waitman. "Large corporations and governments built their own generators and used them for single-purpose applications."* (http:// www.informationweek.com/big-data/news/big-data-analytics/big-datas-new-buzzword-datafication/240149288)

We predict that companies will become largely dependent on structured and unstructured data to analyze and understand their customers and business as well as bring about new products.

The "hype cycle" for Big Data

Figure B-1 provides a small, dated peek into the number of technologies and tools that have surfaced. These numbers will stabilize as we see the development or evolving solutions for Big Data. Additionally, although Gartner places Big Data as approaching its "peak of inflated expectations," in 2012, Forbes magazine provides direction in the form of charts for how and who will benefit (now) from investments in Big Data strategies (*http://www.forbes.com/sites/louiscolumbus/2012/08/16/roundup-of-big-data-forecasts-and-market-estimates-2012/*).

> **Note** The Hype Cycle graphic has been used by Gartner since 1995 to highlight the common pattern of overenthusiasm, disillusionment, and eventual realism that accompanies each new technology and innovation. The Hype Cycle Special Report is updated annually to track technologies along this cycle and provide guidance on when and where organizations should adopt them for maximum impact and value (*http://www.gartner.com/newsroom/id/2124315*).

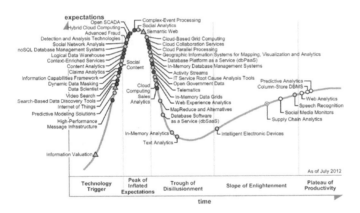

FIGURE B-1 The Hype Cycle for Big Data (*source:* Gartner [July 2012]).

The Big Data toolset

This section describes products and tools that will help you to understand the role Microsoft plays in deriving value from what we have defined as Big Data.

Hadoop, MapReduce, and HDFS

At much less cost, Hadoop brings the ability to process large data sets regardless of structure. This is different from enterprise data warehouses and relational databases, whose purpose is to process structured data.

In a more formal definition, Apache Hadoop is an open-source software framework that facilitates distributed processing of large data sets across clusters of computers by using a simple programming model. It consists of two primary components: Hadoop Distributed File System (HDFS), a reliable and distributed data storage; and MapReduce, a parallel and distributed processing system. A Hadoop cluster can be made up of a single node or thousands.

In short, Hadoop = MapReduce + HDFS.

MapReduce

The idea behind MapReduce is to divide and conquer in a way that you can add nodes to your cluster to help handle data. The MapReduce programming model establishes a core abstraction that provides closure for map-and-reduce operations. The MapReduce programming model views all of its jobs as computations over key-value pair datasets. So, both input and output files must contain datasets that consist only of key-value pairs. Figure B-2 shows a conceptual rendition of a MapReduce job wherein there are inputs, mapping instructions, reducer instructions, and ultimately an output that is typically aggregated data.

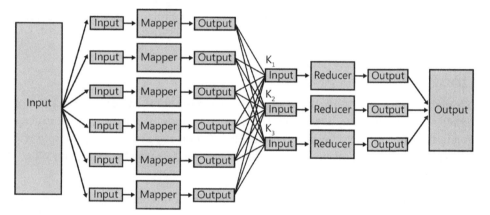

FIGURE B-2 A diagram of a MapReduce job.

Pig and Hive

Other Hadoop-related projects such as Pig and Hive are built on top of HDFS and the MapReduce framework and are used to provide a simpler way to manage a cluster than working with the MapReduce programs directly. With Pig, for example, you can write programs by using JavaScript that are compiled to MapReduce programs on the cluster. It also provides fluent controls to manage data flow. Hive provides a table abstraction for data in files stored in a cluster that can be queried by using SQL-like statements.

Pig

Pig is a high-level platform for processing Big Data on Hadoop clusters. Pig consists of a data flow language, called *Pig Latin*, supporting writing queries on large datasets and an execution environment running programs from a console. The Pig Latin programs consist of dataset transformation series converted under the hood to a MapReduce program series. Pig Latin abstractions provide richer data structures than MapReduce; they perform for Hadoop what SQL performs for RDBMS systems. Pig Latin is fully extensible. User Defined Functions (UDFs), written in Java, Python, C#, or JavaScript, can be called to customize each processing path stage when composing the analysis.

Hive

Hive is the glue between the world of Hadoop and the world of BI In effect you can make Hadoop look like another relational data source. Hive is for analysts with strong SQL skills, providing an SQL-like interface and a relational data model. Hive uses a language called *HiveQL*; a dialect of SQL. Hive, like Pig, is an abstraction on top of MapReduce, and when run, Hive translates queries into a series of MapReduce jobs. Scenarios for Hive are closer in concept to those for RDBMS; thus, they are appropriate for use with more structured data. For unstructured data, Pig is a better choice. The HDInsight Service includes an ODBC driver for Hive, which provides direct real-time querying from BI tools such as Microsoft Excel into Hadoop.

Other tools

Sqoop is a tool that transfers bulk data between Hadoop and relational databases such a SQL or other structured data stores as efficiently as possible. Use Sqoop to import data from external structured data stores into the HDFS or related systems such as Hive. Sqoop can also extract data from Hadoop and export that data to external relational databases, enterprise data warehouses, or any other structured data store type.

Flume is a distributed, reliable, and available service for efficiently collecting, aggregating, and moving large log data amounts to HDFS. Flume's architecture is streaming data flow–based. It is robust and fault tolerant with tunable and reliability mechanisms as well as many failover and recovery mechanisms. It has a simple extensible data model, enabling online analytical applications.

Mahout is an open-source machine-learning library that facilitates building scalable matching learning libraries. Using the map/reduce paradigm, algorithms for clustering, classification and batch-based collaborative filtering developed for Mahout are implemented on top of Apache Hadoop.

What is NoSQL?

A NoSQL database provides a simple, lightweight mechanism for storage and retrieval of data that provides higher scalability and availability than traditional relational databases. The NoSQL data stores use looser consistency models to achieve horizontal scaling and higher availability.

Big players (companies)

Because the terms and names of companies tend to blend, we thought it would be a good idea to include some of the larger companies that provide enterprise solutions for Hadoop.

Cloudera provides an open-source Apache Hadoop distribution called CDH (Cloudera Distribution Including Apache Hadoop).

Hortonworks develops, distributes and supports enterprise Apache Hadoop and is Microsoft's partner in all things Hadoop. They recently released a beta of its own distribution of the Hortonworks Data Platform (HDP) for Windows. This more "vanilla" HDP for Windows will coexist with Microsoft's HDInsight distribution of Hadoop, which itself is based on the HDP for Windows code base.

MapR is an enterprise software company that develops and sells Apache Hadoop-derived software. The company contributes to Apache Hadoop projects such as HBase, Pig (programming language), Apache Hive, and Apache ZooKeeper.

There are many others in addition to Microsoft's products.

Using Microsoft's Big Data tools

Microsoft has developed tools that help customers to realize value from their investment in Hadoop. This section discusses these tools.

You can imagine that Microsoft's integration of Excel/PowerPivot and Hadoop through Hive and ODBC means that any Excel user will be able to analyze Big Data by using the familiar spreadsheet tool that has been established for decades.

HDInsight

HDInsight is Microsoft's Hadoop-based service that brings a 100 percent Apache Hadoop–based solution to the cloud. HDInsight gives you the ability to gain the full value of Big Data with a modern, cloud-based data platform that manages data of any type, whether structured or unstructured, and of any size. There is also an on-premises HDInsight solution.

With HDInsight you can seamlessly store and process data of all types through Microsoft's modern data platform that provides simplicity, ease of management, and an open, enterprise-ready Hadoop service, all running in the cloud. You can analyze your Hadoop data directly in Excel by using new capabilities like PowerPivot and Power View.

The on-premises version of Microsoft's HDInsight distribution of Hadoop will integrate with Active Directory, System Center, and other back-end products. The Azure cloud-based version (see Figure B-3) integrates with Azure cloud storage and with the Azure SQL Database offering, as well.

After you have signed up for Windows Azure, Figure B-3 shows that you can then try Azure HD Insight.

FIGURE B-3 Azure HDInsight Preview.

Microsoft is putting SQL Server BI tools on top of Hadoop to make Big Data analysis work with familiar, accessible Microsoft technologies. The following sections provide an overview of Big Data, Hadoop, and Microsoft BI stack integration. You can use this information to see how to apply your skills to this rapidly growing part of the industry.

Setting up in Windows Azure

The following steps are outlined in Getting Started with Windows Azure HDInsight Service (*http://www.windowsazure.com/en-us/manage/services/hdinsight/get-started-hdinsight/*). To set up Windows Azure perform the following procedure:

1. Subscribe to Windows Azure and enable the HDInsight Service.

2. Create and configure a Windows Azure Storage account.

   This will be used by the HDInsight Service (see Figure B-4).

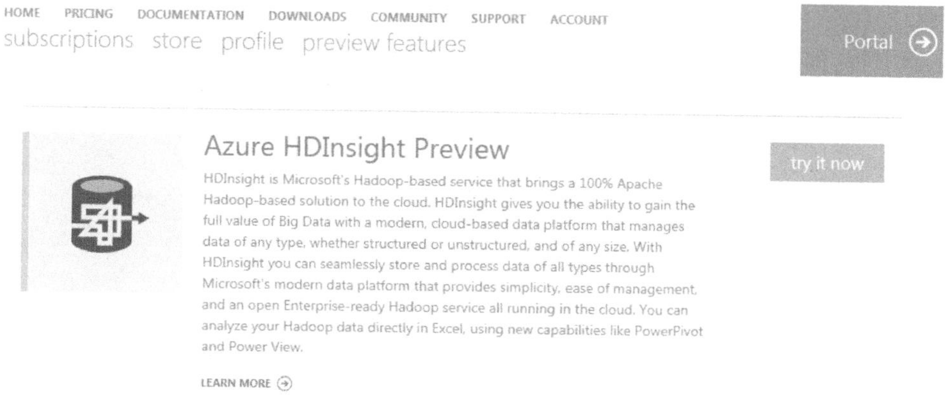
HOME PRICING DOCUMENTATION DOWNLOADS COMMUNITY SUPPORT ACCOUNT
subscriptions store profile preview features
Portal
Azure HDInsight Preview
HDInsight is Microsoft's Hadoop-based service that brings a 100% Apache Hadoop-based solution to the cloud. HDInsight gives you the ability to gain the full value of Big Data with a modern, cloud-based data platform that manages data of any type, whether structured or unstructured, and of any size. With HDInsight you can seamlessly store and process data of all types through Microsoft's modern data platform that provides simplicity, ease of management, and an open Enterprise-ready Hadoop service all running in the cloud. You can analyze your Hadoop data directly in Excel, using new capabilities like PowerPivot and Power View.
LEARN MORE
try it now

FIGURE B-4 The Welcome screen for Windows Azure.

3. Provision an HDInsight Service cluster from the Windows Azure portal.
4. Use the HDInsight Service dashboard and sample gallery.
5. Run a sample MapReduce program.
6. Use the interactive console to examine the output from a MapReduce program.

Getting value from Big Data

Even though we have discussed at length Excel 2013 and the built-in features of PowerPivot and Power View, there are two add-ins that help you to extract further value from your investment in Hadoop, and a third that helps you clean data:

- Excel-Hive
- Excel Data Explorer for Excel Add-in (a preview as of this writing)
- Data Quality Service for Excel Add-in

Excel-Hive Add-in

One key feature of Microsoft's Big Data solution is solid integration of Apache Hadoop with the Microsoft BI components. A good example of this is the ability for Excel to connect to the Hive data warehouse framework in the Hadoop cluster. Figure B-5 shows how to populate Hadoop with Hive. You can follow the instructions in How to Connect Excel to Hadoop on Azure via HiveODBC (see *http://social.technet.microsoft.com/wiki/contents/articles/6226.how-to-connect-excel-to-hadoop-on-azure-via-hiveodbc.aspx*).

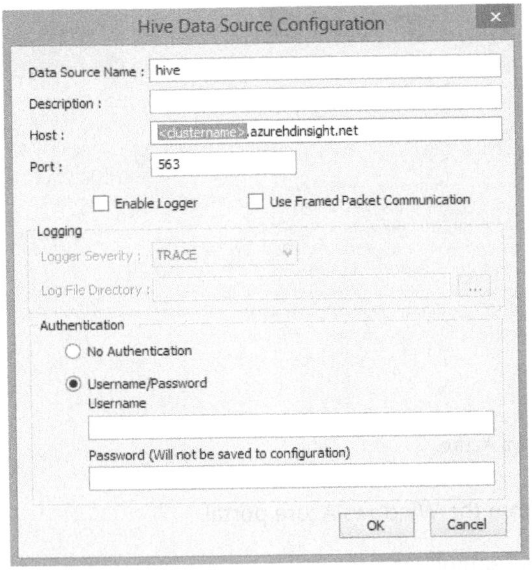

FIGURE B-5 The Hive Data Source Configuration dialog box.

You can download the Excel-Hive Add-in from *http://www.windowsazure.com/en-us/home/scenarios/ big-data/*.

The Data Explorer for Excel Add-in (preview)

Data Explorer for Excel 2013 is an Excel add-in that enhances the self-service BI experience in Excel by simplifying data discovery and access.

With Data Explorer for Excel, you can do the following:

- Identify the data you care about from the sources with which you work (for example, relational databases, Excel, text and XML files, OData feeds, webpages, Hadoop HDFS, and so on).

- Discover relevant data by using the search capabilities within Excel.

- Combine data from multiple, disparate data sources and shape it to prepare the data for further analysis in tools such as Excel and PowerPivot.

Figure B-6 demonstrates how you can import data from both HDFS and Windows Azure HDInsight.

Figure B-7 shows how you can perform an online search in Excel and hover your mouse over the result to see a preview of the data that is extracted from a website shown in a worksheet.

You can download the preview from *http://www.microsoft.com/en-us/download/details. aspx?id=36803*.

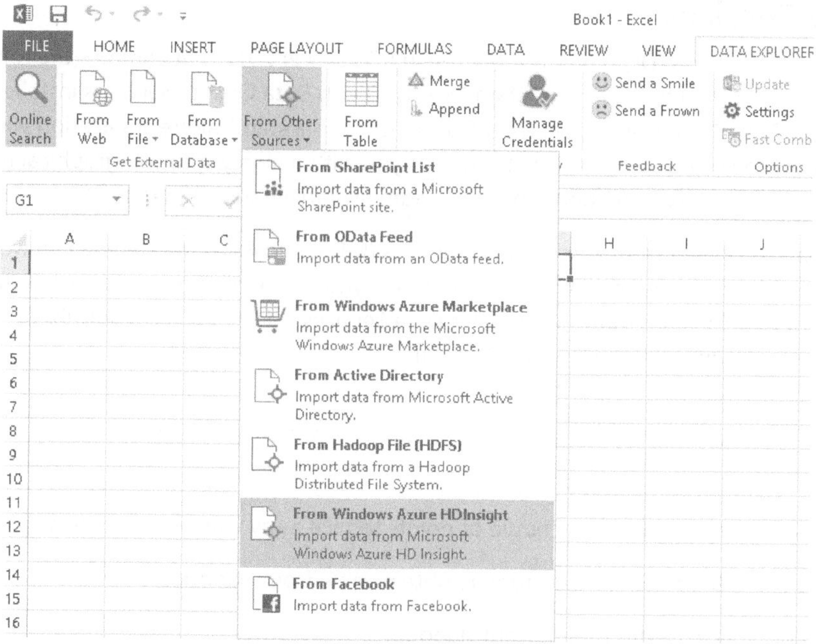

FIGURE B-6 Data Explorer Other Sources Add-in: Windows Azure HDInisghts.

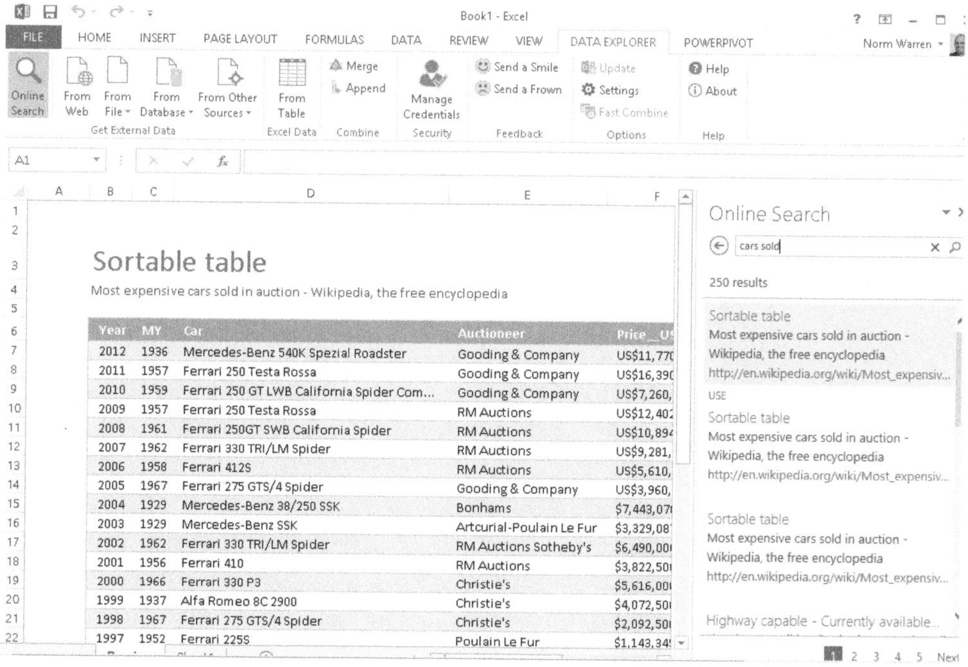

FIGURE B-7 The Online Search feature in Data Explorer.

Data Quality Services

SQL Server Data Quality Services (DQS) is a new feature in SQL Server 2012 that contains the following two components: Data Quality Server and Data Quality Client. Data Quality Server is installed on top of the SQL Server 2012 Database Engine. Data Quality Client is a stand-alone application with which you can connect to Data Quality Server. It provides you with a highly-intuitive graphical user interface to perform data-quality operations and other administrative tasks related to DQS.

You can load filtered lists of data from Master Data Services (MDS) into Excel, where you can work with it just as you would any other data. When you are done, you can publish the data back to MDS, where it is centrally stored. To learn more, see Master Data Services Add-in for Microsoft Excel (*http://msdn.microsoft.com/en-us/library/hh231024.aspx*).

Summary

We hope you got the message. Here are a couple of points to take away with you from this appendix:

- Microsoft is committed to helping customers obtain value from Hadoop.

- Excel plays a big role in getting value from Hadoop.

You could say Excel is becoming the center of the universe at Microsoft. We should give it just as much attention with its add-ins for exploring data from the web, databases, HDFS and HDInsights, cleaning data, modeling, creating visualizations, and so forth.

Index

Symbols

= (equals sign) operator, 116

A

Absolute Value option, 148
Actions area, PowerPivot Management Dashboard, 204
Active Directory Content Pack Demo 2.0, 333
Active Directory Demo Build 2.1
    hardware requirements, 334
    installing content pack, 334–336
    overview, 333
    post installation, 336
    software requirements, 334
ActiveDirectory.zip file, 335
Add-Ins tab, Excel 2013, 113
Add Measure Columns dialog box, 253
Add Measure Filters dialog box, 253
Add Part To list box, 323
Add This Data To The Data Model check box, 102, 104
Add Trusted Data Source Location link, 230
ad hoc tool
    Excel Services 2013 as, 162
administration
    of Excel Services 2013, 164–166
adult stage, Business Intelligence Maturity Model, 40–41
AdventureWorks data warehouse, 76
AdventureWorksDW2012 database, 342, 343
AdventureWorksDW2012 sample database, 122–124
AdventureWorksIT database, 346
<a> element, 185
All SharePoint Locations option, 231
Also Refresh As Soon As Possible check box, 198, 199
Analysis Services cube, 28
Analysis Services Cube data source, 236

Analysis Services OLAP cubes, 14
Analysis Services Tabular Project option, 75
analytical competition, 42
Analytic chart report type, 216
Analytic grid report type, 216
Analyze In Excel option, SSDT, 81
APIs (application programming interfaces), 28
application programming interfaces (APIs), 28
Apps, SharePoint. *See* SharePoint Apps
architectural enhancements
    infrastructure improvements. *See* infrastructure improvements
architecture. *See also* infrastructure improvements
    for BI, 10–11
    infrastructure improvements. *See* infrastructure improvements
    of PerformancePoint Services, 223–224
audience
    understanding, 22–24
authentication
    settings for, 171
    in workbooks, 168–171
Authentication Unattended Service Account, 239
authoring tools
    for BI, 12–19
Automatically Link button, 300
Automatic Link Wizard, 300, 301
automating data processing
    for SSAS, 85–89
AutoSalesModel model, 343
AutoSalesSourceDW database, 342
AutoSPInstaller.bat file, 341
AutoSPInstallerDemo15.2.zip file, 341
AutoSPInstallerLaunch.bat file, 341
Average Instance CPU view, 206–207
Average Instance Memory view, 207
Azure Marketplace, Windows, 108, 119

B

C

E

About the Authors

 NORMAN P. WARREN works for Ancestry.com, which helps people discover, preserve, and share their family history. There, he works as a BI specialist and to implement guided and managed self-service business intelligence. He is organizer and coauthor of *Business Intelligence in Microsoft SharePoint 2010* (2011, Microsoft Press). He earned his Master's degree in computer information technology and recently earned his MBA with an emphasis in financial accounting. He was previously a writer for PerformancePoint Server 2007 and SharePoint Server 2010 at Microsoft and has written articles on PerformancePoint Server and business intelligence for the information worker, IT Pro, and SQL Server BI developer audiences. He is an active member of the community to provide the right content about Microsoft business intelligence. When not writing, Norm loves spending time with his family, mountain biking. Additionally, he shares his passion of business intelligence at conferences.

 MARIANO TEIXEIRA NETO is originally from Recife, Brazil. He has a Bachelor's and Master's degrees in computer science, with research on data synchronization on mobile databases from Universidade Federal de Pernambuco, also in Brazil. He has more than 10 years of experience on software development implementing complex systems for search engine, mobile telephony, and oil companies. At Microsoft since 2007, Mariano is a software development engineer in test on the Analytics team at the SQL Server Business Intelligence, and has been a part of PowerPivot since its incubation. He has authored scientific papers, whitepapers, and is a coauthor of *Business Intelligence in Microsoft SharePoint 2010*. When not working or enjoying his family, he can be found running, biking, or swimming.

 STACIA MISNER is a MCITP-BI and MCTS-BI with a Bachelor's degree in social sciences. She is a consultant, educator, author, mentor, and principal of Data Inspirations. Her career spans more than 25 years with a focus on improving business practices through technology. Since 2000, she has been providing consulting and education services for Microsoft's business intelligence technologies. In addition, she has authored or coauthored several books covering different components of the Microsoft SQL Server database and business intelligence platform. Stacia has presented at the Professional Association for SQL Server (PASS), Microsoft's TechEd, SQL Server Magazine Connections, and various Microsoft events. She currently lives in Las Vegas. She is also a coauthor of *Business Intelligence in Microsoft SharePoint 2010*.

SCOTT A. HELMERS has been a Microsoft MVP for Visio since 2008 and is the primary Visio expert at Experts-Exchange.com. The author of *Microsoft Visio 2010 Step by Step* (2011, Microsoft Press) and *Visio 2013 Step by Step* (2013, Microsoft Press), he has taught thousands of people to use Visio and other technologies more effectively. Scott is a partner at the Harvard Computing Group, a software and consulting firm that assists clients with understanding and implementing business process solutions. He is a co-inventor of TaskMap (*www.taskmap.com*), a Visio add-in that allows anyone to document all of the important aspects of any business process. For more than a decade, he was an Adjunct Professor at both Northeastern University and Boston University, during which time he wrote *Data Communications: A Beginner's Guide to Concepts and Technology* (1989, Prentice-Hall). When not working or spending time with his family, Scott can usually be found on his bicycle or working with a local community-theater company.

IVAN SANDERS is a SharePoint MVP and independent consultant with more than 15 years of broad-based, hands-on experience. He has focused on delivering Microsoft SharePoint solutions since 2004. He specializes in the design and development of mission-critical applications and innovative information management strategies for the enterprise deployment of Microsoft products.

Now that you've read the book...

Tell us what you think!

Was it useful?
Did it teach you what you wanted to learn?
Was there room for improvement?

Let us know at http://aka.ms/tellpress

Your feedback goes directly to the staff at Microsoft Press,
and we read every one of your responses. Thanks in advance!

CPSIA information can be obtained at www.ICGtesting.com
Printed in the USA
LVOW01s1931040214

372303LV00020B/79/P